J. Barrell
N.C. 2008

The VIOLET QUILL Reader

*The Emergence of Gay Writing
After Stonewall*

EDITED BY DAVID BERGMAN

St. Martin's Press   New York

For John

and

in Memory of George Stambolian

THE VIOLET QUILL READER. Copyright © 1994 by David Bergman.
All rights reserved. Printed in the United States of America. No
part of this book may be used or reproduced in any manner
whatsoever without written permission except in the case of brief
quotations embodied in critical articles or reviews. For information,
address St. Martin's Press, 175 Fifth Avenue, New York, N.Y.
10010.

Design by Sara Stemen

Library of Congress Cataloging-in-Publication Data

The Violet Quill reader / David Bergman, editor.
    p. cm.
  ISBN 0-312-11091-X
  1. Gay men—United States—Fiction. 2. American fiction—
20th century. 3. Gay men's writings, American. 4. Gay men—
United States. I. Bergman, David.
PS3501.U25S79 1994   94-425
813'.540809206642—dc20   CIP

First Edition: May 1994
10 9 8 7 6 5 4 3 2 1

Permissions

Contents

*Published for the first time

Acknowledgments

I must thank a large number of people for their help in putting this book together. After finishing *Gaiety Transfigured*, my study on gay self-representation in American literature, I noticed George Stambolian's references to the Violet Quill, and although I had heard the term, I had not paid much attention to it. In a panic, I wrote George Stambolian, Edmund White, Felice Picano, and Andrew Holleran, asking for additional information. George, whom I had known for several years, was already quite sick with AIDS and recognized that he could not write the book on the members of the Violet Quill, his friends and associates, that he had hoped to produce. He invited me to his home in Amagansett, where he told me about his involvement with and his thoughts on the VQ. We had spoken about being co-editors on this volume, and since he could no longer write, I intended that the interviews I conducted with him over that September weekend would form the basis of an introduction. Unfortunately, George did not live long enough to help in the selection of the works or in the planning of the volume. Nonetheless, I dedicate this book to his memory.

Edmund and Felice wrote, supplying what information they could remember, and asked me to carry on the work that George had always planned to do. Andrew Holleran, in his many letters and his frantic and hilarious phone calls, has been a continuous source of information, amusement, and good sense. I am grateful for all the help and encouragement I got from these men. In addition, Victor Bumbalo, George Whitmore's friend and literary executor, has been generous with his time and support.

One of the monumental tasks this project has entailed is reading through the unpublished material of these writers. For a week, Michael Ferro, Robert Ferro's father, permitted me to live in his home, where

Robert's and Michael Grumley's papers were then stored. Putting up with a writer is never easy, but it is especially difficult when he is sifting through boxes of dusty manuscripts and photograph albums, boxes that have stored many memories—not all pleasant. I greatly appreciate his patience and his hospitality. I am particularly grateful to Robert's two sisters, Camille Burns and Beth Quigley, who looked after me as if I were a brother, even sending me a new copy of Michael's diary when my photocopy disappeared into the Bermuda Triangle of my study. Robert's nieces Cathy Barrett and Jennifer McGuinley kindly answered my questions.

No one, at first, seemed to know where Chris Cox's papers had gone. After a week of calling around, I was given Chris's sister's number in Alabama. When I explained my reason for telephoning her, Nancy Cox replied, "I've been waiting for this call for five years." Over a period of months, Nancy sent me her brother's papers. She has been an extraordinary help.

Two students, Mark Cheshire and Kasey Edison, have been faithful research assistants. Kasey has been especially enthusiastic, transcribing handwritten letters and journals with what seems to me incredible accuracy. The late Allen Barnett was an enormous source of inspiration, giving me transcripts of interviews he had conducted with Edmund White, Andrew Holleran, and Robert Ferro. Richard McCann, David Román, and Jeff Newton were sources of support and encouragement. John Lessner, who puts up with me on a daily basis, has been especially heroic in meeting this challenge of tolerance. His advice has been especially helpful.

I want to thank the Faculty Research Committee of Towson State University for granting me time to work on this book, time that was simply invaluable. Sue Smatt and Carrier Gibson, the English Department secretaries, were extremely helpful. My chairman, Dan Jones, has been extremely supportive, and Donald Craver, who retired in the middle of this project, has been everything that a mentor should be.

The material for the Violet Quill is being collected at the Beinecke Library at Yale University. I want to thank Patricia Willis, the curator of the American Literature Collection, and Stephen Shutt, a cataloger for the Edmund White Papers, for their help.

I also want to thank my editors at St. Martin's, Michael Denneny and Keith Kahla. It was Michael's suggestion to do this particular reader, and it was Keith who followed through and made the path smooth.

Introduction

American cultural history is filled with mythic moments when groups of artists came together—the Stieglitz circle, the Actors Studio, Gertrude Stein's Paris salon, the New York School, the Harlem Renaissance, the Beats. These labels are convenient, and they help make sense of the flux of history, and yet they can be intimidating obstacles—legends that freeze our understanding of the work. Artists coming on the scene later live in the afterglow of these moments. Abstract painters today must contend with the shadows of Willem de Kooning and Jackson Pollock. Black writers do battle with the ghosts of Langston Hughes and Zora Neale Hurston. Generations of the restless young have gone "on the road," aware that Jack Kerouac, Allen Ginsberg, and Neal Cassady have been there and done it all long before them. So when I began to do work on the Violet Quill—that circle of writers who in the late 1970s and early 1980s was considered the gay literary mafia—one person after another—their friends, associates, and editors—warned me, "They're not the Bloomsbury Group," and, by making such an analogy, showed that the urge to put the Violet Quill in its place was as strong as the need to mythologize it.

What, then, was the Violet Quill? It was a group of gay writers joined by friendship, ambition, and concern for their art, who got together—eight times, in fact, in 1980 and 1981—to read to one another from their works in progress. Not much to mythologize. Except that several of these writers became the most important gay authors of the decade, setting a standard for gay fiction against which the present boom in gay writing is always compared. When we consider the first generation of gay writers to emerge after Stonewall, theirs—with the addition of Larry Kramer's and Paul Monette's—are the names we remember. Collectively they produced a vision of gay life that haunts us still—a vision of beauty, privilege, friendship, sexuality, loss, and lyricism. Edmund White, Andrew Holleran, Robert Ferro, George Whitmore, Felice Picano, Michael Grumley, and Christopher Cox have together left their mark on how we will come to view American literature and American culture in the last two decades. Theirs was a brief but important moment that we need to understand before it gets hardened into myth or lost in the way so much gay culture gets lost. The Violet Quill has come to epitomize the dozen years of gay life between the outbreak of the Stonewall Riots—when everything seemed possible—and the first reports of AIDS, a disease that has already killed four and infected a fifth of the group's seven members. This twelve-year span has been execrated for all that is worst in gay life—its shallow hedonism, its mindless trendiness, its self-indulgent irresponsibility, its empty narcissism—and has been celebrated as a period of rare freedom, intense communion, unsurpassed energy and creativity. The VQ never sought the role as symbol of that time, nor, after we take a close look at their work, can they be seen to sustain such praise or blame. They were seven individuals who were as much the products of their time as its creators, seven men who struggled with their own problems and limitations while they tried to produce the best works they could, seven serious writers honing their craft to produce a body of work that would speak out of their experiences as gay men. This collection of their work should help us to judge how much they succeeded, both individually and as a group.

The actual meetings of the group were, in fact, the least important part of the Violet Quill, whose members began to refer to themselves as the Violet Quill even before they began to meet formally. Just how those meetings started is not clear. Edmund White recalls that they may have been suggested by Robert Ferro and Michael Grumley, lovers who eventually lived together for some twenty years. Ferro and Grumley had attended the University of Iowa's Writers' Workshop, where they met Andrew Holleran. The Violet Quill readings were meant to re-create some of the atmosphere of mutual help and study the three had found in Iowa. As Felice Picano recalls, the VQ members came together because they were having difficulty getting useful advice about style and technique. Straight editors, agents, and fellow writers seemed so hung up by gay subject matter that they couldn't respond helpfully to the quality of the writing. The VQ members felt that the only readers they could trust were gay readers, who would not be shocked or put off by their tales of gay life. For as much as they were involved in gay politics—and it is important to note that Edmund White and Chris Cox were both at the Stonewall Riots—what they were most concerned about was becoming the best artists they could be. Looking through the countless drafts of their work, their laborious processes of composition, one cannot but be impressed by how seriously they took the art of writing. From March 1980 until March 1981 they met at intervals to read from their work. Usually, two people read each night—a half hour each—one before, the other after dessert. If today what the surviving members recall most is the desserts, which became more and more elaborate with each meeting, the reason may be that dessert was the least demanding and most unanimously enjoyed part of the evening.

To appreciate the Violet Quill, one has to understand the condition of gay fiction as its members found it. Before Stonewall, novels that contained gay characters and themes fell into four categories. The first two categories take in novels written primarily or ostensibly for straight readers. In the first type, gay characters and themes play minor roles in stories whose main concerns and characters are heterosexual; the second type are those sentimental and sensational novels in which gay characters live lonely, tragic lives that end in murder or suicide. The third group of novels, usually foreign, are of such high literary value that they were given allowance by heterosexual critics. André Gide, Jean Genet, Marcel Proust, and Thomas Mann, for example, were given special dispensation to discuss gay subjects. But beyond this special class of highly literary fiction, novels that dared address gay readers were relegated to pornography, the fourth class. In *Homosexual Liberation* (1971), John Murphy complained that the gay reader finds that "the choice of books dealing with *his* sexual concerns are limited to a few serious 'classics,' some sensational popular novels, and pornography."

To be sure, a number of books before Stonewall provided models for the VQ. In a lecture he gave at Oberlin College, Robert Ferro referred to some of the gay writers and works that were important to him. Despite its special pleading for tolerance, John Rechy's *City of Night*, for example, had presented a raw look at a certain aspect of gay life, Ferro noted, and William S. Burroughs's *Naked Lunch* assumed a homosexual outlook with a kind of unself-consciousness the Violet Quill aspired to. But still, both Burroughs and Rechy depicted homosexuality as a kind of twilight world of the marginal and insignificant. The books are violent and the sex they depict is impersonal.

Burroughs's drug-induced paranoia made homosexuality seem especially antisocial, and Rechy celebrated a netherworld of one-night stands. (The work that most inspired the authors of the VQ, the work they unanimously praised, was Christopher Isherwood's *A Single Man*, whose middle-aged, middle-class central figure represented in some ways a frontal attack on the homophobic mythology of the gay man as weak, predatory, effeminate, and unproductive, as a person of marginal value in a marginal life.)

The VQ did not arise in a vacuum. The 1960s brought a number of gay writers to light, among the most prominent James Purdy, Sanford Friedman, Hubert Selby, Alfred Chester, and Gore Vidal. Yet pre-Stonewall gay works did not represent a gay literary movement. They were published as individual books, not as part of a continuous gay list or publishing focus. No literary publisher—large or small—published a line of gay books before the 1970s. Indeed, as Roger Austen pointed out in *Playing the Game* (1977), one of the first books on gay literature, the sixties and early seventies were a falling-off period. "With the upsurge of pornographic and gay-liberation literature," he claimed, "there has been a corresponding decline in both the quantity and quality" of what Austen considered to be serious fiction.

Forgotten today is the hostility and disdain with which homosexuality was treated in straight literary circles. In a 1970 article that inspired one of the first demonstrations of the fledgling Gay Activists Alliance, Joseph Epstein wrote, "Private acceptance of homosexuality, in my experience, is not to be found, even among the most liberal-minded, sophisticated, and liberated people. Homosexuality may be the one subject left in America about which there is no official hypocrisy." Epstein concluded his attack on gays in this way:

> *Cursed without clear cause, afflicted without apparent cure, they are an affront to our rationality, living evidence of our despair of ever finding a sensible, an explainable design to the world. . . . I find I can accept it least of all when I look at my children. There is much my four sons can do in their lives that might cause me anguish, that might outrage me, that might make me ashamed of them and myself as their father. But nothing they could ever do would make me sadder than if any one of them were to become homosexual. For then I would know them condemned to a state of permanent niggerdom among men,*

> *their lives, whatever adjustment they might make to their*
> *condition, to be lived out as part of the pain of the earth.*

This apocalyptic message didn't come from Jerry Falwell, nor did it appear in *The National Review*. These words were penned by a man who at the time was a leading liberal intellectual (even if today he is known for his neoconservative views), and they appeared in *Harper's*, one of the most thoughtful and liberal journals of the time.

Gay writers speaking openly about their experiences were sure to meet this kind of reaction. In 1972, Shane Stevens felt free to write in *The Washington Post* that John Rechy's *City of Night* "was loved mostly by homosexuals and amorphous polyglots who like to believe they can accommodate every shade in the human spectrum." Only other homosexuals and "amorphous polyglots" (whoever they may be) could be interested in gay people. Moreover, the appearance of such a book was the result of "the strong homosexual lobby in publishing and the literary life." Stevens asserted that only a conspiracy of faggots and their fellow travelers could account for the success of *City of Night*. In 1978, John Yohalem, writing for *The New York Times Book Review*, complained that Edmund White's *Nocturnes for the King of Naples* "is a narcissistic novel—which is not to deny the rareness of its beauty, only the breadth of its appeal." And because "external constraint imposed on creativity . . . can itself be an inspiration," Yohalem wished that the openly gay White would once again "disguise his own sexuality . . . to give his art a nervous, mysterious charm, a bewildering but wonderful evasion of certainty." No wonder so many stayed closeted.

Yet within the gay community there was enormous pressure to write openly and positively about gay experience. One of the most moving documents of the period, Mike Silverstein's "An Open Letter to Tennessee Williams," appeared in *Out of the Closet: Voices of Gay Liberation*, a groundbreaking collection from 1972. Silverstein began by praising Williams as "one of the few people who told me I [as a gay person] was beautiful, and showed me how to be courageous and endure." But still, Williams had failed Silverstein:

> *I'm writing to you now because what you told me wasn't*
> *enough. What you told me I was, what you told me I could*
> *be, what you told me you are, are still too close to what*
> *my parents told me I was, what the critics tell you you are.*

You helped me free myself, but I can see you are not free,
because you still tell me we can never be free.

The Violet Quill can be seen as the most important group of gay
writers after Stonewall who rejected the accursed lot that critics like
Joseph Epstein would have doomed them to, and who tried to articulate
the belief that gay people can be free, not of their history of oppression,
but of the feeling that they are forever condemned to "the pain of the
earth."

Although no formal charter was ever written for the Violet Quill,
the members shared several impulses: a desire to write works that
reflected their gay experiences, and, specifically, autobiographical fiction; a desire to write for gay readers without having to explain their
point of view to shocked and unknowing heterosexual readers; and
finally, a desire to write, to paraphrase William Wordsworth, in a selection of the language really used by gay men.

The Violet Quill is associated with New York, and particularly the
stretch that ran from Christopher Street to Fire Island. But only one
member of the Violet Quill—Felice Picano—grew up in New York.
Edmund White spent his formative years in the Midwest—shuttling
between his mother's home in Chicago and his father's in Cincinnati.
Chris Cox came from Alabama, dropping out of the University of
Alabama to try his luck as an actor (and hustler) in New York. Michael
Grumley came from the heartland (he was a Missouri farm boy), and
George Whitmore grew up in Denver. As his novel *Nights in Aruba*
indicates, Andrew Holleran as a boy spent time in the Caribbean, until
his family moved to the South, and Robert Ferro was reared in northern
New Jersey, in the suburban sprawl that covers much of the Eastern
Seaboard. That they came to New York to live is explained by the
drawing power New York has—or at least had—for both writers and
gay men.

As the excerpts from Picano's journal make clear, the VQ grew out
of interlocking friendships, some quite old, some newer and lasting
only a very short time. The VQ members' work, in fact, testifies to
the importance of friendship for gay men, who in the 1970s were
feeling the first flush of being part of a community made up almost
exclusively of gay people. In some respects, the theme of friendship
unites all the fiction of the Violet Quill. Not that gay friendships aren't
strained by jealousy, envy, and greed. Indeed, romance is threatened
by the interlocking threads of friendship, which can bind more strongly

than the passions of the moment. But time and again these works indicate how gay friendships often create an alternative to family, a link more compelling than blood. The theme of gay friendship is a theme that, more than any other, separates gay fiction from straight fiction. In fact, straight readers find depictions of gay friendship most puzzling because they have no immediate contact with it. For straight readers, gay relationships must by definition be sexual (as the present debate about gays in the military makes clear). In an essay by Edmund White not included in this volume, an otherwise savvy female New Yorker asks the author whether gay men have friendships, and the question strikingly shows him the cultural gap between even fairly sophisticated heterosexuals and gay people. Perhaps it is the gay and lesbian capacity for friendship that has made possible such groups as Bloomsbury, the Harlem Renaissance, Stein's Paris salon, and the Beats, since, as in the Violet Quill, gay men and lesbians dominated each of these movements.

This collection can be divided into three parts: writing composed before the formation of the Violet Quill; writing executed during the period of the Violet Quill or read at its meetings; writing completed after the breakup of the Violet Quill. The parts are not equal in size—in fact, the last section is the longest—but I have tried to give a representative sample of the work, emphasizing the best material. I should also add that not all of the writers are represented equally: Some of the writers were and continue to be very prolific, while others wrote relatively little. Some of the writers produced, dare I say it, better work than others. Finally, some of the writers wrote pieces that could fit more easily into a volume like this one.

I have in all cases, save George Whitmore's and Andrew Holleran's, gone back through the members' papers, combing their files for unpublished material. I'm happy to say that everyone but George Whitmore is represented by unpublished material (and Whitmore's story "Getting Rid of Robert," which Robert Ferro saw as a personal attack that hastened the breakup of the VQ, has appeared only once, in a magazine). Excerpts from Felice Picano's journal, which is the finest and the most accurate record of the period, and from Michael Grumley's diary have never appeared before. These give a remarkable picture of how these writers lived day by day during the most active period of their association and at its end. Picano is also represented here by a portion of a new novel that dramatizes the conflicts between pre- and post-AIDS generations of gay men. Chris Cox's "Aunt Persia and the Jesus Man" has never appeared before; this story—"Doe's Pillow," the title under which Cox read it at a VQ meeting—is reconstructed out of literally hundreds of pages of rewrites. Cox rewrote each paragraph individually, going through at least a dozen drafts. The version contained here is not meant to be a final rendering of this story, but only my best attempt to get this hilarious southern gothic tale into print. Except for a lively guide, *A Key West Companion*, Cox wrote no other books. Instead, he entered publishing, first as an assistant to Bill Whitehead—who edited Edmund White and Robert Ferro—and then as an editor in his own right, encouraging a new generation of writers, including Matthew Stadler, the author of *Landscape: Memory*, who worked briefly as Cox's assistant.

I should say something about Andrew Holleran's "Sleeping Soldiers." Holleran read two stories at the VQ, "Sleeping Soldiers" and "Someone Is Crying in the Château de Berne." Felice Picano published the latter story in his remarkable anthology *A True Likeness*, which contains work by all of the VQ except Chris Cox, but Picano admitted that even after a decade he remembered "Sleeping Soldiers" as the better story. I asked Holleran to send me the story, but he was unwilling to do so until he had time to work on it again. The present version is a reworking of that early tale and recalls Holleran's youthful period in the army.

Robert Ferro is represented by letters and an essay never before published as well as by sections of *The Family of Max Desir, The Blue Star*, and *Second Son*. The lecture "Gay Literature Today" was given at Oberlin College, and the energy he put into this last critical statement is recorded in Michael Grumley's journal. Ferro wrote very little criticism, but the little he wrote is striking.

We usually regard fiction as a mirror held up to reflect life, and it is true that much of the work here is meant to preserve and reflect the life of gay men at the time these pieces were written. Current literary theory goes further and argues that the language and the shape of a text is borrowed from and "constructed" by earlier texts; therefore, no work can produce anything "new" or anything that would challenge the existing power structure. But in the case of the VQ—although much of the work is reflective of the social order and indebted to past concept—the very act of representing gay life altered that life, by indicating that it was worthy of depiction, of creative energy. The VQ represented to other gay people a way of living a gay life that might not have otherwise seemed possible to them. The VQ writers depicted a community that was not available. And after the appearance of AIDS, they worked to imagine a way of living with the disease even as they tried to cope with it.

In an early essay, Edmund White wrote, ''When I was a teenager, I recall . . . the intramural loathing extended to all public figures who were reputed to be gay—'Oh, he's not a good conductor; he's gay.' '' One of the prejudices that the Violet Quill fought against was the notion that gay fiction, because it was gay, could not be good. It lacked, straight critics were quick to point out, the universality, the depth of feeling, the connectedness to normal human life, that was the privileged condition of straight writers. The Violet Quill writers fought against this prejudice and showed that by exploring with ruthless honesty and craft the experiences of gay men, they could produce a body of work as important as the straight novels of domestic life or of business affairs, the tales that had dominated *The New Yorker* and had become the approved mode of American fiction. It is time to look at their accomplishment, and form a more complete sense of what they did and of the era in which they lived and wrote.

The Violet Quill Reader

A Letter to Ann and Alfred Corn

Edmund White

Ann and Alfred Corn were close friends of Edmund White's, who dedicated his first novel, Forgetting Elena, *to them. In the summer of 1969, they were living in France when White wrote this account of his participation in the Stonewall Riots. Alfred Corn has since become a major American poet; his books include* All Roads at Once, Notes of a Child of Paradise, *and the recent* Autobiographies.

July 8, 1969

Dear Ann and Alfred,

Well, the big news here is Gay Power. It's the most extraordinary thing. It all began two weeks ago on a Friday night. The cops raided the Stonewall, that mighty Bastille which you know has remained impregnable for three years, so brazen and so conspicuous that one could only surmise that the Mafia was paying off the pigs handsomely. Apparently, however, a new police official, Sergeant Smith, has taken over the Village, and he's a peculiarly diligent lawman. In any event, a mammoth paddy wagon, as big as a school bus, pulled up to the Wall and about ten cops raided the joint. The kids were all shooed into the street; soon other gay kids and straight spectators swelled the ranks to, I'd say, about a thousand people. Christopher Street was completely blocked off and the crowds swarmed from the [*Village*] *Voice* office down to the Civil War hospital.

As the Mafia owners were dragged out one by one and shoved into the wagon, the crowd would let out Bronx cheers and jeers and clapping. Someone shouted "Gay Power," others took up the cry—and then it dissolved into giggles. A few more prisoners—bartenders, hatcheck boys—a few more cheers, someone starts singing "We Shall

1

Overcome''—and then they started camping on it. A drag queen is shoved into the wagon; she hits the cop over the head with her purse. The cop clubs her. Angry stirring in the crowd. The cops, used to the cringing and disorganization of the gay crowds, snort off. But the crowd doesn't disperse. Everyone is restless, angry, and high-spirited. No one has a slogan, no one even has an attitude, but something's brewing.

Some adorable butch hustler boy pulls up a *parking meter*, mind you, out of the pavement, and uses it as a battering ram (a few cops are still inside the Wall, locked in). The boys begin to pound at the heavy wooden double doors and windows; glass shatters all over the street. Cries of ''Liberate the Bar.'' Bottles (from hostile straights?) rain down from the apartment windows. Cries of ''We're the Pink Panthers.'' A mad Negro queen whirls like a dervish with a twisted piece of metal in her hand and breaks the remaining windows. The door begins to give. The cops turn a hose on the crowd (they're still within the Wall). But they can't aim it properly, and the crowd sticks. Finally the door is broken down and the kids, as though working to a prior plan, systematically dump refuse from waste cans into the Wall, squirting it with lighter fluid, and ignite it. Huge flashes of flame and billows of smoke.

Now the cops in the paddy wagon return, and two fire engines pull up. Clubs fly. The crowd retreats.

Saturday night, the pink panthers are back in full force. The cops form a flying wedge at the Greenwich Avenue end of Christopher and drive the kids down towards Sheridan Square. The panthers, however, run down Waverly, up Gay Street, and come out *behind* the cops, kicking in a chorus line, taunting, screaming. Dreary middle-class East Side queens stand around disapproving but fascinated, unable to go home, as though torn between their class loyalties, their desire to be respectable, and their longing for freedom. Sheridan Square is cordoned off by the cops. The United Cigar store closes, Riker's closes, the deli closes. No one can pass through the square; to walk up Seventh Avenue, you must detour all the way to Bleecker.

A mad left-wing group of straight kids called the Crazies is trying to organize the gay kids, pointing out that Lindsay is to blame (the Crazies want us to vote for Procaccino, or ''Prosciutto,'' as we call him).* A Crazy girl launches into a tirade against Governor Rocke-

---

*Mayor John V. Lindsay was that summer involved in a reelection fight against

feller, "Whose Empire," she cries, "Must Be Destroyed." Straight Negro boys put their arms around me and say we're comrades (it's okay with me—in fact, great, the first camaraderie I've felt with blacks in years). Mattachine (our NAACP) hands out leaflets about "what to do if arrested." Some man from the Oscar Wilde bookstore hands out a leaflet describing to newcomers what's going on. I give a stump speech about the need to radicalize, how we must recognize we're part of a vast rebellion of all the repressed. Some jeers, some cheers. Charles Burch plans to make a plastique to hurl at cops.

Sunday night, the Stonewall, now reopened—though one room is charred and blasted, all lights are smashed, and only a few dim bulbs are burning, no hard liquor being sold—the management posts an announcement: "We appreciate all of you and your efforts to help, but the Stonewall believes in peace. Please end the riots. We believe in peace." Some kids, nonetheless, try to turn over a cop car. Twelve are arrested. Some straight toughs rough up some queens. The queens beat them up. Sheridan Square is again blocked off by the pigs. That same night a group of about seventy-five vigilantes in Queens chops down a wooded part of a park as vengeance against the perverts who are cruising in the bushes. "They're endangering our women and children." The *Times*, which has scarcely mentioned the Sheridan Square riots (a half column, very tame) is now so aroused by the *conservation* issue that it blasts the "vigs" for their malice toward *nature*.

Wednesday. The *Voice* runs two front-page stories on the riots, both snide, both devoted primarily to assuring readers that the authors are straight.

This last weekend, nothing much happened because it was the Fourth of July and everyone was away. Charles Burch has decided it's all a drag. When he hears that gay kids are picketing Independence Hall in Philly because they're being denied their constitutional rights, he says: "But of course, the Founding Fathers didn't intend to protect *perverts* and *criminals*." Who knows what will happen this weekend, or this week? I'll keep you posted.

Otherwise, nothing much. I've been going out with a mad boy who tried to kill me last Friday. He's very cute, and I'm sure it'd be a kick, but I think I'll take a rain check on the death scene.

---

the conservative Democratic candidate Mario A. Procaccino. Left-wing radicals believed that the election of a clearly repressive mayor might ignite the larger-scale civil unrest that the more moderate Lindsay had kept from starting.

Finished the first act of my play and outlined the second. My sister has a new boyfriend who's got $30 million, two doctorates, working on a third. She met him in the bughouse (shows the advantages in sending your daughter to the *best* bughouse in town). I'm going out to Chicago in two weeks to help her move.

I miss you both frightfully. No more fun dinners, no endless telephone conversations, no sharing of exquisite sensations, gad, it's awful.

Love,
Ed

Early Correspondence of Andrew Holleran and Robert Ferro

Andrew Holleran and Robert Ferro met at the University of Iowa's Writers' Workshop and studied with, among others, José Donoso and Kurt Vonnegut, Jr. After graduation they kept in touch as Holleran went to law school at the University of Pennsylvania and then into the army, and Ferro traveled to Rome. In 1970 the letters stopped, since both men were living in New York. However, they began writing again quite frequently starting in 1979. The letters printed here are from the early period of correspondence, 1967–70.

ANDREW HOLLERAN TO ROBERT FERRO

October 23, 1967
Philadelphia

O Robert—

Things couldn't be worse. Go read this in the catacombs, or a crypt. (Did I ever ask you, why don't you set your novel in Rome instead of Florence? I mean aside from the news value of the flood and all.)

About my novel: It's appearing serialized in the Sunday *Times* under Obituaries.

I mean I am at last taking EVERYBODY's advice and putting it aside. And starting a new one. Set in the Moffit Apts. You have the opening scene, dangling a string of imported Viennese sausages from your second-floor aerie. Listen: to the tune of "Good Day Sunshine." Listen again: A man at Harcourt read it this summer, sent it back saying I had talent (he was being nice to his secretary—who is a friend of mine and whom he was dictating the letter to). (Don't believe a

5

word of it.) (Of course I have talent, don't we all.) And that he'd read it again if I corrected certain things—like all the characters were lifeless. Well, after spending the summer writing a play called *Promise You Won't Say You Love Me** (I see a part for you in it opposite Tuesday Weld or Hermione Gingold), which is now at an agency in N.Y. gathering mold, I came to Law School (more, much more about that later) and wrote the book again—this time, very excited (oh hell I get excited when I write a grocery list), thinking, Baby Kiddo, you have got characters. And I did get characters. Which is one reason the rewriting was valuable; I convinced myself I can do characters. But anyway, Robert, I get it back *tout pris* with a letter saying Now he thinks the book is about the "difference between the ordinary and beautiful people" (and could I write a treatise on that [for which one, you're giggling]) and the "pressures on kids to get into good colleges" or some such really elegant and Nobel Prize–winning theme; well, I was a little crushed—but am going to send it out to Random House or somebody while I start this 2nd novel, just to have it off my mind. Have also written 2 stories—in fact, I've done as much, if not more, writing here than in Iowa; the fact is I know when I stop writing I have to do Property or Torts and that keeps me writing.

O Robert—Law School is not to be believed. I mean it's OK in the sense that there's lots of time to write, but the kids, aside from a few witty bright ones, are of another race; I mean I guess I didn't realize that some people have no imagination—I mean, you know, that other faculty that sees a little more to life than the usual routine that fills ninety-nine percent of everyone else's. But no more—they're all decent and civilized but not Souls.

Yesterday I went up to see John Wideman out of desperation.[†] He was reading the *Sat. Review* review of his book which just came out; very nice guy, kind of pleasantly gentle with success, if you know what I mean—Robert, they are starting a second printing, I mean a second printing—which means paperback ultimately—which might mean MOVIE RIGHTS. This is all my construction, he only modestly entertains the remote possibility—but good reviews in the *N.Y. Times,*

---

*Holleran did in fact write this play, which has never been published or produced.
[†]John Edgar Wideman was a student at the Iowa Writers' Workshop at the same time as Ferro, Grumley, and Holleran. He has since become one of the leading black novelists in the country.

Sat Rev, all others—congrats letter from Kurt Vonnegut. Not that it eats me up anymore. I haven't the energy left at this stage to feel envy—but it does something when you then walk to the library, pick up the *Atlantic Monthly,* and find Mary Kathleen O'Donnell's story in the issue; and then two other friends from Harvard in two other mags. Well, no wailing.

We'll see . . .

And now we come to your Thing—

I mean aside from drinking champagne from Jacqueline de Ribe's Playtex Living Gloves and wading nude in the Trevi Fountain for a crowd of hysterical paparazzi and gushing American Express tourists from Billerica, Mass., how has the rest of life been going? I do mean THE BOOK. LE LIVRE. EL LIBRO. Please don't tell me it's accepted; or if you do, tell me in a nice way. I do hope you're having luck with it.

We don't want the entire company wiped out. Ooo . . . a little bitter, there. Watcha yaself! Robert, have you seen *Reflections in a Golden Eye*? Certainly the movie you should have been in; I mean people rode horses and everything—*

No, really a movie that knocked me out.

Have been bopping out to Bryn Mawr, where all the girls are not Katharine Hepburn; actually, Penn girls are quite stunning. Yesterday I was so desperate to get out of the large fart of polluted air in which the Law School rests that I streaked down to the train station and told them, Give me the next train to the Country. They, of course, thought I was nuts. After long explanations, I got a ticket to Paoli, went out and finally found peace huddling under a rock on the ninth fairway of a golf course breathing again and looking at bugs and leaves. Last night saw Herbie Mann at the Showboat—such a phony.

And how many decadent fêtes have you been to at which the hostess makes sure the guests issue out onto the beach to see the dead manta ray she had ordered from the fishmonger that morning for the celebration?

Tell me what you're doing.

---

*This running gag is based on a dare that Robert Ferro would ride a white horse naked in a parade down Michigan Avenue when both he and Holleran became famous writers.

I do miss Iowa—especially, you and José [Donoso] and Chap and Lorraine.* I really do, and I never even contemplated it.

I thought, Fly Fly away to the East and Live Again! But all ah wanna do, chile, is run around on a bicycle telling people about my last short story. Oh baby how sick. Luv it. This next novel has got to be good. I think what you need absolutely in this game, besides talent, is stamina. Just stick it out. Oh can't you see me sending in stories to the *Post* at age ninety-two when the magazine has ceased publishing for twenty years. As Tom Lehrer said, It is a sobering thought that when Mozart was my age, he had already been dead two years.

WRITE WRITE WRITE WRITE oh I do need a letter. Can't tell how the elegant little *tarjeta postal*† made me dissolve into tears over the oatmeal in the Law School Cafeteria—Oh, they all whispered, it's the crazy novelist. Oh, who wants to play their game? It's so easy, and so dull—Robert, I must have an island in the Caribbean quick.

Andrew

ROBERT FERRO TO ANDREW HOLLERAN

January 23, 1968
Rome

Dear Andrew,

Thanks for the soothing letter. It's impossible what the human mind can endure. *You* were *crushed!* For a while I felt like an asparagus.

I've solved [in my novel], I think, that nasty problem with point of view. The first half is rewritten to my satisfaction, and the second half, started before I went to Florence to return to the scene of the crime, looks entirely possible.‡ It's scary to see all my characters running around in the flesh behaving beautifully. I had to watch myself and refrain from calling them by their fictional names. I'm afraid Fiore is not what she has become to me, but that's her fault, not mine. My characterization is a great improvement on the original. It will take me a while to get the real one out of my mind. What my memory does

---

*Chap and Lorraine Freeman, husband and wife, were also students in the writing workshop. They were especially close friends of Robert Ferro's.

†The postcard is lost.

‡Ferro is referring to a novel that has not been published. The episode he discusses appeared in the opening of *The Blue Star*, reprinted elsewhere in this volume.

to life is a huge improvement on life itself. So it was a great mistake to go and stay in the pensione, but it also gave me some new stuff on Rena that I can use. But I did things like ask Rena about her magazine articles, then realized that I had made that up. When the houseboy came into the dining room with a new silver soup tureen, I asked what had happened to the old china one. In the book he drops it. It turned out he did drop it, but only after I left. Many other things, plus a big bill. Spooky.

You sound your usual vulgarly productive self. "Oh, yes, today, I wrote a play and six short stories, but that's only because I got up late. Was up until four, you see, finishing off the novel." How are Torts? Or is it tortes? I think it's all nonsense. You don't need money, so why not drop everything and write, if only to commit yourself irrevocably. I'm at the point where the only way I can survive (without my father's money) is to write and sell my body. Soon no one will want to buy that, and then I will be left to do—as a last resort—that which I want to do, the only thing I can do. But you will be a lawyer and a teacher and a savant and a Renaissance person. Andrew, drop out before it's too late. It's so much easier to suffer in a four-hundred-year-old palazzo than in the University of Pennsylvania Dining Hall. Studying all that stuff will addle your brain. Your characters will start saying things like "I've just fallen in love with the party of the first part," and "behoove," and "right of way." And so on.

It bugs me slightly that you're writing so much even though you eat with philistines. You always did. Write a lot, I mean. Maybe you're right to pick up insurance along the way. Could it conceivably be that you will change your mind about writing? You see I had literally no choice. Never will.

Rome is a cold, wrapped-up city, very private, very closed. As it should be. Someone like you, as industrious, would find few distractions. I'm pleased with it for that reason. I will be able, starting tomorrow, to work all day every day and finish the book by the middle of May. That's my plan.

Must rush—tea with the countess.

Robert

ANDREW HOLLERAN TO ROBERT FERRO

Feb. 23, 1968
Philadelphia

Robert—

So much has happened. None of which is worth telling about. Point: Book is returned with suggestions of other editors to send it to; but coupled with reaction of a literate friend here, I see nothing worked. (However, I just KNOW that if I switch it to the 3rd person, it will be a masterpiece.) However, I did please myself; that is, I did all I thought I could do to it, and achieved, I thought, some utterly brilliant set pieces (I don't know if that's the phrase; the point is a lot of great individual scenes, but no one seemed to get that feeling which is more than scenes, which is the general movement of a piece of art), and so I can put it away. When I think of all the people who suggested I do that long ago, I . . . Well, I cry a bit. Laugh a bit. Fall into a coma a bit.

However, am now working on another. This is frankly facile. But that is what I do best, I'm afraid. I mean it's facilely a major piece. What the hell. It involves America. She is seen on Wabash Avenue directing the picture in which YOU were supposed to ride naked on a horse. Ah well, there will be other cameras. You betcha sweet ass.

(At least I don't SOUND like a lawyer.)

(That's another moral—and I do mean moral—crisis altogether.)

Listen. Got a letter from *The New Yorker* (I know you got them when you were six) full of sweet praise and a generally rather arrogant suggestion that I try something more simple and straightforward on my next story. Piss on them. I *will* try the difficult and SUCCEED with the difficult and be difficult with them ALL when they try to crash my palazzo for interviews.

Robert—write no book. Your letter was a masterpiece. I read it countless times. I quoted it to people here. I pored over phrases. ("Rome is a cold, wrapped-up city, very private, very closed" is now the first line of my new novel. Even though it occurs in Chicago. So be more *careful* next time.) I mean it was most enjoyed. Write another now.

What's the story anywhere? I am glad about your book. You will be done soon apparently and I wish you better results than mine.

(Bitter? not at all.)

OH *SHIT*.

The draft is a sweet situation. ROTC now has a claim on these precious fingers. Robert, you can imagine, I don't care about this novel, but it's there and I have to write it, and I can't wait to get to the next one, which is about [line inked out]—say nothing to no one.

Went out to the suburbs here to see a thing called the Barnes Collection. Amazing Cézannes. Why aren't we painters? But we ARE—you are destined to be one of the great stylists, you little shit. José told Lucy [Rosenthal, another Iowa student] and me that we had no poetic faculties whatsoever, or at least a very low quotient in that department.

The world press may give little notice, but it is a matter of some portent that rock 'n' roll in America has split into two bifurcating streams: West Coast phony psychedelic, and Negro Motown Soul. I don't think you should wait too long to come back. The situation is grave.

What is your body going for these days? A plate of spaghetti—

I spent an hour this evening in the lib[rary] reading back copies of *Variety* to see what songs were popular the summer my book takes place.

O Robert, writing is such a pain. There comes a time in every book when you sag—I mean you know you've got so much to go still, and just lose for a while the reason that made you whip through the first two chapters. I do hope it's temporary. What is it about writing? I mean the hesitance to get down to work—the resistance to compose? It's so illogical and yet it happened in Iowa, it's happening here. There comes a time when you have to make yourself work. On something you love and enjoy every other time.

Robert, have been reading *The Importance of Being Earnest*—so good—would give everything to write another one even close. You have a part—do *not* sign with Ponti.*

Battily,
Andrew

---

*Carlo Ponti (b. 1913), the great Italian film producer and husband of Sophia Loren.

ROBERT FERRO TO ANDREW HOLLERAN

March 8, 1968
Roma

Oh, Andrew, mistake number one: mustn't write me at American Express. One takes an apartment in Rome to avoid places like that. It is only by the merest chance that I came upon your letter at all. Otherwise it would have sat there thirty days, then been returned to you. As it was, it sat just the right amount of time. You remember that Samuel Clemens threw all incoming mail into a basket that he kept by his bed—it always takes, he said, a few days for a letter to ripen. As it was, your letter was very ripe, a bit past mellow, really, but I enjoyed it anyway.

Yours was one of those letters that spur me to write back right away (a great stylist would have said "immediately" instead of "right away," you little shit). So many questions.

I quoted you on the difficulties of writing great books to my parents in a letter today. They'll love it. I'm introducing my parents into the delights of letter writing lately. Sample line: "I'm convinced that all it takes to be really happy is a good wardrobe and a decent occupation." That's family jargon for "send more money." My mother invariably replies with "darling"'s and mommy patter.

I'm so glad you're writing through all of this Tort shit. You completely ignore my advice, and I can only surmise that you know something I don't know. If you had spent half the time educating my parents that you have spent educating yourself, you'd be propped up here in Rome in a small, rather inexpensive, but nice flat down the street from me. But maybe that wouldn't work for you. You've certainly produced ten times more than I have (having produced nothing myself) and yes, a degree in law, coupled with an MFA and an MA and BA in English at Harvard,* well! All that earning power. If you turn into a high-priced agent, I'll murder you, you little shit.

Why go on about my book. I haven't looked at it for a week although I plan to finish it in the next two months. This time for good. I'm going to send it around and not rewrite it anymore. I'm itching to get on to something else. It's been almost three years with this damn thing, and it's only two hundred pages long. Now really. Write me

---

*Ferro is not exactly correct. Holleran has both an MA and an MFA from Iowa.

immediately about the Curtis Brown agency.* They have a story of mine, and I want to know if they're worthy. It seems that the agent I had at William Morris moved over to them, and my story (a lovely bit of froth I whipped up one night) was forwarded to her. She'll probably say she likes the story just so she can get a look at the novel. It's eleven pages of surface perfection, a conscious effort at stylistics that was an experiment related to the novel.

I've always thought that *The New Yorker* magazine tries so desperately to imitate itself that, like a man who looks at himself in the mirror, it gets everything backwards.

Have been reading Wilde myself—*De Profundis.* It's a shock to find him without, for once, his sense of humor. I think it was his real disgrace—not the trial and prison, etc.—but that treatise on gloom and sadness. He should never have admitted to us that he was wrong. Because, of course, he wasn't. What will life do to us, if it did that to *him*?†

I've just put on my white tie and white tails and white hat and there's all those steps to go down, out into the city, dancing. Oh Budapest!

Robert

ANDREW HOLLERAN TO ROBERT FERRO

April 2, 1968
Philadelphia

Robert—

I'm glad I can write to you at last. I have just finished my new novel.‡ Stop screaming and calling me a slut. The fact that I work fast means nothing as I have explained at length—how obvious can the record be—it has nothing to do with quality. I have now the

TERRIFYING

---

*An agent at the Curtis Brown literary agency had been reading one of Holleran's plays.

†Although this reference appears to indicate that Ferro and Holleran were open about their homosexuality, they were still at this point in their lives keeping it hidden from each other.

‡*How to Ride a Motorcycle with Humility* was never published.

job of reading the damn thing. I am scared (a) that it will be a piece of shit or not a novel at all (I've only worked on it in sections—God knows what will happen when you put them together), and (b) that there will be maybe 12 pages I have to redo to make it right. I'd almost prefer nothing to that. I can't labor on any more typing.* It's called *How to Ride a Motorcycle with Humility* (used to be the title of that story Marna Klein hated—you were the only one in the class amused—thank god for taste) and has 2 quotes (W. J. Bryan—you shall not crucify mankind upon a cross of gold!, and H. James—I have always thought the raising of a woman's eyebrow across the dinner table more dramatic than the fall of Rome) and an Invocation of the Muse and 12 chapters. Very funny last scene, but—crap!—is it continuous—a novel?!

I dread looking. I always rush into stuff, discover I overlooked something. Anyway you get the benefit of my creative post-coital elation (no, it's depression, isn't it—I no longer separate the 2 feelings—I can maintain them absolutely simultaneously—I know you've been doing it since you were 3).

I think I am going to slip out of Law School without ever having briefed a single case. Let's face it, I have stopped writing since arrival—the law is such a drag. I have been excited by 2 cases all year out of a total of maybe 8,000.

(Papa suggested I should "give the law a chance"—after all, he said, you have no way of earning a living—oh the heart went thump thump thump.)

Write promptly.

Andrew

ANDREW HOLLERAN TO ROBERT FERRO

Nov. 19, 1968
Ft. Benning, GA

Robert—

Where the shit are you? Diving for coins thrown by fat tourists in Guadeloupe? Herding sheep in Mallorca? Waiting for the cameras to roll with you doing the Life of Christ as a musical comedy?

Oh weak—weak—

---

*This letter is handwritten.

But then I am weak, and terrified, and trapped; Robert, I am at Ft. Benning, not for the pecans or country music, though there is plenty of both here, but rather because I was carried kicking and screaming into the modern action army on Aug. 28. Having made it through basic training thinking I would be a spy in Cannes for the rest of the hitch, I am scheduled to go to Advanced Infantry Training at Ft. McClellan, which is, tootsie, Vietnam. I was luckily held up [from going to Ft. McClellan] for a security check (if you've traveled outside the country, you're a Red) so I missed the shipment, but I could go any day. I am frantically trying to change my classification from Infantry.

I have not seen a typewriter in 10 weeks, but I have been writing poems out the ass (everything around here produces an angry ode). You are so fortunate to be out of the clutches of this Kafkaesque nightmare. All because you were swathed in bandages like the Prince of Peace when you were 5 years old. I will not harm a single Vietnamese. After a propaganda film drove me to the library, I am appalled at how illegal, contrived, murderous our being there is, and that is not just liberal/pacifist cant. It really is on a par with the Nazis.

ANDREW HOLLERAN TO ROBERT FERRO

[The following letter is in two parts. The first part, written in South Carolina, is undated and typed. The second part is handwritten and dated May 28, 1969, from Heidelberg, Germany.]

Ferro:

I am sitting in the Piedmont of South Carolina: Ft. Jackson. Tonight I board an omnibus, motor down to Charleston; after dinner on the quay (a pale lavender seafood affair) the troops are boarded with cattle prods into a capacious C-141 where we spend the flight sitting on our duffel bags, eating C-rations, and watching others vomit. No in-flight flick. I deplane in Germany. I am to be a ghostwriter for Marlene Dietrich; the Army doesn't know it, but I'll convince them it's necessary to the national defense.

The point is, babycakes, I escaped through a fluke of the computer system from going to where everyone I know is going: Nammy. The point is that I'm stuck in the motherfucking organization for only one more year, when I'll emerge really depressed but convinced that the only way is up. This summer, a friend is making his own real full-length honest-to-god movie in the Mediterranean and I will take leave to see that. Also plan to hitchhike as far as I can on Air Force planes (the imperial fleet, with flights to Anchorage, Tahiti, Kabul, and Reemy Air Force Base in glorious San Juan: You walk in and take your pick). I know, I know you have been dawdling from sandbar to sandbar for the last six months, and though surrounded by Babbitts I cannot shed a tear: You can always just fling the rope from the moorings with an Oh really! and sail off immediately into a Bahamian sunset. Rome—Bahama—Manhattan. What an axis! Really, you could rule the world. And you will, you will.

It is close. Clammy. Outside, the barracks peel. The southern sky is overcast. I have turned in my bed linens, I have to make the 2000 formation, pick up my records, tote duffel bag, laundry bag, and small elegant leather suitcase embossed with my brother-in-law's initials to the fucking bus and then endure the hideous cattle transport to Germany. The only funny thing all the troops did in basic was when they'd get us into trucks with wooden railings to take us out to the rifle range, everyone would join in a concerted chorus of bleats and moos: perfect. At first I didn't mind being stuck with these people. It was like traveling in another garden, all new and exciting. Now it gets on my nerves. I just don't speak to anyone. They're all much younger for one thing, and I am filled up on picturesque charm, and, need I say, our interests are somewhat divergent.

May 28, 1969

Roberto:

Am stationed in Heidelberg, headquarters of the whole damn operation. Why aren't you in Rome, dummy? I have no one to visit. We live in the old SS headquarters. In Frankfurt I slept in the former Nazi prison for top-ranking Allied prisoners, right next to the railroad station but not touched by bombs. Shall I go to Paris this weekend? Stuttgart? Berlin? Muncie, Indiana? Do return to the shores of light and we'll discuss Rilke as we walk through the grape arbors.

ANDREW HOLLERAN TO ROBERT FERRO

15 April 1970
Heidelberg

Dear Mr. Ferro:

Here it is, Robert, the sun has finally broken through the clouds, the clouds that cover Heidelberg all year round till, when the sun comes out, you learn not to rush to the window and gush because in one second it will go right back behind the clouds, thus making of you a prize fool, gushing over NOTHING. Robert, while looking for my W-2 form last night, I came upon your inimitable letter, written from the poop deck of some mammoth sailing vessel becalmed in the Encantadas—or merely a yacht marina in Boca Raton—and fumed anew at to why you are such a prize schlep of a correspondent; or perhaps I have bad breath, I don't know. But I would like to hear from you very much, no more said. Robert, I am no longer at Ft. Benning; no, I am just downriver from the bridge Goethe called the most beautiful in the world (when viewed from a certain angle) fresh from skiing at Garmisch, cruising the Aegean, in between trips, yes the next one will be a quick hop from Zurich to Mombasa, where I will sleep among the giraffes and wildebeests waiting for that first tangerine flush of sunlight on Mt. Kilimanjaro—then, yes, to Paris for the summer. AND I'M STILL IN THE ARMY, O shit. Robert, I have written since last we met 456 three-act plays, 26 long novels, 19 novellas, 2,345 unpublished short stories, and a very few brief volumes of poetry and collected *pensées.* How's your production?

I'm sure you took that all seriously. Robert, what can I say? I am in Heidelberg, charming university town on the banks of the Neckar, among whose graduates is Joseph Goebbels, I read last night. We go hiking in the hills for edelweiss and cow patties, return to have drinks on the Happstrasse, or perhaps a concert of sonatas and ballades tonight on the Zeegarten. (Yawn.) Then there's cleaning the latrine in the mornings and running off personnel rosters on the mimeograph machine all day in the basement and not being able to eat breakfast because the mess sergeant said I came too late to sign the head count. Whatever you're doing, Robert, I hope it stinks. I went to London and saw *Lonesome Cowboys, Z, Funny Girl, The Reckoning, Last Summer,* and *Way of the World, Hadrian VII, Richard II,* and oh shit, I spent 7 days in theatres from 2 in the afternoon till midnight, I returned suffering from exposure—chill winter winds in Piccadilly as I stood checking the newspaper before descending into the odious Underground.

Robert, much has happened: That is, I finally finished *Remembrance of Things Past* and I don't know what to say—the idea that Joyce ended the novel is so absurd; it's Proust who ended the novel, simply by doing something so complete, monumental, perfect, that what the fuck can you do afterwards? Really, Robert, I remember your remark about all you were doing at Iowa's being "finger-exercises" and this idea that one is just preparing for the magnum opus near the end of one's *vie*—I mean, why write a book, even a good novel, of course there is *Bovary*, etc., but after *Remembrance*—well, I'm not through thinking, but that certainly is the major event in my education, consciousness, etc., thus far. Robert, I finally placed a story (never say "sold," dummy) to *The New* something or other, you know the one with the pastel seasonal covers and all the glossy ads and clever cartoons, and—I guess—they publish Creative Writing too yes, but it doesn't come out till next Christmas.* I await the Nobel Prize the following spring. Robert, am working on a novel which has taken all year and may be a piece of schmozola but it takes me so long now to finally do anything, draft after draft a way of writing I once utterly despised. Robert, what is happening to the world? Are we totally out? OR do you wear bell-bottom trousers, coat of navy blue, scarves, a water pipe, and paint your belly button pistachio-glisterine? WHERE ARE YOU

WHERE IS ANYBODY

who has taste, wit, a heightened sensitivity to life. Robert, a winter twilight on the Kurfürstendamm, listening to the bells of the various animals high in the hills of Mykonos, watching General Goodpaster award The German Grenadiers the best rocket division—oh what are these to the replies of friends you wish to hear from? Write, you shithead. And I do hope you are reasonably pleased with the direction of ... things ... and that you feel ... well, what can I say? I've been unhappy so long I think I'm getting bored with it.

---

*Holleran's story "The Holy Family" was published in the January 2, 1971, edition of *The New Yorker*.

FOR THE DEPUTY CHIEF OF STAFF, COMMUNICATIONS-
ELECTRONICS:

Andrew

ROBERT FERRO TO ANDREW HOLLERAN

July 19, 1970
Largo Febo

Dear Andrew,

Yes, I am in Rome, to answer your last question first (as though I just received your letter yesterday—it was sent, as near as I can figure, three months ago). (But one had better let A. H.'s letters sit about for a while, to ripen, as Mark Twain advised, to mellow; and meanwhile use the ether to correspond. I pick up all sorts of messages from you on the ether all the time. Don't you mine?)

But then one runs the risk of losing one's quarry. Has in fact the Army sent you elsewhere? Are you reading this in Darjeeling in 1971? Three months is a long time in the Army, they tell me. Anything can happen. Well, your mother and I hope for the best.

Heidelberg. A city in northwest Baden-Württemberg, in southwest West Germany. Its university was founded in 1386 and its population is 126,500 (now 501). It is also famous for the discovery, nearby, of a bit of human lower jaw, found in 1907, from which was reconstructed (no mean feat) what is referred to as Heidelberg Man, a primitive of the Middle Pleistocene Age (making it in actuality 502). But never mind. One does not have friends or family there so I really can't help you in any way to make yourself more comfortable than you have already managed by yourself.

Yes, the whole thing is a debasing affair. How you managed it is beyond all of us. But soon, very soon, you'll be a free man again, and of course you've heard the rumors, which no doubt have leaked by now out of Rome, that your name is on the list of the Pope's secret cardinals. (Am I amusing you? This is a bit like visiting a friend in the hospital.)

Now for a bit of splashy news. Where to begin? I think you are already familiar with the early facts of the biography: The yacht, the *Tana*, was my father's (still is, we didn't sink it, contrary to expectation all the way around) and we took it (Michael Grumley, whom you know from flat Iowa, and I) on a five-month voyage down and into the

Bahamas in search of the fabled Lost Continent of Atlantis. Subsequently (Nabokov), we found it. Covered with the ooze and slime of the ages (we all know people like that) it suddenly was there, just beneath the bow, unnaturally geometric and strange, and one had only to don one's pink aqua-lung and mask, drop over the side, and hover a bit, to establish for all time one's place in the annals of important archaeological achievers. Troy (Ilium, to you and Vonnegut), the graves at Marathon, Heidelberg Man—what are they in comparison? Very little, said the editors at Doubleday as they commissioned us to write a book about it. *(Tiens!)*

We returned to New York in May 1969 and collaborated, rather brilliantly, on *Atlantis, the Autobiography of a Search* (to be published this coming October). One has learned so much from the experience (including the art of parenthesis), but if I were pushed to pinpoint the single most exciting moment of the trip, discovery, and ensuing ramifications, I would have to say it was the first five minutes of holding the book's galleys in me hands—that, my dear, was the real discovery.

Why detail the trip, the discovery? You'll read about it soon enough. One admits there is great fright involved, usually conveyed in the subtle cinematic way with a close-up of flaring nostrils, to think that one's baby is to be picked over (unfortunate associations of metaphors) by the world (U.S. first, and then England) and that, for once, you will not be able to watch the face of every reader of your work, as he is reading it. So after all the hoo-ha of six different degrees in creative writing, one's first book is nonfiction.

And now the stunner: We are returning to New York in September to promote it, to behave, as best we know how, like Jackie Susann, to appear on the fabled (yes, he, like Atlantis, rates that word) Johnny Carson show, David Frost, Dick Cavett—the big ones, and a host of other, smaller, day- and nighttime attractions and divertissements, designed to soothe and edify, to entertain and titillate those who have not. One is preparing one's answers and wardrobe at the very moment. There are only a few weeks of anonymity left, at best.

Meanwhile, we are propped up in a very showy, though empty, five-terraced apartment, high above Rome, close by the Piazza Navona, wondering the while, if it would be wise, financially, to let our New York apartment go (the address would never do for Cult heroes). Like the rest of us, I couldn't bear New York for the nine months we were there (though I miss it a bit now), nor the rest of the country, which if it were a musical comedy would have closed in New Haven on the second night (between the first and second acts). I have gotten myself to the point where I loathe crowds of more than three people, except sexually, and this of course lets out the entire United States. Here, in Rome, one floats above the language (a line from the book) and, up in this blimp of an apartment, one floats above everything. It is divine, and there's a nook here for you when you come.

We will be away from mid-September until the end of October, I think, though with Mass Media as it is, one never knows. We might come fleeing back after a week of it or one gaffe-ridden half-hour spot on the tube. Eventually the book will be made into a movie, the witches here tell us, so there's money to be made. But the movie will not be very good. It will be terrible, in fact, and we are instructed to take the money and run with it, to Switzerland, where one's life is digital and cool, and where, I'm told, there is a pleasant lake.

José has struck it big. We should all learn. He finished his *Obscene Bird of Night* (retitled something else very badly—like *Fallen Archangel*) and he and Maria Pilar and their adopted daughter are living in Barcelona.* We spent a few days with them in Marbella in March. Very happy. He is receiving prize after prize and many offers of translation and foreign publication. In short, the crest of the wave.

I am writing a book about the assassination of the Pope and the destruction of the Holy Roman Catholic Church, in the year 1999, called *The River of the City of Dream.*† Cairo figures very importantly in the narrative so a trip there is planned for early next year or late this year. Also London is in the offing, where one has friends. I am bearded and rather slim, still under my father's protection (though he has warned me lately that we are all going to be wiped out) and still in favor of the election of Edward Kennedy to the presidency. I write him encouraging notes periodically. I read Gide and Nietzsche, Bulgakov and Dinesen (the first and last have taught me how to write letters, and the second and third how to read them). You, on the other hand, had better lay off Durrell for a while.

The fan opens, flutters, and snaps shut.

Michael sends his best.

Robert

---

*José Donoso (b. 1924) published the book as *The Obscene Bird of Night*.
†The book was never completed.

P.S. I am very pleased about the placing of your story with that magazine. It's a step in the absolutely right direction. Now, for God's sake, do something about your address, which is exposing you to comment on the platform.

ANDREW HOLLERAN TO ROBERT FERRO

17 August 1970
Florida

Robert, what can I say? The whole letter was a joke? I fervently hope so. If you're a success, I cannot say what I'll do. I watch Dick Cavett: every night—last night Mort Sahl viciously attacked John Simon for sexual deviations too common to be mentioned here—and that bastard Cavett, though I think he was genuinely stunned, refused to stop the bloodletting. It was like watching a human cockfight for an hour and a half. One sat on the couch in horrors eating chocolate chip cookies, fudge ripple ice cream, and watched these men destroy each other. I am tremendously impressed. I know your nonfiction book will be elegantissimo prose even if it is about looking for Atlanta while on a trip through—but that's in GEORGIA, for heaven's sake—(?) the Bahamas. You shithead, berating me always for my diligent work (I have just finished my 3rd roman à clef) you seduce me into thinking you are wasting magnificently your life on the poop deck and then you obeat me to publication. (The Freudian phrasing of this sentence now strikes me—"you seduce me" is followed later by "you beat me"— to publication . . .) There are many years ahead of us, Robert, not all of them salad.

Have you any idea what this entry into the world means? Floating, as you so nicely say, above Rome in your empty apartment, I suspect you haven't the slightest idea what you will be subject to after you expose your slim, bearded personage to the vulgar appetites of the American people. Here alone in the small town in which I live, we have been thrown into a TIZZY at the news—my mother is selling space in our den for the show this September. As Warhol says, "In 5 yrs everyone will be famous for 15 minutes," but Robt, though I realize we must all offer ourselves to the U.S. public eventually, the question is as *what*? Cereal, author, improved gas exhaust? Life is little more nowadays than a question of packaging. But your father is in that racket, isn't he? Therefore, you must be wiser than I thought, upon first hearing of this rash exposure to the vast population of *boobus americanus.*

Secondly, thanks so much for telling me you were right there in Rome, a city I skirted too many times to mention in my big travels this spring (Formentera to Arusha, Mombasa to Basel, Memphis to St. Joe). (I went to Africa, lived with the Masai in an extinct volcano; don't think for a minute you won't see it all in *Holiday.*) In May I was in Ibiza and Formentera suicidally lonely and if I had only known José The Happy, Successful Chilean Novelist was in Barcelona I could have brought my duffel bag to him. Is there any English version of his book yet? What the hell, I would have enjoyed Marbella in March too. Neverthelessbethatasitmay, I am now out of the Army, looking forward to free dental care for the next entire year at the V.A. Hospital, and writing in Florida. In 2 weeks I go north, either to take Accounting and Federal Income Tax at Penn Law School or write for *The Mary Tyler Moore Show*. I do hope to see you if you come to New York, for this sick fantasy of appearing on talk shows to promote a book which your mind (by now rotted with ambition) only invented over this morning's pasta . . .

Near the Piazza Navona . . .

What joy success brings to your friends—and how deodorizing. Could we have exchanged letters at all if I had not sold to That Magazine, and you had not overcome the staff of Doubleday? I doubt it.

Robt your time is near. Has come. Comb your beard and come out iridescent, witty, elegant, intelligent, even arrogant in a charming way, from behind that panel. I think you should try for Petronius Arbiter. I think you and Kellogg's Bran Flakes could be the biggest thing that has happened to this country in the last 30 years. Who knows, Jackie Susann may pick you for the Love Machine—

> Just one of your vast Viewing Public,
> Andrew

Notes.

1. My regards to Michael, whom I do remember from Iowa.

2. I read all of Proust this past year, and to my profound embarrassment my style is now influenced not even by an Author, but a Translator; I write like C. Scott-Moncrieff. I also read Dinesen's *7 Gothic Tales*. They are pure form, no substance . . . the only literary equivalent I know of abstract art. They read like a story, have a story's characteristics, yet have no relation to life. Why did José have you read them?

What do you think of her? Also who the hell is Bulgakov? Have I offended you? (Do illuminate Dinesen for me. I haven't spoken to anyone but supply clerks for 2 yrs.)

3. Your letter was—indescribably delicious—it must have been a third draft—I estimate that at your present cycle I should have a reply to this one by October of 1975? WRITE and tell me when you will be in the Big Apple. May I talk to you for 5 minutes at the main elevator in the Seagram's Building? Have you ever tried writing a scenario? Mine is irresistible . . .

4. Since, if this entire extravaganza is even remotely true, you must have done it all with a beaver-intense Agent, could you now pass on to me some info about that? I mean, how does one get an agent?

5. I agree that galleys are better than Sex, Food, Truth, Love, and just about anything you care to mention.

6. I think that's it.

A bientot.

This letter is so neat because I typed it over. I don't like letters that are too neat, however, since my brain is more scattered, and one must, to thine ownself, be true . . .

FOR YOUR FILES
A service of Transamerica Inc.

Robt, as a literary historian—me, that is, of little note, I just thought you might be interested to know that of your 3 letters in my possession (I turned down an offer from a woman in New Orleans of $658.90 apiece) which are in my library (bound, gilt letter, FERRO, Robert. *Letters from Abroad: The Impossible Years, 1968–1970*) I have one from the days of via dei Giubbonari 98 (remember those fondly or otherwise), which ends with the following closure, peroration:

"I've just put on my white tie and white tails and white hat and there are all those white steps to go down, out into the city, dancing. Oh Budapest!"

And your more recent work, dated Largo Febo (is this *real*; what is a febo?) is ended on this note:

"The fan opens, flutters, and snaps shut."

Students at my conservatoire littéraire are divided as to whether the marked change in style means anything in terms of your larger corpus. The move from whiteness to motion (i.e., the fan's very real activity) suggests many things, all controversial. Simply for your notes . . .

P.S. Run, do not walk, to Michael Holroyd's biography of Lytton Strachey (2 Vols, recent). If you think you have ever been decadent (and don't we all) wait till you read the 2nd vol. of that life—Good Grief . . . I will say no more. The fountain has to be turned on. The colored lights have burnt out.

Maximo

ANDREW HOLLERAN TO ROBERT FERRO

Philadelphia
Labor Day, September 8, 1970

Robert:

All right, goddamn you, if those letters *aren't* third drafts then you *do* type very well. *And* your mind is an absolute Fabergé Easter egg, and it's oh so appropriate that you live on the Square of the Sun God, since a correspondent such as yourself could not live anywhere else. In fact I am tempted not to call you when you return since talking will be such an anticlimax after this. (*The entire preceding paragraph costs $5.46.*)

You persist in The Fantasy. I will answer in kind. (Really, the last thing in the original—now donated to the British Museum—was virtually a mural, scrawlings in the margin were so excessive and loop-de-loop.) BROADWAY BEAT: I have just virtually stayed up all night beside my silent telly to be there this morning when David Frost came on, so as to see, announced in the paper in advance, John Updike (waiting all week for this). He was NERVOUS. They ALL are. I began to imagine the moment of coming out around that gray pissoir-partition they have on all talk shows, the moment of having Frost lean toward you with his eyes impounded into crystalline insets by all the klieg lights, and I, too, would swallow my gum at the first "Hello." After all, out there, like a huge, blue whale floating on the Pacific swell, IS the Audience, breathing, salivating, chewing *its* gum in contentment because YOU're up there to while away the hour for them. I think Frost is a nullity; he sits on the edge of his chair with that clipboard looking like a gym instructor trying to psych up his guests to swim the 100 freestyle in record time. He should be most routine for you. The only reason he has the show is because he's ENGLISH. After two hundred and some years since THAT relationship, we still fall down in a mass of slobber of the British being so much more————than we are. Cavett, shrewd muskrat that he is, put his finger on this fact last night when Barbara Walters (I hope you have put down your orange juice and are reading this mass of material with the attention it deserves) undiplomatically recited an anecdote from her appearance on Frost (making the whole thing a little inbred, a trifle incestuous, I thought; can you imagine the day when all talk shows' conversations will consist of what happened on other talk shows?). Cavett said: Is this another show? And ended, Well, that foreigner. Of course this is Frost's sole raison d'être for holding the seat. But the real BULLETIN is this: We have entered a new era in the American mind; we have not only Cavett, Frost, Carson, Mike Douglas (won't you go on that? a pushover, and not far from home), but now Tom Kennedy (erstwhile M.C. of the afternoon game show *You Don't Say*) and—hold your buns—DINAH SHORE—have broken into the racket. When DINAH SHORE starts her own talk show, called, magnificently, *Dinah's Place*, then you know the gospel has reached the hinterland. I foresee in 2 years everyone famous à la Warhol simply because all TV will be one continuous talk show virtually going out on the street—as I could swear Cavett does some weeks, his guests are so paltry—and pulling the first five pedestrians in to converse. Simultaneously the United States will evaporate on a boiling sea; where once stood the Great Plains will be a lot of bobbing TV sets and people in inner tubes watching Carson interview Monty Rock III. But about all this: General discussions are a bit irrelevant at this point, I guess, since if you are reading this letter at all, you are no doubt reading it on a plane, which in a moment will be hijacked to Beirut. You are thinking less of cultural speculations and more of ties, haircuts, opening lines. Cavett, if he is not in a silly mood—sarcastic about EVerything—should do you very straightforwardly. I think Griffin is an impressed name-dropper, should fawn all over you; in fact, you are quite lucky in a sense; you see, you can hide behind this Escapade; they don't want *you*, they want the man who dived for Atlantis; you can almost forget your personality as irrelevant. You are a man in an aqua-lung. Be sure to have a tan and some kelp in your breast pocket. Besides, this is hardly your Major Image, your long-term offering to the bored consciousness of America. Just remember not to pick your nose on the air, and say thank you when it's over.

I *am* afraid to meet you this fall since Emily Dickinson's (with whom I identify more and more each day) refusal to meet Emerson, though he was visiting one day next door, has its points. You understand. Life is so disappointing when the forms are ordinary, as they tend to be in living. Do you lunch, by the way, with Gore Vidal? William Humphrey? Federico Fellini? The American Consul for Commercial Contracts? The less said about where I am now, the better. It is supremely tentative. . . . Though I DON'T know what to do with my life, after I send this (yawn) novel in.

Anyway after seeing Updike I realize how gutsy an experience this is to anyone of taste and sensitivity—the Walling Out (of course another huge point in your favor: there will be two of you—and The Tub) before the studio. (Of course you are theatrically inclined, as we know, having been willing to ride down Michigan Ave naked on a horse—and this will no doubt stimulate you to empyrean realms of wit.)

So I close.

The Duc de Guise

Incidentally I have begun to think that novels may be mere excuses for publishing of letters; having read now Proust to his mother, Proust to Antoine Bibesco, John Addington Symonds to everyone, and who else . . . But novels are such work. There must be an easier way to have one's letters published.

Rough Cuts from a Journal

Felice Picano

Throughout most of his writing career, Felice Picano has assiduously kept a journal. By now comprising well over twenty volumes, the journal contains notes about writing projects, ideas for stories and novels, and reminders about what to do. But it also contains the most reliable and precise account of the events concerning the Violet Quill. Picano has an eye for detail and a nose for news, as well as an ear for gossip and a taste for the juicy story. He records who was where and what they said and did. The following extracts are culled from hundreds of pages of this invaluable literary document. Of all the members of the Violet Quill, Picano has been the most prolific. He is the author of a series of psychological thrillers including Eyes *and* The Lure. *He is also the founder of the Sea Horse Press, a small publishing house dedicated to gay literature.*

1978

9/2/78, Fire Island

Sunset calm: only a distant stereo and an eight-point antlered buck in the bushes at the side of the house. The sky is blue—with a darker scrim of clouds from the west, and underneath that the mauve/taupe of the sunset sky.

I'm afraid I won't see any deer next summer. I heard that the lot that includes the sea-level deer runs has been sold. Instead there will be a house where the deer now gather. It makes me sad, like summer coming to an end, like a beautiful day half wasted in lovemaking, like the indefinable sadness that suddenly become a hole around the smooth-limbed body of Scott Facon.*

9/6/78, Fire Island

Last night at the Jim Peters' Crazy Ladies house (where I last attended a dawn pool party *cum* orgy two years ago) I went to a largish, rather disorganized dinner party at which, however, I had the good fortune to meet Andrew Holleran.

Holleran is the author of the stunning first novel *Dancer from the Dance*, which may be the first crossover commercial best-seller. Published by Morrow, it's already in another printing up to 25,000 copies and Bantam bought the paperback rights for $175,000—excellent auguries for the future of an excellent book.†

Holleran, it seemed, also wanted to meet me, thus the arranged meeting by our host. We were together most of the evening—with great pleasure—and promised to see each other back in Manhattan.

Andrew is tall, not slender, not heavy, with the awkwardness of an oversized adolescent. He must be at least my age—though he seems much younger: fresh, naive, innocent in many ways. Shy, too, perceptive, curious to find out from me—whom he knows about either through hearsay or whatever—what he ought to do next about his success. I told him what I did—I refused to be pushed into changing my life, yet accepted the inevitable changes with as much grace as I could. And above all—I tried my best to *enjoy* the advantages.

He wanted to meet George Whitmore and I promised to connect them. It's not beyond possibility to have some literary coming out for Holleran at my apartment in October. It might even be fun. I'll see what he says. It could be one of those salons where *everyone* was present.

Curious my meeting Holleran on that day. One of the predictions [in my horoscope] was increased contact with artistic, literary, social types. Also a more active love life.

---

*Scott Facon (b. 1956), artist, photographer, and onetime protégé of Robert Mapplethorpe.

†The actual figure is widely debated, but by accounts it was unusually large for the time.

9/14/78, Fire Island

Last night I went to a literary party, invited by the guest of honor himself, Andrew.

Everyone was there: faggots I'd seen around for years, publishing people I'd never met and never hoped to meet; celebrities such as Pat Loud*—Andrew's agent—Taylor Mead,[†] Fran Lebowitz[‡]; friends and authors such as Marty Duberman,[§] Barry Kaplan,[‖] George Whitmore, Larry Kramer; and others, Bob Wyatt and Susan Moldow of Avon Books.

I had fun with friends, enjoying Andrew's success. At one point we went around hand in hand and introduced ourselves to everyone famous or handsome we wanted to meet.

During the evening I had interesting chitchat: introduced Andrew to George and to Michael Denneny[¶]; talked with Pat about the now-legendary Norman Fisher**; mended fences with Marty; continued to get to know Denneny; got a complaint and a half-joking offer from Bob Wyatt (he'd read my story "The Interrupted Recital," loved it, and said something about stealing it from Delacorte when I said I was beginning to collect my stories); and above all, I watched Larry Kramer make a fool of himself.

Now, I'm not the most modest person, but in some company I feel comfortable, arrived—if you will—and so I'm usually on very good behavior. I stay with those I like, meet others shyly, keep quiet with strangers. Larry, however, is in hysteria. His novel *Faggots*, four years

---

*Pat Loud (b. 1926), one of the subjects of the PBS documentary series *An American Family*, which although designed to show the strength of family life ended up chronicling the demise of Loud's marriage.

[†]Taylor Mead (b. 1931), a writer and performer associated with Andy Warhol's Factory.

[‡]Fran Lebowitz (b. 1951), the author of *Metropolitan Life*, a collection of her hilarious magazine articles and essays.

[§]Martin Duberman (b. 1930), a professor of history and a distinguished playwright, biographer, and historian.

[‖]Barry Kaplan (b. 1944), a classmate of Holleran's and Robert Ferro's at the University of Iowa.

[¶]Michael Denneny (b. 1943), an editor at St. Martin's Press and a founder of *Christopher Street* magazine.

**Norman Fisher, a painter connected to both the Andy Warhol and Frank O'Hara circles.

in the making—also agented by Bernstein/Loud—is in deep trouble. Although Random House paid 50 G's for it, and there's a paperback floor of 150 G's—the book has not yet gone to auction—no one else bid. Everyone hates it. Not only because it's politically retrograde or repulsive (which it is), not only because it's slanderous, self-hating, homophobic (which it is), but also because it's poorly written, even after four years of writing and one of editing. And so Larry heard that Wyatt hated it, declined to bid on reprint rights, and with no previous acquaintance or anything Larry literally got him up against the wall for half an hour. The most humiliating of possible things for himself or for his reputation. If he can't hack it with the N.Y. literary big boys he ought to turn his misused typewriter in and split. And he can't.

The gay media is all set to rip his book to shreds, with the same enthusiasm that they'll raise *Dancer* to a height it doesn't belong in—excellent as it is. Herein lies a lesson. For once the straight publishing people are listening to gay tastemakers—after all, who should know better about the book world *and* the gay world? Evidently Larry hasn't given up, though he grovels in front of all who he wanted to be his peers.

September 1978, New York

Last night Andrew Holleran and I met at Central Park, where an international display of fireworks was given. Afterwards we had dinner on the Upper West Side in a diner-style restaurant, then sauntered down Columbus Avenue to Harrahs, where *After Dark* magazine was giving a party in honor of Nathan Fain's new article on "Mock Chic"—whatever that is.* From what I saw in the current issue and at the party, I guess it's disco, a cleaned-up rock/punk look with bad rock-music accompaniment.

Everyone, needless to say, was at the party and I suppose that was pleasant. My position in gay society was shown to be quite solid, though only respectable, not fabulous. Which is fine by me: I'm a person first, writer second, socialite last.

Aside from dancing and minor socializing Andrew stayed back from the crowd. I shook hands with a half dozen men before I could get away. He's already learned the art of vanishing.

Afterwards we had coffee in Burger King and talked a bit more. He

---

*Nathan Fain, a Texas-born writer, later died of AIDS.

was reticent about his next project and a little upset about the "slump" his book has hit in recent weeks. He's sort of despairing as to whether it will break away from the Gay audience.

Andrew is a curious combination of innocence and shrewd common sense. Excited, thrilled as he is by his success, he still has both feet on the ground and sees exactly how much things can get out of hand.

He's a nice man: I hope we can become friends.

Last night reading Edmund White's new novel, I was once more attracted to the idea of doing something autobiographical and "literary" myself.

The project is *Artificial Memoirs*.

But last night I got a clue as to what to do . . .

September 1978, New York

A late meeting, drinks with Edmund White. This was a first meeting George Whitmore instigated. We got on well, easily after a while. I enjoy his storytelling, his humor, his seriousness. He invited me to speak to his writing course on "suspense" down at the Johns Hopkins University. He also asked to interview me for his "Travels in Gay America—New York" section. I agreed to both. On my part, I asked if he and I could do a project for Sea Horse Press, putting a bee in his bonnet. We'll see if anything comes of this—he's talented, prestigious, and his new novel, *Nocturnes for the King of Naples*, is a lovely book, one to cherish and reread.

Oddly I feel very much in the middle of things these days, so much so that when I recognized the poet Edward Field at my neighborhood newspaper stand I had to introduce myself and convey my admiration.

Somehow we will all look back at this time as the coalescing of some acme in literature—I really think so, and I'm trying to make others feel so too.

October 1978, New York

Got a very nice call from Edmund White. He'd gotten hold of *The Deformity Lover*,* and read it through in one sitting.

The Deformity Lover, a volume of poems by Felice Picano published by the Sea Horse Press in 1977.

During our telephone visit, he reiterated plans for me to guest-lecture down at Johns Hopkins. I'm looking forward to it.

Last night I had the fruit of my "literary" dinners.
Present were Bob Lowe,* George Whitmore, and Andrew Holleran.
Aside from George going under the table at one point and biting Andrew's ankle, nothing extraordinary occurred.
Bob and Andrew know each other as acquaintances for several years.

I still haven't done any work on *The Lure*. My only consolation is that neither has my editor.

Saw Scott [Facon] three times this week over the art for the book cover. The first time we balled, the second time I comforted him over his argument with the art director, today we got high and talked.
I like him a great deal. He's smart, intuitive, talented—and often very kind to me.

11/12/78 New York

George [Whitmore] and Bob Lowe and I went to the Flamingo last night at 2:30 a.m. Thick boogying until 7 a.m. then home to crash. It was a good, hot crowd. And Richie Rivera generally broke out the best music at about 5—a lesson to us all.
Woke up at 3 p. m. this afternoon. Coffee, breakfast, a bath, and Alessandro Scarlatti's oratorio *S. Filippo Neri*. Already it's getting dark.

11/13/78 New York

A meeting of gay men and women gathered by Andrew Holleran (whom I increasingly like) to see a screening of Helen Whitney's film *Youth Terrorism—The View from Behind the Gang*.
An excellent film, often touching and always real. But it answered no questions about what she would do for ABC-TV News Documentary in an hour on gays and gay life.

---

*Bob Lowe (1948–91), the longtime companion of Felice Picano. Lowe was an attorney who co-authored the New York State Law Board's Rules on Adoption, a project he was working on at the time of his death.

After the film we had an intense meeting or encounter: intelligent, wide-ranging, humorous, down-to-earth, active, real.

Among those present were Andrew, Robert Ferro and his lover Michael Grumley, Larry Kramer, Barry Kaplan—the writers; Mike Denneny, his friend John [Preston], also an editor; Joan Peters, who teaches at Rutgers U.; another educator, Andrew's pal Donald Sullivan;* and Eddie Rosenberg† from sociability.

Later, nine of us had dinner uptown from the ABC screening room with Helen and her assistant Laurie. I was seated between Robert and Michael—both serious, intense, sexy, intelligent, humorous men in their mid-thirties. I fell instantly in love with both of them, as well as with Helen Whitney.

I can't say what were the results in terms of the film, except that Helen's first taste of the gay community through this group was of a high caliber and enough to sustain her through the fear, suspicion, and shit she will later encounter doing the film.

But Michael and Robert are new acquaintances, possibly new friends. They said to Andrew what I've felt so much—how last night was a "dream" evening: gay writers together discussing themselves, each other, books, all together.

It's something we must try to keep together as much as possible now that it's beginning.

11/22/78

The holiday season has begun with parties all around. I went to a chic gay literary cocktail party given for Edmund White's new novel, *Nocturnes for the King of Naples*, a lovely novel.

Present were a great many older, very dressed-up forty- and fifty-year-old queens whom I didn't know, and a equal number of the newer literary gay set mostly in jeans. Among the older group were Edward Albee, John Ashbery, and David Kalstone. The latter was the only one I spoke with at any length, and he was charming.

In general, however, that older group was highly reserved, off to

---

*Donald Sullivan (1941–90?), a close friend of Holleran's. Possible model for Sutherland in *Dancer from the Dance*.
†Eddie Rosenberg (1942–83), a friend of Holleran's, Ferro's, and Grumley's, and a center of social life and gay events in the New York/Fire Island circuit. He wrote a gossip column for *The Fire Island News* as "Rosatic."

themselves, and, in the largest sense, uninterested in others. Not very good for anyone, I think.

Later on, Bob Lowe and I had dinner at his apartment then taxied up to New York, New York for the "Night of the Panther" party. A very mixed party, everything from formal black to T-shirts and jeans with a few costumes and some leather trips, and every shade in between—the straight/gay mixed party scene.

11/23/78, New York

Dinner here last night with Andrew Holleran, Michael Grumley, and Robert Ferro. I made Thanksgiving. The evening began at 9 p.m. and went on until 2 a.m. There was so much to say, to discover, to exchange.

Michael and Robert have been lovers for several years, and it's a fascinating relationship—very close, with a great deal of space too. Tensions and disagreements exist, but so do shared ideals and unspoken beliefs. Michael is evidently the Cancerian mother—Robert the spoiled child constantly exerting his independence, then returning to the womb again. I suspect he also does this with extramarital affairs, one of which he'd like to have with me—unless I'm totally misreading him.

11/25/78

Robert Ferro is an interesting man—indeed a fascinating one to me since our first meeting about two weeks ago: author of a novella, *The Others*, which I haven't read, and co-author with Michael [Grumley] of *Atlantis: Autobiography of a Search*.

He is both intense and mystical. Very physically and compellingly so, yet with strong charmed links to the unseen. His face, his voice—especially face, it wrinkles when he laughs—and his eyes very much remind me of another friend, Steve Charnow, from college days who recently resurfaced in my life. I suppose Robert is in some ways representative of a physical/psychological archetype in my life. It's difficult to say right now whether he will have more to do with my life than Steve did. Like Steve, he is very sexy, but unbeautiful, and perhaps some sexual connection is possible. Or it may be otherwise. He did ask me several intensely personal questions I somehow eluded answering. But maybe I won't always be able to elude them. They may be exactly the questions I need asking because they are the questions I ask myself—but to hear someone else ask them makes those questions sound extra important.

At any rate, Robert and I are due to go out tonight to the Flamingo. That ought to be interesting if—that is—something doesn't come up to interrupt the plan. Behind his interest in me also lies a set of fears of something I can't yet know. I have the strong feeling that this is the last year of his and Mike's relationship unless something is done. I might be the sacrificial victim—or the chosen catalyst.

12/1/78

I've spent the last two days in Baltimore, a first for me. I taught Edmund White's advanced fiction-writing class for a two-hour period, injecting the realities of the publishing world and explaining how writing careers are built, how business is done. I'm fairly certain mine was a different view than the one they've received from both Ed and John Barth—the two stars of the writing department. I had been invited specifically as a commercially successful novelist in order to help counteract the "artsy/literary" business they'd gotten so far.

I know to an extent I fascinated many in the class. I also know that I outraged and annoyed the others. In general the responses were limited. Edmund tells me this is not unusual as this generation of college students are a bland lot compared to us raucous, riotous 60s students.

Edmund was very pleased and said the next day students had come to him about what I had said. So it's all to the good.

Later that evening I had dinner in academia. Our host was Stephen Orgel, whose specialty is Jacobean lit and who is responsible for a huge two-volume book on Inigo Jones and the theatre. Also present were Edmund, a handsome young associate professor named Chip,* and an elderly philosophy professor named David Sacks.

Edmund White, whom I talked to a lot on the ride down and back on the Metroliner, is a charming man given to stringent self-analysis, but hiding it behind a lovely surface of shifting polish and childlike delight. I find him quite one of the easiest people to get to know and yet one whose various levels will take years to uncover. I suspect he is unsure whether he wants pure love or respect more. I can love him

---

*Chip Tharsing (b. 1953) was in fact a graduate student at the time.

more easily because I so much respect his work. But I have yet to hear an unkind word from his mouth, and I suspect I won't.

12/10/78

An endless night beginning at 8 p. m. when a hot 25-year-old from North Carolina, Mike Waycaster, came by after work for sex. He is warm, attractive, with a leggy, long-limbed body, sweet face and huge cock. We fucked until about 10.

Don Eike* joined us then to go to George Whitmore's party. Mike didn't stay, however—having come twice (once while I fucked him). He went home exhausted. Meanwhile, Don and I bounced over to George's.

Ed White, Coleman Dowell, Andrew Holleran, Arthur Bell, Byrne Fone, and Howard Moss.† All the literary gay men were there too: [Bob] Wyatt, [Michael] Denneny, a few people from Dell, Seymour Kleinberg,‡ who knows!

Also present were two friends of Edmund from Houston, Texas, Rick and Steve. Steve is here for an interview to become the president of the National Gay Task Force. He helped organize the gay scene quite successfully in Houston; a strong, ambitous, down-home, sensible young man. Also sexy and attractive in the blond/southern way.

Don and I took them and George to the Flamingo, which was loose and very hot. At 5:30 Steve and I left and went to Ed White's apartment to fuck and sleep. The phone kept interrupting us. Finally at noon we got up. Ed walked in with coffee, donuts, his authorial dizziness, and general delight.

The party was very literary dish. Arthur and Andrew were just back from tours. Edmund had a book review in today's Sunday *Times*. I met several people who claimed to be admirers of my novels.

---

*Don Eike (b. 1948), a friend of Picano's, shared a house with Picano on Fire Island Pines, 1977–79.

†Coleman Dowell (1925–85), a novelist who committed suicide in part because of the failure of his work; Arthur Bell (1938–1984), a gay activist and columnist and the author of *Dancing the Gay Lib Blues* (1971); Byrne Fone (b. 1936), a scholar and author; Howard Moss (1922–81), a poet and editor for *The New Yorker*.

‡Seymour Kleinberg (b. 1933), a professor of English at Long Island University, Brooklyn, the editor of *The Other Persuasion*, an important early anthology of gay fiction, and the author of *Alienated Affections: Being Gay in America.*

Bell apologized for offending me. I set him straight. He hasn't insulted me—yet. It was pleasant meeting him—drunk, maudlin, egomaniacal as he is. At least he knows who I am for future reference.

I was up with a total hangover: wine, vodka, coke, grass, poppers. But I'm feeling fine now.

12/12/78

A sumptuous afternoon with Scott yesterday. This was the first time since he's returned that we've made love. It was splendid despite the fact that I fucked all weekend.

How pleasant to be able to have him in my bed with me even if it's once or twice a week.

1979

1/2/79 Manhattan

I had a rather crazy although pleasant New Year's Eve, despite my general bad mood these two days.

Andrew and George and I went from place to place via subway, taxi, and car. At one point there were six of us writers, including Larry Kramer, Robert Ferro, and Mike Grumley. Larry and George are *arch* enemies because of George's terrible review in *Body Politic* and so there was tension, tension, TENSION.

George and I ended up at Richard Howard's, which was delightful.* We spent a good time chatting with Stephen Greco and Barry Laine.† Barry will be producing *A Perfect Relationship* in March,‡ and so we talked about co-operative ads and selling copies of the play in the lobby.

---

*Richard Howard (b. 1929), poet, translator, critic, and teacher, winner of the Pulitzer Prize in poetry and the National Book Award for translation.
†Barry Laine (1951–87), who died of AIDS, was a founder of the Glines, an important early venue for gay theater. He knew Picano since grade school, when Laine's sister and Picano had attended the same class in Queens.
‡Doric Wilson's play was published by Picano's Sea Horse Press in *Two Plays* (1978).

1/20/89 Manhattan

Transiting Saturn has been going over my mid-heaven yesterday and the day before, depressing me terribly. The next time it happens will be in early August of this year, when other aspects will be offsetting its dour influence. This movement of Saturn is absolutely a clear-cut example of "vibrations" or "emanations" affecting my mind.

In what way? I said depressed, but though that is partially true it isn't all of it. Anxiety is the major factor—fear for the future, fear about the past, an inability to face people, places and, matters, an unrealistic evaluation of things, an inability to do anything helpful or constructive—a burden, in short.

All this is coming pretty much out of nowhere—out of context, even. If anyone ought to have the fewest fears, the greatest satisfaction in accomplishment, it is me. Aside from Scott, there is nothing in the past five years of my life I could have wanted differently or better. Even that disappointment was not fully unexpected. In short, I have no complaints.

My personal life is filled with loving friends, many of the closest being only six months old—Andrew Holleran, Mike Grumley, Robert Ferro, George Whitmore, Ed White, and Rick Fiala.* I have moved right into the center of the gay literature movement, where my poetry and fiction have given me a respected place.

March 79 Manhattan

Although the Sea Horse Press will possibly do some of my books, I really hope that I can find different publishers for them, so that I can publish other works. The two projects I have on hand are an anthology and an expanded version of George Whitmore's *The Confessions of Danny Slocum.*

Last night, George and I and Edmund White and his lover Chris Cox† had dinner at George's apartment. Ed was talking about doing a big, new novel very different than *Nocturnes* and *Elena.*‡ He's right

---

*Rick Fiala, a writer, editor, and cartoonist, served as the first art director of *Christopher Street* magazine.

†Christopher Cox was the last member of the Violet Quill Picano met.

‡*Forgetting Elena*, White's 1973 novel.

to think that way. He certainly has the name and the talent to pull off something extraordinary.

I am impressed by the entire academic/literary set that Ed aspires to conquer, preferring to build a basic audience and allow the others to discover what they've been missing. He has a greater sense of self-importance—of mission, I suppose you could call it—tempered by a far harsher view of reality than I have. His own treatment as an author has been widely different than mine. He has not yet been able to live off his books and has always had a small, highly vocal, very elite audience who praise and pamper him mercilessly. This has led to great expectations and great disappointments.

My disappointments have been minor by comparison. *Eyes* was sabotaged by the publisher, yet it went on to become a most popular book, translated into a half dozen languages. *The Mesmerist* did poorly in hardcover, but seems to be coming back in paper. *The Lure* may be a commercial breakthrough. Or it may sink upon publication. To date, I have about a million copies of my books in print, but how much better it would have been for me to have sold a million of just one title.

March 79 Manhattan

Last night, Mike Grumley and Robert Ferro joined Dino di Gherlando and me for dinner here. We were so into talk that it was 3 a.m. before anyone realized how late it had become.

4/1/79 Manhattan

A good party at Flamingo last night. The right number of people—not too crowded. A party at 12 West kept the surface party people away. Only the regulars were there. Richie Rivera's music—much of which was new—bordered on genius. I danced from 3 until 5:30.

My landlord from Fire Island called to say that since his property dealings are still in abeyance, he is issuing a lease to me for the entire summer for the cottage—at last year's price!

The house opens May 18th and runs until September 18th. I will have Don Eike as one housemate and possibly Bob Lowe as the other. At any rate I'll be there again and at home again.

*   *   *

George Whitmore and Andrew Holleran, bless their souls, are so excited about *The Lure* that they are exciting others about it too. Yesterday, George met with his editor at St. Martin's, Mike Denneny, who is vaguely connected with *Christopher Street*, and did a number on Denneny on how they are missing the boat by not taking the book.

Today, I'm taking a preview copy to Edmund White, who called to say he got my publisher's letter but not the book. Over the phone, he read me some hilarious sections about Upper East Side queens from his new book, *States of Desire*.

5/18/79 Manhattan

Dinner last night at Whitmore's. Present were Bob Wyatt and Pat Loud. Pat seems to be doing just fine as an agent. When I first met her—at a Hollywood party—she was fresh from Santa Barbara although she's been around a bit in the gay world thanks to her son Lance's connections.*

She is the same tolerant, curious, open-minded, equable woman, although more New York–appearing, naturally. She's very serious about what she's doing, *loves* being an agent, is dying to know more people in the business, and above all seems dedicated to her authors. A few exchanges between her and George showed how much she *really* was on his side.

Her relationship with Bob Wyatt is another matter. Bob—whom I met through dear Susan Moldow—is a person I value more and more, despite the fact that I can't stop occasionally making him uncomfortable. Bob is a cynic, on top of it, and a very successful publisher.

5/29/79 Manhattan

During Memorial Day weekend, Andrew Holleran dropped by briefly to visit George Whitmore and me. He told me that he gave Dell an excellent book-jacket quote for *The Lure*, which doubtless will be used at the ABA when the book is presented this week. Sunday, I returned Edmund White's phone call. He's also received a galley copy to read, and liked it so well he offered to review the book for *The New York*

---

*Lance Loud, Pat Loud's son, came out to his parents on national television as part of the *An American Family* series. He is currently a columnist for *The Advocate*.

Times Book Review. I thanked him in advance and hope the review comes across—although it's questionable.

Sunday, I read George the introduction to *The Final Flowering of Thomas Wyndeslade.* It was enough to give him a good sense of the book. He praised it. But even better praise was nonverbal. All Monday morning he was restless, and finally he decided to leave early. His excuse was that hearing me read the introduction had given him the urge to get home and work on *The Confessions of Danny Slocum.*

I read the core article of about 20,000 words and several subsequent smaller portions of the book, and they mark a real departure for George in terms of a new maturity and confidence. This weekend, I read a fully revised and expanded version of *The Rights,* the one-act play he wrote last year. Like *Danny Slocum,* the play is authoritative, mature, perceptive, funny, sad, touching, and wonderfully characterized.

George had a few critical remarks about my introduction, which I am taking to heart.

5/31/79 Manhattan

I had drinks yesterday evening with Richard Howard. As I walked into his apartment, he told me that I was "famous," explaining that his other guest, a young gay English professor from Baltimore, knew my work.

June 79 Manhattan

Yesterday at noon, Don Eike and I went over to George Whitmore's for a fast brunch before the Gay Pride March up Fifth Avenue. The Ferro-Grumleys, Ed White and Chris Cox, Mike Denneny and friend, were there. Andrew never showed up.

The parade was huge—fifty blocks long—and the crowd estimated between 90,000 and 100,000 marchers, one out of ten gays in the New York metropolitan area. It was extraordinary.

Once we reached Central Park for the Rally, it was, however, banana-oil political rah-rah. After a rest we all went for lunch, then downtown to the Christopher Street Carnival, where another 20,000-odd people were enjoying a street festival which in effect exists every day.

6/28/79 Manhattan

Back in New York. I came into the city for two reasons—one, to have a dinner party with Edmund White and his friend Chris Cox and with Andrew Holleran. A charming, delicious, delightful evening.

Andrew and Edmund are similar men—highly intelligent, sort of quirky, either very strongly enthusiastic or else down, warm, modest, real. They are also two of the best writers I've read.

They differ in their thinking. Over the years, Edmund has, I suppose, developed an entire system of thought devoted to understanding the world around him in a practical and theoretical level. He is worldly in the best sense. Also angry at the foolishness around us. Also committed to a socialist restructuring of society. On several occasions we've discussed exactly how awful matters seem to be, and how almost every positive change is really an inverted bow into the overarching capitalist framework.

On matters like these Andrew is almost naive. His thinking has not yet opened out. He has not focused his selective intelligence on anything more than people, and most recently on social and cultural mores.

When I return to the Island, I will take this journal. I hope to be spending more time there than here in New York.

June 79 Fire Island

I'm more and more knocked out by the idea of writing about all the wonderful portraits and characters from my current gay life. I've only touched on a few in my stories, but now I want to do rather fuller portraits: the boy who wants to become a D.J. and finds everything, the beauty who goes sour, the sweet farm-boy hustler who becomes a butcher.

7/1/79 Fire Island

Guests visiting the house this weekend. The general guest is George Whitmore, who has been out all week finishing a first draft of *Danny Slocum*, which St. Martin's will probably publish next spring. Pat Loud came out, bringing goodies galore—a filet mignon for six, fresh fettuccine and pesto, ripe tomatoes, avocados, kiwi and prosciutto, an Explorateur cheese too divine for words, pâté, and her pleasant company.

Last night instead of going out (ho-hum) I read some of the stories in the *Dell Anthology of Great Irish Stories*. Two ideas immediately came to me: the first, a portrait of a Greenwich Village homosexual whom I had seen for 13 years and who last fall had either a stroke or heart attack on Sheridan Square and had to be taken away by ambulance. The other, already titled "Rose and a Kiss," is about an incident from my past involving ignorance of emotion and how the relationship between two men I was friendly with, George Sampson and Chuck Partridge—and George's life, in fact—changed drastically as a result of his coming upon Chuck kissing me by a rosebush.*

I will be going into the city tonight for some banking and Sea Horse Press business. Luckily the weather has continued unseasonably cold.

Andrew Holleran, who has a full house of friends, roommates, and guests, came by at about 2 p.m. and remained here for sanctuary most of the day. We read, talked, had lunch. I'm really delighted that we have become friends.

Last night was memory night for me at the Sandpiper. I got into the spirit of the place for the first time this summer, and as a result was in a good mood for reencountering several past affairs: Steve Adams of 3 summers ago, Neal Ralph of 2 summers ago, and, of course, Scott Facon.

Scott was accepted at the School of Visual Arts. His grades weren't very good, but his portfolio was. I'm delighted. I think he has the imagination and devotion of a great artist, all he needs is the learned skills.

We danced a bit, and the old magic returned, including "Could it Be Magic," which the D.J. thoughtfully played. In the thirty-five years of my life I have never found a person physically more to my taste, and I'll be surprised if I ever do again. He is almost magically beautiful to me.

I separated from him at the end of our dance set when he offered to buy me a drink. We could have spent the night together—again—if I wanted. We parted with a warm kiss and a clasp.

---

*The incident is recounted in Part III, "The Jane Street Girls," in Picano's *Men Who Loved Me*.

7/10/79 Fire Island

I'm going into town this evening for dinner at Ed White's. He's finished *States of Desire*, and this will be a sort of celebration.

It's just as well that I'm leaving. I've been very by myself out here since Bob Lowe left Sunday night after dinner. Yesterday, I visited Nick and Enno and Ray Ford at their house, but soon enough even that became tiring. I spent the rest of the day reading, thinking.

8/8/79 Fire Island

Today is the culmination of my Saturn's travel over mid-heaven. Last night was a full moon in Aquarius in conjunction with Mercury.

8/11/79 Fire Island

It's raining after an afternoon of cloudy gray. George Whitmore is my guest this weekend. Matinée idol Joel Crothers* came by, bored to death by his housemates. We chatted, discussed bridge, and then played Scrabble for hours while I misbaked a cake.

8/13/79 Fire Island

The entire weekend was dominated by a huge storm which began Friday and did not end until last night. This morning the sky is still filled with heavy, low-hanging, but fast-moving clouds. We've had a fire in the Franklin stove all weekend to get some of the dampness out of the air.

It was sort of too bad that the weather spoiled George's weekend, but we did read each other's new work. I read his new short stories "Black Widow" and "How to Marry a Zillionaire," and he read "Expertise" and the prologue to the new novel, *Paul.*†

George has really hit his stride writing these days. Turning the

---

*Joel Crothers appeared in the Broadway production of *Torch Song Trilogy* opposite Harvey Fierstein, and on the TV soap opera "The Edge of Night."
†"Expertise" became part of *Slashed to Ribbons in The Defense of Love*, but not as the penultimate story. "The Black Widow" was published in *Christopher Street* and in the collection *Aphrodisiac*.

"Danny Slocum" articles* into a book seems to have opened him up. He is writing more easily, more gracefully, more humorously, and with a great deal of point. St. Martin's will do *Danny Slocum* next spring, and his play *The Rights* will be given an Equity Showcase by the Glines this fall. It is amazing how it's all falling into place for him.

We talked about "Expertise," which I hope will be the penultimate piece in my short story collection *Gay / Tragic / Romances*. I have problems with the way it moves from a humorous beginning to a rather harsh conclusion. Bob Lowe read it last week and wasn't upset by the dichotomy, but he thought it needed a bit more objective / narrator / humor at the end. George's feeling was that I might leave the end alone, but go through it eliminating the humor and writing it as starkly as possible.

I don't know which to do, but I *do* want the story collection ready by next summer so Sea Horse Press can publish it next December [1980] in order that it can profit by whatever success *The Lure* enjoys in paperback.

8/23/79 Fire Island

Andrew Holleran was over for dinner last night. He seems to be undergoing with uncanny similarity the hassles, depressions, irritations, and confusion I've been feeling.

As I had several months ago, Andrew has just finished an affair with someone he's persuaded was the most important affection in his life. Like me, Andrew is both successful and yet pressured and limited by the very elements that had provided that success. I know he's having difficulty with his new novel, and he said last night he's decided to be patient with it.

9/8/79 Fire Island

A gorgeous day yesterday. This morning, cloud cover. Only the real Island people are here, or at least that's what it seemed like at Tea Dance last night.

George Whitmore is out this weekend. Last night, Andrew Holleran came for dinner. One of the things we talked about was the exploration

---

The Confessions of Danny Slocum began as a series of articles that appeared in *Christopher Street* magazine in 1979.

of the planets via robot satellite. Andrew believes this is one of the most important happenings of our time and decries that so few of us are really taking it seriously. He thinks that it is the only important thing to be writing about today. I agree and don't. I think writers have to present all of our current mental/social evolution in order to show how we've gotten to this stage of interplanetary exploration—that is the real task.

Yesterday, I rode out to Fire Island with Scott Facon. He was unavoidable on the train—alone, shirtless, and wearing a straw cowboy hat. Our conversation was mostly "safe" topics: what I've been doing (a lot!); what Scott's been doing (not much); how the summer has been (OK).

Scott has not been motivated to draw, so I revived the idea of his illustrating my short stories. He seemed enthusiastic about it, so I guess next week I'll give him some of the stories and set him to work.

He's to come to dinner tonight. Mike Denneny may also show up.

9/9/79 Fire Island

A glorious night at the Ice Palace with George Whitmore, Scott, Mike Denneny. The place was almost perfect, as indeed the Island is almost perfect now that most of the tourists are gone.

I dropped a Mandrax halfway through the night and got very sleazy. Walking home, I made George drop me off at the Grove meat rack. He was hesitant, afraid I was too looped. But I was just fine and carried on for about an hour. As it happened, getting home was quite difficult because I was completely exhausted. But I did drag my ass into bed. Woke at 1 p.m.

9/11/79 Fire Island

Andrew stayed overnight and left on the last boat yesterday. We're now on the Early Fall schedule. The Sandpiper opens at midnight for dancing, but not on Tuesday and Wednesday. Hardware—the L.A. boutique at the Botel—is closed until next year. The Crow's Nest only opens weekends. Houses everywhere are closed. More than half of the renters' seasons were over yesterday. Today the sun was hot, the night cool. Odd to have such wonderful weather now since it was such a nothing summer. "The summer that never was," Andrew called it.

Perhaps this month will be like some Early Romantic Symphony, a long furious coda to a trivial final movement.

9/15/79, Fire Island

Back out after 2 1/2 days in town. Andrew was and is not here: working (thankfully) on his new book.

I finished work on the novella, had it photocopied, and got a copy to Jane,* who is supposed to be reading it this weekend. I don't know what the result will be. Ideally, I would like Delacorte to publish the novella. The *I Ching*, however, has not given the best omens. Hexagram #5, Waiting, with no changes, is the most clear-cut of all: It signifies future success, but much delay.

A finished copy of *The Lure*, the first off the press, sent to me by messenger on Thursday.

Wednesday night, at Chuck Adams/Pat Cool's going-away dinner for Ed White and Chris Cox, the cover of *The Lure* was shown around, the book talked about with much anticipation of assured success. *I'm* not so sure. However, Whitmore, Holleran, the Ferro-Grumleys, were present, the latter two suffering financially and feeling it. I made an offer. It was put on hold. Andrew has already helped them.†

10/12/79, Manhattan

The ups and downs continue—periods of busyness followed by quietude.

The week began with a letter from Ed White. After being refused the assignment of reviewing my novel for the Sunday *Times*, he contacted *The Washington Post Book World*. Now they, too, have backed out, claiming "other plans" for the book. He's disappointed and so am I at seeing the last chance fly out the window for my book to get serious consideration. I'm angry too about the obvious continued discrimination against me by these so-called "tastemakers." I suppose the only retaliation I have is on tour publicly to declare them homo-

---

*Jane Rotrosen was Picano's literary agent.
†This is the first occasion when all the members of the Violet Quill found themselves together.

phobic. More than anything now I want this book to be a best-seller and have at least *that* satisfaction.

I made new contact in publishing with Ed's editor at Dutton, Bill Whitehead, a very educated, caring man. He hinted that he would be interested in me as a client at Dutton when he returns from his sabbatical in 1981. He has been editing mostly "heavy" nonfiction, but working with Ed has shown him the pleasures of working with a real writer, and he wishes to return to more literary fiction.* He may be an excellent contact especially if *The Final Flowering of Thomas Wyndeslade* runs into problems at Dell. Or if I decide to move after this two-book contract is over.

1980

1/1/80

I've improved my material life a good deal in the past decade. For the moment, at least I'm financially secure. I have things in a way I'd never thought possible. I travel, I buy clothes, books, records, gifts for others.

What about internally? The past decade provided two major romances—neither successful. The first degenerated into an odd dependent friendship. I felt so burned by the relationship that I couldn't give my love again until 1978. My affair with Scott Facon was more satisfying all around. The tables were turned in many ways, and now I am open to future love. Cautious, discreet, discriminating as always. But open.

Friendship remains a volatile area of my affections. My friends from the 70s remain. I've made new friends—Bob Lowe, Don Eike, Linda Gray, George Whitmore, Andrew Holleran, Edmund White, Mike Denneny.

My family has also changed since 1970. My parents divorced. My father has a common-law wife. My mother married again and was widowed. My younger brother married and had a son. My older brother married and had a daughter. This was the decade in which my sister Carol and I became the bulwark of the family.

---

*Until his death (from AIDS), Bill Whitehead was Edmund White's editor. Edmund White won the first Bill Whitehead Award for lifetime contribution to gay fiction.

1/20/80

I just read George Whitmore's *The Confessions of Danny Slocum*, and while it's not great, it is rather successful in its own terms.

Unlike William Golding's classic triptych structure in *Darkness Visible*, Whitmore has chosen a forward spiral to shape his book. This makes sense, since his book is about a psychological illness (or disability) and its therapeutic cure: a process that mixes past and present and takes in various areas of life. It's extremely readable—by turns funny, moving, informative, erotic, and filled with comments on the current gay scene.

1/21/80

A party yesterday afternoon and early evening given for Bill Whitehead, Dutton editor, and Ben Short, who will be taking a multi-month tour of the world. Present were the Ferro-Grumleys, Ed White, George Whitmore, George Stavrinos,* Fran Lebowitz, and scores of people I did not know.

This morning Ed White's *States of Desire* got a *New York Times* review from John Leonard. It wasn't terrific, but considering the source, I'd say it was just fine. I called to congratulate him, but got the machine.

1/30/80

Edmund's excellent book *States of Desire* is to be reviewed in the Sunday *New York Times Book Review*, and like my own novel, which was reviewed there in November, Ed's is savagely attacked.

It's no surprise to me. Only one important gay book in the past few years has gotten any kind of good notices there—*Dancer*—and that was connected with a complete dismissal of Larry Kramer's *Faggots*. Most gay books are quite blithely ignored. Now that major writers are doing major gay books, however, even the blindfolded *NYTBR* feels obliged to review them—attacking as viciously as possible.

The entire experience points out that we must persevere in what we are doing. Evidently the furies of reaction are gathered and willing to

---

*George Stavrinos (1948–90), an illustrator, designed covers for Picano's *The Deformity Lover* and *Late in the Season*.

stoop to anything in order to ensure that gay books are not considered important enough to read. But they are. And soon everyone will know it.

2/7/80

Dinner at the Ferro-Grumleys' last night. Delicious and excellent company—George Whitmore, Ed White, Chris Cox, Ed's editor, Bill Whitehead, and Whitehead's lover, model Ben Short—the last two are off to an eight-month round-the-world trip beginning next week.

There was a great deal of talk, but once Bill and Ben had left we turned to the Lavender Quill Club,* of which we are all active members, and how word of it has been bruited about so that in interviews recently both George and Ed were asked about it.

Edmund told interesting little tales of artists. Among the most precious was that of Virgil Thomson talking to the young Pierre Boulez. "You have a very complicated style, young man," Thomson is reported to have said, "but you'll be sterile at forty unless you decide never to lose sight of the subject you wish to render." Ed took this as a motto all of us—complex stylists that we are—ought to keep in mind.

2/24/80

Going for 3 books every two years at Sea Horse Press. If I can publish the anthology [*A True Likeness*] by November of 1980, I'd like to bring out by the following May a collection of stories, and if that works and Gay Presses of New York does not publish the second collection, then that one ought to be out by November of 1981.

Only when Sea Horse can print 3,000 copies of a book can we hope to make a largish profit. For the next title, the anthology, I plan to sell 10% in hardcover, but the profit would only be $1,300—not much. Whereas printing 5,000 copies of the stories at $1 a book would bring profits of close to $8,500. Evidently Sea Horse must begin to switch into higher-sales, high-profit fiction in the next year if it's not to become a drag on my own finances.

---

*This appears to be the first mention of the Violet (or Lavender) Quill Club—the names were used interchangeably.

2/26/80

High tea at the Ferro-Grumleys' yesterday. Guests included George Whitmore; an editor from Crowell, Larry Ashmead; author José Donoso* from Spain; and Barry Kaplan, looking better than I'd seen him in years.

The real treat was Julia Markus and Larry. She and I talked about novel writing, starting a small press (hers is called Decatur), jackets on paperbacks. Very pleasant, smart, real woman. Certainly a welcome member of the Lavender Quill Club.

I read the first two parts of *Window Elegies* to George Whitmore after tea and before dinner. He thinks I should be less literal and more figurative, that I ought to retain as much mystery as possible in the poem. He seemed satisfied with the poem's movement, flow, and, most important, its tone. He thinks it could be longer, but it works as an elegy should work—instructing through sadness and loss.

2/27/80

Last night at the Millennium 4 workshop on the East Side, where last week I gave a lecture to a small audience on gay poetry, there was a huge audience for George Whitmore's symposium on the gay novel.

Besides George, the panel contained Edmund White, Seymour Kleinberg, Byrne Fone, and Scott Tucker. Byrne is a historian and teacher of gay literature. Seymour is also a teacher, essayist, and social critic of the gay scene. Scott Tucker is a young leftist radical writer whose critiques of gay literature have just begun to appear in print in the past year.

The room was half filled with writers—Arthur Bell, Mike Denneny, Arnie Kantrowitz, Richard Goldstein, Larry Kramer, and others. It was—as they will say in the future—a glittering company. Only Andrew Holleran—slated to be on the panel—was missing.

Much of the evening was given over to taking stands. Scott took the radical position, while Edmund in his Olympian sanity declared that literature had nothing to do at all with propaganda or with politics.

What most interested me—besides the turnout and the passions that

---

*José Donoso taught Robert Ferro, Michael Grumley, Andrew Holleran, and Barry Kaplan when they were all students together at the Iowa Writers' Workshop.

arose—was each panelist's choice of a pre-Stonewall gay voice and how that novel represented a tradition.

Ed chose Genet's *Our Lady of the Flowers*, Scott chose Isherwood's *A Single Man* (for its calmness), Seymour selected Selby's *Last Exit to Brooklyn*, and Byrne talked about a variety of 19th-century books that he felt developed basic themes. I found these themes intriguing. They are:

1. the romantic relationship of seducer to innocent,
2. counterpart to that—the older gay lover as Platonic teacher and guide,
3. the search for a gay Arcadia,
4. the raising of homosexuality to a superior kind of love,
5. the gothic and rapturous aspects of the hidden life.

These are still important themes, and *Dancer* and my book are popular simply because they continue to deal with them. Oddly, no panelist chose Rechy's *City of Night*, which I would have selected. Moreover, no panelist mentioned the new genre of gay literature—"the witness." Perhaps nonfiction is doing that rather than the novel.

Edmund said several times that he felt that in order to build a literature that every niche of genre need to be fitted up. George talked about how the expansion of pornography in the 70s deeply affected the reading of many novels.

3/9/80

If Edmund is on my mind these days, it's hardly surprising. *States of Desire* has generated controversy and praise. He is currently in the midst of a promotional barrage as hectic as the one I went through in the fall. It seems that any gay book worth anything at all must be accompanied by its author going out and meeting the press and the people. I hope this won't be necessary in the future, but as gay literature is still a hotly disputed subject—*The New York Times*, for example, doesn't believe it exists—such promotion is probably a good thing.

His literary roots are unusual since he's a few years older than Andrew Holleran or me, and far more precocious. His early days in New York were spent in the Frank O'Hara crowd—artists, poets, art critics. Edmund's parties and receptions invariably include friends of that era—Ned Rorem,* John Ashbery, Richard Howard, etc.

However, in the last three or four years—perhaps more, since I've known him only a year—his work has stepped out of the East Side literary closet. *The Joy of Gay Sex* and *Nocturnes for the King of Naples* are distinctly gay and could not be taken any other way. His "Travels in Gay America" series in *Christopher Street* for the last year or so has kept his name before the public and solidified his reputation as a gay writer.

One has to remember that Edmund was the darling of a certain set of writers in the 60s. His play and his first novel, *Forgetting Elena*, were especially highly praised, extolled even in *The New York Times*. Nabokov praised him. He had expectations to fill and a place reserved in the literary establishment.

That he has been reviled in reviews since he came out is no surprise. *Nocturnes* was called narcissistic—a key word in the homophobic vocabulary. His new book was attacked. In the *Times Literary Supplement* review of *The State of the Language*, his essay "The Political Language of Homosexuality" was singled out and called "illiterate," when in fact it is both literature and revolutionary. In short, having been set up, he is perceived as the object to be shot down by the establishment for failing to fulfill *their* expectations of him.

So much do reputation and politics color his life that it is often difficult to assess the work. What is clear to me at this moment is that he is the most important voice of gay literature today, with impeccable credentials and a large body of achievement. Of the rest of us, only Andrew Holleran has a good literary reputation, and he has yet to undergo the trials of a second novel. George Whitmore is certainly making inroads, but his *Danny Slocum* will not be reviewed outside the gay media. My own reputation is spotty.

3/19/80

The Violet Quill Club was so excited by my reading of "Absolute Ebony" last week at Three Lives & Company that we've decided to hold smaller readings of our work.† We'll probably meet twice a

---

*Ned Rorem has been described as "the world's greatest composer of art songs," and he won the Pulitzer Prize for music in 1976. His diaries, with their explicit homosexual references, were highly controversial when first published.

†Three Lives & Company is a prominent Greenwich Village literary bookstore.

month—once at the Ferro-Grumleys', once at mine—for coffee and dessert and the reading of three or four pieces.

The first reading is March 31st at the F-Gs'—Andrew Holleran, George Whitmore, and I will read then. The following week, Edmund White, Mike Grumley, Robert Ferro, and Chris Cox will read.

Whether we will read new works or old is not decided—works in progress, experiments, etc., *seem* to be the most likely things. I, for example, will probably try out either "Teddy—the Hook"* or "To the Reader," a reworking I began last night of the first part of the 1st-person section of *Shadow . . . Master*, which seems to be on its way to becoming something quite distinctive, if only vaguely related to how I actually will begin the book.

Another question is criticism. Since we all do comment on each other's work, it will naturally occur, but before reading, we may either solicit criticism or not.

The experiment may utterly fail or work out pleasantly. We'll see.

3/22/80

Plans are for me and Andrew to join the Ferro-Grumleys for a two-and-a-half-day stay at Robert's family beach home on the New Jersey coast, beginning late Sunday night.†

I'm sort of looking for a change of pace and of place. I especially hope that the weather, which has been rainy and cold for the last two days, will warm up so that I can get a little sun, a little color.

What I miss not going to Fire Island is sitting out sunbathing to beautiful music, smoking and reading. It's not certain whether I will go out to Fire Island. All indications are pointed against it at the moment. I'm not actively looking for a place now that the house I've rented for years is no longer available—or valuable—its view destroyed, the peace gone, neighbors everywhere. Nevertheless I'm sort of hoping that Kismet brings me a place out there.

Its name comes from Gertrude Stein's book, and it has showcased gay and lesbian writers in the store's early years.

*"Teddy—the Hook" is included in *Slashed to Ribbons in Defense of Love*.

†This house, Sea Girt, known to Robert's friends as "Gaywyck" plays a central role in both *The Family of Max Desir* and *Second Son*.

3/27/80

Although the weather reverted to February, I enjoyed the Jersey Shore. Robert's family home is on a private beach on an inlet between two boardwalks fronted by public beaches.

We read, wrote, cooked, played cards, talked, walked, jogged.

I brought a notebook hoping to work further on a new story, "Fantasy and Fugue," which I re-began the Sunday before in N.Y.C. Instead, I began to write the opening of a novella, *A Summer's Lease.** I hope to get both the story and the novella done this month and then leap ahead to work on *Shadow . . . Master.*

Possibly this Sunday Andrew and I will go off to Fire Island to look for a tiny house in the Grove. I'm not terribly hopeful about finding one.

3/28/80

Finally! At last! Surprise! What does one make of it?! *Christopher Street* magazine has taken one of my stories—"Slashed to Ribbons"—one of my first, written as long ago as 1972.

Naturally, the achievement was not without its minor stresses. Chuck Ortleb† and Tom Steele both felt the piece ought to end before I go off on the Aztec fantasy. So I cut it right before then. I will be anxious about how other members of the Lavender Quill Club deal with the publication. I haven't yet told George, but Andrew was delighted.

Moreover, Tom brought up their anthology of short stories to be issued in August, prepared by Thom Miller of Coward, McCann. Tom thinks the story ought to be in the anthology and has sent it off to Miller. Should this happen, I will join Andrew, George, and Edmund— all of whom have stories in the anthology.‡ It gives me a little more reason to go on writing these damn things.

A Summer's Lease became the novella *Late in the Season.*

†Charles Ortleb, (b. 1950), is the founder and publisher of *Christopher Street* and *The New York Native.*

‡"Slashed to Ribbons in Defense of Love" did indeed appear in *Aphrodisiac: Fiction from Christopher Street.*

4/1/80

Last night the Violet Quill Club met at the Ferro-Grumleys' for our first night of readings. Ed White suggested we call it "First Drafts," which would be fine, except that I was the only one who read a first draft.

Andrew began the evening with a story called "Sleeping Soldiers" about his experiences in the earliest days of basic training in the army and of an affair that arose between two very different soldiers he encountered—a sergeant whose tour of duty was almost up and another recruit. The real story, however, was about privacy in differences—how we take away from our experience, no matter how strange and unprecedented, something of value to us alone. Beautifully written in his incomparable style—reflective, factual, evocative—it certainly is very Holleran and was greeted by us as such.

The third reader was Robert Ferro, who co-authored a nonfiction book with his lover, then published a curious novella, *The Others*, two years back. He read the opening chapters of his autobiographical novel, titled *Max Desir*. The writing was a real departure for him. The utter restraint of this first novel is modified somewhat so that scenes, ideas, characters, can step forward and come to life. Horses—imaginary, real, and in statuettes—form a thematic link in the writing and are beautifully used. Several scenes stand out even more—the boy's rapid seduction by a black nurse, his grandmother's funeral, an all-night pinochle game. The book is still bereft of the subjective, but it is wonderfully relaxed, and compared to *The Others* I think it might make a fine novel.

I read in between, daringly, a quickly revised draft of "Fantasy and Fugue"* off the manuscript notebook. As it is an internal monologue, it read pretty well. It came out funny, touching, accurate, and original. "Damon Runyon in a D.J. Booth," Andrew called it. Both he and Edmund insisted that it ought to get into print as soon as possible.

4/7/80

I face the summer without the pleasures and envies of Fire Island Pines. I might well be invited there and to Branford, Connecticut, and to Westhampton, but unless matters change drastically in the next

---

*Retitled "Spinning," it is the first story in *Slashed to Ribbons*.

month or so, I will be living in my apartment in the Village, not at the beach.

I'm of two minds about this. Naturally, I feel deprived. The Island can be terrific, and at its worst is still better than most places in the world. In the past, it's been awfully good to me and for me. I've met splendid people, made excellent friends, entertained effortlessly, and written extensively, made love, loved, and was loved there.

Last summer, I got bored a great deal. I spent a lot of time in Manhattan, but September especially was a magical month for me, I consummated a new friendship with Andrew and Edmund and the Ferro-Grumleys.

On the other side of the coin, I may enjoy it more if I'm there only a week or two at a time. I enjoy the rocky shore of Connecticut, the straight scene at the Hamptons, the beach down at the Jersey coast.

It is not change I fear or detest—it is that change moves in ways that are strangely ambiguous to me. Do the Fire Island years represent some kind of apex in my life from which it is now turning? If so, what formed that apex?

I've seldom been so social, so open to all comers, so full of friends. The years before were more alone. Are the next ones to be alone, too?

I've had five most creative years. Three novels have been written partly or entirely at the Pines as well as innumerable stories, poems, novellas. Of course I've done work away from there too. As much? Will I do as much work in New York this summer?

While I have had plenty of sex and solidified many relationships at the Island, only one love affair resulted and little business. I can't believe my career is tied up in the Island cycle.

4/8/80

The Violet Quill Club met here for readings last night—the second in our series.

George Whitmore read the opening chapter of his new novel, *Slights and Offenses*, and it seems as though it will be a good one. Its early chapters go back to college in the late 60s and detail a curious ménage between a couple and their male friend.

Michael Grumley also read an excerpt from his novel *A World of Men*,* the section entitled "Public Monuments," which I will be putting in the Sea Horse anthology.

A World of Men became *Life Drawing*.

There were various criticisms of details of both these excerpts—I found little wrong with either of them. Then we talked about various subjects in writing. For example, Edmund brought up Penelope Mortimer's comment to him about not using brand names in a book unless you want seventy-five years hence to be extensively footnoted and thus hard to understand. We discussed objects in Austen, James, and Proust. We decided that objects ought to be "rendered" if used, as Proust renders the telephone and the airplane in his novel.

We decided that after next week's readings we would take a break for a few weeks, then start up again. In June, John Rechy, Paul Monette, and Christopher Isherwood will be in N.Y.C. We will probably invite them to our readings; otherwise, readings will be kept in the circle—exclusive—if only because they are more than show-and-tell. They are actual work sessions wherein ideas are distributed, discussed, critiqued—and where we are *faute de mieux* forced to think about what we and others are writing. The more we open our readings to people who are not actually writers, the more the session will be for display and the less for work. Yet to have the use of so many talented men— and hopefully women too—will be invaluable.

I'm wondering whether my next reading ought to be of a story— say "A Stroke"—which I think is finished or of an excerpt from my novel in progress. It will depend, I suppose, on how much I do before the next reading.

4/9/80

Yesterday afternoon, I sat down to revise the opening pages of *Summer's Lease*, which I'd written at the Ferro-Grumleys' in Sea Girt a week or more ago, but I encountered so many interruptions I had to put it away.

4/17/80

The third set of readings of the Violet Quill Club were held at George Whitmore's apartment on Washington Square North last night.

Andrew read a new, funny, very wonderful story called "The House of Dead Queens" (title subject to change?) about the journey of two New York queens in their mid-thirties who visit friends who've retired to upstate New York and how they come up against aging and all its concomitances. The crux of the story is not what happens, but what could possibly happen. And that seems a great deal: our imaginations being richer in possibilities than life often is. A wonderful character, Hadley Vernon, stands next to Sutherland from *Dancer*.* Hadley is the preeminent New York Queen—realistic, sophisticated, tolerant (to a point), eccentric, and utterly lovable. He is given to seducing his best friends' boyfriends with the allure of the city. Yet he is capable of saying, "When I die I want it to be on my knees in some back room with my lips filled with dead babies." The house party is almost hysterically dull, except for the various guests' machinations. A very courtly story.

Edmund also read the second chapter from his autobiographical novel. This one begins, "I was fourteen years old when I bought my first hustler," and is set in the Midwest.† It is almost impossible to describe, being from White's densest, richest, and most personal work. Suffice it to say his powers of description are magical, his delineations of youth brilliant (complete with follies, fears, and misunderstandings). This chapter is darker by far than the sunny estival first part.

Various discussions took place around these readings. One concerned the described "beauty" of some of our characters. Both Edmund's *States of Desire* and my novel *The Lure* were attacked in *The Advocate* for being too concerned with beautiful guys—the popularity of our books was attributed to this.

I see nothing wrong with describing someone as beautiful—straight or gay—if they are. Even more to the point, after reading of themselves as powerless freaks and criminals, gays need to read of other gays as dynamic, bright, successful, powerful, handsome, and able. To have set *The Lure* with unattractive characters would have been a lie.

Last night, Edmund told us he is receiving an award from the National Gay Task Force for *States of Desire*. This is great news. We are still under attack from most gay politicians. It is very important that gay literature begin to be recognized for its positive achievements, its influence, its ability to help others.

---

*A version of the story appeared as "Someone Is Crying in the Château de Berne" and is included in *A True Likeness*. Hadley Vernon's name was changed to Hadley Van Ness.

†The story was published as Chapter 2 of *A Boy's Own Story* and as "A Man of the World" in *A True Likeness*.

4/18/80

One of the matters we discussed at the Violet Quill Club was the role of the writer of fiction. The day of our last meeting, Norman Mailer had been awarded the Pulitzer Prize in fiction for *The Executioner's Song*, a biography of the life and times of Gary Gilmore, a third-rate criminal. I was outraged. Mailer had first foisted this book off to his publisher as a novel to satisfy a contractual obligation. Then, following Truman Capote's footsteps, the publisher foisted the book off to the public as a "true-life novel," whatever that means. It worked with the *NY Times*, which is befuddled by the what-is-or-isn't chic and defended putting it on their fiction best-seller list, well knowing that it would never get on the nonfiction list. As it is, it never rose above #8. Of course the other books were Philip Roth's *The Ghost Writer*, a failed novella that happens to have some of his best writing, and *Endless Love*, a bizarre literary device which the public isn't buying either.

True enough, there are many classic examples of mixing genres— Goethe's *Sorrows of Young Werther*, Flaubert's *Sentimental Education*, Joyce's *Portrait of the Artist*, Proust, of course. But in every case the autobiographical element has been transformed into the universal. And this may be the crux of the modern problem. For if our writers see themselves as incapable of being rendered so intensely, they must then turn to other subjects. Oddly, Capote and Mailer have turned to minor criminals rather than to great and admirable characters, afraid to show how they would fail in comparison. But of them Capote is the least culpable; he at least came to love one of his subjects and worked with them rather than just exploiting them.*

Another problem with the contemporary autobiographical novel is what stance to take, how much distance to put between one's present and earlier self. In Edmund's new book, he is the character—he is the boy, but also the grown-up writing about it. His recapture, like Proust's, seems to be enlarging a life he admits was "bleak."

On the other hand, Andrew's story "The House of Dead Queens" has a distant narrator, one who ought to be a bit closer to the story, we all thought. We want to know things about the narrator—who his friends are, what he thinks of them, what he'll do to interfere, what not. He is otherwise uncommitted and only affected secondhand, apparently, by the story he tells.

---

*Picano has since changed his mind.

Last night, George Whitmore read from his *Confessions of Danny Slocum* at Three Lives & Company. He chose to read the heart of the book, those parts dealing with his relationship to his father. It made for a depressing evening. Afterwards he remarked to me that he didn't realize how bitter those parts were until he read them aloud. But the problem stands: Where does one fictionalize, how much, and how closely or distantly do you stand to the action?

4/24/80

The fourth meeting of the Violet Quill Club provided a surprise and two fulfillments.

The surprise was my haircut—which was well received. Only George was nonplussed at first. He didn't recognize me and looked at me aslant—suspicious. Obviously my big-brother image was shattered for him.

Robert Ferro read from his novel *Max Desir*, the second chapter— a good one with Max at 37 in the city, struggling. The writing is more assured, easier to follow.

Chris Cox's presentation was "Doe's Pillow," or at least the first third of it. This is a novella, written à la Eudora Welty of "Why I Live at the P.O." but with more depth of emotion, more complications, and more detail. The quality of the writing is quite excellent—the monologue stylistically is brilliant. I only wonder whether the plot can sustain such a baroque framework.

5/7/80

Talked with David Rieff* yesterday at Farrar, Straus about permission to reprint James Schuyler's poems in the Sea Horse anthology. He asked about my novel, and I told him that instead of the *Wyndeslade* book I'd been writing *Late in the Season*. He said it didn't sound much like a Dell book, and I had to agree. He seemed very interested, and I promised to show it to him.

Later on I talked with Robert Ferro, who had brought over pieces of his novel for me to select for the anthology. Robert said that David Rieff was interested in his work too—and in Ed White's. I didn't tell

---

*David Rieff (b. 1952), a writer and an editor at Farrar, Straus & Giroux. He is the son of Susan Sontag and Philip Rieff.

Robert that I knew that David had just declined George Whitmore's story collection (it looks as though I will be publishing them).

5/21/80

Last night was the second reading connected with the Gay Arts Festival. The first had Richard Howard and Frank Bidart reading, and I understand it was poorly attended. Not last night's reading, with Ed and George Whitmore.

Ed read "A Man of the World," the piece he's included in the Sea Horse Press anthology. He was dressed nattily in a blue-black blazer, pale blue shirt with white collar, white ruck slacks, black tie, and white shoes.

George was more restrained. He read two stories from *Out Here: Tales of Fire Island*, "The Guermantes Way" and "Scrabble"—the two linked by an interlude. These two stories were extremely effective, and I have to say I find it almost unbelievable that his agent, Pat Loud, has not yet found a publisher for them.

5/22/80

Last night, Andrew Holleran and I went to Joe Mathewson's to be an audience for a first reading of his one-act play *Canned Soup,* a comedy about the changing roles of the sexes. Austin and Katina Pendleton took roles and Stephanie Murphy was the protagonist. This was the second version of the play, which I accepted for the Sea Horse anthology.

5/30/80

The readings at the Glines went off rather well, despite all the initial difficulties surrounding them. Dennis Cooper* was first, by choice. I read after the intermission.

Dinner beforehand with Ed White and Dennis, Chris Cox, John Ashbery, and David Kermani.† I sat on John's left at dinner, and we struck up a good conversation until the wine hit him (and me) and then torpor set in.

---

*Dennis Cooper (b. 1953), author of *Safe*, *Closer*, and *Frisk*.
†David Kermani was John Ashbery's companion and bibliographer.

6/20/80

Spent the last three days at Sea Girt, New Jersey, at the summer home of Robert Ferro's family. Present were Robert, Michael, Andrew Holleran. Chris Cox and Ed White did not arrive as planned. Instead on Monday night Chris called to say Ed had returned from his trip promoting *States of Desire* and had told him he wanted to break up their two-year relationship. Much brouhaha over this and sadness.

We swam, jogged, played tennis, cards, ate seemingly all day. I got my first summer tan. Read a bit of Walter Benjamin. I brought the novel manuscript for Ed to read. Andrew picked it up. By the train trip back, he'd read about one third of it, but would offer no impression of it. I will be on pins and needles until I receive some kind of response to it.

6/25/80

Last night, John Rechy—in from California—read at the Westside Mainstage Theatre as part of the Glines 1st American Gay Arts Festival.

George Whitmore said Rechy had succeeded best in *City of Night* because he had Miss Divine to be his drag-queen representative, and through her to see his macho stance as another kind of drag.

I think all of us in the Violet Quill have an edge over him in sheer craft and complexity. I did find his remarks about the formal structures of his books both touching and a plea for professionalism.

6/29/80

Today was the eleventh Gay Pride Day. The Glines 1st Gay Arts Festival was a financial and critical success.

7/20/80

Dinner last night at Edmund White's apartment. Present were Edmund's old friend Stan Redfern, the harpsichordist Andy Appel, Australian critic Dennis Altman, and the American essayist Richard Sennett. This next week must be spent completing the Sea Horse anthology.

7/21/80

Ed called. Turns out I was the hit of his dinner party. Richard Sennett liked me a great deal and so did Andy Appel. Edmund is matchmaking again.

7/30/80

Meeting of the Violet Quill Club last night. George Whitmore read his story "Last Dance"; Andrew read a section—a character portrait of George Lash—from his new as-yet-untitled novel; I read "Xmas in the Apple."

Andrew's portion got the best response. It is wonderfully inventive and flows beautifully. He still seems to have a problem with structure, but his reading was the purest pleasure.

7/31/80

Last night the Violet Quill Club met here for the second of our summer readings.

Michael Grumley read the opening chapter of his unnamed Beaches of the World book, which he hopes to sell to Viking this month. The chapter was about St. John the Baptist Day in San Juan, P.R., a big beach holiday in that country. The writing was quite fine (although some of the commentators thought "too high"), the perspective was an Olympian one.

Robert Ferro read chapter three of his novel in progress, *Max Desir*—this one titled "The Ripple Effect." It is the best writing he has done to date—warm, personal, terrifying—very autobiographical. His family, especially his mother's illness, is rendered splendidly.

Ed White finished off with a long third chapter from his novel in progress.

9/10/80

Spent the last three days at the Ferro family house in Sea Girt doing little or nothing.

10/29/80

Monday, Andrew and I and the Ferro-Grumleys took a drive up the Hudson for fall foliage. We spent some time at West Point. There the natural beauty of the setting almost allowed me to forget the enormous, dull gray institution behind. Almost, but not quite. Of all the hundreds of cadets we saw on parade, jogging, walking to class, or playing at various sports, only one had a smile for us. It must be an awfully depressing place.

11/10/80

An interesting weekend, even an adventurous one for a change. On Saturday I got a call from a man named Randy Shilts, who'd gotten my number from Mike Denneny. Randy is a journalist in San Francisco, visiting New York for a book contract on the life of Harvey Milk for St. Martin's Press.* He said he was a great fan of *The Lure* and would like to meet me. He came by and was cute—a bearded, active little teddy bear. We got high and taxied to the Flamingo, which looked dead, and then to the Saint, where we talked and danced for several hours. Finally we agreed to come here to fuck. We did, and did again about five hours later, and then again the next afternoon after a late breakfast.

11/18/80

I've been reading Leon Edel's book on the Bloomsbury Group. What is most astonishing about them all is that they attained such power in so short a time. By 1922 Virginia Woolf could write to a friend, "We are all famous," she the least of them, although it is through her that we now approach the others.

I thought of the Violet Quill Club in comparison. We are a far younger group—only one year old—smaller, seven members to Bloomsbury's ten; far more cohesive—all in literature, all male, all homosexual. We don't share a common background such as the Cambridge of the Bloomsbury Group. Still, many see us as just as powerful, at least in gay literature.

---

*Randy Shilts has written not only *The Mayor of Castro Street* but also the bestsellers *And the Band Played On* and *Conduct Unbecoming*.

11/20/80

Well, it was bound to happen. Yesterday, when I went to Three Lives & Company to check the sales of Sea Horse books, the ladies began to sympathize about "the Soho piece . . . " Since I had no idea what they were talking about, they showed me the article in the new *Soho Weekly*. The cover headline reads, "Fag Lit's New Royalty," and the subheading is "A Moveable Brunch—The Fag Lit Mafia."

12/17/80

Dinner party at Ed White's. Delicious meal. He is a splendid cook—roast beef, spinach soufflé, a shrimp appetizer, and special pie for dessert.

Present—the Ferro-Grumleys, in good spirits; Stan Redfern with his new boyfriend Brendan, a handsome, bright, blond midwesterner of about twenty-five. Also on hand before dinner was Ed's own new beau, met the previous night—Matt Ward.*

1981

1/1/81

The best New Year's Eve party in a decade! I went up to the F-Gs' to exchange Christmas gifts. They had already received the *New Yorker* subscription, and I added a recording of Schubert's Impromptus played by Wilhelm Kempf. I received a pound box of Godiva chocolates—yum.

1/3/81

The new year is certainly off to a start. Yesterday the IRS called, looking for my 1978–79 tax forms, still not filed, thanks to my accountant. I owe them almost ten grand.

Good news on the money front from the F-Gs, who've somehow

---

*Matt Ward (1951–90) was an editor and translator of such writers as Roland Barthes and Colette. He is the model for Luke, the main character in Edmund White's story "Running on Empty," published in the collection *The Darker Proof*.

come up with enough cash to pay me back the $600 they owe me. Between that and payment for the *Blueboy* story and the *Advocate* reviews, I should take in almost a thousand dollars this month. Perhaps Sea Horse Press will repay me another fifteen hundred. My first priority this month is preparing the opening four chapters and a working proposal for Delacorte so I can gather some real money in the next few months.

1/10/81

At the St. Martin's party last night at the Roosevelt Hotel, I was taken aside by Robert McQueen of *The Advocate* and asked to write 2,500 words on Manhattan for their New York supplement.

"What can I do?" I asked him.

"I really just want your name and your work in it!"

Up early to appear on an Editorial Contents panel, then the luncheon for the formation of the Gay Press Association. I'm to meet Vito Russo there for the interview he's doing for *London Gay News*.

My *I Ching* for today: #1 with no changes.

1/11/81

#1 The Creative stands for a Historical Moment—which is exactly what happened at the Hotel Roosevelt yesterday, where some eighty people representing fifty or so publishers got together to form the Gay Press Association.

1/17/81

Yesterday a friend, Nick Rock, died.* He'd been ill for the past few months with what was finally diagnosed as cat-scratch fever.† Hyperallergic for years, his immunological system couldn't cope with it. Before the illness was diagnosed he wasted away, formed lesions on the brain, etc., fell into a coma.

He and his lover of seven years, Enno Poersch, were a standard of

---

*The deaths of Nick Rock and his housemate Rick Wellikoff are chronicled in Randy Shilts's *And the Band Played On*. Picano shared a house on Fire Island with Rock and Enno Poersch in 1975.

†Nick Rock did not have cat-scratch fever. His was one of the first cases of AIDS.

the Pines at Fire Island in the seventies. One of the golden couples. Nick was bright, sharp, sarcastic at times, always no bullshit, but soft and yielding, too, curious, interested, open to new ideas. I valued him as a friend and a good man.

1/18/81

I saw Mike Grumley briefly for tea here. He'd been down at the Leslie Lohman gallery, where his illustrations are on display. Last week he and Robert went down to Sea Girt, where Michael did a lot of work on his novel in progress, *A World of Men*, a chapter of which is in the Sea Horse anthology, another to be published this spring in *Christopher Street*.

1/26/81

Yesterday *Publishers Weekly* did the Sea Horse Press story, "The Unauthorized Life of Novelist Felice Picano." It was all I could have wished for. The best possible publicity.

2/15/81

Last night, Chris Cox and George Whitmore came by for dinner. I roasted a leg of lamb, baked acorn squash, casserole of Bruxelles sprouts, green salad, chocolate ice cream and cookies.

We talked about journalism. Chris recently had a portrait of Iris Love in *Soho Weekly* and one on Henry Geldzhaler for *CS*. I asked whether *Soho* would be interested in a piece on the closing of the Flamingo tonight after six years. He'll ask the editor.

2/23/81

Vito Russo and Clovis Ruffin gave me a birthday party in Clovis's penthouse overlooking Abingdon Square. It was my first birthday party in perhaps twenty years. Vito showed a terrifically funny movie, *Roxie Hart*, 1942, upon which the musical *Chicago* is based. At the party were the VQ Club—Ed White, Chris Cox, the Ferro-Grumleys, George Whitmore—and Eddie Rosenberg, Bob Lowe, two people from Washington, Arthur Bell from the *Voice*, Doug Ireland from *Soho Weekly News*, Mike Denneny, and Joe Mathewson.

3/1/81

George Whitmore has dropped out of the VQ Club. He was here last night for dinner, attempting to explain why. It is all a ridiculous tempest in a teapot, of course, but it does open the VQ up to guest participants, which I've always wanted not only for the good publicity but for the new blood.

It's odd but, I suppose, unsurprising that it was the lesser known of the group—George and Robert Ferro—who kicked up a rumpus last July that caused the break.

George, of course, *is* a problem. He is the most nakedly ambitious of us all—the least secure, the one most involved in the scene from the past. The complaints against him are his opportunism and what Robert perceives as his very minor talent. He is in many ways derivative and superficial. While his stories often don't dig deep enough— his best, "Black Widow," "Scrabble," "Getting Rid of Robert," work the surface of life—*The Confessions of Slocum* does dig deeply, revealingly. Perhaps George ought to return to playwriting, which he prefers anyway.

Robert wants nothing but critical success. He has a vision of himself as a sort of Flaubert, working away in the dark at the hard rock of literature. When his work is good—as in the first chapters of the new novel—it's very good indeed. Otherwise it can be icy and impenetrable.

For my part I'm just interested in writing and discovery. Tonight or tomorrow I will be reading "A Stroke" to the VQ.* It will be interesting how it is received since technically it poaches on their territories.

3/2/81

At the VQ meeting at Ed's house last night, Mike Grumley, Robert Ferro, and I read. Michael read "Subways" from his novel in progress, Robert the fourth chapter of his novel, "The Beach House."

Robert's was the most intensely personal and complete, I thought. It was a minute, almost day-to-day reconstruction of his mother's cancer from the first radiation treatments to her death. Mike's chapter wove the past and present with a beautiful rendering of his childhood and some Czech displaced persons in the Midwest.

---

*"A Stroke" appears in *Slashed to Ribbons*.

My story was well received, especially by Edmund, who felt I should send it to *The New Yorker*. He said it was tight, surprisingly powerful, and anything but ordinary.

3/3/81

The VQ Club met here last night. Edmund White read a splendid 4th chapter from his novel *A Boy's Own Story*. Vito Russo—our first guest—read two chapters from his book *The Celluloid Closet*, which Harper and Row will publish this summer. Christopher Cox read excerpts from his book on Key West. It seemed the perfect wedding of author and subject.

We all missed Andrew and some of us George.*

3/12/81

The first group reading from *A True Likeness*, the Sea Horse Press anthology, was a success last night at Three Lives. We had to turn away thirty people. George Whitmore read ''Sunday Lover,'' a longish story, which wandered a little at the end even though it was published in *Blueboy*. Shirley Powell read a story from *Parachutes*, and Joan Larkin read about a dozen poems. There was a brief intermission, then Robert Ferro read a chapter from his novel; the section was called ''The Mummy,'' but it didn't have the depth of the earlier chapters.

3/13/81

The second evening of readings at Three Lives was not as crowded as the first, but it was a much tonier audience—Ed White, Richard Sennett, Mike Denneny, Tom Steele.

Dan Diamond opened the evening with his poetry. Mike Grumley presented ''Media,'' an excellent section of his novel. Chuck Ortleb broke his public reading virginity and did quite well. After the break, Jane DeLynn and Bob Heron; he read from *Moritz*.†

---

*This would be the last formal meeting of the Violet Quill.
†Bob Heron (1930–86) published *Moritz* with Calamus Press (1986). Picano has written about their relationship in *Men Who Loved Me*.

3/15/81

A party given by his lover, Enno, and friends of Nick Rock last night. About two hundred in attendance including both Enno and Nick's families. Naturally, almost everyone from the Fire Island crowd was there. There were many reencounters, and it's fascinating to see how we've turned out. Nick's mother, Rose, cut the cake (baked to duplicate one of Enno's colorful Hawaiian-shirt cards) and she said, "I didn't want to come tonight. I was afraid to. But I'm glad I did because I got to see what a great group of friends Nick had and how well he remains in your memory. This is the happiest day since the birth of my son."

3/21/81

Tea at the Ferro-Grumleys'. Chris Cox was there but coming down with a fever. Ed was just back from a triumphant tour of Toronto, which just had its Stonewall. Joel Crothers was there too and Diane Cleaves, the F-Gs' new agent, whom I persist in distrusting.

3/25/81

Right in front of me at the Met's new production of *La Traviata* were Ed White, with Susan Sontag, Roger Straus of FS&G, and his wife, the Macy's heiress. She had her hand in a cast. Edmund was in heaven.

3/30/81

I had drinks with George Whitmore last Saturday. Brief and painful. It is fairly clear to him that we are no longer close friends, and he is distraught. But he is so neurotic that he is unable to see that he has, step by step, arranged it this way. His unawareness is what pains me— not the mental acrobatics, which he evidently enjoys.

The three most recent steps disintegrating our relationship were (1) his stepping out of the VQ Club (which I accepted), and his attempted manipulation to destroy it completely (which I abhorred); (2) his taking advantage of the *True Likeness* reading, where he read for 40 minutes even though he was supposed to be on 15–20 minutes (he denies this, but I timed it); (3) his failure to come to my own poetry reading after I had given him my spot at Three Lives.

All of this is annoying, but most annoying is trying to deal with a person who doesn't see what he's doing. We all are—Andrew, Ed, and I—tired of playing nursemaid to someone whose only return to us is to steal our work and ideas, fawn over us so much it seems insincere, and then lie and manipulate behind our backs.

3/31/81

Andrew's letter with interview and preface arrived yesterday, and it was pure Holleran. I have retyped it and answered the questions. The interview will appear in dozens of gay magazines and newspapers, I hope, and will be the major push behind *Late in the Season* since Delacorte seems so uninterested in it.

4/1/81

Literary homophobia continues. Richard Sennett told me he tried to review *A True Likeness* for the Sunday *Times* book-review section and the editor, Harvey Shapiro, turned him down. That's the second time it has turned down a review, and all the more galling because Avon's anthology of Jewish poetry, *Voices from the Ark*, got a two-page spread.

5/2/81

Drove down to Sea Girt for the weekend. This was supposed to be a meeting of the VQ Club, but it didn't turn out that way. Andrew canceled—he's still in Florida. Then Ed White canceled; a reading of his play is to be done on Saturday with the perfect cast before he rushes off to Europe. Chris Cox naturally failed to show. So it was me with the F-Gs. Read a chapter from Robert's novel which is both more imaginative and less relevant that any of the other chapters, and a short story of mine, "In Which the Average of the Particular," and they liked it very much. I read Michael's proposal for a new book of nonfiction, "Brothering," which I found small, unspecific, and inadequate to the subject.

1982

1/1/82

Well, here it is—a new year—and I'm much the same as I was last year. I'm still alone, with no one to love, and memories of previous loves are as sharp as ever. Friends remain—Susan, Jane, Bob, Don, the Ferro-Grumleys, Andrew—while others have gone—George Whitmore to find a lover, Ed White for ambition, Linda Gray for a better job. No new friends this year, and I lost many whom I loved—my mother, Nick Rock, Rick Wellikoff, my neighbors Sheldon and Doug. With Hal Seidman and David Jackson ill with KS, I may lose them soon, too. At the beginning of March, Uranus goes retrograde, and Neptune follows at the end of the month. With constant, dexterous, complicated work, I ought to have my next book done by the spring.

From *Dancer from the Dance*

Andrew Holleran

Dancer from the Dance *(1978) evokes as no work has the poetry
and pain of gay New York in the 1970s. It tells the story not just of
Malone and Sutherland, whose friendship towers above and destroys
their relationships with everyone else, but the whole tribe of
"doomed queens." "I realized the other day," one of the characters
admits, that "everyone I know is gay, everything I do is, all my
fantasies are, I am [one of those] people we used to see in the
discos, bars, baths, all the time . . . I am a doomed queen." This
chapter presents a world as funny as anything in Waugh, as
brilliantly witty as anything in Firbank, and as deeply touching and
self-destructively glamorous as anything in Fitzgerald.*

Long before journalists discovered the discotheques of Manhattan,
long before they became another possession of the middle class, in the
beginning, that particular autumn of 1971, two gentlemen whose
names I forget opened up a little club on the twelfth floor of a factory
building in the West Thirties. The West Thirties, after dark, form a
lunar landscape: The streets that are crowded with men running racks
of clothes down the sidewalk during the day, and trucks honking at
each other to get through the narrow passageways of factory exits, are
completely deserted at night. The place is as still as the oceans of the
moon. The buildings are all dark. There isn't a soul in sight—not a
bum, a mugger, or a cop. But late on Friday and Saturday nights,
around one A.M., flotillas of taxis would pull up to a certain dim doorway and deliver their passengers who, on showing a numbered card,
would go up in a freight elevator to the twelfth floor. Everyone who
went there that first year agrees: There was never anything before or
since so wonderful.

In a town where clubs open and close in a week, no one expected it to last more than one winter. The second year it was too famous, and too many people wished to go. Film stars and rock stars, and photographers, and rich Parisians, and women from Dallas came to look, and it was finished. There were arguments in the lobby about who was whose guest, and there were too many drugs; and toward the end of it, I used to just sit on the sofa in the back and watch the crowd.

The first year contained the thrill of newness, and the thrill of exclusivity—that all these people who might not even know each other, but who knew who each other were, had been brought together in the winter, in this little room, without having done a single thing to bring it about. They all knew each other without ever having been introduced. They formed a group of people who had danced with each other over the years, gone to the same parties, the same beaches on the same trains, yet, in some cases, never even nodded at each other. They were bound together by a common love of a certain kind of music, physical beauty, and style—all the things one shouldn't throw away an ounce of energy pursuing, and sometimes throw away a life pursuing.

Within this larger group—for some of them came but once a month, or twice all season—was a core of people who seemed to have no existence at all outside this room. They were never home, it seemed, but lived only in the ceaseless flow of this tiny society's movements. They seldom looked happy. They passed one another without a word in the elevator, like silent shades in hell, hell-bent on their next look from a handsome stranger. Their next rush from a popper. The next song that turned their bones to jelly and left them all on the dance floor with heads back, eyes nearly closed, in the ecstasy of saints receiving the stigmata. They pursued these things with such devotion that they acquired, after a few seasons, a haggard look, a look of deadly seriousness. Some wiped everything they could off their faces and reduced themselves to blanks. Yet even these, when you entered the hallway where they stood waiting to go in, would turn toward you all at once in that one unpremeditated moment (as when we see ourselves in a mirror we didn't know was there), the same look on all their faces: Take me away from this. Or, Love me. If there had been a prison for such desperadoes, you would have called the police and had them all arrested—just to get them out of these redundant places and give them a rest.

There was a moment when their faces blossomed into the sweetest happiness, however—when everyone came together in a single lovely communion that was the reason they did all they did; and that occurred around six-thirty in the morning, when they took off their sweat-soaked T-shirts and screamed because Patty Joe had begun to sing: "Make me believe in you, show me that love can be true." By then the air was half-nauseating with the stale stench of poppers, broken and dropped on the floor after their fumes had been sucked into the heart, and the odor of sweat, and ethyl chloride from the rags they clamped between their teeth, holding their friends' arms to keep from falling. The people on downs were hardly able to move, and the others rising from the couches where they had been sprawled like martyrs who have given up their souls to Christ pushed onto the floor and united in the cries of animal joy because Patty Joe had begun to sing in her metallic, unreal voice those signal words: "Make me believe in you, show me that love can be true."

(Or because the discaire had gone from Barrabas' "Woman" to Zulema's "Giving Up," or the Temptations' "Law of the Land." Any memory of those days is nothing but a string of songs.)

When the people finally left, the blood-red sun was perched in the fire escape of a factory building silhouetted on the corner, and the cornices of the buildings were all gold-edged, and they would strip off their T-shirts, in the cold fall morning, and wring them out over the gutter. And the sweat would fall into the gutter like water dripping from a pail, the sweat of athletes after a long and sweaty game of soccer on some playing field to the north, on a fall day as pure as this one; and they would walk up Broadway together, exhausted, ecstatic, their bones light as a bird's, a flotilla of doomed queens on their way to the Everard Baths because they could not come down from the joy and happiness.

They looked, these young men gazing up toward the sky with T-shirts hanging from their belts, like athletes coming from a game, like youths coming home from school, their dark eyes glowing with light, their faces radiant, and no one passing them could have gathered the reason for this happy band.

Toward the end, I used to sit on the sofa in the back of the Twelfth Floor and wonder. Many of them were very attractive, these young men whose cryptic disappearance in New York City their families (unaware they were homosexual) understood less than if they had been killed in a car wreck. They were tall and broad-shouldered, with handsome, open faces and strong white teeth, and they were all dead. They lived only to bathe in the music, and each other's desire, in a strange democracy whose only ticket of admission was physical beauty—and not even that sometimes. All else was strictly classless: The boy passed out on the sofa from an overdose of Tuinols was a Puerto Rican who washed dishes in the employees' cafeteria at CBS, but the doctor bending over him had treated presidents. It was a democracy such as the world—with its rewards and penalties, its competition, its snobbery—never permits, but which flourished in this little room on the twelfth floor of a factory building on West Thirty-third Street, because its central principle was the most anarchic of all: erotic love.

What a carnival of people. One fellow came directly from his tour of duty in the Emergency Room at Bellevue on Saturday nights, and danced in his white coat sprinkled with blood. A handsome blond man whom the nation saw on its television sets almost every day eating a nutritious cereal, came to stand by the doorway to the bathroom, waiting for someone to go in whose piss he could drink. Chatting with him was a famous drug dealer from the Upper East Side who was sending his son through Choate and his daughter through Foxcroft, and who always dressed like a gangster from the forties. They were talking to a rich art collector, who one day had resolved to leave all this, had cursed it and gone to the Orient the next day to live there; within a year he had reappeared standing beside the dance floor, because, as he told his friends, Angkor Wat was not nearly so beautiful as the sight of Luis Sanchez dancing to "Law of the Land" with his chest glistening with sweat and a friend stuffing a rag soaked with ethyl chloride into his mouth.

The art collector walked up to talk to a handsome architect who had also tried to escape this room and the life, and society, which flowed out from it, as a river does from a spring. He had decided one night he was dissipating himself, he had looked in the mirror and decided he was going to waste physically. And so he bought a car and drove west till he found a little shack high in a mountain pass with not a single mirror in the house. Four months of snow, and two of flowers, in the pure mountain air, however, did not arrest the progress of these physical flaws. They were age itself. And so one morning in May, with flowers on the meadows and the valley beneath him, he decided to go back to Manhattan and rot with all the beauties in this artificial hothouse of music and light. For what was this room but a place to forget we are dying? There were people so blessed with beauty there they did not know what to do with it. And so the doctor who came direct from the Emergency Room (whose dark, bearded face was that of a fifteenth-century Spanish saint), the archangelic son of a famous actress, the man who had driven west to leave time behind, breathed now the air of Olympus: Everyone was a god, and no one grew old in a single night. No, it took years for that to happen . . .

For what does one do with Beauty—that oddest, most irrational of careers? There were boys in that room, bank tellers, shoe salesmen, clerks, who had been given faces and forms so extraordinary that they constituted a vocation of their own. They rushed out each night to simply stand in rooms about the city, exhibiting themselves to view much as the priest on Holy Saturday throws open the doors of the Tabernacle to expose the chalice within.

Nevertheless Malone, the night Frankie nearly beat him up on the sidewalk outside the Twelfth Floor (a commotion I was unaware of long after it had occurred, since I had arrived early that night to watch the place fill up with dancers and hear the music that began the whole night, as an overture begins an opera, and that the dancers never heard) and had to be taken off by the police, had by that time come to loathe being looked at; could not bear the gaze of amorous strangers; and the only reason he came out at all, during that period after he left Frankie, when he wanted to go away and hide forever, was the crazy compulsion with which we resolved all the tangled impulses of our lives— the need to dance.

Everyone there, in fact, like Malone, was a serious dancer and they were by no means beautiful: Archer Prentiss, who had no chin or hair; Spanish Lily, a tiny, wizened octoroon who lived with his blind mother in the Bronx and sold shoes in a local store—but who by night resembled Salome dancing for the head of John the Baptist in peach-colored veils; Lavalava, a Haitian boy who modeled for *Vogue* till an editor saw him in the dressing room with an enormous penis where a vagina should have been; another man famous for a film he had produced and who had no wish to do anything else with his life—all of them mixed together on that square of blond wood and danced, without looking at anyone else, for one another.

They were the most romantic creatures in the city in that room. If their days were spent in banks and office buildings, no matter: Their true lives began when they walked through this door—and were baptized into a deeper faith, as if brought to life by miraculous immersion. They lived only for the night. The most beautiful Oriental was in fact chaste, as the handmaidens of Dionysius were: He came each night to avoid the eyes of everyone who wanted him (though for different reasons than Malone ignored their gaze), and after dancing for hours in a band of half-naked men, went home alone each night refusing to tinge the exhilaration in his heart with the actuality of carnal kisses. The gossips said he refused to sleep with people because he had a small penis—the leprosy of homosexuals—but this explanation was mundane: He wanted to keep this life in the realm of the perfect, the ideal. He wanted to be desired, not possessed, for in remaining desired he remained, like the figure on the Grecian urn, forever pursued. He knew quite well that once possessed he would no longer be enchanted—so sex itself became secondary to the spectacle: that single moment of walking in that door. And even as he danced now he was aware of whose heart he was breaking; everyone there was utterly aware of one another.

For example: I sat on the sofa watching Archer Prentiss dance with two other men in plaid shirts and moustaches, who looked as if they had just come down from the Maine woods—two people I had seen for years and years, yet never said a word to, as was the case with Archer Prentiss. This technical distance did not keep us from knowing a great deal about each other, however. Although I had no idea who the two strangers on my left were, nor had ever been introduced to Archer Prentiss, I knew, to the quarter inch, the length and diameter of each one's penis, and exactly what they liked to do in bed.

But then so did everyone else in that room.

If one of the figures in this tapestry of gossip woven at the Twelfth Floor vanished—like the man who fled to Cambodia, or the one who drove west—such a disappearance was, in that crowd, less mysterious than most vanishing acts. If a face in that crowd vanished, it was usually for one of three reasons: (1) he was dead, (2) he had moved to another city whose inhabitants he had not all slept with, or (3) he had found a lover and settled down, spending his Saturday nights at home with his mate, going over the plans of the house they hoped to build in Teaneck, New Jersey.

The two strangers in plaid shirts who had sat down on the sofa to my left were discussing at that moment such a move. The big, blond fellow (whose face decorated a dozen billboards on the Long Island Expressway, smiling at a Winston cigarette) said to the dark one: "He wants me to move in with him, after he comes back from Portugal."

"Oh, God, he lives on Beekman Place, doesn't he?"

"Yes, but Howard lives off Sutton, and he wants me to move in, too. Damn, I don't know what to do."

"Marry John! Sutton Place is all Jewish dentists."

And they burst into laughter over their solution to this problem; while at the next instant, the creature who, for a reason I could not put my finger on, fascinated me more than any of the habitués of that place came in the door: Sutherland. He swept in trailing a strange coterie of Egyptian cotton heiresses, the most popular male model to come over from Paris in a decade, a Puerto Rican drug dealer, and an Italian prince. Sutherland was dressed in a black Norell, turban, black pumps, rhinestones, and veil. He held a long cigarette holder to his lips and vanished among the crowd. The dark man began to debate idly whether he should go to bed with Archer Prentiss, who was (a) very ugly, but (b) had a big dick.

In the midst of their deliberations, Zulema's "Giving Up" suddenly burst out of the recapitulations of Deodato, and the two woodsmen got up to dance; at their rising, two other boys in black with tired, beautiful eyes, sat down immediately and began discussing the men who had just left: "I call him the Pancake Man," said one. "*He* doesn't use makeup!" said the other. "Oh, no," the first replied. "The opposite! Because he's the kind of man you imagine waking up with on Saturday morning, and he makes pancakes for you, and then you take the dog out for a walk in the park. And he always has a moustache, and he always wears plaid shirts!"

"I agree he's gorgeous," said his friend, "but someone told me he has the smallest wee-wee in New York."

And with that, as if the boy had snapped his fingers, the big, blond woodsman standing by the dance floor in all his radiant masculinity, crumbled into dust.

"Oh please," said the one, "I don't need that." He covered his face with his hands. "I'm already on downs, why did you say that?"

"Because it's true," said the other.

"Oh, God," the first moaned, in the nasal wail of Brooklyn, "oh, God, I can't believe that. No, he's my Pancake Man."

"They *all* wear plaid shirts, and they all have moustaches," said his friend. "You might as well pick one with a big dick. None of them will look at you, anyway."

He looked out between his fingers at the woodsman, who was now talking animatedly to Sutherland in his black Norell and turban and long cigarette holder, and said, "Who is that woman he's talking to?" And the other said: "Her name is Andrew Sutherland, and she lives on Madison Avenue. She's a speed freak. She hasn't long to live." At that moment, "Needing You" began, buried still in the diminishing chords of "You've Got Me Waiting for the Rain to Fall," and the two boys on the sofa—with hearing sharper than a coyote's, and without even needing to ask each other—bounded up off the sofa and headed for the dance floor. Instantly their seats were taken by an older, gray-haired man and his friend, an even older fellow who because of his hearing aid, toupee, and back brace was known among the younger queens as Spare Parts. "I find him so beautiful," said the man of the boy who had just left, "like a Kabuki, that long neck, those heavy-lidded eyes. He never looks at me, do you think because he's afraid?" They began to discuss a friend on the dance floor who had recently learned he had cancer of the lungs. "No, no," said Spare Parts, "he has cancer of the colon, I think, his mother has cancer of the lungs." "Yes," said the friend, "he used to scream at his mother for smoking too much, and she used to scream at him for eating too fast. And now look." "He flies out to the clinic tomorrow," said Spare Parts. "Do you suppose he wants to go home with someone?" "You know," said the friend, "I would think the fact that he's dying would give him the courage to walk up to all these boys he's been in love with all these years but never had the nerve to say hello to." "Well, he has a look about him," said Spare Parts. "He looks . . . ethereal." At that moment two Puerto Rican boys, oblivious to everything but their own heated discussion, stopped to snuff out their cigarettes in the ashtray beside the sofa.

"And the reason you don't know any English," the one said suddenly in English to his friend, "is because you waste too much time chasing dick!"

And they hurried off into the crowd, the accused defending himself excitedly in rapid Spanish to his friend.

The gray-haired man on the sofa rolled his eyes, sighed a long sigh as he snuffed out his own cigarette in the ashtray, and said: "My dear, whole *lives* have been wasted chasing dick." He sat up suddenly. "Oh!" he said. "There's that song!"

At that moment, "One Night Affair" was beginning to rise from the ruins of "Needing You," and they both put down their paper cups of apple juice and started toward the dance floor.

For a moment the sofa was empty, and two tall black boys wearing wide-brimmed hats eyed it as they moved, like sailing barges, very slowly along the edges of the crowd, but before they could cross the space of carpet to its comfortable cushions, I heard a rustle of silk and a distinctive voice. I turned and saw Sutherland sitting down with a thin, pale young fellow in horn-rimmed glasses who looked as if he had just stumbled out of the stacks of the New York Public Library.

For an instant Sutherland, as he fit a cigarette into his long black holder, and the pale boy in spectacles eyed the black boys in hats across the rug; and then the blacks, seeing they had lost their harbor, turned and continued moving along the crowd like two galleons perusing the Ivory Coast on a hot, windless day.

"I find it perfectly expressive of the whole sad state of human affairs at this moment of history, I find it a perfect *sym*bol of the demise of America," said Sutherland in that low, throaty voice that always seemed breathlessly about to confide something undreamed of in your wildest dreams, "that dinge are the only people who take hats seriously!" And he turned to the boy with the cigarette in its rhinestone holder, waiting for a light.

"Dinge?" said the boy in a cracked, earnest voice as he tried three times to finally get a flame from his lighter.

"Oh, darling, are you one of these millionaires who go around with ninety-nine-cent lighters?" said Sutherland as he waited for the flame to ignite.

The boy—who, we later learned, was the heir to a huge farm implement and nitrogen fertilizer fortune—flushed scarlet, for he could not bear references to his money and was terrified that someone would ask him for a loan, or assume that he would pay the bill. Sutherland puffed on his cigarette and removed it from his lips and said through a cloud of smoke, when the boy repeated his request for a definition of *dinge*: "Blacks, darling. *Shvartzers*, negroes, whatever you like. Why are they the better dancers? For they are. They get away with things here that no white boy could in a million years. And why do they get to wear white hats? And all the outrageous clothes? When gloves come back," he said, pulling at his own long black ones, "and I'm sorry they ever went away, you can be sure they will be the ones to wear them first!"

The boy was not looking at Sutherland as he spoke—his eyes had already been caught by something ten feet away from him; his face had that stricken, despairing expression of someone who has seen for the very first time a race of men whose existence he never suspected before, men more handsome than he had ever imagined, and all of them in this tiny room. He looked as if he were about to burst into tears. He leaned closer to Sutherland, who was at that moment just finishing with his gloves and who looked about himself now, with a gossamer cloud of stagnant cigarette smoke forming a double veil over his face. "My face seats five," he sighed, "my honeypot's on fire."

The boy, transfixed and terrified, leaned closer to Sutherland and said, "Who is that?"

"His name is Alan Solis, he has *huge* balls and does public relations work for Pan Am." They looked at him together for a moment. "Ask me about anyone, darling, I know them all. I have been living in New York since the Civil War."

And it was true: Sutherland seemed to have been alive, like the Prime Mover, forever. He had been a candidate for the Episcopalian priesthood, an artist, a socialite, a dealer, a kept boy, a publisher, a film-maker, and was now simply—Sutherland. And yet—behind the black veil his face was still as innocent and wonder-struck as it was the day he arrived in New York; his face, though everyone was waiting for it to crumble—from the speed he took—was open, honest, friendly, and looked, even more than that of the boy on his left, as if it were gazing on all of this for the first time.

"I used to be in love with Alan Solis," he said in his low, breathless voice, "when I came to New York. I was so in love with him, with him," he said (for he stuttered, and repeated phrases, not through any impediment of speech, but for effect), "that when he used the bathroom on the train to Sayville, I used to go in right after him and lock the door, just to smell his farts! To simply breathe the gas of his very bowels! A scent far lovelier to me than Chanel Number Nine, or whatever the ladies are wearing these days."

"You know," said the boy, bending over as if in pain, his eyes on Alan Solis with all the intensity of a mongoose regarding a snake, "if I can only find a flaw. If I can find a flaw in someone, then it's not so bad, you know? But that boy seems to be perfect!" he said. "Oh, God, it's terrible!" And he put a hand to his forehead, stricken by that deadliest of forces, Beauty.

"A flaw, a flaw," said Sutherland, dropping his ash into the ashtray on his left, "I understand perfectly."

"If I can just see a flaw, then it's not so hopeless and depressing," said the boy, his face screwed up in agony, even though Solis, talking to a short, muscular Italian whom he wanted to take home that night, was completely oblivious to this adoring fan whose body was far too thin to interest him.

"I've got it," said Sutherland, who turned to his companion now. "I remember a flaw. His chest," he said, "his chest is so hairy that one can't really see the deep, chiseled indentation between the breasts. Will that do, darling?"

The boy gnawed on his lip and considered.

"I'm afraid it will have to. There isn't a thing else wrong with the man, other than the fact that he knows it."

"You know," the boy said, "when my family was living in England and I came home from school on vacation, there was a boy who worked at our butcher's in the village. And he was astonishing! He had white, white skin, and rosy cheeks, and the most beautiful golden hair! He was as beautiful as an angel! I'm not exaggerating. And all that winter I used to dream of him, walking over the fields, at home at night. And at Princeton, a boy who used to dive at the pool. I was in love with him, and I used to ache walking home in autumn from the gym and think of him for days! And that's why I'm here, I guess, I'm looking for the English butcher boy, the diver at Princeton," he said as Alan Solis wandered onto the dance floor, "because I'm so tired of dreaming of faces and bodies. I want to touch one this time," he said, his voice suddenly choking.

"Well, how about that one over there?" said Sutherland, waving his cigarette holder at a tall, square-jawed fellow who taught English to children of the Third World in Harlem. "Greg Butts. I've always found him very Rupert Brooke; however his cock is very small, they tell me, and would hardly sustain a major fantasy on the scale of yours."

"You know, I hate being gay," said the boy, leaning over toward Sutherland, "I just feel it's ruined my life. It drains me, you know, it's like having a tumor, or a parasite! If I were straight I'd get married and that would be it. But being gay, I waste so much time imagining! I hate the lying to my family, and I know I'll never be any of the things they expect of me," he said, "because it's like having cancer but you can't tell them, that's what a secret vice is like."

Sutherland was speechless at this declaration; he sat there for a moment, with the cigarette holder to his lips, perfectly still; and then he said, "Perhaps what you *need* ... perhaps what you need," he said, in a speculative tone, "is a good facial." He turned quickly to his friend and said: "Oh, darling, for heaven's sake, don't take it so seriously! Just repeat after me: 'My face seats five, my honeypot's on fire.' "

"My face seats five, my honeypot's on fire," said the boy with a constipated smile.

"That's right, that will get you into the spirit of things! And please don't feel you have an obligation to be secretary of state!" he said, as his two Egyptian heiresses came by. "Their great great great great great great grandfather was a Pharaoh, while yours was just a potato farmer in Würzburg!" And he waved at his two Egyptian women, who were wandering around the French model, wreathed in the happiest of smiles. The floor had cleared momentarily to watch a tall, thin girl dance who came dressed each night in the latest work of a famous designer, and who prided herself on sleeping with all the handsomest homosexuals in New York. "Perhaps what you need is this."

He held out his black-gloved arm, and a little red pill sat in the center of his palm.

"What's that?" said the boy.

"Oh don't ask, darling," said Sutherland. "If it's a pill, take it."

The boy looked askance at the rosy pebble in Sutherland's palm, glowing like a ruby on black velvet in a vault at Bulgari. "I don't . . ." he said.

"Don't you trust me?" said Sutherland. "I would never ask you to take anything that does not enhance lucidity."

"But . . . speed kills," blurted the boy, looking up at Sutherland over his glasses.

"And Dial prevents wetness twenty-four hours a day," breathed Sutherland in his lowest tone. "Darling. Don't believe everything you hear. You mustn't for instance read the newspapers, that will destroy your mind far faster than speed. The *New York Times* has been responsible for more deaths in this city than Angel Dust, *croyez-moi.*" He put the red pill on the arm of the sofa and said: "There are many drugs I would not have you take. I am not like these queens whose names I wouldn't mention, but who, if you glance at the dance floor, you can certainly pick out, and who are on *hog tranquilizer*. My dear," he breathed, nodding toward a certain Michael Zubitski, a blond man wandering past the sofa now with no awareness of where he was: a sleepwalking queen whom Sutherland had not spoken to since he alienated a boy with whom Sutherland had been in love. "I do not pickle myself in formaldehyde or drench my brain pan in a drug used to tranquilize pigs, I have no desire to be turned, like Ulysses' men, into beasts, I am not envious of the profound ease felt by a Nebraska hog about to be castrated and bled to death," he said, straight into the face of Michael Zubitski, who, trying to see who this person was, had stopped and bent down to stare into Sutherland's black veil, five inches from his forehead, and hung there now like a huge sea gull poised above a swimming fish, "for the tables of all-American families in Duluth and Council Bluffs, no, you'll have to forgive me, darling, I am old-fashioned, I believe in General Motors and the clarity of the gods . . . "

And here, raising his ponderous blond head, Michael Zubitski withdrew from Sutherland's face and began moving, like a zombie, across the rug till he came to rest against the wall beside a potted plant.

"Who was that?" said the boy, ogling.

"A woman of no importance," said Sutherland, expelling a stream of cigarette smoke. "A vengeful queen. For that great blond beast, that Nazi storm trooper, has a cock that if it were any smaller would be a vagina, and if people, for whatever reason, go to bed with him, they inevitably leave in the middle of it, saying 'I'm tired,' or 'I've already had sex today,' or one of those classic excuses. The boy became so bitter about his fate that when he developed a case of syphilis he went to the Baths and infected everyone he could who sported an enormous organ. Well, darling, I guess it's better than assassinating a president." He expelled a long stream of smoke. "For don't you see, even after the dinge are taken care of and the amputees and Eurasians and the fags, even after all of them are provided for, who will ease the pains of that last minority, that minority within a minority, I mean those lepers of New York, the queens with small cocks? Truly Christ blessed the lepers and the whores, but there is *no* comfort in the Bible for boys with small winks, and they are the most shunned of all. People go to bed with me once, and I never hear from them again!" he said with the bright eyes of a koala bear, confessing what others in his situation spent a lifetime concealing. "What will the government do for *them*? Ah well, no matter," he sighed, "it's certainly not your problem." He squeezed his hand and smiled. "There are three lies in life," Sutherland said to his young companion, whose first night this was in the realm of homosexuality and whose introduction to it Sutherland had taken upon himself to supervise. "One, the check is in the mail. Two, I will not come in your mouth. And three, all Puerto Ricans have big cocks," he said. And with that he leaned forward and cupped the young man's hand in his long black gloves and said to him in that low, breathless voice: "You are beginning a journey, far more bizarre than any excursion up the Nile. You have set foot tonight on a vast, uncharted continent. Do let me take you as far as I can. I shall hold your hand as far as we can go together, and point out to you the more interesting flora and fauna. I will help you avoid the quicksand in which you can drown, or at least waste a *great* deal of time, the thorn-thickets, the false vistas—ah," he sighed. "We have many of those, we have *much* trompe l'oeil in this very room!" he said ecstatically, cocking his cigarette holder at a sprightly angle. "So let us go upriver together as far as we may," he resumed, once more cupping his charge's white, slim hand, "and remember to ask questions, and notice everything, the orchids and the fruit flies, the children rummaging for food in piles of shit, and the ibis that flies across the moon at dusk. Let us go at *least* as far as the falls. What a journey! If only I can help you avoid the detours, culs-de-sac, fevers, and false raptures that *I* have suffered." He squeezed the fellow's hand and said, echoing the signal phrase of a Bar Mitzvah he had once attended in the guise of a Jewish matron from Flatbush: "For tonight, my dear, you are a homosexual!"

And with that he returned his attention to the men coming through the doorway, of whom they had the only unobstructed view from that sofa by the coat check. In the midst of this late-arriving throng (for the desire of everyone to arrive after everyone else had created a ripple effect so that no one could go out anymore before two A.M. at the earliest), in a kind of rest between the arrivals of two of the larger "families," a young man appeared in the doorway by himself; and the fertilizer heir said, "Oh, who is *that*? Find a flaw, I can't find a flaw."

"That is Malone," said Sutherland in his lowest, most dramatic voice, "and his only flaw is that he is still searching for love, when it should be perfectly clear to us all by now that there is no Mister Right, or Mister Wrong, for that matter. We are all alone. He used to be a White House fellow, darling, and now he talks of suicide, if a certain Puerto Rican maniac doesn't kill him first."

I watched as this individual walked into the room and was immediately greeted by several of the handsomest boys there, the ones so handsome they never looked at anybody, but went to the darkness of back rooms merely to piss on perfect strangers and have their asses licked. They were the first to go over to Malone. He put an arm around their shoulders or shook their hands, with his almost old-fashioned manners. He put his head close to theirs when they spoke to him, as if he didn't want to miss a word, and when he replied he spoke almost against their ear: a charming gesture ostensibly to defeat the noise of the room, but one that made you feel you were being winnowed out, selected, for some confidential revelation. The courtesy with which he moved on through that crowd of zombies who stepped on one another with the oblivious brusqueness of a crowd in a subway, and stopped to talk to whoever tugged at him, was reflected in his smile. He had a face you liked with the certainty that, though you had no idea who he was, he was a good man. He introduced his admirers to one another and then left them new friends and vanished in the crowd. I had no idea who he was, he was just a face I saw in a discotheque one winter; but he was for me the central symbol on which all of it rested.

"He had the misfortune to fall in love with a thug," said Sutherland when the fertilizer heir asked him again about this man, "who has threatened to kill Malone simply because Malone no longer loves him and was foolish enough to say so. Another rule, *caro*, which may help you—if blacks are the only ones who wear hats anymore," he breathed, raising his cigarette holder to his lips, "then Latins, my dear, are the only ones who take love seriously. Malone is now being chased around Manhattan by knives and bullets. He *never* has sex."

The two Egyptian women came up to Sutherland, leaned down, and spoke rapidly in French to him for a few moments; they shrieked with laughter and went on their way. When the fertilizer heir asked what that was all about, Sutherland replied: "They want to know if they should paint their cunts. What do *you* think?"

"Me?" said the boy, his face alarmed.

"Does the thought of cooze make you vomit?" said Sutherland, blowing out a stream of smoke. "Well, to be dead-honest, I find it, the very thought of it, loathsome beyond words! However, I love my girls! They are being driven mad by the presence of so many handsome young men—so many handsome young men who have absolutely no interest whatsoever in dining between their legs this evening. But, *croyez-moi*, my friend, there is steam rising from those pussies!"

The boy sat back, white as a sheet, and Sutherland proceeded to greet a group of five who had come up to talk to him, among them the blond man being pursued by the Puerto Rican maniac, the Egyptian heiresses, and the model who had come over from Paris. For a second, in glancing over, I found myself looking straight at Malone. Our eyes met. His were blue-gray and calm. It was, I noted much later that morning in my journal, like that melodramatic moment in historical novels: when the protagonist, in a crowded marketplace, on a dusty road, on Golgotha, suddenly meets the eyes of Christ, and he is forever changed. Well, I was not changed, but I was singled out—enough to write about it for a while later that day, to record that moment when I looked at Malone and thought: His eyes are like Jesus Christ's.

But at that moment Sutherland turned to the fertilizer heir and said: "Darling, come, we're going uptown! A small Crucifixion at Park and Seventy-fifth, nothing heavy." The boy, pale and stricken, got up and followed the Egyptian women, the French model, and a couple of Halston assistants out of the dim room with Sutherland in his black Norell and turban, leading the pack. With them went Malone, and with him went the magic of the room, which consisted, I realized then, not of the music, the lights, the dancers, the faces, but of those eyes, still, and grave and candid, looking at you with the promise of love.

From *Nocturnes for the King of Naples*

Edmund White

*Nocturnes for the King of Naples was Edmund White's second
published novel and his first to be overtly gay. Of course, by then he
had co-authored* The Joy of Gay Sex, *and some of the articles that
were to become* States of Desire: Travels in Gay America *had begun
to appear. The year 1978, in which* Nocturnes for the King of
Naples *was published, was a turning point in the history of gay
fiction. It was the year that Larry Kramer's* Faggots, *Andrew
Holleran's* Dancer from the Dance, *and Felice Picano's* The Lure
*also appeared. The critical and financial successes of these four
novels signaled to publishers that gay fiction ought to be a regular
part of the books they issued.*

*Nocturnes is written as a long letter to the older former lover of
the nameless narrator. The narrator is a rich, self-destructive young
man who learns too late that he has rejected the person he loves
most and who treats him best.*

A young man leans with one shoulder against the wall, and his
slender body remains motionless against the huge open slab of night
sky and night water behind him. He is facing the river. Little waves
scuttling shoreward from a passing, passed scow slap against boards:
perfunctory applause. On the other side of the water, lights trace sense-
less paths up across hills, lash-marks left by an amateur whip. He turns
toward me a look of hope tempered by discretion, eyes dilated by a
longing too large—as large as this briny night panel behind him—to
focus in on any single human being.

I have failed to interest him. He turns back to his river as though it were the masterpiece and I the retreating guard.

For me there was the deeper vastness of the enclosed, ruined cathedral I was entering. Soaring above me hung the pitched roof, wings on the downstroke, its windows broken and lying at my feet.

A wind said incantations and hypnotized a match flame up out of someone's cupped hands. Now the flame went out and only the cigarette pulsed, each draw molding gold leaf to cheekbones.

There are qualities of darkness, the darkness of gray silk stretched taut to form the sky, watered by city lights, the darkness of black quartz boiling to make a river, and the penciled figures of men in the distance, minute figures on—is that a second story? What are they doing up there? A cigarette rhymes its glow with my own across the huge expanse that has shattered its crystal lining to the ground.

I told myself to stand still in the shadow of an immobile crane, its teeth rusted shut, to stand still and watch. What I was looking for were the other men secreted in corners, or posted on dilapidated stairs, or only half-visible behind tarred bollards. The wind died and in my hiding place a bowl of fragrances was lifted like a potpourri culled from leaves, cloves, tar, burned rubber—droll hobby. I could scarcely get past the preserving odor of brine. But just beneath it hovered the smell of trapped sweat on bodies. Beneath everything else I smelled (or rather heard) the melancholy of an old, waterlogged industrial building, a sound as virile but at the same time as sexless as a Russian basso descending liturgically from low G to F to E, on and on down on narrow steps below the stave into a resonant deep C.

The men I was searching for now became palpable. They leaned out of the low shelf of night. They whispered, if they were in twos, or shifted their weight from foot to tentative foot if alone. At the far end of the vaulted room in a second-story window, one gnat-sized man knelt before another.

I had moved out from under the crane to walk the length of the pier, intrigued by the symmetrical placement of people on the faraway landing deck. They stood at attention, motionless—ah! posts. They were posts, but the sound beside my right hand was human breathing. Through the glassless window of an office I saw a man sitting on the floor, breathing. I didn't speak but rather rested my hand on the sill, which was grained as fur. He plopped his hand over mine: not dry, not clean. Beneath the concealing ridge of his brow his eyes could have been staring up at me.

Congeries of bodies; the slow, blind tread on sloped steps; the faces floating up like thoughts out of ink, then trailing away like thoughts out of memory; entrances and exits; the dignified advance and retreat as an approaching car on the highway outside casts headlights through the window and plants a faint square on the wall. The square brightens till it blazes, then rotates into a trapezoid narrowing to the point of extinction, its last spark igniting a hand raised to hit a face. A new square grows on the wall but when it veers off it reveals not the stunned face, nor the punishing hand—ooze on old boards, nothing else.

Down the steps, past the polite, embarrassed face of someone I know, I mount a loading ramp onto a platform where an insubstantial shack, doorless and windowless, shelters another cigarette. I stop at the doorway. He turns to the wall, causing me to retreat. There is another dubious figure, tall, face visored. I won't risk encountering him now. He can wait—that he *will* wait is the bet I'm willing to place. A shed at the extreme end of the platform glistens and sweats with water; running water can be heard, muted, sloshing through moss-slick pilings. Into that wet vault I take a step. A hand; a bearded face; the smell of whiskey; another hand. My motionless shoes turn cold— no, wet. A vagrant wave wallops against the pier like a blanket someone shakes out during spring cleaning. A boy with pale arms bruised by shadow is caught in the cross-currents of fear and curiosity. Something behind me is ticking, an electrical timer in good running order within a building I had assumed was long ago defunct.

Retracing my steps, I notice that the sentinel I'd left posted by the door to the shack has been relieved but not replaced. Down a ramp I go into the central hall, which not only reports but also magnifies the waves drumming the dock in triplets of eighths over the sustained crescendo-diminuendo of a passing barge. As it passes, the barge pivots its spotlight into our immense darkness; two voices, male, call back and forth to one another from bow to stern over tons of clean gravel. Instructions. Orders.

Our orders, scattered by the prying beam, emerge out of hiding places. A hand-rail, wrenched away from the stairs it was designed to guard, stencils opposed pairs of black S's on absorbent gray air. A protective sheathing of corrugated tin, torn free from the clerestory, rattles stage thunder above us.

Yes—us. A moment before the barge's beam invaded the cathedral we were isolated men at prayer, that man by the font (rainwater stagnant in the lid of a barrel), and this one in a side chapel (the damp vault), that pair of celebrants holding up a flame near the dome, those communicants telling beads or buttons pierced through denim, the greater number shuffling through, ignoring everything in their search for the god among us.

This glorious image I've made, sustained like a baldachino on points of shadow above the glass mosaic on the floor, gently folds under the sun. The sun is rising. It recalls us to work, play, reputation, plans, to guilt, and sends everyone away until only I remain, hugging my knees, my eyes unfocused into the refracted dazzle of water. The red line painted on a boat's hull rises and dips, its reflections flaring on the waves like flames from the sun's corona, scorching the mystic vacuum.

On my way home I see one last man pressed against the wall, gathering about him the last tatters of darkness to be had. He is very rough with me.

"Do you want to go to my place?" he asks.

"Yes."

"Promise you won't change your mind when you see me in the light?"

"Do I know you?"

"Promise?"

I nod.

And then, once we're in the light, I see he's one of your old admirers, the crazy one who gave you the dog. We smile and begin to talk about you.

Can't sleep tonight. I was lying in bed reading the biography of a great man whose genius deserted him. Then I switched off the light and tried to sleep, but I was afraid of something. I got up and made scrambled eggs in the dark, standing there naked and cold, watching the slime from the bowl churn up into gray curds in the pan. They looked like brains on the plate. I ate them and they were delicious, perfumed with tarragon. I poured myself a glass of milk and felt like a good little boy, though the glare from the refrigerator revealed that my body's no longer boyish—odd, troubling reminder. Good boy in a man's body.

I sat by the window on a cold metal chair and looked out at a black building across the way pressing its bulk against the wintry haze, which was bright enough to suggest dawn, though surely that's at least an hour away. The genius who deserted me was you.

A psychiatrist I once knew told me that the unconscious, that irritating retard, can't distinguish between abandoning someone and being abandoned by him. I guess he meant that even though I left you, it's come to seem as though you left me. That rings true. He also said that I was making myself into a "quiet disaster" in order to force you into returning to save me—once again a dimwit stratagem hatched by the unconscious, which doesn't recognize any of the ordinary dimensions such as time, distance, causality or your indifference.

I never kept a diary. I never saved up witty things people told me. I never even bothered to remember my own past, the events that mattered most to me. Nor have I tried to piece things together. I'm a master of the art of pruning, you might say, as though I'd heard that plants should be cut back to make them flourish—except I keep hacking them down to the roots and wonder why they die.

Not all of them do. You're tenacious. Like a tree in paradise heavy with birds.

The leaves hang against the summer sky, real, not stirring, transected by the evening sun; the birds circle and light on its branches weightlessly. You know not to touch me, though I can sense you want to. We're both in jackets and ties, feeling formal after so many days on the beach in swimsuits. I can't be more than . . . twenty, but I look younger. Everyone says I do except you. You've learned to avoid describing me to myself, since everything you say provides me with another excuse to be vexed. It's a holiday and we've strung lanterns and put out flags along the walkway in honor of the occasion. The decorations, too, lend formality to the evening.

Belle comes toward us across the lawn, smiling, her nose and temples red with today's sunburn. Now she's dressed and has a cardigan over her shoulders. She kisses my cheek, as she did the first time we met, though this evening I catch her darting a glance in your direction the moment she pulls away. Have you told her we're having one of our little disagreements?

Over supper the Captain, the only man who looks natural wearing an ascot (his is yellow with age and the ends hang straight down in crumpled afterthought), neglects my glass and my remarks, which is not like him. And he brings up names I don't know but that you and Belle do. He's excluding me from your old circle, reminding me that there are dozens of people who have admired you for years—tribute-bearers assembled before the throne in their native regalia (gauze leggings over gold pants, woven-feather bodice above a hairless stomach, a short military skirt), their origins so exotic and the precise degree of their vassalage so old and various that only a historian could explain it—but the Captain explains nothing and you're invisible behind the incense rising from the bronze tripod.

All during the festival and the fireworks after supper I avoid you and stay with the Portuguese family who take care of your house. When you catch up with me and ask me where I've been, I say, "It's impolite for couples to stick together."

"Are we still a couple?" you ask.

"Maybe. You should know. You've known so many people whose names I can't even recognize—"

"I don't know *why* the Captain—"

"Why shouldn't he talk about anyone he wants to? Isn't it a little artificial to pretend I'm part of your old gang?"

As we walk out to the end of the dock, our feet sounding a different note on each slat of this crooked xylophone, your hands sketch out several possible replies, none to your satisfaction. From a distance we might look like a patriarch and his heir in our nice summer jackets, out for a stroll on a resort island. That's what a stranger would think. Your friends might say, "They've reconciled. Thank God we didn't let slip anything nasty about the boy while they were quarreling." We stare across the bay toward the lights of a town that rise in a curved band like the crown of a child coming toward us, candles in her hair to celebrate the festival.

The gleam of that bright town in the distance, intensified here and there where a car's headlights shoot out over the waves for a second, fills me with a longing to flee you.

Now, years later, how easy it is to interpret that urge as a loveless boy's fear of a perfect love that came too late, but back then it seemed (my longing to get away) almost metaphysical. In fact I said to you, as we stood on the dock, "Doesn't it ever strike you as strange to be a man rather than a woman, to be here rather than," pointing toward the crown of candles, "there, for instance? Sometimes I want to explode into a million bits, all conscious, and shoot through space and then, I don't know, rain down on everything or, well, yeah, actually catch up with the light rays that bounced off people thousands of years ago. Somewhere out there," my lifted hand was pointing straight up, "Solomon is still threatening to cut the baby in half."

You turn silent and I'm afraid, once again, that I'm boring you. Oh, now, my friend, I can see you loved my enthusiasm but didn't know what to say nor where to begin. So you looked away and I thought you were bored. The hot ingot I had become cooled and hardened.

"Shall we head back?" you asked.

"Go on," I said. "I'll stay in the beach house tonight. I want to play records very loud."

"You can do that—"

"*My* records. Anyway, I don't want to be anywhere near you to-night."

"Have I done something wrong?"

"Of course not," I said and looked you in the eye and smiled ever so brightly. I was so angry at you, but you climbed in my bedroom window and I relented.

Old friend, you studied me too closely, as though deeper scrutiny would finally reveal my mystery. But there was nothing more to learn, nothing definite in me beyond one surge of emotion after another, all alike and of the same substance, though this one broke early and fanned out timidly across the sand whereas that one broke late, right beside the reef, and shot spray up against the solicitous sky.

On the ferry the next day as we headed back toward the mainland and home, I was caught between regret for the difficult summer and anticipation of the fall. We all sat on the top deck under the sun and even the noisiest holiday-makers grew silent and breathed in the salt breeze.

Once we had docked in that surprisingly vernal inlet, the foliage to the west, where the sun had just set, was already black whereas the trees on the other side were still somberly green. Motionless up to the very moment of our arrival, the branches, once we landed, began to churn and revolve—rides in a somnolent amusement park that function only for the paying visitor. In the taxi to the train station we were jammed in with other vacationers, none of whom we knew, and I was happy to sit scrunched up beside you with one arm around your neck. But I didn't turn to look at you.

Back in the city I had more freedom than on the island, more free-dom from the surveillance of your friends. You changed everything to please me. Took down the curtains, rolled up the rugs, stored furniture, painted every stick and surface white—I was in my stark, simple pe-riod. Now I've lived so long in hotels I can't imagine caring about my surroundings. They're things to accept, like people, not to change.

One night that fall I brought home a man I'd met during intermission at a theater. We, you and I, had an unspoken rule not against infidelities but against adventures that were conspicuous, intrusive. But nothing pleased and frightened me so much then as to cast aside all our rules.

I set up a little campsite in the kitchen for him and me, that is, I dragged in a brass lamp (one that could be dialed down to near extinction), a scratchy radio and a Chinese red blanket. I bolted the doors and that man and I became drunk and raucous. Once, near dawn, I thought I heard you pacing the hall. Cheap music, cheap wine, fumbling sex with someone who was homely, grateful, not even very clean—what fun and anguish to defile the polished tiles of that kitchen floor beside the room where the maid slept. Just before she was due to awaken I saw my visitor out, though I prolonged the farewell by the front door, whispering and giggling. Lurching about I then restored the lamp to its proper place (my "study" as you called it), threw out the empty bottle and the cigarette ashes and cloaked myself in the red blanket. You were awake and dressed, sitting on the edge of our bed, talking and smiling but inwardly subdued and angry.

"Don't pretend with me!" I said, still drunk. "What are you really feeling?"

"Toward you?"

"Yes, of course, toward me."

You stood and looked out the window at the tree whose leaves were not coloring with autumn, just drying and curling. "This can't go on, can it?"

"What can't?" I wanted the full scene. "What can't go on?"

"I don't need to elaborate," you said and left the room.

The next day as I was walking my bicycle down the hall you stopped me at the door on your way in and invited me to dinner on the following evening. "Okay, maybe," I said casually. After all we lived together.

"Maybe?"

"All right!" I shouted. That was good, wasn't it? We needed to shout, didn't we? "Black tie? White tie? Shall I bring flowers?"

"Eight o'clock. Here." Only when I looked back did I see you watching me with the big brown eyes of a child—the child in a sailor suit you had been and whom I knew from that old photograph in the family album up at the cottage.

I had so much power over you. If I would touch you, as I did once in a while (just a touch, nothing intimate), you'd get excited. I could insist you cancel your social engagements for a week in a row and you would comply, but then that full, powerful life you led away from me would gush in through a crevice I'd neglected and inundate you and, yes, me as well. The telephone would ring, at a restaurant someone would stop by our table, people would drop in, on the street you'd be recognized and friends would draw us away.

You possessed a genius for friendship, a gift you'd refined through energy and intelligence. Your intuition was so keen that you could even sense when a shy person needed to be *ignored*. Yet there was nothing slavish about your politeness. You were cool and, among old friends at least, demanding not of favors, never favors, but of wit, if that means saying something interesting. I have not, now that you've left me, tried to imitate your style, nor could I; I'm simply carried about from place to place. When I was with you I did try to say interesting things from time to time. Not now. What I've learned is that people will get me home no matter how much I drink and pick me up no matter how little I said or offered the night before. As with possessions, I've given up conversation, but everything still goes on.

We gave a party in honor of an old musician visiting our city. The visit was only a pretext; we scarcely knew the man. Hundreds of guests came. Everyone wanted to meet him. We wanted, I suppose, to show your friends how much we loved each other all over again. I stood at the door and shook hands and told people where to put their coats. Then I passed a tray, which I liked because it gave me an excuse to keep moving. Finally I joined a group and asked our guest of honor to tell me the significance of the red thread in his lapel, and people seemed pleased by the naiveté of my question and the modesty and humor of his answer.

But I couldn't keep it up. Suddenly I was tired and even angry. I rushed to the back of the house and sat on the sooty ledge of the storage room. A few people found me in there and we had, after a while, a band of renegades among the old cans of paint and the tools and firewood. The renegades agreed parties were a terrible bore and they drank a lot and I was quite free to become silent and inch still farther out the window. To me the atmosphere seemed rebellious and one I alone had created. I was very happy until someone asked me, ever so casually, a question. She was a young woman in a black gown. She had lovely breasts and diamonds in her ear lobes, and she wasn't much taller or older than I. "What's it like," she asked, "living with him?" I could tell how much she admired you and envied me. I tore off my tie and jumped off the ledge into the alleyway and ran to the corner with a cocktail shaker in my hand—silver and engraved with your initials entwined in mine. I drank right from the frosted spigot and tossed the empty pitcher in a trash can, but only after I'd lit a match to look at those initials incised in white metal. The engraver had worked cleverly; at first glance the design seemed to be a flourish in a scroll. The letters became apparent only after—ouch! I dropped the pitcher and it made a pathetic clang against the bottom of the trash can.

I ran and ran until I reached a promontory overlooking the city and the river. There I sat on a stone and stared at the cars below as they flowed across the bridge, their lights infusing the water like the blood of an antique senator in a tub. The cool moist earth tried to talk to me but it didn't have a mouth, just something through which it exhaled. Maybe it breathed through its pores. I took off all my clothes and clasped my skinny body, shivering. At my feet lay that little puddle of garments you had bought me. At last I was free of them, the dress shirt, the shoes and socks, the coat and trousers. I studied the watch and its black Roman numerals that circuited through its round ("I," "Aye, Aye!," "eye, eye, eye," "ivy") past the ecstatic shriek "VIII" and on to the dignified "X my sign." Now it was 1:30 and the hands said "I vie," as I did with you and your light yoke, your silk shackles. I threw the watch on top of the pile and strode away, still clutching myself, into a chilling fantasy of freedom. For a moment I had the illusion I was walking through a true forest until I came to a metal grille sunk into the ground through which I could see more cars streaking down a tunnel. The warmth and odor of the exhaust filtered up around me and I stood on that grating I know not how long. Could I pry it open and drop onto the shiny roof of a car, crawl to its hood, shrink and turn silver as the ornament breasting the wind? Or slip into a window, surprising a contented family, Dad vigilant and responsible behind the wheel, Mom reading a map by the faint glow of the open glove compartment, the kids and the collie a dim, dozing heap in the back seat?

If I said nothing they might take me home to a bungalow in a development and clothe me and keep me and you would never find me. They might consign me to the back seat and I, too, could become implicated in that tangle of fur, doggy breath, cool hands and cheeks as smooth as glazed fruit, our upturned eyes seeing only the tops of buildings, then trees, then after a while the stars and our ears catching only the murmur of grownups navigating us safely to our beds.

From *The Confessions of Danny Slocum*

George Whitmore

The Confessions of Danny Slocum *exists in two versions: a shorter version published in two parts in* Christopher Street *magazine and a full-length version brought out by St. Martin's Press. The following is the first part of the shorter version. Whitmore published* Danny Slocum *in the magazine anonymously because it was so closely autobiographical. Only when it was published as a book did he feel comfortable enough to add his name. In many ways* Danny Slocum *epitomizes the efforts of the VQ. It speaks of gay experience from the inside to insiders. It uses the language gay men use among themselves. It describes a relationship that has no analog in the straight world, a relationship of the deepest intimacy, and the greatest tenderness, and without any trace of the traditional marriage plot.*

My name is Danny Slocum. I am a homosexual male—college educated, U.S. citizen, thirty-three years old, not bad-looking at all, resident of New York City. I've been around. I'm no dummy.

Yet at first I didn't realize I had a problem, a "condition." In the past two years, I've cum exactly twice—in company, as it were—with two different men. I don't know how many men I've "failed" with in two years. . . .

But this is starting to sound like an A.A. speech, isn't it? What I want to do is give you the record of my sex therapy.

I'm aware that I'm another statistic, a contributor to the rising line of male impotence and dysfunction sexologists are graphing out across the face of the sexual revolution. I have no idea how many people share my problem. Since I can get it up and (if I'm alone) jack myself off without difficulty, my problem didn't become apparent to me for quite a while. Then Virgil, my shrink, suggested that I "work with someone." Until then, I didn't think he took my "problem" seriously—at that point there were a lot of other things to talk about. But when he did, I felt like falling to my knees and covering his hands with kisses. No shit. I was that grateful.

"A surrogate?"

"No," he said. "A partner. Someone with the same problem."

My heart was racing. I felt like crying. I hadn't realized how awful it had become.

At first, I was too embarrassed to tell anyone. It had been hard enough to admit I had to go into therapy in the first place. I was sure my friends would laugh at me.

When I told my novelist friend, he said, "How fabulous! Sex therapy! How downright *American*!"

"Go ahead. Laugh."

"But darling, I'm not laughing. It's just that I can't imagine any other nationality going about it in quite the same way. Self-reliance. How-to. Know-how. All that. Of course, it *is* rather humorous. *Anything* having to do with erotic life is humorous. Don't look so chagrined. You have a problem. If you're going to change, then of course you'll have to work on it. Of course. What a marvelous adventure. I almost envy you."

But not quite.

I suppose it all began with my ex-lover. You've heard the expression "go to Hollywood"? Labelle used to sing about it: "Can I speak to you before you go to Hollywood?" Meaning, can I talk to you without your attitude?

Well, one Halloween Max was in Los Angeles on business and went dancing with Sandy Duncan at Studio One. Went Hollywood, in other words. Oh, he came home. But essentially, Max was in Hollywood even when he was in New York with me.

Money and fame. The old story.

A classic passive-aggressive type, Max asked, when I said I was leaving, "What do you want me to do?" For two years he had been asking me that.

"Nothing," I said. "Just let me out of here."

Perhaps modern relationships should be counted like cats' and dogs' lives. In feline terms, then, Max and I lasted eighteen years. I felt like every one of them had been taken out of my hide.

Anyone, however monogamous he may have been, can learn all over again how to cruise, seduce, sparkle, and shine. (Sing out, Louise!) My obligatory period of mourning slid into the obligatory period of fucking and sucking—but there was one problem I'd never had before.

During my last six months with Max I had cum two or three times among the dozen or so times we actually got around to having sex. Max's mind was on money and fame. I don't know where mine was. On Max's money and fame, I guess. Eventually, I began to consult my friends. With all the charity of a registered nurse about to plunge a hypodermic needle into an upraised and defenseless buttock, my friends told me to "relax."

I relax. I breathe deeply. I can't feel a thing.

"Anything wrong?"

"No. That's nice." A lie.

Think of a cool stream, slender trees, just unbudding, fleecy clouds. Salem country. Marlboro country. Think of the Marlboro man. God, I want a cigarette. . . .

"You sure?"

His face is flushed and damp.

(*Note: Sainthood to those who labor over a hard cock in vain.*)

Kiss him. Now *that's* nice.

He sits back on the bed and smiles at me. A small crease appears between his eyes. "You seem to want to . . . "

"What?"

"Do something," he says, "you haven't told me about."

"Oh, no. Do *you* want to do something?"

He reaches for his cigarettes, puts one in his mouth, shakes one out for me. We light up.

He lies back on the bed, exhaling smoke. (*Note: Register for Smokenders: smoking is not, repeat, not sexy.*) His profile is to me, a good, clean profile. Blond forelock, smooth forehead, straight nose, full lips (a bit "too" full, the ounce of imperfection worth a pound of beauty), foursquare jaw (no nonsense), and a sprinkling of freckles (far more fatal than his struggle to make a life far from home, his intelligence, his newfound sophistication).

I shake my head.

"What's wrong?"

"Nothing."

"You were shaking your head."

"Oh."

"What's wrong?"

"I don't cum."

He doesn't laugh. Looks at me directly, candidly. "Well maybe next time, then."

"Maybe." Another lie.

My trusty *Joy of Gay Sex* (for all the good it's done me) tells me that a "late comer" like me "exercises such tight control over his feelings as well as his body that he avoids anxiety but may suffer from such displacements of anxiety as an upset stomach or a tendency to skin rash."

My stomach hurts. I learned long ago what this means: that I am unhappy. But a new symptom accompanies it: My balls, my cock, the muscles between my legs ache, my asshole aches; the pain is fierce; cramps, coming in waves (as my women friends, God help us, have described their periods).

It's because I'm going to meet *him* tonight. My "partner."

All Virgil would tell me about Joe is that he is Italian (The Italian Stallion!), twenty-six, and "not what I believe you call a troll."

Joe is not a troll. He is a nice-looking guy, about six feet tall, slender, with warm brown eyes, a head of thick brown-black hair, and great forearms. He is dressed in "the uniform" (I too wear a flannel shirt and jeans tonight) and sunburned from last weekend at the beach.

He lives with his parents in Massapequa, Long Island. He sells men's clothes at the local Korvette's. He is, it seems, "drifting."

He twitches and blushes with anxiety in Virgil's office, barely able to answer Virgil's innocuous questions.

I feel like screaming at him: Relax! I am cool as the proverbial cucumber. The cramps have abated somewhat.

But, oh, his problems. An ambiguous relationship with a woman that ended badly about a year ago. The constricting circle of friends at his local bar, his jealousy of the sex they're getting. His parents. Aimlessness. Not cumming.

I know I'm no prize, but Joe's problems seem disconcertingly to magnify my own. While Joe's anxieties make me feel "healthy" in comparison, I wonder if I will have to deal with his problems. Do we have to go through with this?

With what? What is "this"?

A weekend at the Pines with my Fire Island friend. So near to Joe but so far away. Light-years from the disco where Joe and his friends dance—wearing the same clothes we wear, dancing to the same music, getting off on it as we do.

Joe seldom goes to the City, has never been to the Island, looked rather stricken and envious when I told him I was coming out this weekend.

And here I am in Disneyland. My last fling. Once Joe and I begin therapy we can't have sex with anyone else. (Virgil: "It only reinforces bad habits.")

My Fire Island friend not only takes me into his house but into his arms, and the "problem" is no longer a problem . . . almost.

Thinking how for Joe and me sex is synonymous not with physical release but with a frightening intimacy. Cumming is the final sign of accepting that intimacy. For us sex is full of static, like a busted radio.

Virgil asks for our decision. Blushing, tentative, virginal, and shy as we never are in "real life," we agree to try.

When we are sixty-five, we joke, we will be running ads in *The Advocate*:

Older Gentleman
Fit and Willing
Wants Younger Gentleman Willing To
SHOWER AND TALC
No fats, Fems, Dopesters, Bikers
Good Clean Fun

We have been showering and talcing twice a week for three weeks now. (Virgil calls it The Prune Stage.) We are very clean.

First we soap each other thoroughly in the shower, then we get out and dry each other. Finally, we talc. We are forbidden to go beyond this. We report our feelings, fantasies, thoughts in detail to Virgil—as we will do with all our exercises in the months (months?) ahead. The sensations in each part of the exercise are very different. Joe and I call this process "desensitization." (Virgil himself dispenses no cant.)

I have ceased to look upon Joe as a sex object. The first time we stepped into the shower (at my apartment, for obvious reasons) I had a raging hard-on. Joe was limp. What fantasies I had! Joe had none. Now I get hard only when he soaps or dries my cock.

My vanity has been sorely tried. I want Joe to look at me, lust after me, compliment me. He doesn't. He wants no compliments, no come-ons from me. They make him nervous. He says he's "selfish, in this for myself." One night I complained to Virgil that Joe was cold. Virgil encouraged me to "voice other fantasies."

Shower and talc. Shower and talc.

We see Virgil for an hour or less each week. He is brisk and busi-nesslike, half shrink, half recreation director. He tells us not to worry, though he knows we will. Every week new anxieties—all over show-ering!

Joe doesn't have stomach problems. He has acne.

Joe and I have agreed that neither of us is the other's type. That is, we would not cruise each other in a bar. Neither of us quite knows whether to be offended by this or not.

The men on the street are driving me crazy. Joe reports the same reaction to guys trying on clothes in Korvette's.

"But what if you run into the love of your life at the Cockring?" my actor friend asks.

"I don't know. Maybe I can get his phone number."

"But what will you say? 'I'm in sex therapy and can't sleep with you'?"

"God, no."

"Well, you ought to think of something. Unless you're getting enough sex from Joe as it is."

"It isn't sex, for godsake. I told you."

"But what is it then, if it isn't sex?"

Massage.

We are massaging now with baby oil. It's nice to be out of the shower, though we still shower together afterwards. Joe philosophizes that it's a bit like the multiplication tables and says that eventually, you see, we'll work our way up to trigonometry. But we should never forget addition and good old subtraction. (Joe likes the showers. He's a water sign.)

For the first time in years (to Joe's obvious delight) my skin is breaking out. All that fucking baby oil.

At first we were forbidden to do nipples, asses, or cocks and balls. We're supposed to talk a lot, just as Virgil encouraged us to do when we were in the shower. I realize how little I used to talk in bed, especially with Max. Talking per se is not, of course, the issue. Communicating our desires is—"down a little further on the left," etc. Everyone knows that, you're saying. Yeah. But I suppose this is one of the things Joe and I have to learn, or re-learn.

My political friend says Virgil is a "fascist" for not letting Joe and me have sex with other people, that our therapy is really the lowest, most corrupt kind of behavioral modification—"deprivation brainwashing."

The rest of my close friends seem to think it's all a little dizzy and more than a little unnecessary. They pretend to be interested but hearing about my sex therapy bores them as much as hearing about therapy in general. I think they're secretly of the opinion that all I need is the love of a good man.

Perhaps they are threatened by what I'm doing. The answers to my problem are easy and evident to them. Fear of men. Fear of getting hurt. Fear of losing control. Fear of not performing. Fear—yes, even now—of succeeding.

Joe and I talk, talk, talk.

Not always about clothes.

Tonight he sat on my back, massaging my shoulders. He was hurting my back but I was too "shy" to ask him to get off. So I suffered and was mad at him for being so inconsiderate. "Why didn't you just tell me?" he asked afterwards. That seems to be the $64,000 question.

"You absolutely must tell each other everything," Virgil says. "No matter how trivial or stupid, how embarrassing it might seem at the time. And things no lovers would tell each other. That's our only rule."

So we try.

Thoreau said something to the effect of, "If I knew a man were coming to my door with the express purpose of doing me good, I would not be at home." Joe must feel that way about my nagging. I give Joe lots of advice—get out of that house, make new friends, get a new job.

I am fighting my desire to lecture, to patronize Joe, to keep him at arm's length, to deny we are having a relationship. A most peculiar relationship, but a relationship all the same.

We're getting in deeper and neither of us likes it. Joe is often sullen and snappish, bored, silent. Then there are spats. All very childish. Not like lovers at all.

My ass.

Joe has never cum with another person in his life.

He told me about the last time he had sex—saying the word with that wry turn of inflection identical to mine.

The boy (he couldn't have been more than nineteen) followed Joe around from bar to bar. Joe had no real interest in him, though he was attractive and friendly—and so hot. But the boy couldn't get enough of Joe and was so persistent that at two a.m. Joe agreed to go to the motel with him.

Joe sat down on the bed. The boy took off his clothes, sat down beside Joe, and began unbuttoning Joe's shirt. Joe was very hard, very excited. He wasn't drunk. He never drinks.

The boy lay on top of Joe. Joe hoped he would get it off quickly. He was so hot Joe knew he would cum right away, but if the boy found out *he* couldn't, it would be a drag. Better fast. Better now.

The boy urged Joe to finish undressing, and he did. They sucked each other. Kissed a bit. Sucked. Joe sucked the boy a long time. "Don't you want to cum?" he asked the boy.

"I'm waiting. I want to cum with you."

"That's all right," Joe said. "I'm a little tired tonight."

Eventually, under protest of sorts, the boy came.

They left the motel and said goodbye on the sidewalk outside, shaking hands rather formally.

Joe found his car and started it up. He thought about the boy, the boy's body. He was more frustrated than he'd been when he'd left home after showering, dressing (big deal, big night out at the bars, sure), and driving twenty miles to the bar. He was more frustrated than he'd ever been in his life, if that was possible.

He took out his cock, driving home in the dark. He jacked off, thinking about the boy and the boy's body.

That was the week before we met. Joe says he looked forward to meeting the nice older man, me, who was "more experienced" than he.

* * *

Fire Island again this weekend. Utter serenity. I danced with my friend at night and sat on the beach during the day, watching the passing bodies with appreciation and detachment, the way one might view a fine Monet, or better yet, a Winslow Homer landscape/seascape. All that turbulence, so far away, viewed through this remote lens. . . .

Joe and I sit naked on the floor, porno magazines spread out around us. We have each been through these magazines before and know the models intimately. We have favorites, of course. Different types. Joe, the Italian American, likes the All-American Football Jock, preferably hairless. I, the Midwestern WASP, like the dark-eyed Latins, lightly muscled but mature, preferably hairy. Every once in a while we surprise each other. This is the first time we have "compared" together, not an assignment but a friendly inspiration, to share our fantasies. We are turning into "sisters."

"What about him?"

"Naw. Him."

"*Chacun à son goût.*"

"What?"

"Nothing."

After Joe left tonight I flashed on Max. Don't think of him much lately. But in my mind's eye he is standing there with his hand on the doorknob, talking. At least his mouth is moving. I'm fixated on the fact that he has his hand on the doorknob, as if, like 007, he must be ready to make a quick escape. Throughout our entire relationship he was on the verge of taking a powder. At least that was the threat, ubiquitous, omnivorous. He warned me at the beginning that he wouldn't fight, that he would walk out if we fought, that he had no stomach for fighting. But we were just talking, so why was his hand on the doorknob? I was the one who was leaving. Ah, yes. We were talking about money. Fifty-fifty. As it was in love, so was it in parting. I was grief-stricken. He was relieved.

Joe and I have fought in the past few weeks more openly and recklessly than Max and I had fought in two years.

Of course, we feel we are in a fishbowl of sorts—or a lockup, forced into this unnatural proximity with so much at stake. Our sessions have become little psychodramas, symbolic versions of our dealings with other men and the rest of the world. I suppose a certain amount of decorum is necessary for lovers to remain friends as well. Joe and I can't maintain that decorum.

It's clear to me now that what we're engaged in is nothing less than a complete restructuring of our sexual responses, and a reevaluation of all the suppositions and mythologies that have accompanied them. We are formulating new principles to replace old, rigid Rules we carried into sex before this. To what extent everyone operates off those Rules (an unwritten, self-policing code of sexual etiquette) I don't know. Joe and I aren't typical, of course. But we feel there *is* something typical, some kind of behavior we can't live up to or fulfill. We can't be so atypical in that.

Part of it is learning to say no, which comes hard for us. Part of it is learning to say, or indicate, what we want. Part of it is learning what we want.

With all the ritual concentration of bullfighters suiting up for the ring, Joe and I prepare for our first night of "sex."

As usual we are going to massage. But we have also pre-selected and set close at hand our porno—pictures for Joe, stories for me. When we finish massaging, we are to begin to jack each other off. Then, when we get hot, we're to finish the job in separate rooms.

The theory, as Virgil's outlined it for us (and as we've read in *The Joy of Gay Sex* half a dozen times by now), is to approach each other gradually over a series of sessions from the other room, from across the room, with our backs to each other, then side by side—and eventually arrive at mutual (if not simultaneous) orgasm.

We are giggly and self-conscious. I can't look Joe in the eye. I get hard immediately. Joe takes a little longer. As he pumps me, I feel . . . if he . . . does it just a bit longer . . .

The idea that I might cum then and there is terrifying. I ask Joe to stop for a while. I felt that I *could* have cum, but I have thrashed around on that particular plateau many times before. Was it an illusion this time as well?

Joe's eyebrows rise on his tanned forehead. He is thinking, I find out later, that I am less fucked up than he. He must struggle for a moment to remember that not cumming is my problem too. Feels faintly betrayed, a sinking disappointment. Will I pass him up? What kind of game have I been playing all these weeks? He falls back on the quilt and closes his eyes.

We begin again. When we can stand it no longer, we separate. I go to the bathroom, Joe stays where he is. I close the flimsy door, cursing my studio apartment. Put down the toilet seat and sit. Open my magazine. *Playguy* (Vol. 1, No. 5). Turn to "Pit Stop," one of my favorites.

I can hear the *Man's Image Calendar* (1977) pages rustling in the other room as Joe searches out his companion.

The shower next door comes on and I hear voices. The toilet seat is cold and hard. I am semisoft.

He is staked out spread-eagle in the grease pit to roast under the hot Texas sun

Next door, a woman's voice: "I could just go down there tomorrow and tell them . . ."

The younger garage attendant takes out his cock and pisses a long hot stream into the pit, over his face and chest. He doesn't want to, but his raging thirst drives him to open his mouth, to lap up the golden liquid

From the other room, a moan. My foot jerks and taps against the bottom of the door.

" . . . and if they won't, then I'll just . . . "

Trussed up, bent double over the belt, the grease gun unceremoniously thrust up his asshole

"You done, Danny?"

Jesus H. Christ! He's finished! I just about came in the living room with him and now I'm not going to cum at all . . .

Riding back and forth on the big one's cock

On the fucking toilet seat. . . .

"Umf," he protests, as the kid's cock swells in his mouth, stifling his cries

Cumming. . . . Cumming. . . .

What the fuck is Joe doing? Making coffee? He's making coffee! Tight. . . .

So ironic. I was so hot in there. . . .

"Let me have a turn," the kid says

Cumming. . . .

Pulls out with a slurp

Ah. . . . Ah. . . . Ah. . . .

I cum.

"Joe?"

"Yeah?"

"You done?"

"Yeah. Want some coffee?"

"Too fast."

"Like that?"

"Yeah. Harder."

"Show me how you do it. . . . "

"It says in the book you aren't supposed to look at it."

"Oh?" (He's been reading *The Joy of Gay Sex* again.)

"That feels good." Then, "You want me to do you a while?"

"Sure." Joe lies back and picks up a leaf of the now dismantled calendar.

"Do you have to look at that?"

"Yeah," he says. "Why not?"

"Are we supposed to?"

"Yeah," he says.

"I thought we were going to—you know. Do each other."

(Finally side by side. The big night.)

"We are. But we can use our porno, can't we?"

"I don't think so."

(He *needs* his pictures. He can't do it without his pictures. Why won't he look at me?)

"Well, I'm going to use them," he says, fed up with me inventing new Rules.

I pick up my *Drummer* (Vol. 3, No. 22) and read "The Corporal in Charge of Taking Care of Captain O'Malley." Jacking myself off, I cum. ("All over the place," Joe comments dispassionately; Joe cums in white blobs, three or four of them, doesn't squirt.)

Joe is concentrating on Mr. April—bulging biceps, Jockey shorts with a nickel-sized splotch on them, hard hat on his head for the sake of this one photo session. In reality he's anything but a hard hat: an amiable bodybuilder.

Joe is jacking himself off, remembering that "this is not a race," trying to picture that green glade to "relax." He can't. But finally he cums.

"What was your fantasy?" I ask, even though he hates to share his fantasies.

"I don't know." He wipes off his stomach with a towel. "I just thought of him . . . undressing." He turns over to throw the towel onto the floor, mumbles something.

"What?"

"In front of a bunch of women," Joe says, low.

"Oh."

Forget the fact that Joe has cum in the presence of, aided and abetted by another human being, for the first time in his life. He wants more. More!

He calls our therapy his "avocation." He no longer wants to go to the bars. "What for?" He misses his friends, most of whom he hasn't told about his problem, let alone the cure. His parents (who don't even know he's gay) have no idea why he drives into the city twice a week. He looks hassled, tired, and depressed. His narrow life, without the bars, without Friday and Saturday nights, is pressing in on him as never before.

Secretly I agree with him: this is taking too long. These past few weeks, we have tried to jack each other off and failed. But I big-brother him (and anger darts around in his black eyes) that we have all the time in the world—that, as Virgil says, "the tortoise and the hare" and "too fast is slow in the end." Worrying, I say like a prissy Boy Scout, will guarantee our failure. In any case, we have not failed, merely suffered a setback because we thought we'd be able simply to jerk each other off and that would be the end of it. . . .

"Do what you know you *can* do," Virgil says. So tonight we bring ourselves off.

(Says my actor friend, "But being jacked off is one of the hardest things to do! No one does it like I do it to myself." Nevertheless . . .)

Side by side, tense and angry, we work at ourselves.

Using "Last Day on the Track" (*Numbers*, Vol. 3, May 1978), I cum. I curl up next to Joe. He asks me not to. He doesn't know why. Just don't.

He never wants me to touch him, look at him.

Finally, tonight, when I couldn't bear to talk any longer, I got up off the couch, knelt next to Joe, and put my arms around him. I told him everything would be all right.

Something much more enormous than whether or not we can bring each other off is occurring between us. Is it knowing we can only help each other so much? This something overshadows our dreary "exercises." Success, failure . . . no longer quite the point. The whole enterprise has turned black, revealed something cold, alienating, depressing. Joe is beyond my reach, especially when I hold his cock in my hand. We still avoid each other's eyes. Our fantasies (poor, tattered, exhausted fantasies) remain private, as remote as we are from each other.

To G.G.'s Barnum Room with my dancing friend. A ten-dollar disco on 45th Street. A small room and bar letting off the main room. Stage and runway for drag shows. Trendy straights, transvestites, Latin crowd, suburban gays, twosomes, threesomes, Punk-Rock kids looking for something to bash their brains out on. The big room is two stories tall, surrounded on three sides by a balcony. At railing level, a net. Above that, trapezes and bars.

We buy our drinks and I follow my friend (who has sprinted up the stairs ahead of me) to sit "ringside." Three boys and a girl (can one be sure?), all in gold lamé G-strings trimmed with black fur, swing from the bars or go-go on the narrow ledge over light panels that rise up from the floor below. A huge mirror ball in the middle of the ceiling turns slowly above the sequined and strobed discomaniacs below.

We sip our drinks, revving up to dance, taking in the place. "It was so fabulous the first time I came," my dancing friend says. "I was sure it would be a downer the second time around, but isn't it fabulous?"

We indulge in some reprehensible speculations on where the boys come from and what they want out of life. Real slumming stuff. Then, in the darkness, one team replaces another. When the lights pulse up, we see an S&M tableau. Two boys stand over a girl, one pretending to beat her with a studded "belt" (a black satin sash set with silver beads), the other pretending to fuck her face. The shape of the boys' breasts under their satin vests reveal they are in the midst of sex changes.

Buttocks convulsing in time with the music, sweat running down their backs and chests, the boys mime fucking the girl from every angle, in every conceivable position. But their studded crotches, violently thrusting, bumping, never touch her thighs or face. For the benefit of us here on the balcony, she opens her mouth and lets her red tongue flop out onto her chin, rolls the tongue around, rolls her eyes, makes faces that parody orgasm and insatiability as lewdly and coldly as those on satyrs in Roman frescoes.

Onto the trapezes. I watch an ass gyrating and pumping not five feet away from me, so close I can see the hairs gleaming wetly along the crack, the root of the balls between the legs. The spine is a deep indentation like a finger rut in soft clay. The muscles of the upper back fan out hard and well-defined, like the roots of the angels' wings poets place on beautiful boys' shoulder blades. . . .

My dancing friend turns to me and smiles. Am I enjoying myself? I nod. He turns back to the acrobats. The music screams "Do or die." I have no desire to fuck this boy or anyone else.

I love Joe and I believe Joe loves me. But he's not infatuated with me, suffers no illusions about me, dislikes me a great deal as well, pities me to an extent that romance is out of the question. Our love exists in both of us like a hard kernel, like a seed buried away in an arid tomb—still capable of germination after thousands of years, but buried away in obscurity nevertheless. Our love for each other is an abstraction, an idea whose time will never come. Our caring for each other is substantial, empathetic. But our love for each other grows weekly more vestigial. We are, after all, in this lover-like position only in order to seek out our own lovers freely. If our love achieves its purpose, it will no longer be needed.

I know now that however far we go together Joe and I will never kiss each other on the lips. Between us there will never be either that passion of the movie screens or that passion of the grope and spit-swap in the dark doorway.

My Fire Island friend half-worries: "Will it transfer over to other people if you make it?" Then laughs. But he is serious. "Or will you be stuck with each other?"

I can't tell. This experience is devouring the past and the future, somewhat as a smaller cell takes in and incorporates a larger one.

Tonight Joe was lying on his back flipping through his magazine and I was sitting up reading mine and jacking him off (just a quiet evening at home with the folks), taking it easy, waiting for him to wrap his hand around mine and guide it (Virgil calls this the "passive hand" technique), when his legs stiffened, his cock throbbed, and he came.

He came.

He put his magazine down and we exchanged a brief, disbelieving, rather fearful look. Then we both smiled. "Where did that come from?" I asked. "I don't know," he said, wiping himself off. "It just happened."

Was it total relaxation or total boredom? How do we do it again?

Then, when we showered together and Joe was rinsing, I touched him on the side with my index finger, to point out a glob of lather he'd missed. He flinched.

Later, he told me he'd flinched because I was standing behind him and he was fantasizing that I was going to kill him—knife him, like *Psycho* or something. When I touched him his heart stopped.

"Why?"

"Maybe I thought you were jealous," he speculated.

I was upset. I didn't know what vibes I might have been throwing off, though I knew I was happy for him. "I must be jealous," I said. "I don't feel it very strongly, but I must be."

I'm lying on my back with my head propped up on the pillows reading "Studs and Suds Go Down at the Garage" (*Numbers*, November 1978), about this mechanic and his young friend who have lured this bodybuilder into the garage and he has pulled down his trousers ("hot in here") to reveal a pair of black bikini briefs packed tight with meat and after one blow job, sprawled out on the hood of a car, he is ready to cum again, so the boy goes down on him, then the bodybuilder pushes the boy's head away, stands him up, and shucks down his pants and the boy sits on the bodybuilder's cock and the mechanic (getting a sudden inspiration) dips a broom handle in motor oil and shoves it up the bodybuilder's asshole, and I am about to cum. . . .

I mean to ask Joe to take my prick in his hand and bring me off (if I can get him there in time; haven't been able to yet, or his hand has turned me off) but the only name I can think of is *Max*.

I drop back. I begin again. The mechanic is sticking an inquiring finger into the bodybuilder's asshole, the white buns squirm and squeak on the car hood, the boy rides the monster cock, the broomstick is pushed into the hole. . . .

Who is he? Joe. Right.

"Joe?"

His hand grasps my cock and I am cumming.

"Simple," Virgil says. "You've been saving your cum for Max."

* * *

What a night! I finished massaging Joe and then he sat beside me and, very lover-like, ran his hands over my chest, cock, and balls, in circles around my cock, an abstracted look on his face, watching what my body was doing, doing the things I like.

I closed my eyes and immediately a fantasy popped into my head, as I remembered "Father Figure" (*Playguy*, Vol. 1, No. 10), where this guy comes home from the navy and (Mom comfortably out of the picture) makes it in the kitchen with the Old Man ("He was looking at my pecs straining through my T-shirt. . . . "). Then, alarmingly, *my own father* was in the picture, sitting at the kitchen table, feeling me up under the table. Whoa!

Joe was doing delicious things to my cock; we'd worked on that the other night.

In the kitchen in Nebraska . . . I conjured up my Uncle Bob the sailor, but my father wouldn't go away, his fingers fumbling for my fly, taking out my cock under the table, pretending to stir his coffee. I was rock hard. Go with it, I thought, and gave a little involuntary snort. Joe's steady-unsteady rhythm didn't falter.

Outside the window, leafy green trees. Sounds of insects in the bayou. Sun buzzing. "Let me give it to you, at last, Dad. . . . "

My hips thrust up. Joe stepped it up. My God, if he only knew . . . Go away. But he wouldn't.

My father stands up and comes around behind me. Stands me up. Opens my pants and lets them drop around my thighs. Chair legs scrape over the linoleum. Works it into me.

With a groan, I shot all over myself, chest, face, all over the pillow. Opened my eyes. Joe's face, curious, above me.

"Wow," he said.

I told him about my fantasy. "Outrageous," he said. I was very happy, if embarrassed.

Joe lay with his eyes closed, hands behind his head, legs slightly open, while I jacked his cock—long, rather flexible, a real handful. At one point he opened his eyes and I thought he'd pick up his porno, but he didn't. He turned his head to one side and I smiled at him, holding his balls in one hand. He tossed his head again and I asked, *à la* Mayor Koch, "How'm I doin'?" "Do the head more," he replied, and closed his eyes.

He opened his legs further and they began to quiver. I smiled to myself, thinking of the dildo he'd bought (good old *Joy of Gay Sex*) to "practice" and get to know his asshole. He is incredibly industrious, I thought. And as I was thinking of the applications he'd been filling out for Pan Am and Eastern—what a scrumptious steward he'd make—he heaved and came, a monster orgasm that almost didn't happen—there was a pulse, a pause, then he came.

I whistled. He opened his eyes. His mouth was agape. His eyes shone with that primordial, post-orgasmic glaze.

"We get the prize," I said. I'd cum too.

"Oh, really?" he said. Immediately downplaying it.

Mustn't hope too much.

Virgil congratulated us, "Though I know you'll probably use your success as an excuse to worry about the next time."

He's very pleased with us. "You might be interested to know now," he said, "that all the literature says retarded ejaculation is the hardest thing to cure. That it takes at least six months before the patient will ejaculate. . . . " (Well, it felt like six years.) "That those who suffer from it are invariably angry people, which you two aren't, and that it has to do with resentment"—he looked at me—"towards the mother."

I laughed and Virgil smiled. We both knew it had nothing to do with my mother. Or my real father, for that matter. But with the father of my childhood and adolescence, who hadn't been able to love me. Or me, him. That the issue was one of giving, nurturing.

Thinking of my father, now dying of cancer. Who wasn't there. Max, who wasn't there.

Halloween evening. After leaving me, Joe drives down Christopher Street. (Destination dirty-book store, to buy a new dildo. This after Virgil's warning that the one he'd bought on Long Island, having no "balls," might get lost up his ass. Practice.) Or *trying* to drive down Christopher Street. There is an enormous crowd on the street, masked and costumed. (Oh, yes, like any other night.) In a festive, whacko mood. A zonked-out transvestite is stopping cars, or rather, assaulting their occupants with attitude and good humor while they stand stranded in the traffic jam.

Joe is three or four cars back from the TV, the knot of people who surround her, and the car whose hood she dances on. A man in a black

Stetson stops, does a double take at Joe, smirks, cups his basket, and settles in for a long cruise.

Joe is rather liking it—the attention of the cowboy, who has now gotten verbal about it, the carnival swirling around his car, even sweating out his turn with the TV.

The cars inch forward. Men, men, men flow around Joe like water around a ship's prow. Some smile. Some give him the deadeye cruise (pretending not to notice, pretending not to cruise, saying, "Look at me, eatcha heart out"). Some stop and lean against his car. His fenders are being polished by a dozen Levied butts! What attention!

From being so out of it, so Long Island, so down—he is suddenly *in it*, right smack dab in the middle of it, a million miles from Korvette's and his room with the dumbbells and the closet mirror, the porno hidden beneath his underwear in the drawer, his mother's silent questions as he slips out the door.

He has told me this and I've wanted to take him in my arms, for this is what he's been moving towards. Not the Christopher Street carnival, not a stranger's denim *tushe*, but this sudden sense, this rush of freedom, this glimpse of a future.

We are wary. It's working and we don't want to rock the boat. I complain to Virgil that we're too involved. I feel, like Joe, that this is somehow sucking up the rest of my life, that I've brought too much of myself into it for comfort.

"But that's just it," Virgil says, smiling patiently.

"What?"

"To put yourself into it."

I sit back and think while Joe is talking. Yes. To put myself into it. I was trying to fuck with all those guys just like they tell you to do in the porno magazines, or like we assume you have to be able to do in the decade of the zipless fuck. Keeping myself out of it, though my body was in it. And the body said no.

I am dancing at Flamingo with my dancing friend when I spot a man standing not far from us on the edge of the floor, looking at me, clapping his hands along with the beat, smiling. I smile back, but, embarrassed by his unwavering cruise (at Flamingo, of all places), steer myself around so I'm not directly facing him.

It is four o'clock in the morning and I am high.

He moves and soon I'm looking into his eyes again. Even the pulsating lights and shadows on the dance floor don't obscure the amusement, interest, and—oh, Jesus—intelligence in his eyes. He is obviously a mirage.

I take a hit of amyl. He's still there.

Perhaps forty, great build, salt-and-pepper hair cut short, the obligatory mustache. And that face. Not the cattle-prod-jolt-to-the-balls face, but the "I am Gatsby, won't you join me on my yacht for a cool drink" face.

So it's a fantasy. I may be stuck with Daddy for a while, but I'll be damned if I have to take on Alan Ladd too.

There is a sheen on his bare $200 Sheridan Square Health Club chest. There are those straight white teeth. There is the unremitting, ironic cruise.

What with the Quaalude and the poppers, I am slow to admit that this is what I want. Yes. Now. Him. This great, corporeal manifestation of a wet dream.

He is dancing with us now, I have a silly, senior-prom grin on my face and my stomach is flopping. I wonder what the fuck I'm going to do with this gorgeous man who is—yes—interested in me, running his palms over my chest.

In me. Danny Slocum.

Ever mindful of my social obligations, I offer him the popper bottle. He shakes his head no thanks. I take another hit and put the bottle back. My dancing friend is intensely involved in this byplay. I know because he is elaborately pretending not to be. As he spins around he shoots me a look that says, Your round, Miss Thing, and dances away.

The rush hits me, bringing me down more than it pumps me up. But I am a little bit higher than I was before he joined us. And he is still there, fingers caressing my nipples, trailing off along my stomach.

"Wanna take a break?" I pant, desperate for some strategy to get Mr. X into my bed—bed, hell, into my shower—sometime, sometime in the future.

"What?"

I repeat my ploy.

"Naw," he says. "I think I'll dance with my friends."

He weaves away through the crowd. I am down now. All the way down. Romance-schromance. I won't let this happen again.

* * *

Joe kneels between my legs. With a look on his face of curiosity mingled with distaste, he takes my cock in his mouth. A flutter. Then he is off and jacking it with his fingers again. A pause. He lifts the glass of water to his lips, takes two or three sips, then goes down on me again.

None of this has been prescribed by Virgil, this sipping and jerking, hand to mouth, so to speak. He has not sucked cock much and when he has he's been heavily face-fucked, the last time by some dude in the back seat of a Ford Pinto.

I have billed myself as a terrific cocksucker. Joe has not been persuaded.

We are not angry people. We *are* fearful people (the flip side). Fearful, complicating . . . paranoid? Fearful of coercion. Fearful of unleashing dark forces within ourselves. Fearful of this act with all its mythology and its associations. We can't feel it.

Flutter-flutter. Sip-sip. Tuggings, scrapings, tonguings, warmth, coolness—all vague, pastel, not red-hot. I'm shy (again) about giving instructions.

I go down on Joe. "Um-humph?" Hard to ask questions with your mouth packed full of cock.

We jack each other off. I cum first (old hat); the beat before Joe cums is elongated into two, three, four pulses.

"Weird," I say.

"What do you mean?"

"You mean you didn't feel it?"

"What?"

"It was as if you almost didn't cum."

"Well, I *did*."

"What's wrong?"

"Fuck you" (from under the arm he's thrown over his face).

"What's wrong?"

I rub his belly.

"Stop it. I can hide if I want to."

I leave him lying there and go pee. He wanted to be praised and petted. So I lie down beside him, praise, and pet him a bit.

In the shower we both agree we're tired and pressured. We feel weepy. Blowing. Joe has a lot to learn and I a lot to unlearn. Same thing. Whenever this happens, this lack of progress, each of us blames the other.

* * *

At Virgil's suggestion Joe has been practicing blowing—whether with a cucumber or his dildo, he won't tell me. "How's it going?" I ask over the phone.

"Now I have to practice cocksucking," he says, exasperated. "I have to practice putting a dildo up my ass to get fucked. I have to suck on a cucumber to learn how to cocksuck. I have to practice filling out employment applications for my group therapy. I have to practice dancing in front of the mirror to see how my ass looks at the disco. If everyone had to practice as much as I do, there wouldn't be any homosexuals."

We try different positions. Virgil says our necks might be tense, that we might not feel in control in certain positions, that we will learn how to breathe in due time. Practice, practice. Neither one of us gets at all close. Joe is getting pretty good.

I have just had the interesting experience of having my therapist offer me his lover for sex. I declined. God knows what it might do to my "transference."

But Joe took him up on it, rather liking the idea. "I don't know," he said. "It's kind of like going to bed with *him*."

"You realize what you just said?"

"I don't mean that. I mean he'll get it straight from the horse's mouth now."

Glorioski.

The idea is that we gradually transfer onto other people now, the answer to my Fire Island friend's perennial question as to whether we'll be stuck with each other forever. We were beginning to wonder about it ourselves. It is now November and we've been doing this since July.

The supply of male sex surrogates, I take it, is limited. (*Note: Remember to tell actor friend this is not, repeat not, easy work, and that it takes the dedication of a Salvation Army captain and the patience of a Sister of Charity.*) Virgil's lover is well trained, I take it, and comes highly recommended. . . .

Joe appeared at the door at precisely the appointed hour, a little box of pastries in hand, and Virgil went out to see a movie.

They talked about Michael's studies and looked at some of Michael's drawings. ("I have some more in the bedroom." Heh-heh.) Michael suggested they massage each other. They took off their clothes. Joe lay down on his back as he would with me. "How about your back first?" Michael suggested. Joe turned over. Michael didn't use any oil. His touch was light and feathery. At one point he ran the hairs on his arm down Joe's back. Joe shivered, not sure how much he liked it. He realized then he wasn't saying anything. His mind was so full of the admonition to say something, anything, that he couldn't think what to say.

He turned over and Michael leaned down and licked his nipple. Joe's body jumped a bit. He hadn't expected that at all. Then Michael sat back on his heels and began massaging Joe's thighs. Every once in a while a hand would stray away from the center of Michael's attention to rest on a nipple or a shoulder or next to Joe's balls. Every once in a while Michael would lightly feel his way around the head of Joe's prick.

Joe just lay there, passive. Being with Michael was so different from being with me—or anyone else he'd been with, for that matter. He didn't know what was coming next. Inwardly he laughed at himself and his predicament. It wasn't that Michael was in control of the situation, but that they were both drifting towards their destination— Joe's orgasm—without knowing *how* they would arrive there.

Just like real sex.

Joe felt paralyzed. He knew he was supposed to give Michael a hint as to what he wanted him to do, but the words wouldn't come to him.

Michael asked Joe to massage him and Joe did. Then Michael blew Joe for a while, then jacked and blew him. But Joe couldn't cum. Michael lay down for a rest, his hard cock sticking out from between his slender thighs. He took Joe in his arms and held him and Joe sighed. He felt the evening was going to be a total washout. He wanted to say "Oh, Michael"—as he sometimes says "Oh, Danny"—meaning, "What am I going to do?"

"Do you mind if I cum?" Michael asked. And then he jacked himself off.

"It must be very frustrating work," Joe observed.

"Yes, it is," Michael replied.

So Joe said he wanted to jack himself off. He lay back on the bed with a new copy of *Mandate* with a hunky guy in it. As he was about to cum, he took Michael's hand, but Michael didn't know Joe wanted him to finish him. Joe came.

They showered and had coffee and the pastries. Virgil called, asking if he could come home. Joe left before Virgil got there, accepting Michael's congratulations but feeling mildly depressed about the whole thing.

"But you came!" I said over the phone.

"Yeah."

Silence.

"Joe, where'd you get that? That never-give-yourself-a-break thing."

"I don't know."

"From *your* father?"

"Mother, I guess."

"Well, if we're both stuck with it, at least we don't have to act as if we are. *You came.*"

"Yeah. It wasn't real sex."

Boy, if Sammy wasn't real sex, I don't know what is. Nonstop talker—Studio 54, his childhood in Brooklyn, his design classes, the shoes he wears to dance in, all the jobs he's had, his girlfriends, his boyfriends—yak yak yak. And all the while, steering me through my paces.

I feel like I've just come back to the old homestead from Kansas City. That boy turned me every which way but up. Gave me organs I never knew I had. Played me like a calliope.

"You like that, don't you, you should see yourself there, laying there with that grin on your face, here, put it there, that's it, terrific, that really feels good, let's kiss."

"A cock like that has to have a name," I say.

He hefts it in his hand. "How'd you know? Thumper."

He jacked me every which way but off, blew me every which way but away, and then jacked me up to the Mega-O. Had me screaming. Rolling in the aisles. Then dashed away to catch forty winks before Studio.

Sammy's report to Virgil: "Very cerebral. Very repressed. I'm surprised he even came."

* * *

And, boy, was I in trouble. I knew it even before the door slammed behind Sammy. I would have to tell Joe I had a terrific time. I downplayed it at Virgil's, but it didn't do any good. On the way to my place Joe was silent. At home I bustled around, getting coffee and unpacking the brownies. Joe sat languid in the chair, staring at the rug.

"What's wrong?"

"Nothing."

"You're jealous."

"Yeah."

"You're not me."

He snorted.

"Look, Joe, I'm not going to let you bring me down. I'm sorry you're pissed, but I'm not going to let you bring me down." I was getting strident. "When I try to cheer you up you get mad at me. You have to be coddled." (And why not? What's so wrong about that?) "I don't know what you want."

"I'm tired of being alone all the time," he said.

He said it so simply, so without affectation, I was stung by it. I said something to the effect that I understood, but it was a throwaway. Then I said, fast, "Let's go lie down."

He followed me listlessly. We lay on the bed. I took him in my arms and kissed him on the neck. He kissed my neck. We were quiet for a while.

"Why don't I massage you for a while?" I asked. "I don't think we have everything worked out between us, but we can do that. Maybe you'll feel better. And we don't have to do anything else if we don't feel like it." Sounding like Nurse Greer Garson, but softly.

So I massaged him without the oil, then he massaged me a bit, and it was quite different, quite good. He's something of a mind reader by now—he unbuttoned my jeans as I hoped he would, and rubbed my belly.

"I like that," I said. "I'm very—uh—responsive tonight." We laughed.

Lying together a bit later, I asked him if I could lick his ass. He stiffened. "I'm not going to rim you," I said, half-joking. "I just feel like licking your ass."

The idea didn't especially turn him on, but he let me do it. Since I'd been massaging his ass through his jeans while he lay on top of me and he'd been pretty hot over that, as he usually is, I figured he'd like a little ass work. He loves to have his ass pushed and pulled when I massage him.

So we took off our jeans and shorts. He lay facedown on the bed and I licked up and down his legs, then lay down between them and licked and bit and kissed his ass—which was really quite picturesque in the light from the bedside lamp, that ass, every mole and hair of which I know so well. How anyone could lick that ass and not dive into the crack to the asshole is beyond me. But I resisted.

I turned him over and began to blow him. He hardened up in my mouth, then we traded off a while. Then I went—as they say in the porno magazines—"crazy on his cock." And he came! Hurrah!

He jerked it out of my mouth, laughed, and shivered up and down the length of his body.

He blew me for a while, then. But I was pretty enervated by this time, and generally just glad for Joe, not so interested in it. So I jacked myself off. And though I wondered for a while there if I'd make it, I did.

Sammy said, "People can only go as high as you go yourself." And, sticking his finger up my ass, "People can only get as hot as *you're* hot."

Tonight I was eating dinner and watching TV. A story about a pediatrician. The kindly doctor was filmed on his rounds.

All day long something had been flickering about the edges of my consciousness, and somehow the doctor did it. I began to cry. I managed to swallow the food in my mouth. The doctor cut through a child's ribs on the operating table. I put my napkin over my eyes and cried. . . .

I grew up in a small Western city where one of the summer attractions was a musical comedy performed in the city park and sponsored by one of the newspapers. From age eleven until well into high school I acted and sang in these shows, which for us kids usually meant cavorting and mugging around the stage while the Wells Fargo Wagon was a-comin' down the street or everyone was declaring in four-part harmony what a real nice clambake it had been.

The year I was thirteen I began riding to and from rehearsals with a schoolteacher who lived a ways out of the city, in one of its eastern suburbs. Taking the bus all the way downtown alone and then back home in the dark was an ordeal. It was much more fun riding with Ted.

He was a popular amateur actor who usually played comic parts in our summer shows and, during the winter, appeared in little-theater productions. Everyone loved him. He was a card. I liked him because he was funny and intense. He looked like he'd stepped directly out of *The Inspector General*: long, string-bean body, Adam's apple like a fist, prematurely balding.

Driving home one night, Ted brought up the subject of hypnotism. Casually.

"Ever been hypnotized?" His eyes alit on me briefly, then returned to the street.

I said I hadn't. He said nothing more. Shifted gears. Silence.

Why? I asked.

"It's just . . . kind of a hobby with me."

Again, shifting gears, busy concentrating on the traffic, street signs—like a man miming driving a dummy car.

I asked him about it the next evening, of course. Did he think *I* could be hypnotized? What made some people easier to hypnotize than others? Are you unconscious, in a trance?

He smiled indulgently at my questions (keeper of the mysteries), answered with a patient air, and saved his proposal for the next night.

"Would you like to?"

Be hypnotized?

"Yeah."

I didn't know. It might be fun, I said.

"I don't hypnotize just anyone. I think I'd only put you in a light trance"—as if deciding—"to begin with."

And so he did.

That night and the following night—and the next night, after rehearsal in the marble pavilion in the park. He drove to the other end next to the reflecting pool, behind a stand of pine trees.

I have no doubt that he put me in a real trance and that it was impossible to move my arm, that the pinprick in the back of my hand (the pin drawn from under the collar of his jacket) didn't hurt, that his hot breath in my hair, as he put his arm around me to raise my right hand above my head and leave it dangling there, thrilled and frightened me almost inexpressibly.

One afternoon on the way to rehearsal Ted parked the car under a red maple (like the two trees in our front yard at home) and hypnotized me. He had me rub my face in his crotch, over his dark brown serge trousers. Then he opened his fly and had me rub my face in his underwear. I remember the smell.

That night he had me do other, painful things, though I asked him not to make me do them.

"You won't do anything you don't really want to do," he said in his hypnotist's voice.

I knew that was true and that I had wanted him to do something I wasn't quite sure of in the beginning. I knew who, what I was, what I wanted. Vaguely.

"Is this guy Ted all right?" my father asked the next day.

"Oh, sure," I said to my father. "He's a nice guy."

Tonight, with the napkin over my face, remembering what I'd so desperately and successfully forgotten for twenty years, I realized why I don't trust men.

Not dead yet. My father at seventy, dying of cancer. But not dead yet. As I write this, the cancer is spreading through him like dye through water, but he's not dead yet.

I no longer await his death impatiently, to get it over with—as if he would die and I could dust off my hands, walk briskly away from the grave, and be rid of him at last. But it's easier for me to think of him dead than it is to force myself to realize he is alive, thousands of miles away, but dying; that he will die painfully, not long from now, far away.

I asked myself over and over again that night how he could do nothing, when he knew. How he could ask again, and still do nothing. I held the pillow tight and beat it as if it were my father. But finally I set the pillow aside. I lay in the middle of the bed. The tears and snot dried on my face.

So, in a way, all my men—Max, the others—have been reflections of those two. And all of them reflections of myself. The little drama has been repeated as if by rote, right down to the final betrayal. Until the body refused to perform.

* * *

Sitting in the living room tonight, I watched Joe through the bathroom door, combing his hair. The part. The points behind his ears. Preoccupied.

Joe is not my lover. We're moving apart. He'll be himself without me.

Aunt Persia and the Jesus Man

Christopher Cox

Cox wrote and rewrote this story, later titled "Doe's Pillow," for at least a decade, but he never finished it. Each paragraph was rewritten at least a dozen times. The following version, the most complete, is based on a draft from the summer of 1971, but it does not reflect Cox's last wishes for the story. Although the story does not have a gay theme, its farcical drama of sibling rivalry bears a striking resemblance to George Whitmore's "Getting Rid of Robert," which appears later in this volume. Indeed, the small-town world of rural Alabama in which Cox grew up mirrors in a striking fashion the tightly knitted gay community in which he found himself in New York. After all, Eudora Welty, who is so obvious an influence here, is not so distant in manner from Ronald Firbank. This is the first publication of "Aunt Persia and the Jesus Man."

1.

I tell you it's just one thing after another.

The girls in my car pool had no sooner let me out from the church picnic than my people told me that sweet Aunt Doe was none too well and that I'd better get to her room right away. Never in a million years thought she'd go so fast but you just can't tell about things like that. It's not for us to reason why. Otherwise I wouldn't have even gone—to the picnic, that is—but I'm special-events chairman of our Women's Bible Class and absolutely had to be there. Planned, executed, and cleaned up the whole mess with these two hands and not one "thank you" from a single WBC member. So afterwards I just pranced up to Mrs. Rita Underwood, our president, who has never lifted a finger or dirtied her hands for anybody far as I know, and told her not to expect my help next year and not even to ask. And don't you let them hog-tie you into joining one of them committees. They always take advantage of newcomers.

Well, I was going to say I was up in my room checking for chiggers when one of my cousins came into the room and says, "Hon, it's real soon. Real soon," and puts her hand on my arm like this. I tell you I ran down the hall lickety-split, still in my pedal pushers. Real cute ones, too. Didn't even think of changing, I was so upset. And none too soon.

I had just closed the door when Doe opened her mouth and whispered something. Everybody got real close to the bed and cocked their heads sideways like this. Then Doe started to rise up from her pillow with her hand stretched out toward my Aunt Persia. Somebody said, "Isn't that sweet. Trying to say good-bye." But uh-uh. Up she went like a flash! Up in the air and snapped the gold locket and chain right off Persia's neck! Just like that! Then she let out a smiling scream and fell over deader than a doornail right there in front of God and everybody!

Well, honey, I tell you I never seen anything like it in my life. Aunt Persia, who had just realized what happened, jumped on top of poor Aunt Doe, who was getting colder by the minute, and started pulling out hair like she was weeding a garden! Honey, she was beatin' a dead woman! And it took me and the rest of the people in the room to pull her off, and even then we wouldn't have gotten her off if I hadn't said, "Aunt Persia, please. She won't be bothering you no more."

You see, I'm her favorite relative and she's mine, though I had my doubts for a while. Wouldn't you? I mean she's really harmless and all but she did scare me that day. But I have to admit I'm glad she went on and got it out of her system. And as if that wasn't enough, Other-Mama, who's about as blind as a bat and deaf as a crazy man with wax in his ears, turns around and says, "I want my pot." I just nearly died on the spot! No pun intended.

Other-Mama, you see, is about a hundred years old and thinks she's still living in Shiloh. Honey, the lady talks about the Civil War like it was yesterday! My grandmother really, Other-Mama is, but she raised me when my mother died, along with Aunt Persia and Aunt Doe. So that's why I call her Other-Mama.

So, anyway, Persia—who's taken care of sweet Other-Mama for years—very smugly took the handles of the wheelchair and shot out of the room like a light. Other-Mama's been in a wheelchair since she tripped on one of my roller skates. It wasn't my fault. Everybody just looked at each other with their lips all tight and mad as hornets. One of them said, "I knew this was going to happen. I knew it sure as shootin'," to which I said, "Shut up or get out," and left the room myself, slamming the door in their faces.

I just had to get out so I decided to sit on the back porch for a while. No sooner had I got comfortable than I see Miss Curtsy Neagle hot-tailing it over from next door with a pecan pie.

"Oh, honey," she said, "the minute I saw them stick that corsage on the door, I popped this in some foil."

Sure, I said to myself, she just wants to get in that house and see a dead body. People are strange that way. But I didn't say anything except that I thought it was sweet of her to bring that pie over and she kept rattling on about how she lost a sister recently and all the time looking over my shoulder trying to see what was going on.

"Miss Neagle," I said, cutting her off, "there's Dr. Puckett right now and I gotta run and tend to gettin' Doe down to the funeral home so as you and everybody can pay your respects there."

Well, let it be known that she took that as an insult and got all huffy and left without a "thank you, ma'am." Not that I cared. If you'd ever tasted her pecan pie you'd know why.

So Dr. Puckett comes tromping up the steps, very calm and professional-like because it's a death and all, says "Hello, Fancy June" and "Where's the deceased?"

When we got back to the bedroom, Other-Mama was sittin' next to the bed with her hair down talking about anything and everything that came in her head. Persia was brushing that old mane, and I swear nobody has hair that long anymore. It ain't human. Reached all the way to the floor, around and under her wheelchair, and if Other-Mama had taken a mind to wheeling the chair back she would've yanked her head off.

When Dr. Puckett felt of poor Doe's heart, all the men in the room turned the other way. Other-Mama told everybody about the day Granddaddy died until Persia said, "Hush up," and told "Doc"— that's what I call him when I want to see a blush—what happened. I noticed that she had that locket back on her neck with a Band-Aid around the clip.

While Dr. Puckett finished examining Doe, he told us about old Lucy Taylor, who died a few weeks ago. She had pneumonia, you know, and would have been out of bed in a few weeks. But one day she had a visit from one of her grandchildren: Judy and Mack Bowen's little girl, and the little thing brought her grandmama a Snickers. You know children and their little presents. Well, just to be sweet, I suppose, Lucy took a bite out of that Snickers, tossed it around her mouth, and choked on a goober. Dead, honey, and that is straight from the horse's mouth! And that's not all. Before that little girl called anybody, she finished off that Snickers, threw the wrapper in the wastebasket, and swore she didn't know what in the world happened. Took them eight hours to get the truth out of her.

By then Persia and I were in hysterics and just couldn't stop laughing, although I suppose we shouldn't have laughed, since Lucy used to be in our Bible class. So, at the request of our relatives, we left the room in respect for the dead. We just hightailed it to the back porch for a cigarette. Now, I am not a smoker or a drinker but that day I needed one.

It was out on the back porch that Aunt Persia told me why she and Aunt Doe never got on. Before that I had only heard bits and pieces 'cause nobody wanted to talk about it. But that day she let it fly. I mean, it was good for her to get it all out in the open, you know. And I am her favorite relative and she's mine. I suppose you could call me her confidante.

2.

Now, Aunt Persia is one of the nicest and most good-natured ladies I've ever known, only she just doesn't fool around. If she don't like you she'll tell you so. If she likes you she'll hug you on the main street of town. She's tall as I am, maybe taller, and pulls her hair back like yours only it's darker. Darker from the bottle, that is—now, that didn't mean you, honey—but don't you dare say I told. And she has these real long legs like those pretty birds in Florida that only stand on one. I mean that as a compliment—I said "pretty birds." I guess she must be sixty-something now and cute as a button. I'll introduce you sometime.

Just the opposite from Persia was Aunt Doe. Tiny as a midget, five feet even, with naturally curly hair. Runs in the family and is where I got mine. And I know for a fact that she only weighed eighty pounds 'cause she told us every night at supper. Weighed eighty pounds when she graduated from Catawba County High School and hadn't gained a pound since except when she had her tonsils out and could only eat ice cream and Jell-O and she got rid of that in a hurry. And smile? Honey, talk about someone who smiled a lot. Persia used to swear she'd get lockjaw one day.

But even though everybody thought Doe was just as sweet as pie, she was also just as lazy as an old dog. Never helped clear the table or wash a dish or anything. She just sat around smiling and painting her toenails dark red.

They weren't always on different ends of the rope, though. No siree—they were just as close as two sisters could be born two years apart. Other-Mama never played favorites, although she knew who she could depend on to get things done. And in those days, Other-Mama was a mighty strong lady. Of course, all this was long before my time, so I can't swear to everything I'm going to tell. But this is straight from Persia's mouth and she should know.

Mind you, I'm only telling you this because you're new here. If you tell anybody I'll just deny it up and down and swear you're just trying to get in with everybody. So you'd better cross your heart not to tell and we'll stay friends. You're sweet, honey, and I like you and that's why I'm talking about this to you. Mind you, I don't do this with most strangers. It's not easy to get to know me.

3.

I don't know about where you come from but here, every summer, this evangelist used to come through town and put up a tent on the north side of town close to the Merita bakery. Since I've been here there's been a different one every year, but back then there was only one who covered this territory. That is, until he got himself involved with certain people.

This man called himself Smiley Fitts. The Reverend Smiley Fitts. He first came to town when he was eleven years old. They called him "the Youngest Disciple" and he was supposed to be one of them kids that have religious dreams or something. Can you beat that? Somebody dug up a picture of him taken back then: this little boy dressed up in a suit with his mother standing next to him outside the tent, looking up at the sky like he was holding a conversation with Him. Took it with him when he left, but not before everybody and their brother had laid eyes on it.

Now, Smiley Fitts was said to be "a man among men," and from the way Aunt Persia described him I can believe it. She says he stood six feet three, had little black watermelon-seed eyes, a nose like Valentino, long fingers, and hair as red as a Coca-Cola sign. Don't you wonder about people like that? But apparently there was something good and decent about him,'cause Persia isn't fooled that easily.

They say he came into town in a blaze of color. He rode on top of a wagon that was painted all different colors with signs all over it: God Found a Good Man in Smiley Fitts. They say he drove through town while all these little girls from our Training Union class followed behind, handing out leaflets that told where and what time the services would take place. Also listed quotes from various newspapers where he had spread the word. They called him the ''Roosevelt of Bibleland'' and Boaz claimed there hadn't been a true religious person since Sister Aimee.

Following the Reverend down the road was this quartet that called themselves the Fishers of Men. They always traveled behind and arrived late, just as the service started, smelling of whiskey and mouthwash. Made a name for themselves round here with a little wax-cut of ''Do, Lord.'' If I had a copy I'd play it for you. Just use your imagination.

So out to the campgrounds they went: dressed in black suits and butterfly bow ties. Smiley, they say, always smelled like spicy eggnog and smiled like a crazy man. Never stopped waving to people, shaking hands and saying ''Howjado!'' Other-Mama always said: ''Now, that's a man with teeth.''

Minute she heard he was in town, Other-Mama was telling everybody to get dressed for church. She literally made Persia go. Doe went just so she could get dressed up. And go they did, walking all the way.

4.

The tent was only about a mile away from the house, so by the time they arrived, Smiley was still out in front shaking hands: ''Howjado!'' Then he would take each person by the arms and pass them to those little Training Union girls, who had changed into usherette outfits. Persia did admit that she threw a glance toward Smiley, but Other-Mama slapped her on the thigh and said, ''Behave yourself in church, girl.''

But, sugar, smile on while you can. If you've ever been to one of them tent meetings you know what I mean. They sit you in those metal fold-up chairs and somebody always brings a bunch of tacky snapdragons to go under the pulpit. And anybody knows snapdragons wilt almost immediately. You go in at six-thirty, and if you're lucky, you're out by ten.

Reverend Fitts began the service with a short prayer that lasted fifteen minutes. Then there were the announcements and welcome-backs—you know, all those people in the hospital. Then the Fishers of Men did a medley of "Onward, Christian Soldiers," "Ivory Palaces," and finished up with "Do, Lord." Well, that got the ball rolling and the hallelujahs rising. Persia said it was so hot that she was surprised anyone could breathe, let alone shout. Said Doe got a cramp in her wrist from fanning so hard. And mosquitoes and gnats! Said it felt like you was sittin' next to a picnic table where somebody ate watermelon yesterday.

But no matter what everybody else felt, Other-Mama was in hog heaven 'cause she'd been raised in those sticky tents. There just aren't good Baptists like Other-Mama anymore.

While Other-Mama was emoting, Persia said she was just trying to keep her eyes open. But she didn't make it. Next thing she knew Other-Mama was shoving the offering plate in her stomach and pinching her. Took Persia a second to come to, and when she did she smelled spice. Honey, Smiley Fitts was standing there staring her right in the face! Said she got so nervous she put fifty cents in the offering plate and forgot to get change. He looked at her real sweet-like and said, "Bless your sweet heart, sister," and if you ask me, that's when he got her. There just ain't a woman alive immune to complimentary remarks.

After that, let me tell you, wild horses couldn't have dragged her away. She was shouting hallelujah along with everybody else and getting the spirit like some country Holy Roller. By the time they had sung four more hymns and sweated through one of Smiley's sermons ("Have You Swum Your River Jordan"), Persia was a firm believer.

"There was never," she said, "another man to cross these parts who could preach fire and damnation like Smiley Fitts. But that don't make up for what he did. He is surely an example of not practicing what you preach."

Then Persia had her moment.

One tent meeting ends like any other. This one was no different. The sermon was over and everybody was sitting there like hot lettuce. The piano started playing real sweet and softly, "Nearer My God to Thee." That meant it was time for the altar call. That's when I would have sunk down in my seat. But some people go up just like they walk up the street. That night they were a little slow, it being the first meeting.

Only Jake Slocum got up, but he gets up anytime he can. He's the type that runs across the field when the band's playing at halftime just to get attention.

These altar calls. They're like revenge: You don't come up, you don't leave. So he kept preaching and kept preaching until people started getting a little crazy. But nobody moved. That is, until Persia got her wind up.

Right smack in the middle of the second sermon, Persia jumped up out of her seat and shouted: "Take me into your precious bosom, Lord. I am a sinner!"

Well, Other-Mama nearly dropped her teeth, and for a minute even Doe stopped smiling. And that wouldn't have been so bad if Persia hadn't gone on traipsing down the aisle, just as pretty as you please, and delivered a testimonial fit to beat the bejesus out of you. I hear you had to be there to believe it.

Honey, you couldn't hear a pin drop. Nobody was about to make a face in front of Persia. She would've slapped them silly. And by the time she was finished the whole congregation was sitting with their mouths open. Then she looked them all over one by one and said, "Mrs. Butler—give me some saving music," to which Mrs. Butler replied to the tune of "Battle Hymn of the Republic." The lady got so excited she didn't know what she was doing.

Within the hour, there wasn't a soul in that tent that hadn't been saved. Even Doe trotted up behind Other-Mama, saying "hi" to everybody, while Persia passed them all to Smiley. He took each head in his hands and half broke their necks praying for them. Honey, she was even giving out snapdragons to the old people.

When Alice Donald McGraw refused to go up, Persia just went over, whispered something in her ear (she never said what), and old Alice was up like lightning, screaming, "Save me, good brother. I am ready for Jesus!"

Just when she thinks that she'd got everybody who could be gotten, she thought of those little usherettes. Up the aisle she dashed, and when they weren't there she went outside. Caught them smoking and cussing and brought all of them back 'cept one, Georgia Wise. Probably would have chased that one down, too, but she was too tired. So she just told the little girl's mama.

That was a night this whole town remembers. After it was all over,

Mrs. Butler, the pianist I told you about, said she'd never seen anything like it in all her born days. Persia even stood there with Smiley, saying "Gladtoseeya!" and shaking hands when everybody left. After all that . . . well, Persia has always been susceptible to spells. After all that, she just fainted away on the ground.

The Fishers of Men carried her to Smiley's wagon. He made them wait outside with her while he went in to "clean up a place for her." Someone was sent for a glass of water but all they could find was what was left in the baptismal, and she flatly refused to drink that!

By the time she had pulled herself together she was alone with the preacher. He pulled himself kinda close to her, like this, and said: "Sister, I have never in all my travels seen anything like you. A blessing, that's what you are, a blessing, and we need people with your spirit. Have you ever thought of spreading the Word?"

When she said no, she hadn't been fifteen miles away from here, he looked at her and said: "Do you know you collected thirty-two dollars and seventy-five cents tonight for them orphans in Ethiopia? That's more than we ever made at one meeting. These are hard times on the Dark Continent and we need every penny we can get."

He kept talking all through that night until he finally asked her to fly with him on the road to Heaven. Couldn't you just die? And he gave her this locket with a picture of his mama inside.

"My mama said, 'Give this locket to the woman you find who can take my place in your heart and God's.' "

He said Persia was the spitting image of his mama—spiritually, that is—and that he wanted her to have the locket as a token of his respect. But I think he had a boxful that he gave out all over. You know people just don't go around giving things out to strangers.

Next thing she knew he was making plans for them to travel together. Preaching from the same pulpit. Persia was so thrilled she started crying and said: "Oh, Smiley. Smiley, I will go to the ends of the earth with you. I will go even to Ethiopia as a missionary."

He said he didn't think *that* would be necessary. There was too much work to be done keeping this territory in line. So naturally she got her hopes up. Wouldn't you? I mean the man did everything but put a wedding ring on her finger. She certainly wouldn't travel with a man unless they was married. So she just played coy and said she'd like to speak to Other-Mama about it.

When she got home, Other-Mama met her at the door. Doe was

jumping up and down clapping her hands and saying, "I'll swan, Persia, you was just grand!"

Loves attention, Persia does, and accepts it like a blue blood. She just sat down very calmly and told them what Reverend Fitts said. Other-Mama said she'd think about it but would prefer them to stay at her house 'cause there was certainly plenty to do around this town without going off.

Then Doe, who never misses a thing, eyes that locket I told you about.

"I'll swan, Persia, what a pretty little thing."

"Reverend Fitts gave it to me. Belonged to his mama," and marches up to her room without turning.

Next day and the rest of the week, all three of them got dressed to the teeth and went to the campgrounds. And each night Persia got up and collected a mint of money for the orphans and, more likely, for Smiley Fitts. They were even given a special pew down front.

Then came Friday night. Just as they started to get dressed, Persia realized it was her night to be hostess at the V.F.W. and there was nobody to take her place. She wouldn't have left them people in the lurch, and that is what I call a good woman. On top of that, Other-Mama got sick from all the excitement and had to stay home. Flu, honey, flu—in the middle of summer. So Persia told Doe to go on and get down there and be sure to find out how much they made for those sweet orphans. Then Persia got dressed and left the house with her dried beans and homemade bingo cards. She's creative, too.

5.

Now, I wasn't told every single detail of what happened next except that Persia came home at twelve o'clock midnight screaming bloody murder. Other-Mama nearly had heart failure and tripped down the steps, which is probably what caused her broken hip and not my roller skate as she claims.

Persia just kept saying, "Where is she! Where is that hussy?"

Went crazy, that's what she did.

It seems that Aunt Persia was walking home from the V.F.W. when she runs into Mrs. Butler, who was singing to herself. She looks at Persia, like this with a smile, and says, "Well, where have you been tonight?"

"I been at the V.F.W. doing my hostess duty," Persia says. And Mrs. Butler rattles something off about how could she have missed that night of all nights.

"Sugar," Mrs. Butler said, "Your little sister is something. She is, indeed. Never heard her say a word till tonight. Bet you put her up to it," and giggles.

"What happened?" Persia asked, getting interested, if you know what I mean.

"Well," Mrs. Butler says, nudging Persia in the side with her elbow (Oh, hon, excuse me. I didn't know you had pleurisy.), "Reverend Fitts just couldn't get anybody to come up to altar tonight. Just didn't have it in him. Preachers are just like actors—some nights they just can't get an audience to lift a polite eye. So your sister, who must've gotten something from you, stands up and says: 'I'll make them repent,' and marches right up that aisle in front of the congregation and tells everything she knows about everybody there. Everything, honey! Did you know that Jane Ellen Knowles had a hys—"

But Persia was running. Gone! Ran straight to that campground without stopping.

When she got there, not a soul was left. She looked around and saw a light coming out of Smiley's wagon. Went right over and ripped back the curtain over the door. And there, right in front of her, was that Reverend Smiley Fitts and my poor Aunt Doe stark naked and looking like two peeled and blushing figs! Down on the floor, Persia saw *her* senior-prom dress rolled in a ball and smelled *her* perfume all over the place. She hadn't even opened it yet! Just bought it that same day. And, if that wasn't enough, Doe was wearing the locket Smiley had given to Persia.

Persia took hold of that girl by the hand and flipped her out of that wagon like a buckwheat cake. Right on her stomach in the dirt. Jumped on her back and started plucking the hairs right out of her head one by one. Beat the living daylights out of her, ripped the locket off her neck and left a red mark on her neck. She kept on slapping her until Doe got up enough strength to knock her off and ran to the bushes without a thread to her name.

Ten minutes later, looking like death warmed over, Doe arrived home saying she'd done nothing to be ashamed of and crying because Persia had pulled out so much hair her scalp was bleeding. Doe had also lost two teeth where Persia had gotten her with a foot which just happened to have a high heel on it.

"I just wanted to find out about the missionaries," she said, and went on upstairs.

That went on all night and into the next morning until Doe left for the dentist in Fort Payne to see about some gold caps. Other-Mama had to go to the doctor for another flu shot and some tranquilizers. And while they were gone, Persia moved all her stuff into the guest room and flushed that new perfume down the commode. Never spoke to Doe again far as I know.

And as for the Reverend Smiley Fitts: There was nothing left on the campgrounds for those rows of folding chairs and wagon tracks. He got out fit to beat the devil and never came back.

Persia did say that about a year later she got a postcard from Hollywood, California, signed S.F., but she didn't tell me what it said. She burned it over the stove and told Mr. Burl, the postmaster, that if he ever delivered another postcard to her from anywhere in God's world, she'd break his neck.

So there you have it and you can believe it or not. And remember you promised not to repeat a word, cross your heart. If you do, I'll deny it to your face and swear I never even knew you were in town. But I know you won't. I can tell. I'm just one of those people who can look into someone's eyes and know whether to pass on or tell them my life story. They've always said I have a sixth sense about people. It's just one of those natural gifts.

Sleeping Soldiers

Andrew Holleran

Andrew Holleran read an early draft of "Sleeping Soldiers" at a meeting of the Violet Quill. But he was not satisfied with the story and put it away until, in preparation for this collection, he rewrote it. It is ironic that the question of gays in the military, a question of some importance in 1968, is still an unresolved issue some twenty-five years later. This is the first publication of "Sleeping Soldiers."

The first thing I noticed about the Army the day we were taken to the reception station was an odd detail: There was no advertising anywhere. We were free of commercials. Beyond the chicken-wire fence, the four-lane highway glittered with the traffic of a rich, well-fed nation of consumers, listening to their radios; inside the fence, it looked, that hot August afternoon, like the Escorial. "Think of the Army," said Nelson as we rode over in the bus, "as an expropriation of Time. Think of it as two years in a monastery." I did. In fact, the reception station reminded me strangely of the austere palace Philip the Second had built on a sunbaked plateau outside Madrid; the same air of simplicity and denial characterized the group of barracks where we were to be prepared for six weeks of Basic Training, the same forlorn emptiness, as we walked across the bleached rectangle of grass picking up the remains of cigarette butts, faded by wind and rain, while our sergeant screamed at us.

Poor we were, stripped of possessions, like men entering an order of discalced friars; by sundown we were seated on the curb outside our barracks with shaved heads, watching the dandruff blow off people's scalps in the soft Southern breeze; not saying the Rosary, but polishing our belt buckles with a gooey white paste called Brasso.

In the upward procession of middle-class life, which consisted, in the sixties, of one segment of education after another—laid end to end, like some chain that would eventually tighten around a career—this scene had no place. You could not get a degree in the Army, is what I thought as I sat on the curb. By 1968, you were supposed to have been excused from the draft because you were already climbing the career ladder, or, as befitted a young man with a future, married, or a father. Getting drafted meant you were none of those: still drifting. Indecisive. Not grown up. Lacking purpose. Getting drafted, I felt certain when it happened, meant you deserved to be: If you weren't sure what you were supposed to do with your life, the Army could use it while you decided.

Or so it seemed toward the end of the war in Vietnam—the collection of American citizens who poured out of the buses at the reception station that morning were an odd bunch of leftovers that only the Army could have mixed, a group whose only common element was that, for some reason, they had been careless, or unlucky, or immature enough to be caught. Poor blacks from the slums of Richmond, Virginia, rich whites from the University of Virginia whose deferments had run out, boys from the farms and small towns of north Florida and south Georgia, had all been reduced to a single standard. In our heavy, starched fatigues, with our dog tags, our shaved heads, we felt, by the end of that first day, like children waiting for the ice-cream truck at dusk— which actually came to sell us cones and Popsicles while the sergeants conferred with one another over their clipboards. It was the sort of crowd where eyeglasses were reassuring; they implied reading, books, a bourgeois life. The first pair of eyeglasses I made friends with belonged to Nelson.

Nelson had just finished law school at the University of Virginia, and came there with a classmate, Tully. Nelson was tall and skinny, with a pinched, birdlike face and a nasal, sarcastic voice. He smoked a lot. Nelson immediately got into a fight with Leathers over a stolen lighter.

Leathers was a small, irritable, easily offended man. The whites of his eyes yellow, his mouth perpetually open, his lower lip glistening as it protruded from a face whose permanent expression was one of alarm and umbrage, he had been watching with great concentration the way Nelson held his cigarette—between the tips of his thumb and forefinger, with the wrist cocked—and immediately accused Nelson of racism when Nelson claimed that Leathers had stolen his lighter. Within two minutes they were on the ground trying to push each other's faces into the dirt before others pulled them apart, while I sat there, stunned by the spectacle of something I'd not seen since I was nine: two boys having it out. "You sayin' that 'cause I'm black!" shouted Leathers in his high, hoarse voice as he dusted himself off. "No," said Nelson, in a trembling voice, as he slapped dust from his fatigues, "I'm saying it because you're a thief."

"I ain't no thief!" barked Leathers, as he watched Nelson resume his seat on the curb between me and Tully.

"You are," said Nelson, lighting a cigarette. "You're a mendacious, self-pitying filcher of other people's property."

Leathers put his hands on his hips, looked down at Nelson, and said: "Why you hold your cigarette like that? Why you talk that pussy talk?"

Nelson stared at him. "You mean words you can't understand? Ah," he sighed. "The last resort of the self-centered boor! Words he does not understand are *effeminate*. Words that are the very simulacrum of Western history," he said, pressing the advantage he'd just discovered, "the very civilization in whose penumbra you now lurk." He blew a stream of smoke out and tapped his ash with an exaggerated gesture into the gutter. "You are a paradigm of resentment, Leathers. You are Caliban, and you stole my silver lighter."

"You lucky I didn't steal your dick!" screamed Leathers, his single gold tooth catching what remained of the light. "You can *have* my dick," said Nelson, "if you'll let me Brasso your tooth!" "My *tooth*!" yelled Leathers. "Man, come on," said Leathers's friend Checo in his rich drawl, pulling Leathers up the sidewalk toward the barracks, "he jus' crazy."

"Think of the Army," said Nelson, in the serene voice of someone reciting a mantra, "as an expropriation of time. And sanity."

He was right, of course: Not only was the reception station devoid of advertising, and adult civility, it seemed to be devoid of everything that made 1968, 1968. These plain wooden barracks, this bleak rectangle of lawn, had last been used for the Korean War. The ice-cream truck that came by, complete with recorded jingle, had disappeared from most American towns more than a decade before. Across the street, a shirtless, muscular sergeant was polishing the fenders of a bright-red 1957 gull-winged Chevrolet convertible, while the radio he'd set on the steps played Beach Boys songs that came to us on the summer wind. The Army had both expropriated, and scrambled, Time: We were back in the fifties, which only increased our sense of disorientation, the feeling that we had been pulled back from adulthood, inducted into an institution as hierarchical as the medieval Church, as ancient as the landscape itself: the flocks of blackbirds flying across the reddened sky, the kudzu on the oaks in the ravine, the fact that we were going to bed at sundown.

In fact, we lived that week the life people connected to the land live—not the technological, advertising-soaked society outside the chicken-wire fence: up before dawn, in the cool, humid darkness, to run through the forests of pine, marching over the hot, baked earth to stand in line for belts, canteens, boots, duffel bag, sitting in amphitheatres in the woods while sergeants lectured us as if we were at summer camp, the sergeants themselves in round, broad-brimmed hats that made them look like forest rangers. Push-ups on the scalding asphalt, or forest floor, obstacle courses like those some playmates' father had built for them in the woods, marches through the ravine in clouds of dust stirred by the platoon ahead of us, sudden fistfights, or wrestling matches, like the one Nelson and Leathers engaged in our second afternoon, over the matter of Nelson's lighter, all gave life a sort of Boy Scout simplicity and left us, by the time dinner was done and we sat on the curb waiting for the ice-cream truck, so tired it was easiest to just sit there when everyone else went inside—to brush their teeth, take a shower, and become embroiled in the argument over which floor was entitled to use the buffer first to polish the linoleum we were allowed to walk on only in our socks—like Buddhists who must leave their shoes at the temple door—so that it would shine sufficiently the next day to earn our sergeant's approval.

To argue over the buffer seemed the height of inanity—of the childish silliness in which we felt no more than nine; so Nelson and I sat there till the very last minute before turning in to the barracks, which, the moments before Lights Out, was always as loud and frantic as a train station at rush hour. The two floors of bunks, about equally divided between whites and blacks of every hue, social and educational background, comprised every sort of personality—from an exceptionally polite mulatto CPA who almost never spoke to a boastful, streetwise boy like Checo, who never stopped talking, from members of Charlottesville fraternities to poor boys from farms in southeast Georgia. The collision made everyone nervous. It sounded like a convention; even after Lights Out, when, that first night, the farmers had to listen, groaning, while Checo shocked them with boasts of his prowess at looting TV stores during the Richmond riots—and cunnilinguis—

evoked in the same lyrical, nostalgic tone. Finally someone told Checo to shut up, and silence descended over everything, and I was able to find a quiet moment to forget where I'd ended up—returned to adolescence, back at boarding school, once more in the company of men.

It was an old trick, in fact, I'd learned at school—of savoring that half hour in the dark before one fell asleep, or waking up a bit early before the bell rang. Here in the Army there was one more escape hatch: Around three a.m. every night, I was wakened by Nelson to stand fire guard. This meant sitting at the top of the stairs for an hour while everyone else slept. Like so many duties there—policing the lawn for litter, say—this task was symbolic, and psychological; the fire we were guarding against did not seem likely in that place. But it amounted, I saw immediately, to an hour of solitude—a way to consciously enjoy what one otherwise would have to let pass unnoticed. The minute Nelson tapped me on the shoulder each night that week, and whispered my name, I felt I'd swum up from the depths of the sea, and surfaced in a cool, dark cave; a marine grotto; a place far, far from the Army. Even the air was cooler, moister, as I put on my fatigues and, after taking a drink from the fountain at the top of the stairs, assumed my post on the landing, while my predecessor went back to his bunk.

He went back to his bunk only to get his shaving kit and then returned to the brightly lighted empty latrine to shave—a chore that, next morning in the same room, crowded, noisy, frantic, would be far from enjoyable. I started shaving at night, too. As did Tully, who followed me at four. And the sergeant who polished his car every day at dusk, and sat up all night across the lawn in the administrative barracks, pulling the last duty he'd ever have to perform—for the word was that both he and the cook, back from a tour of Vietnam, had only this week remaining in the Army. The same unit processing us in was processing them out. He came up the stairs, out of the moonlight, his dog tags gleaming against his bare chest, that first night; asked if there was hot water; and, when I nodded, came up the stairs without another word, until I stood up, not knowing if I should salute, and he told me in a dark, impatient voice to "Sit down!"

There was no rank at three-thirty in the morning in a latrine. Each shaver stood before the brightly lighted mirror with intent, self-absorbed concentration: the sergeant—not a limb or eyelash missing after a year in Vietnam; amazingly intact—and the law students. Outside, a moon floated over the umbrella pines in the ravine, and the branches of an oleander bush slapped fitfully against the barracks in the breeze. A tiny stream of water ran from each faucet. What was rushed and often bloody in the morning was at this hour a slow, hypnotic ritual. The shaving cream was lime-scented: some inexpensive stuff which stood for the whole wasteful disposable culture outside the chicken-wire fence. When I pressed the button, it emerged in a white cloud as thick as whipped cream, and I smoothed it on my jaw with a tranquillity felt at no other time. When I rinsed it off, the cheap lime perfume remained on my fingertips, and I thought in the quiet of all those people sleeping: There is always the pleasure of the senses.

Then I returned my razor and shaving cream to the footlocker beside my bunk, and took my place again at the top of the stairs. Nelson even had a cigarette before turning in; sat with me as he smoked and speculated about ways to get out of the Army. We never spoke to the sergeant. We dared not. We merely watched him, head back, drawing the razor up his thick, lathered neck, and said "Good night" when he finally passed us at the top of the stairs, muttering the number of days he had left ("Four to go"), then walking down and out into the moonlight through the door. In the morning, I used the extra time to read. Nelson and Tully went off to an abandoned barracks next to ours, and took a nap, while the rest of the platoon competed with one another for washbasins, toilets, and shower stalls. Even so, most everyone was down on the steps, dressed and ready to go, when Nelson and Tully came walking back out of the fog to get their canteens and belts and stand inspection. The third morning this happened, Leathers spat on the ground as he watched them approach, and said: "Here come the homos."

The first time Nelson heard this, it startled him, as had Leather's calling words he did not understand "pussy talk," and then he decided to turn it to his advantage. Each morning we ran two miles in the predawn darkness, singing a song with the refrain "Jody's got your girl and gone!" (One more reason for us to feel solidarity, one more thing they'd taken away: your girlfriend, now in someone else's arms.) Nelson, running beside Leathers, mouthed a kiss in Leathers's direction after each refrain; and later that afternoon, when Leathers glanced at him during a lecture about bayonet ("What is the spirit of the bayonet?" "To *kill*!"), he mimed the words "I love you." Nelson stared at Leathers every chance he could; let Leathers call him "Miss Nelson" as we sat on the curb after supper, watching the trainees outside the phone booths waiting to call home, while the sergeant and the cook polished the convertible. Nelson explained to Tully in a voice loud enough for Leathers to hear that he had no girlfriend at home to call, and that the greatest warriors of ancient Greece had been lovers who fought at Thermopylae so that they would bring honor to their beloved; while Leathers muttered, ''Now they *really* talkin' pussy talk,'' and spat on the ground.

''You know you ain't suppose to be in the Army,'' Leathers finally said. ''You s'pose to be discharged.''

''For loving another man?'' said Nelson, raising his eyebrows. ''Don't you think it's better for men to love one another than to kill?''

''I'm gonna kill *you*,'' said Leathers.

''Well, that's the problem,'' said Nelson. ''You're going to have to kill a lot more people besides! You're not in the Army to wax floors, Leathers. Remember what Sergeant Clark told us today at bayonet drill. We are being paid to *kill*. Tully and I represent the higher consciousness. We are the true revolutionaries. We prefer to *love*.''

Leathers spat on the sidewalk. ''I better not catch you lookin' at me if I be takin' a crap tonight.''

''But Leathers,'' said Nelson in a hurt voice. ''The sight of you taking a crap, *and* the Sistine Chapel, are the two things I think of every night before I close my eyes.''

''Shit!'' said Leathers as he walked away.

Eventually, the last holdouts started to go in to brush their teeth; the blackbirds flew up from the tops of the pine trees, and we watched the sergeant and the cook draw widening circles with their chamois cloths on the fenders of the Chevrolet, while Nelson pondered the fact that the pair had only two days left in the Army. It was a hard concept to grasp: All that remained for them to do was drive out of the reception station, and resume a life we had just surrendered. ''Two days, then one day,'' Nelson murmured as we sat on the curb, discussing his latest idea for bringing his own servitude to an end: allowing Leathers's fantasy (that he and Tully were lovers) to reach official ears. ''Of course everyone would think I was queer,'' he said, ''which wouldn't be so good. But why do I care? I know I'm not. It's only queers who have to worry what other people think about them.'' ''If I were queer,'' said Tully in a husky voice, ''I'd probably want to stay in the Army. It's all guys.'' ''That's right,'' said Nelson. ''But I'm not. And I want to get out. Now,'' he said. Which put him beside me later that night at the top of the stairs, staring at the rectangle of moonlight on the first floor in which the sergeant would appear. When he did, with his dop kit, his camouflage fatigues, his dog tags, clipped brown mustache, he did not ask if we had hot water; he simply came up the stairs, two at a time. Just as he reached the top, Nelson stood up and opened his mouth to speak. Or so I thought—till I saw the real cause of his parted lips: Leathers, standing at the edge of the darkness in which the rest of the floor was plunged, eyes glaring, saying: "Sergeant! Sergeant! I got sumpin' to tell you! This dude—Nelson—he doin' the Wild Thing with Tully *er*very morning in the empty barracks!" (For some reason Checo and Leathers both said "*er*verybody" instead of "everybody.") "They're queer!"

The sergeant turned, looked at Nelson briefly, then said to Leathers: "So what? In Nam, trainee, they don't care what you are when they shoot at you. Go back to bed." And he walked into the latrine. Leathers stood there for a moment, his lower lip protruding, staring at the sergeant, while the sergeant lowered his face and splashed water all over it. "Shit!" said Leathers, and disappeared back into the darkness.

The same darkness swallowed up a disgusted Nelson a moment later—and then, after he'd finished his last shave in the Army, like some bridegroom before his wedding day, the sergeant passed me, pronouncing, as he did every night, the number of days he had left ("One!"). Then he went downstairs, burnished by the Asian sun, and disappeared. At the base of the stairs—that rectangle of bleached, moonlit grass—the night itself seemed to be flowing, like a river, past the steps; a river that lay between our barracks and the one he'd returned to. The water fountain switched on, then off; the heavy branches of the oleander slapped against the barracks in the breeze, with an almost sexual insistence; as, across the rectangle of grass, the sergeant watched his last hours in the company trickle away. The next morning, he and the cook would drive off in the red convertible, with a string of cans someone had tied to the bumper, like a bridal couple on their honeymoon. Once free, one black, one white, their lives, so close, so intimate now, would go their separate ways; their nuptial vehicle taking them not to a life together, which the Army had created, but a divorce. Leaving the rest of us here, where the light spilling out of the latrine illuminated only the landing, part of the polished aisle between the bunks, a few footlockers, and—like those figures on the Sistine Chapel Nelson had used to make fun of Leathers—the hand or forearm, the bare chest or white T-shirt, of soldiers sprawled in careless slumber; soldiers who, I realized now, could all be divided into those who had lives to return to—like the sergeant, presumably—and those who did not—like myself. Which left our sole connection the river of moonlight flowing between us, the only two people awake in this place on this August night.

And with that, my own sense of purposelessness began to crumble—or rather, into the vacuum of identity which the reception station had so efficiently created, something strange was beginning to seep. What was beginning at the reception station, I understood years later, was the eventual removal of a fake identity; a removal that allowed something else—refused when it was first offered, perhaps, back in the *real* fifties—to grow. Mute, immobile, stripped of their carping, demands, egotism, all of them, like me, about to be jilted by the sergeant, the people sleeping on the bunks I passed on my way to wake Tully up seemed to me, deep in the August night, the dog tags on their bare chests gleaming, almost beloved.

Slashed to Ribbons, in Defense of Love

Felice Picano

The writers of the Violet Quill often chronicled the lives of gay men who lived in the fast world of high fashion, high art, and big money, where beauty was a commodity that could be bought and sold on the not-so-open market. "Slashed to Ribbons, in Defense of Love," the title story of Picano's short-story collection, is a dark tale of how the deadly cost of such a life was glamorized in the minds of those who lived it.

"It's about time you decided to wake up! We have a brunch at one o'clock, as you very well know."

Gary was up, dressed, sitting across the room sipping coffee and smoking a cigarillo. He'd been out: the Sunday *Times* sat unopened on a nearby chair.

"It's almost twelve now. A cab will take at least fifteen minutes. If we can find one. Go shower. You know you take forever in there."

Behind Gary's head, sunlight came in through the skylighted dressing room and pushed through the flecked fibers of the shoji screen. Spence could see the gold flecking on the rice paper very clearly today. The undulating fields of lacquered flowers were backlighted—bright as persimmons. Gary's face was in shadow.

"I want you to know beforehand that this brunch is extremely important to me. Arnie has invited Seitelman, the Oriental Art expert. I've been trying to get near him for months. I want him to come look at those *Monoyama* scrolls I picked up last month."

Gary exhaled blue smoke. It floated into the sunlight, turned gray then yellow then gray again. He exhaled again and a second cloud

151

rose to meet the first in a billow. It spread thinly, forming a tiny tornado around the head of the smiling Shinto statue precariously perched on a wall shelf. The Shinto idol kept smiling; it never seemed to notice the smoke descend again and form a flat halo directly over Gary's head. Spence noticed, though. He laughed.

"I'm not kidding, Spence. Arnie's gone to a lot of trouble to get Seitelman. And it will take a lot of tact to keep him there. So I don't want any interference from you. Is that clear?"

Gary exhaled forcefully and broke the halo. He began picking at the edge of the cup he was drinking from, as though it were crusted with something. It was his favorite china—from the Northern Sung—and invaluable. Spence never touched it. He only used china that could be dropped: or thrown. Gary frowned. Spence turned over in bed.

"As soon as you've met him, go to the other end of the room or table or wherever we are. And stay there. And, Spence, do try to keep your pin-sized knowledge of art to yourself. No one is interested, I assure you."

If Gary weren't dressed, if he were still in bed, he'd be vulnerable. Spence was bigger, stronger. He'd roll Gary over, pin him down, wrestle with him: anything to make him shut up. Sometimes fucking helped. But Gary wouldn't fuck now. He was dressed already. He'd been up for hours. Up, smoking one cigarillo after another. Up, drinking one cup of coffee after another. Up, scheming about the art and Seitelman. Up, thinking, thinking, thinking.

"I don't even know why Arnie and Rise invited you. I suppose as a compliment to me. Either that, or they think it's the enlightened thing to do."

Enlightened, my ass! Spence thought. Ah, enlightenment. Spence could see it all. He and Gary were on the Johnny Carson show. Johnny was asking Gary about his career as New York's most successful male model in decades. Gary was saying how boring it all was—boring and superficial. The only real benefits, he would admit, were the money he made, the investments—the hotel in the Colorado Rockies, the model agency he owned on the Coast—and the freedom it gave him. He was such a prig he wouldn't realize Johnny was looking for a sensational exposé, hinting at it with all those sly innuendoes and lousy one-liners. Gary would begin talking about Oriental Art, detailing the difference between *Kano* and *Genre*, and those with *Ukiyo-E*. Johnny and his audience would be bored stiff. In desperation, the talk-show host would turn to Spence and ask if he shared Gary's interests. "Only fucking,'' Spence would answer. Tumult. Delight. The camera would remain on Spence, as he went on, describing the last orgy he attended, holding Johnny and the audience rapt. Enlightenment ruled all!

''Don't think I'm going to ask you to behave at this brunch. I know that will only incite you to turn it into a three-ring circus.''

Spence turned over again. The sunlight was above the shoji screen now, creeping towards him along the arabesques of the Shiraz carpet. More sun came in through the side windows, lightening up the dark corner where Gary sat in his Regency wing-tipped chair, next to the little Hepplewhite table. Everything Gary had was either antique or invaluable. Everything but Spence.

''Seitelman doesn't socialize much. Arnie says he's very sensitive. So even you can fathom that this brunch ought to be as pleasant as possible.''

Gary's head was in the light now. He shaded his eyes. His arms, neck and face were a perfect tan from Long Island summers and Caribbean winters: so evenly tanned he could be a Coppertone advertisement. Spence was tan too. Spence also passed his summers at Amagansett, his winters in Dominique or Palm Springs or St. Thomas: they were all interchangeable by now.

''The other guests either know you already, or have been warned. Try not to lecture Kate Halliday about Jung today. She's the psychoanalyst. Not you.''

Spence leaned over the bed, opened one of the drawers built into the bedboard, and lifted out a flowered *cloisonné* box. A gift from Gary. Everything was a gift from Gary. A tiny silver spoon was attached to the side of the box by a silver turnaway hasp. Spence removed the spoon, opened the box, dipped the spoon and lifted away a tiny mountain of snow-white powder. Gary always kept cocaine in the house. He said it was the only civilized drug: it cost an arm and a leg, and you needed a bushel basket of it to get hooked. Spence propped himself up against the pillows, held a finger to one nostril, inhaled through the other one; then reversed the process.

''Christ! Spence! You're not even awake, and you're already into that!''

Spence had closed the box. Reconsidering, he reopened it and snorted twice more. Then, carefully—he was already feeling the rush—he closed the box, and replaced it in the drawer. Then he slumped back.

''Didn't you have enough last night? You were like a maniac. Chasing that dark little number around with your spoon all night. He was covered with it when he left.''

Wasn't it Beckett who said that a light wasn't necessary, that a taper would do to live in strangeness, if it burned faithfully? Yes. Beckett. A taper and, Spence added, a spoon of coke.

The sun was playing hide-and-go-seek in the infrequent gray hairs among the chestnut brown of Gary's head. They would glint for an instant, then die away, then glint somewhere else, and die away. Little signals. Maybe a glint was all you needed. And a spoon of coke, of course.

''I hope you're not going to wear these filthy denims again?''

Gary threw the pants at Spence. They hit the side of the bed and fell. Motes of dust had shaken off them: the motes rose in the air and performed an intricate ballet to a silent score.

''When was the last time you washed them? People know you're coming a hundred yards away. You have so many new, clean slacks in the closet, Spence. Why do you insist on wearing these?''

Spence wondered if dust motes had senses of perception.

''I don't care if you make a good impression today. I would rather you made no impression at all. But there are certain rules of hygiene. I'm surprised you don't have lice. And those people you call your friends are no better. God, what a bunch! The Allies' liberation of Bergen-Belsen couldn't have been more unsavory than that party you took me to last week.''

Could dust motes be sentient? Even intelligent? Look how they danced! Spence shook the denims once more. More dust motes flew up into the sunlight. God they were lovely when they danced. Stately.

''While Seitelman and I are discussing our business, why not talk to Rise? She always asks about you. She wants to help you. She really does know a lot of useful people.''

Could man communicate with dust motes? They had to be intelligent to dance like that. So organized!

''Rise thinks I'm holding you back from doing something wonderful. Me?! If they only knew how shiftless you are. Someone who needs an hour just to get out of bed.''

Spence would ask the dust motes to dance for Gary.

''You have to begin to do something with your life. You can't just hang around here and party all the time.''

No. Gary wouldn't recognize a million dust motes dancing for him.

"I'm not saying you have to be a great success. You don't even have to earn a lot of money. But just do something!"

If communicable, and friendly, the dust motes might be persuaded to dance around Gary's head. Then, one by one, without his noticing it, they could enter his ears, his nose, his mouth. One by one. Little by little. So subtly Gary wouldn't notice a thing, until it was too late. At first he would cough a little. Then he'd begin to gag. His multicolored eyes would begin to fill up with tears. Then he'd really begin choking. His handsome, craggy features would be distorted in agony. It would be a sad struggle.

"If you weren't bright, it would be different. But you are. Imaginative too. Why I've never met anyone with so many crazy ideas as you have. Write them down. Draw them up. Make them work for you."

No fingerprints on the throat. No murder weapon at all. Spence wouldn't even have to get out of bed. The perfect murder. He could see the headlines already: "Wealthy Male Model Dies Mysteriously in Uptown Triplex. No Clues!"

Spence would confess, naturally. He'd call the press and explain how he'd entered into a conspiracy with the dust motes. How they'd waited patiently for his signal to attack. He'd explain that dust motes are not only sentient, but intelligent too. He'd reveal their highly organized cultural heritage—based on their major pastime, the art of the sunlight dance.

"We could turn the greenhouse into a studio for you. We hardly ever use it. And that big closet, that could be used as a darkroom. Arnie would help find you a distributor. He knows everyone."

At first his confession would be ignored. Spence might be asked to take a lie-detector test, a mental examination, even. He'd pass it with flying colors, return to the triplex—his, now that Gary was gone— he'd have almost unlimited resources. Once home, he'd contact the dust motes again. He'd study their dance patterns, draw diagrams—he could see them as variations of the double helix already. It would take years of study to get to understand their habits, their customs. But it would be worth it.

"You know I'll pay for whatever lessons or extra equipment you need. It's just that you have to do something, Spence. Man cannot live by partying alone."

He'd compile his findings, edit them carefully and send an article to *Scientific American*. They'd be impressed. They'd print it with four-color diagrams and half-page photographs he'd taken of the dances. In an editorial, he'd be hailed as a pioneer. He'd call his new science Motology.

"Jack and I talked about you last week at Ron's. He thinks this crazy life you're leading is simply compensation for having no real motivation. Everyone needs a goal."

Spence would go beyond science. He'd wait until his work was fully accepted. Then he'd reveal the true meaning of the dust motes' dance—how it embodied their philosophy of life: endless flowing, total dance. He'd try to show how this could be of supreme advantage to people too. He'd be the first and foremost Theomotologist in history.

"Without a goal, you're working against yourself all the time. Kate said so too. And she ought to know."

Naturally, Theomotology would attract many others. To stay ahead, Spence would specialize. He was certain the dust motes held the secret of levitation. He'd learn it from their elders, and apply it. N.A.S.A. would approach him. Imagine floating immense spacecraft on molecular motology. "Man Flies to Pluto on Dust!" the headline would read in *The New York Times*.

"You don't have to be self-defeating, you know. You and I aren't in competition. I'm done now. Retired. It's your turn, Spence."

On Pluto, Spence would make his greatest discoveries: he'd find out how dust motes propagate. Beginning as nonessential carbon crystals from pollution, they develop externally—like all crystalline forms—by simple geometric accretion. On Pluto, of course, there would be no pollution. The motes would have to evolve along other lines to survive.

"What kind of life is this for you, Spence? I have my friends, my businesses, my collections. What do you have?"

At first the adjustment would be difficult—all selective evolution was. Millions, perhaps trillions of them would fail to develop and perish. But one day it would just happen. One mote would make the changeover, and discover how simple it was. The others would follow. Spence would be hailed as a new Darwin.

"Spence, are you listening to me? I asked you a question."

Spence would remain on Pluto. He'd crystallize himself.

"Spence? You haven't fallen asleep again?"

He already suspected the minuscule viruses found in every living body were crystal compounds. He would use them as a point of focus for the process.

"I see you moving. You're awake. Are you getting up today?"

It would take years, possibly decades for the process of autocrystallization to work. Meanwhile he would derive nourishment from airtight gardens in which only nitrogen-high greens were grown. He suspected the crystallization would require absolute stillness.

"It's ten minutes to one, Spence. I'm going. If you aren't getting up, I'm going alone."

Spence might be four hundred years old when his last remaining living tissue—the stomach lining—crystallized.

"And when I get home, you and I are going to fill out that application for registration on the back of the Film School catalogue. If you insist on acting like a child, you'll be treated like one."

On Earth, Spence would be a legend.

"Since classes won't begin for another month or two, you'll have time to get a job. I know plenty of people who need work done in their gardens, or in their apartments. That'll keep you busy."

On Pluto, Spence would be metamorphosized as pure crystal. He'd be immortal.

"I've put up with your nonsense long enough. I will not have you laying around the house stoned all day. And, if you don't care for my plans, you know where the door is."

Spence would disperse into many smaller crystals: all of them immortal.

"That's it. Either go to work, or get out!"

Millions of crystals levitating around the universe.

"Spence! Are you listening? Are you?"

"Fuck you!" Spence said.

"I see it's clear, then. I'll be back by four. You have three hours to make up your mind. And make up that bed when you decide to get out of it."

Gary left the room. A few minutes later, Spence heard closet doors crack open and shut downstairs. Then the front door slammed.

Gary had never talked like that before—never about going to work, or leaving. He must be nervous as hell about meeting this Seitelman. Perhaps if their meeting worked out all right at brunch, Gary would forget what he said, forget this morning's hysteria. Fat chance! That would probably only convince him he was right. Gary was so terrified of being thought inconsistent, he always did precisely what he said he would do: even if it went against his best interest. Ah, well, Spence thought. He'd at least have three more hours of peace. He'd make breakfast, listen to some music, enjoy himself while he still could—until the axe fell.

The sun had already reached halfway up the sheets. Spence threw them off onto the floor. It was warm—hot, really. Hot as Mexico. The way the sun advanced along the room, it would take another hour for him to be completely bathed in sunlight. He wouldn't even have to go out on to the terrace to sun today.

It was hot as Mexico.

He could feel the rough stone surface of the ceremonial altar cool against his back. It almost made him forget the itching hemp he'd been tied with, hand and foot, to the altar. He was atop the highest pyramid in Xochimilco. Above him, the sky was clear blue, cloudless. Below him, invisible, but known from previous occasions when he'd merely witnessed, the immense stone-flagged plaza was filled with people decked out in holiday finery, covered in flowers, chanting. Pennants flew from poles and towers. Children danced in imitation of old legends. Instruments of all sorts whistled, chimed, clacked and stuttered.

His body was the focal point of twenty thousand eyes, of ten thousand minds. He knew, as they knew, that when the sun had completely illuminated his figure through the astronomically precise arch above him, that everyone would suddenly go quiet in the plaza. Everyone would know that the Vernal Equinox had arrived, bringing life again, and once more demanding its payment from them. He would be the absolute beginning of their year: a dot on their calendar: the focus of their collective soul. When the sunlight reached his eyes, the new chant would begin: the people's plea for the sun to accept their votive.

Amidst the hypnotic droning voices, the Priests would gather around him, their gilded masks blinding him with reflections. They too would begin their guttural prayers to the Solar Deity, asking for blessings, good harvest, victory in battle.

When the sunlight had warmed to tips of his long hair, he would know the time was fulfilled. He would be the center of the people, the nation, the world, the universe. He would see the primitive obsidian knife raised in the air, see its final fatal glitter, see it descend and tear out his bowels.

From *The Family of Max Desir*

Robert Ferro

The Family of Max Desir *(1983) was Robert Ferro's second novel, and unlike* The Others, The Family of Max Desir *was highly autobiographical. Ferro and Michael Grumley often divided their literary and family lives from their sexual lives by assuming the names Max and Mickey for their sexual prowlings. Max and Nick are clearly based on that other life. The description of John Desir's house—with its large dining room and two-story den—is an accurate description of Michael Ferro's home. However, Robert Ferro and Michael Grumley did not meet in an Italian prison, but rather at the Iowa Writers' Workshop.*

It seemed a change of venue was needed now that they were going to be a pair, and at Lydia's suggestion and with her help in finding an apartment, they moved to Rome, into a *superattico* near Piazza Navona. To the antiquarian on the ground floor and the local shopkeepers they were brothers, or at least cousins, but likely, as foreigners, to be anything at all. Lydia, with her extravagant costumes and veils, her mute chauffeur, fooled no one. The glint of adoration in everyone's eye when Max and Nick saw her to her car suddenly burst into a flame of respect that soon engulfed the neighborhood. Any official connection might have set them apart; that they should know the sister of the President marked them as *pezzi grossi*. In the market they were addressed as doctor and professor. The antiquarian, seizing a small opportunity, inquired if they had all the furniture they needed for their new apartment.

It was a grand little place with balconies off every room, totally empty. They refused Lydia's offer to swing a few things through the window by crane, the staircase being too narrow for her idea of furniture. Instead they went to the flea market at Porta Portese, Lydia dressed as an English lady and speaking Italian like Ruth Draper. Gorgeous junk accumulated in their wake; when assembled, these objects gave the apartment a religious air, as in the public rooms of a convent, or the sitting room of a priest. Green lacquer walls, extricated grudgingly from the Italian house painter, threw every odd, aged piece into crisp relief—the candlesticks filched from country churches, a marble dog, a one-eyed Saint Agnes, hands clasped miserably before her as if in desperation over her missing eye. A couturier friend of Lydia's who was redoing his studio sent over fifty or sixty varicolored silk cushions no longer needed. This bright pile, in Max's fantasy, might better have been spread upon blazing desert sands beside a passing caravan. Out of the silent, attenuated riot of camels and cloth steps Nick, the dark herdsman. The hot sun through the open windows strikes their backs, the old furniture like bark beside their smooth young skin. Except for food or Lydia's arrangements, they might never have gone out.

His parents' letters from home shrieked with silent alarm. Moved to Rome! Might stay indefinitely! His father took the unusual step of writing to Max directly. Was this the moment to push the bird from the nest? Mr. Desir, larger bird, even threatened to fly over personally if not told immediately what was going on.

So tell him, Nick said. Call him up. Write him a letter. You're with me now.

Impossible to call, only slightly less difficult to put into words, they worked on the reply message together, as they now did everything together. They mentioned *La Stella Nera*, Lydia's help, their intention to stay together always. John received the letter like a cannonball catcher on an off night—not without temporary damage to the midsection. He missed the niceties, the attempts at gentleness, the wish to be accepted, grasping only the headlines of the situation: *Son Gay, Father Distraught.*

Mr. Desir wrote back that he should never have allowed Max to go to Florence in the first place. This had been the basic mistake for which he took all the blame. But to be homosexual was one thing; to be an expatriate was quite another, although perhaps in an unsavory way they were linked after all. In any event, when was he, when were *they*, coming home?

Oh not for years, darling, Lydia exclaimed when told the facts. Home to what? she demanded; to the ideas and sentiments of Queen

Victoria? Let them work it out on their own for a while, in the abstract. You can't rush this sort of thing with Americans.

John wrote, No matter what, you're my son, and Max's allowance continued to arrive each month at the Banco di Roma.

Nick began an acting career with interviews with several Italian directors—set up of course by Lydia. He got extra work immediately, which led to small parts and actual scenes. His good looks were smoothed out by the camera into idealized perfection. You wondered about the director's taste and priorities in letting such a face flash by without lingering; or so Max thought, turning to Nick in the darkened theater with a smile, luxuriating in the mercury profile of his own film star. On occasion in the days of Cinecittà, a studio car would come for him early in the morning. If it were Marilyn Monroe getting into a limousine at five in the morning, Nick said, she would be carrying a pillow and practically walking in her sleep.

A woman named Isabella cleaned the apartment three times a week, a job that consisted mainly of chasing dust mice across the empty floors on drafts from the balcony doors, and of preparing something like eggplant parmigiana or soup for lunch. They sat down to a meal served by a maid in a dining room in their own home, in a place at any rate which they had made themselves, *bent* on inventing a reasonable replica of life either as they had lived it as children or seen it in movies or dreams.

They settled in. This meant ordering suits and buying engraved stationery at Pineider. Max wrote stories. Nick joined a theater company that put on plays in English.

From the railings of their several balconies, set into the mansard roof so as to cut the streets from view, they held each other by the waist and looked out over the rooftops, at the tower of this, the dome of that, at the complacent neutrality of Rome. In the street they were foreigners of consequence; up here they were naked athletes of love, sailing over everything.

Max had been infatuated before this but had never got beyond the first, unrequited, reeflike stages of love. The dynamics of falling in love—so stormy, humiliating, exhilarating and changeable—were now replaced with those of *being* in love, which brought a sense of calm, the image of smooth turquoise water and a pearl beach, a lagoon of ease. This process seemed to have happened on its own.

He was the first to fall. Thereafter he wove a web of sexual and emotional enticement, binding Nick to him in tiny exquisite ways. He angled, as if for a huge fish, the bait being completion, union, the glamour of like minds and bodies, the promise of ambition, the sweetness of constant satisfaction. Every few days Max asked Nick what he wanted, what he missed, regretted, lacked. Max said he would find it, invent it, create it; or if it offended, strip it from his act, like an ugly prop or costume. They must talk. They must identify themselves to each other. They must be clever about their love, avoiding the bone-littered snares and traps set out by a jealous world.

Nick at first did not like to speak of any point further than two weeks in the future. A few years in New York had made him leery of plans, and alert and sensitive to possessiveness. He did not like taking showers together because of the overload of information and sensation—two elements at once. The discovery that he was occasionally skittish, to the edge of paranoia, meant that, at one point, probably in the aforementioned New York, he had been frightened by something, never specified. This weakness was visible only now and then; to Max it meant Nick needed him. He saw it the way he sometimes noticed a tiny scar on Nick's scalp, when the wind blew his hair up in a particular way.

It helped, it seemed, to have met in a foreign country where it was obvious, as it might not even have been clear at home, that they were alone and on their own. Nothing else interested them particularly. Each was incredibly vivid to the other, each being the one point of focus in the other's frame, a focus occasionally replaced on their walks through the city by the details on a monument of antiquity. But only for a moment. Always their attention snapped back to the other's face, to the nape of the neck, the fascinating, specieslike autonomy of the beautiful hands, the sweet, level connection of the eyes.

Lilo in Florence had lied, to intense sexual effect: *Te amo. Ti voglio bene.* Nick was the first to say it in English, the first perhaps ever to feel that way about Max. Max thought at the time that loving might almost have been enough. But being loved in return swept him away completely, and for good. He thought it was as if someone had put a spell on him, that he must always love whoever should be the first to love him back.

Nick loved Lydia like a mother. They had met on the Florentine circuit—the same one Max had glimpsed—which tended to throw together Florence's most sophisticated residents and her best-looking tourists. Nick had gone higher and Lydia had come down a bit, and they adored each other. Nick said they had not slept together nor had they ever considered it. Lydia was his glamorous mother, he her gorgeous son. Had his parents not still been living, back in Iowa, she'd have adopted him legally. Lydia appealed not only to the boy but to the actor in Nick. Her life had been dramatic even in the days before her brother's administration. She gave Nick a wonderful part to play, the cherished of the rich and sophisticated. In return he gave her the constant reciprocation of a quick, sensitive mind and the glamour of his stunning looks.

For man or woman, you're the ideal mate, Max said.

Nick had come to Europe during the first wave of its rediscovery by American youth in the sixties. He had put himself through college in a leisurely way, that is, through six colleges in five states and Mexico, moving on at will, finishing in New York City with, in the end, a philosophy degree from CCNY. He had known of his attraction to and for men since the age of nine, in the days when a man could take you for a ride in his automobile, have sex, and not kill you. During and after the six colleges, he hitchhiked through most of the United States; and then, rather naturally, he moved on to Europe, keeping it simple, traveling like a tourist of the later, *second* wave of discovery— the backpackers and hitchhikers, those seekers-after-good on their long way to India and Nepal. Nick was in no particular hurry, took no particular direction. He appreciated the hospitality of local tricks. The idea that London, Paris, Munich, Hamburg had dealt evenly with young men like him for centuries inspired confidence. He had the feeling that if he wandered from place to place with an open mind and high expectations, important and lucky things would happen to him.

In Florence he was whisked off the street and into Lydia's presence. The combination of shyness, good looks and sophistication in a tourist charmed her. They became friends. She found him a job as secretary to an English novelist so that he could take an apartment and stay awhile. Nothing was permanent or needed to be.

Then the novelist fell for Nick and it was necessary to leave. Nick sublet his flat for six months and went to Paris. Meanwhile the tenant dealt drugs out of the apartment. When Nick reentered the country he was arrested—guilty by association. Two weeks later, in the dark forbidding arms of *La Stella Nera*, he met Max.

They hardly saw anyone but Lydia. They would not hear from her for several weeks, which meant she was in Florence or traveling; then abruptly, irresistibly, she would appear or telephone with The Plan. She strongly favored visits to the country villas of old friends, weekends requiring great logistical migrations of guests and matériel—special food, wine, props, costumes, additional servants, treats, surprises—all the tools of the grand hostess.

We leave Thursday evening by car for Cetona, she announced one Wednesday by phone.

But that's tomorrow night, Nick said.

Don't *say* you're busy or I'll die, Lydia sighed into the phone. You two are the key to the whole thing. None of them would bother to drag their poor tired bones to the country *yet again* except to see you, my two gorgeous boys. And Saturday will be fancy dress. I'm dressing Max as a sixteenth-century Italian prince, for which I am bringing along certain death-defying diamonds.

I'll tell him, Nick said. What am I to be?

An Attic shepherd, darling, stripped down to a few sable pelts and the glories God gave you. I've hired two sheep. If you don't come, I swear we'll eat them.

The sheep stood about, lamplike, where they were put. Lydia's preparations might even have included sheep sedatives. The weekend company included an elderly monsignor who was Lydia's closest friend and principal social beard; a chic, darkly serious lesbian couple; a middle-aged Florentine count who was the monsignor's longtime companion; two American teachers of art, also middle-aged, married and male; and Max and Nick.

Saturday evening's dinner was fancy-dress. Nani, the count, appeared as a nun. This was taken as an amusing and considerate reference to his consort, Monsignor Alessio, who did not dress. The two art professors were simply and tastefully fitted out as European court ladies in evening gowns and tiaras, like elderly princesses. The two lesbians came of course as men, resembling those of the lounge-lizard sort—convincing but not completely reputable. Lydia said she was Maria José, wife of Umberto II, the last Queen of Italy; her dress was made of cloth-of-gold, her hair piled high and gilded. Max wore tights, a black velvet doublet, and long ropes of Lydia's diamonds. Nick, nearly naked with crook and sheep, was awarded the prize for most beautiful and apt.

Monsignor Alessio appeared at every function on Lydia's schedule of dubious social value or political implication. His rank, age, and nearly papal demeanor kept him beyond reproach and out of political reach; this in spite of an open fondness for boys. Monsignor Alessio loved angels as they appeared in the form of young boys, *s'intendiamoci*. Such a party as this would never have been possible in Lydia's life, or even in the lives of her servants, without the correct and reassuring presence of the monsignor.

According to Nick, this evening's gay theme was not the reflection of Lydia's sexual preference but the clever idea of a thoughtful and busy hostess, as on another occasion she might, in the same spirit, assemble eight or ten businessmen or a half-dozen chefs. Lydia believed that theme parties encouraged conversation. In another way, and because of her devotion to Nick, the assembly had been chosen to please him and his new friend. If in some vaguely startling way, there was something jejune about the evening, it was perhaps because the lesbians and the art professors seemed deeply disturbed by the way they were dressed. They had mustered enough sangfroid to cross-dress; not enough to go on with it in company.

The monsignor, who had just taken a sip of wine, now accidentally touched the stem of his glass to his plate with a crystal chime, inadvertently stopping conversation and drawing everyone's attention. Giving them all back a startled look, Monsignor Alessio then fell forward on the table. For a long moment the others wordlessly regarded his slumped figure and purplish face, which rested like a baked apple on his empty plate, the wine he had not completely swallowed dribbling like juice in a pink trickle from his lips. Presently, with a kind of spasm or convulsion, the priest, together with his dinner service, slid from the table and landed without breakage on the thickly carpeted floor. Nani screamed. He pushed over his chair and ran around the table to help his friend.

Get a doctor! Help him! he screamed, holding the priest's head in his nun's lap. He can't die, he cried after a moment. He can't! I couldn't!

The lesbians in tuxedos stepped in, calming Nani, taking the last few beats of Monsignor Alessio's pulse, and even going so far as to blow a few extra breaths into his wilting lungs; but it was clear after a few minutes that the man was dead.

It had been his heart, concerning which this was the last of several incidents, but it seemed at the time, to Nick and Max, to be *them*. What strains had they put on the old man's failing health? Not that they had ever spent a moment alone with him, or thought of it. But it was death at close range, the first for either of them. And it seemed, like so much in their lives—as for instance their meeting in prison—to have some larger meaning. This impression was further developed a few weeks later when the host of a similar weekend house party, at which Lydia was not a guest, just as suddenly dropped dead, this time not actually in their presence but very soon after leaving it.

I'm *swamped* with requests to get you for the weekend, Lydia announced.

That's not funny, Nick said.

Angeli del morte, they're calling you, she went on. Are you both already quite booked up?

It's appalling really, Nick said. We are thinking of leaving Rome.

Leaving Rome! Just because a few old people drop dead? You'll turn into nomads at that rate.

I have the possibility of work in New York, and Max's father has practically ordered him home.

Ahh, Lydia mused.

Or London, Nick said.

Darling, take a few weeks in Positano, to clear the head. London would only put you to sleep and I don't think Rome is done with you, somehow . . .

But the part in New York did materialize and Mr. Desir said Max would have to come back to the United States or get a job. Feeling the way they did, they let the current carry them home.

At the airport and for the forty-minute drive home to Hillcrest, John registered a hard-edged and total silence, leaving Marie—half turned in her seat—to ask the questions and give the news. That no one else had been there to welcome them was deeply ominous.

When he got his mother alone for a moment, Max embraced her and solemnly apologized—not for himself and Nick but for the oddity, the uniqueness of the situation, the unpleasant responses it evoked.

It's all right, Max, she said. As long as you're happy and hurt no one. But your father . . . he simply hates it.

What's going to happen? he asked.

Who knows? You must try not to let him upset you, try not to get angry. He says things he doesn't mean.

Like what? he asked.

You name it . . . Oh God. Oh Max! Her eyes filled up but did not spill over. He made every effort to gauge the precise calibration of her suffering, so that he could hate or excuse himself for it. It appeared that her deepest intention was to protect both him *and* his father at once.

Max went upstairs and told Nick there was going to be a battle royal and that he would take him to Robin's house for a while.

Max's sister was a clinical psychologist and a pretty cool customer. When Max returned, his father was sitting in the big den alone, not watching television.

Where's Nick? John asked.

I thought we'd better do this alone, Max replied. We don't need Nick for this. Where's Mom?

I don't know, his father said. In her room, I guess. She was here a minute ago.

Max walked around the enormous room, went to the window to inspect the lawn, the extra acre of woods they had bought in the back for privacy; everything, inside and out, in perfect order. He turned to his father.

Where do we begin, Dad?

I don't know, John replied, not looking up, then looking up. You tell *me*.

After a pause in which he assembled the words carefully, Max said, I recently faced the fact that I am a homosexual.

I'm aware of that, John said.

Well, I guess it's time you faced it too. I like men and I'm in love with Nick.

You've got a fucking nerve coming in here and saying that to me, his father snapped. What the hell do you have to tell *me* about it for?

Well, you asked why I moved to Rome, and anyway I wasn't going to sneak around and lie about it to you. We're going to live in New York and . . . we'll be right there. Unless you'd rather not see us.

His father didn't answer. Max made another revolution of the room, winding up back at the window, which was a sliding door and therefore an exit. He realized suddenly that he was at an enormous disadvantage, perhaps an overwhelming one. Everything here was his father's.

Mom doesn't seem to care particularly, he said, turning from the window. Why do you?

Because! His father brayed the word. I just don't like it, that's all. Why should I? Who the hell does?

Let's not drag the world into this, Pop, Max said, trying to be as light as possible.

The world is the point, John said. Is *everybody* wrong?

Yes! Everybody's wrong! Max shouted back. And it's not the first time.

That's your opinion, John said derisively. I don't agree with it.

Well, what do you expect *me* to do about it? Max said. Pretend I'm straight? So you won't feel bad?

Yes, John said calmly.

You'd rather I was straight and unhappy than happy with Nick.

That's right, his father said.

And I should keep it a secret.

That too.

Or?

Or nothing. You can do what you want. I don't care, John said.

Max drifted out of the den and into the dining room, which had a dark mahogany table twenty feet long in its center, ten high-backed brocade chairs in slavish attendance, six more against the walls. He wandered into the foyer, which like the den was two stories high. The big chandelier from their triumphant trip to Messina was caught in descent like a crystal parachute. He went back into the den. His father had not moved.

Does Nick make enough money from these films to live on? John asked without preamble.

Usually. He's not established yet. Why do you ask?

I do not approve of this lifestyle, John said, and I have no intention of paying for it.

Well, good, Max said quickly. You can keep your money.

How would you like me to come over there and break you in half? John said.

How'd you like to work this out for yourself? Max replied, thinking of Lydia.

They glared at each other, but neither moved and the moment passed.

Max went into the kitchen and poured a glass of juice from the refrigerator. He turned around and raised the glass to his lips. His mother was sitting at the kitchen table listening, her hand supporting her chin at an angle that caused her to gaze out the front window. She did not look up at him.

It went on like this for hours. At one point Nick called to find out what was happening.

He's cut off the money, Max said, but I knew he'd do that. He thinks you're after the Desir millions.

Nick said, Pick me up. We'll spend the night at Paul's, meaning a friend in Manhattan. Tomorrow we'll find an apartment.

Max said, Oh God . . .

I know it's hard, Nick said. But you have to stand up to them.

No, my mother is fine. She said as long as I'm happy and he said as long as I'm not . . .

Just leave and pick me up. Your sister is terrific. She's filling me in.

Max began to weep and couldn't stop, not for the awful things that were being said, but for the things that had been withheld. He did not try to hide his tears, and in fact broke down completely in front of his father. Of all his efforts this seemed to have the most effect, though not enough to make any difference. John never cried.

Max went up to his room to get his things and Nick's. Exhausted, he sat for a moment on the edge of the bed. His mother came in noiselessly and sat down beside him. She took him in her arms and he sobbed against her.

He wouldn't even bend, Max said.

I know, darling, she said, and held him as he wept.

From *A Boy's Own Story*

Edmund White

A Boy's Own Story *is the first volume of a trilogy (the second volume is* The Beautiful Room Is Empty*) that will depict, according to White, the "unapologetic portrayal of the development of a gay man." It will show how gay men were "oppressed in one generation, liberated in the next, and wiped out in the next." Infected with HIV, White is now working on the third of these novels.*

This chapter shows the unnamed narrator learning from his father to trade money for sex and to betray the ones he loves. As White recalls it in States of Desire, *his father also instructed him on how to fill "in a grand Balzacian canvas of greed, corruption, competition and disappointment" with the details of "everyone's pedigree and pretensions, the scope of their infidelities and true size of their bank accounts."*

My father wanted me to work every summer in high school so that I might learn the value of a dollar. I did work, I did learn, and what I learned was that my dollar could buy me hustlers. I bought my first when I was fourteen.

The downtown of that city of half a million was small, no larger than a few dozen blocks. Every morning my stepmother drove me into town from our house, a fake Norman castle that stood high and white on a hill above the steaming river valley; we'd go down into town— a rapid descent of several steep plunges into the creeping traffic, dream dissolves of black faces, the smell of hot franks filtered through the car's air-conditioned interior, the muted cries of newspaper vendors speaking their own incomprehensible language, the somber look of sooted façades edging forward to squeeze out the light. Downtown excited me: so many people, some of them just possibly an invitation to adventure, escape or salvation.

As a little boy I'd thought of our house as the place God had meant us to own, but now I knew in a vague way that its seclusion and ease were artificial and that it strenuously excluded the city at the same time it depended on it for food, money, comfort, help, even pleasure. The black maids were the representatives of the city I'd grown up among. I'd never wanted anything from them—nothing except their love. To win it, or at least to ward off their silent, sighing resentment, I'd learned how to make my own bed and cook my own breakfast. But nothing I could do seemed to make up to them the terrible loss they'd endured.

In my father's office I worked an Addressograph machine (then something of a novelty) with a woman of forty who, like a restless sleeper tangled in sheets, tossed about all day in her fantasies. She was a chubby but pert woman who wore pearls to cover the pale line across her neck, the scar from some sort of surgical intervention. It was a very thin line but she could never trust her disguise and ran to the mirror in the ladies' room six or seven times a day to re-evaluate the effect.

The rest of her energy went into elaborating her fantasies. There was a man on the bus every morning who always stationed himself opposite her and arrogantly undressed her with his dark eyes. Upstairs from her apartment another man lurked, growling with desire, his ear pressed to the floor as he listened through an inverted glass for the glissando of a silk slip she might be stepping out of. "Should I put another lock on my door?" she'd ask. Later she'd ask with wide-eyed sweetness, "Should I invite him down for a cup of coffee?" I advised her not to; he might be dangerous. The voraciousness of her need for men made me act younger than usual; around her I wanted to be a boy, not a man. Her speculations would cause her to sigh, drink water and return to the mirror. My stepmother said she considered this woman to be a "ninny." Once, years ago, my stepmother had been my father's secretary—perhaps her past made her unduly critical of the women who had succeeded her. My family and their friends almost never characterized people we actually knew, certainly not dismissively. I felt a gleeful shame in thinking of my colleague as a "ninny"— sometimes I'd laugh out loud when the word popped into my head. I found it both exciting and alarming to feel superior to a grown-up.

Something about our work stimulated thoughts of sex in us. Our tasks (feeding envelopes into a trough, stamping them with addresses, stuffing them with brochures, later sealing them and running them through the postage meter) required just enough attention to prevent connected conversation but not so much as to absorb us. We were left with amoeboid desires that split or merged as we stacked and folded, as we tossed and turned. "When he looks at me," she said, "I know he wants to hurt me." As she said that, her sweet, chubby face looked as though it were emerging out of a cloud.

Once I read about a woman patient in psychoanalysis who referred to her essential identity as her "prettiness"; my companion—gray-eyed, her wrists braceleted in firm, healthy fat, hair swept up into a brioche pierced by the fork of a comb, her expression confused and sweet as she floated free of the cloud—she surrounded and kept safe her own "prettiness" as though it were a passive, intelligent child and she the mother, dazed by the sweeping lights of the world.

She was both fearful and serene—afraid of being noticed and more afraid of being ignored, thrillingly afraid of the sounds outside her bedroom window, but also serene in her conviction that this whole bewildering opera was being staged in order to penetrate the fire and get at her "prettiness." She really was pretty—perhaps I haven't made that clear: a sad blur of a smile, soft gray eyes, a defenseless availability. She was also crafty, or maybe willfully blind, in the way she concealed from herself her own sexual ambitions.

Becoming my father's employee clarified my relationship with him. It placed him at an exact distance from me that could be measured by money. The divorce agreement had spelled out what he owed my mother, my sister and me, but even so whenever my mother put us kids on the train to go visit him (one weekend out of every month and all summer every summer), she invariably told us, "Be nice to your father or he'll cut us off." And when my sister was graduated from college, he presented her with a "life bill," the itemized expenses he'd incurred in raising her over twenty-one years, a huge sum that was intended to discourage her from thoughtlessly spawning children of her own.

Dad slept all day. He seldom put in an appearance at the office before closing time, when he'd arrive fresh and rested, smelling of witch hazel, and scatter reluctant smiles and nods to the assembly as he made his way through us and stepped up to his desk in a large room walled off from us by soundproof glass. "My, what a fine man your father is, a real gentlemen," my colleague would sigh. "And to think your stepmother met him when she was his secretary—some women have all the luck.'' We sat in rows with our backs to him; he played the role of the conscience, above and behind us, a force that troubled us as we filed out soon after his arrival at the end of the work day. Had we stayed late enough? Done enough?

My stepmother usually kept my father company until midnight. Then she and I would drive back to the country and go to bed. Sometimes my father followed us in his own car and continued his desk work at home. Or sometimes he'd stay downtown till dawn. ''That's when he goes out to meet other women,'' my real mother told me at the end of the summer, when I reported back to her what went on in Daddy's life. ''He was never faithful. There was always another woman, the whole twenty-two years we were married. He takes them to those little fleabag hotels downtown. I know.'' This hint of mystery about a man so cold and methodical fascinated me—as though he, the rounded brown stone, if only cracked open, would nip at the sky with interlocking crystal teeth, the quartz teeth of passion.

Before the midnight drive back home I was sometimes permitted to go out to dinner by myself. Sometimes I also took in a movie (I remember going to one that promised to be actual views of the ''orgies at Berchtesgarden,'' but it turned out to be just Eva Braun's home movies, the Fuerher conferring warm smiles on pets and children). A man who smelled of Vitalis sat beside me and squeezed my thigh with his hand. I had my own spending money and my own free time.

I had little else. No one I could meet for lunch and confide in. No one who liked me. No one who wanted to talk with me about books or opera. Not even the impulse to ask for love or the belief that such things could be discussed. Had I known in any vivid or personal way of the disease, starvation and war that afflicted so much of humanity, I might have taken comfort at least in my physical well-being, but in my loneliness I worried about sickness, hunger and violence befalling me, as though these fears had been visited on me by the jealous world in revenge against so much joyless plenty.

I hypothesized a lover who'd take me away. He'd climb the fir tree outside my window, step into my room and gather me into his arms. What he said or looked like remained indistinct, just a cherishing wraith enveloping me, whose face glowed more and more brightly. His delay in coming went on so long that soon I'd passed from anticipation to nostalgia. One night I sat at my window and stared at the moon, toasting it with a champagne glass filled with grape juice. I knew the moon's cold, immense light was falling on him as well, far away and just as lonely in a distant room. I expected him to be able to divine my existence and my need, to intuit that in this darkened room in this country house a fourteen-year-old was waiting for him.

Sometimes now when I pass dozing suburban houses I wonder behind which window a boy waits for me.

After a while I realized I wouldn't meet him till years later; I wrote him a sonnet that began, "Because I loved you before I knew you." The idea, I think, was that I'd never quarrel with him nor ever rate his devotion cheap; I had had to wait too long.

Our house was a somber place. The styleless polished furniture was piled high and the pantry supplies were laid in; in the empty fullness of breakfront drawers gold flatware and silver tea things remained for six months at a time in mauve flannel bags that could not ward off a tarnish bred out of the very air. No one talked much. There was little laughter, except when my stepmother was on the phone with one of her social friends. Although my father hated most people, he had wanted my stepmother to take her place—that is, my mother's place—in society, and she had. He'd taught her how to dress and speak and entertain and by now she'd long since surpassed his instructions; she'd become at once proper and frivolous, innocent and amusing, high-spirited and reserved—the combination of wacky girl and prim matron that world so admired.

I learned my part less well. I feared the sons of her friends and made shadows among the debs. I played the piano without ever improving; to practice would have meant an acceptance of more delay, whereas I wanted instant success, the throb of plumed fans in the dark audience, the pulse of diamonds from the curve of loges. What I had instead was the ache of waiting and the fear I wasn't worthy. When I'd dress I'd stand naked before the closet mirror and wonder if my body was worthy. I can still picture that pale skin stretched over my ribs, the thin, hairless arms and sturdier legs, the puzzled, searching face—and the slow lapping of disgust and longing, disgust and longing. The disgust was hot, penetrating—nobody would want me because I was a sissy and had a mole between my shoulder blades. The longing was cooler, less substantial, more the spray off a wave than the wave itself. Perhaps the eyes were engaging, there was something about the smile. If not lovable as a boy, then maybe as a girl; I wrapped the towel into a turban on my head. Or perhaps need itself was charming or could be.

Maybe my need could make me as appealing as the woman who worked the Addressograph machine with me.

I was always reading and often writing but both were passionately abstract activities. Early on I had recognized that books pictured another life, one quite foreign to mine, in which people circled one another warily and with exquisite courtesy until an individual or a couple erupted and flew out of the salon, spangling the night with fire. I had somehow stumbled on Ibsen and that's how he struck me: oblique social chatter followed by a heroic death in a snowslide or on the steeple of a church (I wondered how these scenes could be staged). Oddly enough, the "realism" of the last century seemed tinglingly far-fetched: vows, betrayals, flights, fights, sacrifices, suicides. I saw literature as a fantasy, no less absorbing for all its irrelevance—a parallel life, as dreams shadow waking but never intersect it.

I thought to write of my own experiences required a translation out of the crude patois of actual slow suffering, mean, scattered thoughts, and transfusion-slow boredom into the tidy couplets of brisk, beautiful sentiment, a way of at once elevating and lending momentum to what I felt. At the same time I was drawn to . . . What if I could write about my life exactly as it was? What if I could show it in all its density and tedium and its concealed passion, never divined or expressed, the dull brown geode that eats at itself with quartz teeth?

I read books with this passion, as one might beat back pages of pictures, looking for someone he could love. The library downtown had been built as an opera house in the last century. Even in grade school I had haunted the library, which was in the same block as my father's office. The library looked up like a rheumy eye at a pitched skylight over which pigeons whirred, their bodies a shuddering gray haze until one settled and its pacing black feet became as precise as cuneiform. The light seeped down through the stacks that were arranged in a horseshoe of tiers: the former family balcony, the dress circle, the boxes, on down to the orchestra, still gently raked but now cleared of stalls and furnished with massive oak card files and oak reading tables where unshaved old men read newspapers under gooseneck lamps and rearranged rags in paper sacks. The original stage had been demolished but cleats on the wall showed where ropes had once been secured.

The railings around the various balconies still described crude arabesques in bronze gone green, but the old floors of the balconies had been replaced by rectangular slabs of smoked glass that emitted pale emerald gleams along polished, bevelled edges. Walking on this glass gave me vertigo, but once I started reading I'd slump to the cold, translucent blocks and drift on ice floes into dense clouds. The smell of yellowing paper engulfed me. An unglued page slid out of a volume and a corner broke off, shattered—I was destroying public property! Downstairs someone harangued the librarian. Shadowy throngs of invisible operagoers coalesced and sat forward in their see-through finery to look and listen. I was reading the libretto of *La Bohème*. The alternating columns of incomprehensible Italian, which I could skip, made the pages speed by, as did the couple's farewell in the snow, the ecstatic reconciliation, poor little Mimi's prolonged dying. I glanced up and saw a pair of shoes cross the glass above, silently accompanied by the paling and darkening circle of the rubber end of a cane. The great eye of the library was blurred by tears.

Across the street the father of a friend of mine ran a bookstore. As I entered it, I was almost knocked down by two men coming out. One of them touched my shoulder and drew me aside. He had a three-day's growth of beard on his cheeks, shiny wet canines, a rumpled raincoat of a fashionable cut that clung to his hips and he was saying, "Don't just rush by without saying hello."

Here he was at last but now I knew for sure I wasn't worthy—I was ugly with my glasses and my scalp white under my shorn hair. "Do I know you?" I asked. I felt I did, as if we'd traveled for a month in a train compartment knee to knee night after night via the thirty installments of a serial but plotless though highly emotional dream. I smiled, embarrassed by the way I looked.

"Sure you know me." He laughed and his friend, I think, smiled. "No, honestly, what's your name?"

I told him.

He repeated it, smile suppressed, as I'd seen men on the make condescend to women they were sizing up. "We just blew into town," he said. "I hope you can make us feel at home." He put an arm around my waist and I shrank back; the sidewalks were crowded with people staring at us curiously. His fingers fit neatly into the space between my pelvis and the lowest rib, a space that welcomed him, that had been cast from the mold of his hand. I kept thinking these two guy want my money, but how they planned to get it remained vague. And I was alarmed they'd been able to tell at a glance that I would respond to their advances so readily. I was so pleased he'd chosen me; because he was from out of town he had higher, different standards. He thought I was like him, and perhaps I was or soon would be. Now that a raffish stranger—younger and more handsome than I'd imagined, but also dirtier and more condescending—had materialized before me, I wasn't at all sure what I should do: my reveries hadn't been that detailed. Nor had I anticipated meeting someone so crosshatched with ambiguity, a dandy who hadn't bathed, a penniless seducer, someone upon whose face passion and cruelty had cast a grille of shadows. I was alarmed; I ended up by keeping my address secret (midnight robbery) but agreeing to meet him at the pool in the amusement park tomorrow at noon (an appointment I didn't keep, though I felt the hour come and go like a king in disguise turned away at the peasant's door).

The books in the bookstore shimmered before my eyes as I worked through a pile of them with their brightly colored paper jackets bearing photographs of pensive, well-coiffed women or middle-aged men in Irish knit sweaters with pipes and profiles. Because I knew these books were by living writers I looked down on them; my head was still ringing with the full bravura performance of history in the library-opera house. Those old books either had never owned or had lost their wrappers; the likenesses of their unpictured authors had been re-created within the brown, brittle pages. But these living writers—ah! life struck me as an enfeeblement, a proof of dimmed vitality when compared to the energetic composure of the dead whose busts, all carved beards and sightless, protuberant eyes I imagined filling the empty niches in the opera lobby, a shallow antechamber, now a home to sleeping bums and stray cats, but once the splendid approach across diamonds of black-and-white marble pavement to black-and-gilt doors opening on the brilliant assembly, the fans and diamonds and the raised ebony lid of the spotlit piano.

At home I heard the muted strains of discordant music. One night my stepmother, hard and purposeful, drove back downtown unexpectedly to my father's office after midnight. Still later I could hear my stepmother shouting in her wing of the house; I hid behind a door and heard my father's patient, explaining drone. The next morning the woman who worked the Addressograph machine with me broke down, wept, locked herself in the ladies' room. When she came out, her eyes, usually so lovely and unfocused, narrowed with spite and pain as she muttered a stream of filth about my stepmother and my father, who'd tried to lure her to one of those fleabag hotels. On the following morning I learned she'd been let go, though by that time I knew how to get the endless mailings out on my own. She'd been let go—into what?

That man's embrace around the waist set me spinning like a dancer across the darkened stage of the city; my turns led me to Fountain Square, the center. After nightfall the downtown was nearly empty. A cab might cruise by. One high office window might glow. The restaurants had closed by eight, but a bar door could swing open to impose on me the silhouette of a man or to expel the sound of a jukebox, the smell of beer and pretzels. Shabby city of black stone whitened by starlings, poor earthly progeny of that mystic metal dove poised on the outstretched wrist of the verdigris'd lady, sad goddess of the fountain. Men from across the river sat around the low granite rim of the basin—at least I guessed they were hillbillies from their accents, a missing tooth, greased-back hair, their way of spitting, of holding a Camel cupped between the thumb and third finger, of walking with a hard, loud, stiff-legged tread across the paved park as though they hoped to ring sparks off the stone. Others sat singly along the metal fence that enclosed the park, an island around which traffic flowed. They perched on the steel rail, legs wide apart, bodies licked by headlights, and looked down into the slowly circling cars. At last a driver would pause before a young man who'd hop down and lean into the open window, listen—and then the young man would either shake his head and spit or, if a deal had been struck, swagger around to the other side and get in. Look at them: the curving windshield whispers down the reflection of a blinking neon sign on two faces, a bald man behind the wheel whose glasses are crazed by streaks of green light from the dashboard below, whose ears are fleshy, whose small mouth is pinched smaller by anxiety or anticipation. Beside him the young man, head thrown back on the seat so that we can see only the strong white parabola of his jaw and the working Adam's apple. He's slumped far down and he's already thinking his way into his job. Or maybe he's embarrassed by so much downtime between fantasy and act. They drive off, only the high notes from the car radio reaching me.

A charged space where all eyes take in every event—I'd never known anything like that till now. Maybe in the lobby of Symphony Hall, where as a child I'd gone every Friday afternoon for the kiddie matinee, but there little feudal hordes of children, attached to a mother or nurse, eyed each other across acres of marble unless ordered to greet one another, the curtest formality between hostile vassals who might as well have spoken different languages. But here, in Fountain Square, though two or three men might cluster together and drink from a paper bag and argue sports or women, each group was meant to attract attention, every gesture was meant to be observed and transgressed, and the conversation was a pretense at conversation, the typical behavior of desirable types.

That night, however, I had no comfortable assumptions about who these men were and what they were willing to do. I crossed the street to the island, ascended the two steps onto the stone platform—and sat down on a bench. No one could tell me to leave this bench. No one would even notice me. There were policemen nearby. I had a white shirt on, a tie at half-mast, seersucker pants from a suit, polished lace-up shoes, clean nails and short hair, money in my wallet. I was a polite, well-spoken teen, not a vagrant or a criminal—the law would favor me. My father was nearby, working in his office; I was hanging around, waiting for him. Years of traveling alone on trains across the country to see my father had made me fearless before strangers and had led me to assume the unknown is safe, at least reasonably safe if encountered in public places. I set great store by my tie and raised the knot to cover the still unbuttoned collar opening.

It was hot and dark. The circling cars were unnerving—so many unseen viewers looking at me. Although this was the town I'd grown up in, I'd never explored it on my own. The library, the bookstore, Symphony Hall, the office, the dry cleaners, the state liquor commission, the ball park, my school, the department stores, that glass ball of a restaurant perched high up there—these I'd been to hundreds of times with my father and stepmother, but I'd always been escorted by them, like a prisoner, through the shadowy, dangerous city.

And yet I'd known all along it was something mysterious and anguished beyond my experience if not my comprehension. We had a maid, Blanche, who inserted bits of straw into her pierced ears to keep the holes from growing shut, sneezed her snuff in a fine spray of brown dots over the sheets when she was ironing and slouched around the kitchen in her worn-down, backless slippers, once purple but now the color and sheen of a bare oak branch in the rain. She was always uncorseted under her blue cotton uniform; I pictured her rolling, black and fragrant, under that fabric and wondered what her mammoth breasts looked like.

Although she had a daughter five years older than I (illegitimate, or so my stepmother whispered significantly), when Blanche hummed to a black station only she seemed able to tune in she seemed like a girl. When she moved from one room to the next, she unplugged the little Bakelite radio with the cream-colored grille over the brown speaker cloth and took it with her. That music excited me, but I thought I shouldn't listen to it too closely. It was "Negro music" and therefore forbidden—part of another culture more violent and vibrant than mine but somehow inferior yet no less exclusive.

Charles, the handyman, would emerge from the basement sweaty and pungent and, standing three steps below me, lecture me about the Bible, the Second Coming and Booker T. Washington and Marcus Garvey and Langston Hughes. Whenever I said something he'd laugh in a steady, stylized way to shut me up and then start burrowing back into his obsessions. He seemed to know everything, chapter and verse—Egyptians, Abyssinians, the Lost Tribe, Russian plots, Fair Deal and New Deal—but when I'd repeat one of his remarks at dinner, my father would laugh (this, too, was a stylized laugh) and say, "You've been listening to Charles again. That nigger just talks nonsense. Now don't you bother him, let him get on with his work." I never doubted that my father was right, but I kept wondering how Dad could *tell* it was nonsense. What mysterious ignorance leaked out of Charles's words to poison them and render them worthless, inedible? For Charles, like me, haunted the library; I watched his shelf of books in the basement rotate. And Charles was a high deacon of his church, the wizard of his tribe; when he died his splendid robes overflowed his casket. That his nonsense made perfect sense to me alarmed me— was I, like Charles, eating the tripe of knowledge while Dad sat down to the steak?

I suppose I never wondered where Blanche or Charles went at night: when it was convenient to do so I still thought of the world as a well-arranged place where people did work that suited them and lived in houses appropriate to their tastes and needs. But once Blanche called us in the middle of an August night and my father, stepmother and I rushed to her aid. In the big Cadillac we breasted our way into unknown streets through the crowds of naked children playing in the tumult of water liberated from a fireplug ("Stop that!" I shouted silently at them, outraged and frightened. "That's illegal!"'). Past the stoops crowded with grown-ups playing cards and drinking wine. In one glaring doorway a woman stood, holding her diapered baby against her, a look of stoic indignation on her young face, a face one could imagine squeezing out tears without ever changing expression or softening the wide, fierce eyes, set jaw, everted lower lip. The smell of something delicious—charred meat, maybe, and maybe burning honey—filled the air. "Roll up your windows, for Chrissake, and lock the doors," my father shouted at us. "Dammit, use your heads—don't you know this place is dangerous as hell!"

A bright miner's lamp, glass globe containing a white fire devoid of blues and yellows, dangled from the roof of a vendor's cart; he was selling food of some sort to children. Even through the closed windows I could hear the babble of festive, delirious radios. A seven-foot skinny man in spats, shades, an electric green shantung suit and a flat-brimmed white beaver hat with a matching green band strolled in front of our car and patted our fender with elaborate mockery. "I'll kill the bastard," Dad shouted. "I swear I'll kill that goddam ape if he scratches my fender."

"Oh-h-h . . . ," my stepmother sang on a high note I'd never heard before. "You'll get us all killed. Honey, my heart." She grabbed for her heart; she was a natural actress, who instinctively translated feelings into gestures. The man, who my father told us was a "pimp" (whatever that might be), bowed to unheard applause, pulled his hat down over one eye like Chevalier and ambled on, letting us pass.

We hurried up five flights of dirty, broken stairs, littered with empty pint bottles, bags of garbage and two dolls (both white, I noticed, and blond and mutilated), past landings and open doors, which gave me glimpses of men playing cards and, across the hall, a grandmother alone and asleep in an armchair with antimacassars. Her radio was playing that Negro music. Her brown cotton stockings had been rolled down below her black knees.

Blanche we found wailing and shouting, "My baby, my baby!" as she hopped and danced in circles of pain around her daughter, whose hand, half lopped off, was spouting blood. My father gathered the girl up in his arms and we all rushed off to the emergency room of a hospital.

She lived. Her hand was even sewn back on, though the incident (jealous lover with an axe) had broken her mind. Afterwards, the girl didn't go back to her job and feared even leaving the building. My stepmother thought the loss of blood had somehow left her feeble-minded. My father fussed over the blood on his suit and on the strangely similar Cadillac upholstery, though I wondered if his petti-ness weren't merely a way of silencing Blanche, who kept kissing his whole hand in gratitude. Or perhaps he'd found a way of reintroducing the ordinary into a night that had dipped disturbingly below the normal temperature of tedium he worked so hard to maintain. Years later, when Charles died, my father was the only white man to attend the funeral. He wasn't welcome, but he went anyway and sat in the front row. After Charles's death my father became more scattered and apprehensive. He would sit up all night with a stopwatch, counting his pulse.

That had been another city—Blanche's two rooms, scrupulously clean in contrast to the squalor of the halls, her parrot squawking under the tea towel draped over the cage, the chromo of a sad Jesus pointing to his exposed, juicy heart as though he were a free-clinic patient with a troubling symptom, the filched wedding photo of my father and stepmother in a nest of crepe-paper flowers, the bloody sheet torn into strips that had been wildly clawed off and hurled onto the flowered Congoleum floor. Through a half-open door I saw the foot of a double bed draped like a veteran's grave with the flag of a tossed-back sheet.

In my naïveté I imagined all poor people, black and white, liked each other and that here, through Fountain Square, I would feel my way back to the street, that smell of burning honey, that blood as red as mine and that steady, colorless fire in the glass chimney. . . . These hillbillies on the square with their drawling and spitting, their thin arms and big raw hands, nails ragged, tattoos a fresher blue than their eyes set in long sallow Norman faces, each eye a pale blue ringed by nearly invisible lashes—I wove these men freely into the cloth of the powerful poor, a long bolt lost in the dark that I was now pulling through a line of light.

I opened a book and pretended to read under the weak streetlamps, though my attention wandered away from sight to sound. "Tommy, bring back a beer!" someone shouted. Some other men laughed. No one I knew kept his nickname beyond twelve, at least not with his contemporaries, but I could hear these guys calling each other Tommy and Freddy and Bobby and I found that heartening, as though they wanted to stay, if only among themselves, as chummy as a gang of boys. While they worked to become as brutal as soon enough they would be, I tried to find them softer than they'd ever been.

Boots approached me. I heard them before I saw them. They stopped, every tan scar on the orange hide in focus beyond the page I held that was running with streaks of print. "Curiosity killed the damn pussy, you know," a man said. I look up at a face sprouting brunet sideburns that swerved inwards like cheese knives toward his mouth and stopped just below his ginger mustaches. The eyes, small and black, had been moistened genially by the beers he'd drunk and the pleasure he was taking in his own joke.

"*Mighty* curious, ain't you?" he asked. "Ain't you!" he insisted, making a great show of his leisurely, avuncular way he settled close beside me, sighing, and wrapped a bare arm—a pale, cool, sweaty, late-night August arm—around my thin shoulders. "Shit," he hissed. Then he slowly drew a breath like ornamental cigarette smoke up his nose, and chuckled again. "I'd say you got Sabbath eyes, son."

"I do?" I squeaked in a pinched soprano. "I don't know what you mean," I added, only to demonstrate my newly acquired baritone, as penetrating as an oboe, though the effect on the man seemed the right one: sociable.

"Yessir, Sabbath eyes," he said with a downshift into a rural languor and rhetorical fanciness I associated with my storytelling paternal grandfather in Texas. "I say Sabbath 'cause you done worked all week and now you's resting them eyeballs on what you done made—or might could make. The good things of the earth." Suddenly he grew stern. "Why you here, boy? I seed you here cocking your hade and spying up like a biddy hen. Why you watching, boy? *What* you watching? Tell me, what you watching?"

He had frightened me, which he could see—it made him laugh. I smiled to show him I knew how foolish I was being. "I'm just here to—"

"Read?" he demanded, taking my book away and shutting it. "Shi-i-i . . . " he hissed again, steam running out before the *t*. "You here to meet someone, boy?" He'd disengaged himself and turned to stare at me. Although his eyes were serious, militantly serious, the creasing of the wrinkles beside them suggested imminent comedy.

"No," I said, quite audibly.

He handed the book back to me.

"I'm here because I want to run away from home," I said. "I thought I might find someone to go with me."

"Whar you planning to run to?"

"New York."

There was something so cold and firm and well-spoken about me— the clipped tones of a businessman defeating the farmer's hoaxing yarn—that the man sobered, dropped his chin into his palm and thought. "What's today?" he asked at last.

"Saturday."

"I myself taking the Greyhound to New York Tuesday mawning," he said. "Wanna go?"

"Sure."

He told me that if I'd bring him forty dollars on Monday evening he'd buy me my ticket. He asked me where I lived and I told him; his willingness to help me made me trust him. Without ever explicitly being taught such things, I'd learned by studying my father that at certain crucial moments—an emergency, an opportunity—one must act first and think later. One must suppress minor inner objections and put off feelings of cowardice or confusion and turn oneself into a simple instrument of action. I'd seen my father become calm in a crisis or feel his way blindly with nods, smiles and monosyllables toward the shadowy opening of a hugely promising but still vague business deal. And with women he was ever alert to adventure: the gauzy transit of a laugh across his path, a minor whirlpool in the sluggish flow of talk, the faintest whiff of seduction . . .

I, too, wanted to be a man of the world and dared not question my new friend too closely. For instance, I knew a train ticket could be bought at the last moment, even on board, but I was willing to assume either that a bus ticket had to be secured in advance or that at least my friend thought it did. We arranged a time to meet on Monday when I could hand over the money (I had it at home squirreled away in the secret compartment of a wood tray I'd made last year in shop). Then on Tuesday morning at 6 A.M. he'd meet me on the corner near but not in sight of my house. He'd have his brother's car and we'd proceed quickly to the 6:45 bus bound east—a long haul to New Yawk, he said, oh, say twenty hours, no, make that twenty-one.

"And in New York?" I asked timidly, not wanting to seem helpless and scare him off but worried about my future. Would I be able to find work? I was only sixteen, I said, adding two years to my age. Could a sixteen-year-old work legally in New York? If so, doing what?

"Waiter," he said. "A whole hog heaven of resty-runts in New Yawk City."

Sunday it rained a hot drizzle all day and in the west the sky lit up a bright yellow that seemed more the smell of sulfur than a color. I played the piano with the silencer on lest I awaken my father. I was bidding the instrument farewell. If only I'd practiced I might have supported myself as a cocktail pianist; I improvised my impression of sophisticated tinkling—with disappointing results.

As I took an hour-long bath, periodically emptying an inch of cold water and replacing it with warm, I thought my way again through the routine: greeting the guests, taking their orders, serving pats of butter, beverages, calling out my requests to the chef ... my long, flat feet under the water twitched sympathetically as I raced about the restaurant. If only I'd observed waiters all those times. Well, I'd coast on charm.

As for love, that, too, I'd win through charm. Although I knew I hadn't charmed anyone since I was six or seven, I consoled myself by deciding people out here were not susceptible to the larceny (which I thought grand, they petty) of a beguiling manner. They responded only to character, accomplishments, the slow accumulation of will rather than the sudden millinery devisings of fancy. In New York I'd be the darling boy again. In that Balzac novel a penniless young man had made his fortune on luck, looks, winning ways (since I hadn't finished the book, I didn't yet know where those ways led). New Yorkers, like Parisians, I hoped and feared, would know what to make of me. I carried the plots and atmosphere of fiction about with me and tried to cram random events into those ready molds. But no, truthfully, the relationship was more reciprocal, less rigorous—art taking the noise life gave and picking it out as a tune (the cocktail pianist obliging the humming drunk).

Before it closed I walked down to a neighborhood pharmacy and bought a bottle of peroxide. I had decided to bleach my hair late Monday night; on Tuesday I'd no longer answer the description my father would put out in his frantic search for me. Perhaps I'd affect an English accent as well; I'd coached my stepmother in the part of Lady Bracknell before she performed the role with the Queen City Players and I could now say *cucumber sandwich* with scarcely a vowel after the initial fluty *u*. As an English blond I'd evade not only my family but also myself and emerge as the energetic and lovable boy I longed to be. Not exactly a boy, more a girl, or rather a sturdy, canny, lavishly devout tomboy like Joan of Arc, tough in battle if yielding before her visionary Father. I wouldn't pack winter clothes; surely by October I'd be able to buy something warm.

A new spurt of hot water as I retraced my steps to the kitchen, clipped the order to the cook's wire or flew out the swinging doors, smiling, acted courteously and won the miraculously large tip. And there, seated at a corner table by himself, is the English lord, silver-haired, recently bereaved; my hand trembles as I give him the frosted glass. In my mind I'd already betrayed the hillbilly with the sideburns who sobbed with dignity as I delivered my long farewell speech. He wasn't intelligent or rich enough to suit me.

When I met him on Monday at six beside the fountain and presented him with the four ten-dollar bills, he struck me as ominously indifferent to the details of tomorrow's adventure which I'd elaborated with such fanaticism. He reassured me about the waiter's job and my ability to pull it off, told me again where he'd pick me up in the morning—but, smiling, dissuaded me from peroxiding my hair tonight. "Just pack it—we'll bleach you white win we git whar we gohn."

We had a hamburger together at the Grasshopper, a restaurant of two rooms, one brightly lit and filled with booths and families and waitresses wearing German peasant costumes and white lace hats, the other murky and smelling of beer and smoke—a man's world, the bar. I went through the bar to the toilet. When I came out I saw the woman I'd worked with in a low-cut dress, skirt hiked high to expose her knee, hand over her pearl necklace. Her hair had been restyled. She pushed one lock back and let if fall again over her eye, the veronica a cape might pass before an outraged bull: the man beside her, who now placed a grimy hand on her knee. She let out a shriek—a coquette's shriek, I suppose, but edged with terror. (I was glad she didn't see me, since I felt ashamed at the way our family had used her.)

I'd planned not to sleep at all but had set the alarm should I doze off. For hours I lay in the dark and listened to the dogs barking down in the valley. Now that I was leaving this house forever, I was tiptoeing through it mentally and prizing its luxuries—the shelves lined with blocks of identical cans (my father ordered everything by the gross), the linen cupboard stacked high with ironed if snuff-specked sheets, my own bathroom with its cupboard full of soap, tissue, towels, hand towels, washcloths, the elegant helix of the front staircase descending to the living room with its deep carpets, shaded lamps and the pretty mirror bordered by tiles on which someone with a nervous touch had painted the various breeds of lapdog. This house where I'd never felt I belonged no longer belonged to me, and the future so clearly charted for me—college, career, wife and white house wavering behind green trees—was being exchanged for that eternal circulating through the restaurant, my path as clear to me as chalk marks on the floor, instructions for each foot in the tango, lines that flowed together, branched and joined, branched and joined . . . In my dream my father had died but I refused to kiss him though next he was pulling me onto his lap, an ungainly teen smeared with Vicks VapoRub whom everyone inexplicably treated as a sick child.

When I silenced the alarm, fear overtook me. I'd go hungry! The boardinghouse room with the toilet down the hall, blood on the linoleum, crepe-paper flowers—I dressed and packed my gym bag with the bottle of peroxide and two changes of clothes. Had my father gone to bed yet? Would the dog bark when I tried to slip past him? And would that man be on the corner? The boardinghouse room, yes, Negro music on the radio next door, the coquette's shriek. As I walked down the drive I felt conspicuous under the blank windows of my father's house and half-expected him to open the never-used front door to call me back.

I stood on the appointed corner. It began to drizzle but a water truck crept past anyway, spraying the street a darker, slicker gray. No birds were in sight but I could hear them testing the day. A dog without a collar or master trotted past. Two fat maids were climbing the hill, stopping every few steps to catch their breath. One, a shiny, blue-black fat woman wearing a flowered turban and holding a purple umbrella with a white plastic handle, was scowling and talking fast but obviously to humorous effect, for her companion couldn't stop laughing.

The bells of the Catholic school behind the dripping trees across the street marked the quarter hour, the half hour. More and more cars were passing me. I studied every driver—had he overslept? The milkman. The bread truck. Damn hillbilly. A bus went by, carrying just one passenger. A quarter to seven. He wasn't coming.

When I saw him the next evening on the square he waved at me and came over to talk. From his relaxed manner I instantaneously saw—puzzle pieces sliding then locking to fill in the pattern—that he'd duped me and I was powerless. To whom could I report him? Like a heroin addict or a Communist, I was outside the law—outside it but with him, this man. He didn't attract me but I liked him well enough.

We sat side by side on the same bench. A bad muffler exploded in a volley and the cooing starlings perched on the fountain figure's arm flew up and away leaving behind only the metal dove. I took off my tie, rolled it up and slipped it inside my pocket. Because I didn't complain about being betrayed, my friend said, "See those men yonder?"

"Yes."

"I could git you one for eight bucks." He let that sink in; yes, I thought, I could take someone to one of those little fleabag hotels. "Which one do you want?" he asked.

I handed him the money and said, "The blond."

Dark Disco: A Lament

Andrew Holleran

Since the late 1970s, Andrew Holleran has written his "New York Notebook" for Christopher Street. *"Dark Disco: A Lament" is an early essay in that series. Several of the essays dealing with AIDS that Holleran wrote for* Christopher Street *have been gathered in the collection* Ground Zero.

There's a new accessory in New York now: the large transistor radio cradled gracefully in one arm or hanging from a shoulder strap like a huge metallic communications purse. Like much fashion it started on the street and, as of this writing, is confined to adolescents of the Third World. They take their radios everywhere they go. If you love music, you may find yourself in the curious position of following a young man not because he is sexually interesting (or even sexually possible) but because the radio he carries is playing "Do or Die."

This phenomenon may hit you in one of two ways: either you find the boy on the subway with his blaring radio inconsiderate or you applaud him for wishing to have music beside him every step he takes through life (and which of these two responses you feel often depends on whether you like the song or not).

And if you do like the song and he gets off at the wrong stop, no matter—chances are the radios on the street when you come up will be playing the same song, not to mention the stores on Eighth Street, which you can now traverse from Sixth Avenue to Astor Place without ever completely losing the strains of "Boogie Oogie Oogie," if that's what WKTU-FM is playing. WKTU-FM shocked us all one morning when we got up to turn on "The Mellow Sound" to get us through that first hazy hour of consciousness (John Denver, Cream of Wheat) and found it playing instead the song we had danced to the night

189

before: sometime in the night it had become twenty-four-hour disco Muzak.

Well, all of this—the twenty-four-hour disco station, the radios carried down the street, the music played in shoe stores and gymnasiums—is a tribute to how far disco has come . . . or gone, if you feel that way about its rise from obscure dark rooms to the sunny sidewalk and the shag carpeting of The Athlete's Foot in the Village.

But other things too have changed in that time. When I first came to New York, the radio station we listened to for the music that eventually became disco, WBLS, dispensed positive thinking to its ghetto audience; now that audience tends to drive Porsches. In those days, when you went out to dance, disco had no uniform sound. There was no one word to describe the variegated music we spent the night with. It was distinct enough for the discaire to begin a set quietly, build gradually to a climax, then let you down to start all over again. Do you remember that vanished custom? It happened three or four times a night if you stayed long enough, and you could follow the tantalizing process by which the discaire laid a solid foundation of slow songs and then subtly (if he was good, as they all seemed to be in those days) built you up to the catharsis, say, of Deodato's "2001." One thing for sure: disco was different then. The music was darker, sexual, troubled. Today the dark has vanished and the light is everywhere.

Two winters ago I walked into a discothèque and realized with a mixture of horror and disgust how far things had gone in this business. That was when I heard in the same night disco versions of "I Could Have Danced All Night" and (the mind reels) "The Little Drummer Boy." Why didn't the crowd stampede for the fire exits? Was I the only one who found these songs drivel? I went home that night in a terrible funk: I had seen the death of disco, I felt sure. That winter I let my membership in several clubs lapse and began asking everyone I knew, "What will we be doing *after* disco?" For I was certain that that form of diversion was kaput. The disco beat, which devotees of rock and jazz detest, suddenly seemed idiotic even to me, a certified disco maven.

A terrible uniformity of beat and style had come to dominate all disco music that year, so that when we went out we were never taken up, dropped, and taken up again several times in the course of a night. No, we entered the discothèque and stepped, as it were, onto a moving jet of air that never slowed down until we ourselves stepped out of it—by simply leaving the room. Gloria Gaynor got faster with each song. By the time she did "How High the Moon" there was nothing left, said one acerbic friend, but the tarantella. Stepping onto the floor then was an occasion of apprehension, like gathering your energies to run the hundred-yard dash, for the music, and the discaire playing it, seemed part of a conspiracy to keep me hopping against my will. (What were we to *do* to "How High the Moon"? Use roller skates? Pogo sticks?) But by then disco was big business. What I used to think was as wonderful and mysterious as the dancing madness of the Middle Ages or the rites of Dionysus was now a page in the annual corporate report of Gulf & Western.

There was nothing wrong with Gloria Gaynor, of course—there is nothing wrong with light disco. Some nights you arrive in tennis sneakers and your only regret is that you're not *allowed* roller skates or a pogo stick. Some nights you *do* want to float very lightly. You're feeling fast and cool and breezy, and light disco is just what you need. The wonderful lightness of "Spring Affair" (with its odd tinges of dark disco) is almost ethereal, and you rise and dip with it like a bird coasting on wind. But the dreck that falls in between, the Muzak of disco (which is clearly light), the fast, mechanical, monotonous, shallow stuff that is being produced for a mass market now, the kind of music one imagines hearing poolside at the Acapulco Hilton, beating against the brains of the guests as they squint into the sun looking for the pesky waiter who's bringing them their Margaritas—that is light-years away from the old dark disco, which did not *know* it was disco, which was simply a song played in a room where we gathered to dance.

Deep in a funk the night I decided disco was dead, I began to wonder about the songs we heard no more that, it seemed to me, had created another feeling altogether in those early days. But each time I named a song, I asked myself, Was *that* dark disco? If we were to buy that record and play it, would it really be different? Or was it the time and place and atmosphere, not the music at all? The songs I remembered vaguely, if at all, were not fast and sassy and full of androgynous choral effects. They were not—I was sure—invitations to visit Rio or disco versions of songs from *My Fair Lady*. They were songs you could dance to for a long time, because they concentrated energy rather than evaporated it, songs that went inside you, rather than lodging in your feet and joints the way light disco does. You hardly moved, but suddenly you were closer—ever so slightly—to the person dancing with you, and you became conscious of your limbs, which even, as I remember, became heavier. You lowered your eyes. You closed them finally. It was gripping, real dancing, and the atmosphere in the room was one of surrender. Dark disco was our *fado*, our flamenco, our blues; it spoke of things in a voice partly melancholic, partly bemused by life, and wholly sexual. Dark disco was the song you sang to yourself on the first night of winter in New York walking down one of those long, dark, deserted blocks in Chelsea, when you realized anew that New York is also a winter city, a city where for one long season life turns indoors and we pursue freely our darker desires.

That was dark disco: late nights and love affairs and empty streets, and the sound of Al Green singing "Love and Happiness," and the version of that song by First Choice. It was B. B. King at the Tenth Floor singing "To Know You Is to Love You." It was the *Masterpiece* album of the Temptations, the sinister authority of those opening bars of "Papa Was a Rolling Stone," or "In the Ghetto," or the triumphant gloom of "Law of the Land." It was, finally, a song whose singer I cannot even remember but which is played occasionally today and contains a line that goes: "So you grow up and start a family. . . . " There was nothing strained or inconsequential about those songs. The last was even soft-spoken, exhausted, a song perhaps by a man on downs—not the downs we take as pills but rather the downs we take in life. It told me a little story (and how irrelevant to anything are the lyrics of light disco) of the whole sad progression of a life—the mundane pattern we all follow—but it told it in the most vulnerable mode, and we could all share it. We communed. The music wasn't being done to us; it was being done with us. And that song, so casual, so low-key and easygoing, had in it ten times the power of the fastest showstopper. It was sexual, bluesy, and what can only be called dark. It was not an invitation to fly away or a mad whirl about the room. Oh, give me a slow song any day, one as melancholy as "Love and Happiness," which makes us dance from the pits of our stomachs (the solar plexus, if you will, where a French friend assures me all the major emotions are located) instead of the joints of our arms, the tips of our toes.

A friend who knows this business far better than I do told me yesterday that there will always be dancers in this city—that they were there before disco and they'll be there after disco. Still, wherever I go, I look for what comes next. The roller-skating disco in Flatbush? (The music now is so appropriate to roller-skating, the fast, monotonous, sexless disco that fills WKTU-FM.) Or will we abandon even that and just roller-skate through Central Park, as gay men are starting to do now on sunny weekends? Will we give dinner parties again? Stay home and form book clubs? When I arrived in New York, there were no back rooms and no discothèques; now there are many of each. In five years perhaps they will both have vanished, and we will have what in their place: Betamax societies? Will we all go to bed again at eleven, and do something in the morning? What? Not having been awake before noon in seven years myself, I am at a loss to say.

There is a solution, devotees of dance: dark disco still survives, in a curious way. It is this: To hear it once more, to enter that communion of the blood, don't go out this Saturday night. Eat early, go to bed at ten and set your alarm for five; and then, having showered before you sleep, having chosen your T-shirt and jeans, get up with the bell and dress as quickly as any fireman going to a fire, hail a cab, and go down to the disco of your choice around five-thirty. You will pass the wondering faces of the dancers coming out—pale, white, sweaty, on their way home. You may have to hammer on the door to get the man lurking in the back to come forward and let you in. But do it. Pay your money and go upstairs and you will travel back in time to the days of dark disco. The place will have emptied slightly—depending on the quality of what has gone before—and you, fresh as the morning star, will step onto the floor and find a friend, and start to get the very best of the night. For the best disco is saved (who knows why) for last, as if, under this new regime, the old, dark disco is played covertly, in secret. Then you'll hear ''So you grow up and start a family,'' and maybe ''Love and Happiness'' or whatever else does that to you. You'll dance till seven, or eight, and when you come out you'll have captured what you've missed for so many years now in this tyranny of light disco. Tap dancing went, and the cakewalk, too, and one day our disco will be as quaint as Glenn Miller. But could we not detain its evaporation a bit? That, at any rate, is my plea for dark disco.

Getting Rid of Robert

George Whitmore

Many disagreements broke up the Violet Quill, but most often the conflicts were between Robert Ferro and George Whitmore. One of their bitterest fights surrounded the publication of "Getting Rid of Robert," which Robert Ferro saw as a direct attack on his relationship with Michael Grumley (Ferro and Grumley were the only pair of live-in lovers among the Violet Quill, although Edmund White and Christopher Cox were lovers for several years). The circle of friends in the story do resemble the VQ members in some ways, although there is no real-life parallel to these fictional events. Or, rather, the breakup that the story's most parallels is Edmund White's breakup with Chris Cox, who, like the Robert of the story, had been a hustler. Whitmore does, however, seem to be anchoring the story close to reality when he refers in the last section to Stephen Greco, an actual friend of Robert Ferro and Michael Grumley's.

One rainy afternoon in July, Dan called William and me over to his apartment to break the news. I was well aware of what he was going to tell us. William was not, and therefore his response was immediate and electrifying:

"But you can't do this to me!" he moaned.

One of Dan's eyebrows rose on a perpetually pale forehead. After all, who was breaking up with whom?

"Don't you see?" explained William. "You are the *perfect couple.* This is just devastating. And what about my dinner party tonight? Are you coming? Is Robert coming? Is either of you? Is anyone coming to dinner at all?"

Perhaps Dan had never thought of Robert and himself as "the per-

194

fect couple,'' for I noticed he seemed rather flattered and a pleased smile threatened to rearrange his appropriately soulful countenance.

"No one," lamented William, "stays together any longer."

Then, as if realizing William threatened to steal the scene from him, Dan rose from the couch and crossed the room to stare (sightlessly) out the window into the rain-swept street.

"But Robert's so *perfect*," William groaned.

"*You* understand, don't you, Binky?" Dan asked of me, turning from the spangled windowpane.

"I think I do," I murmured. As he'd explained it, it was over the boy at the baths.

He'd sneaked out to the baths the week before—"Thursday night. You'll remember that Robert made me give them up months ago, my Thursday nights at the baths. Well, there I was, and Robert at the ballet or some such thing, and I was walking around with my little towel wrapped around my waist, feeling absolutely out of my element after such a long time, and I turned a corner and—there before me was one of the most luscious boys I've set eyes on in my life! I just stopped short, breathless. He stepped up to me and, instead of groping me the way they all do, to see if it's real or something . . . '' Dan was, indeed, astonishingly well endowed, a fact which a bath towel conventionally wrapped would hardly have concealed. " . . . this gorgeous Spanish boy stepped up to me and inclined his head so sweetly and kissed me on the lips, ever so gently. Well, I was just *afire*. Hands all over him in an instant. But he drew back, then, with a really *offended* expression on his face and said to me, 'Take it easy. We hardly know each other.' *Well.* So we went to my room and kissed for hours, nothing else, honest. And I think it was the most intensely sexual experience of my life! And then, near the end of the evening (actually, three or four in the morning), I realized that there was no way I would ever see this beautiful boy again. I couldn't even ask for his phone number. Robert absolutely forbids rematches, you know. So I left the baths, where *nothing* had taken place but kissing with this boy, you understand, and I was so depressed at the state of affairs. *Me.* Thirty-five years old. In the prime of my life. And somehow I'd become absolutely chained to what Robert calls 'a primary other'—which means, of course, that there can be room for no 'other' in one's life. How unfair it was! And I realized something just had to be done. So I called Robert yesterday. And the rest you already know."

Indeed, I did know. (William, happily planning his sit-down dinner for eight, did not.) For the jungle tom-toms had begun beating shortly after Dan and Robert's conference. I was only slightly piqued to get the news from Stanley a bare thirty minutes after, but gratified in any case to be only the second in all Manhattan to be informed of the breakup.

"Evidently it was too violent for words," Stanley breathed over the phone.

"Why? What happened?" I asked. "Did Robert slug him or something?"

"Worse," said Stanley. "He threw Dan's Lalique vase against the wall and it shattered into a million pieces."

"My God," I exclaimed. "What then?"

"And then," said Stanley, drawing it out for effect, "then Robert locked himself in the bathroom and Dan was sure he was going to slash his wrists or something, until he remembered that you can't do that anymore, of course, using a Trac II razor . . . "

"And then what?"

"Robert poured every drop of Dan's cologne down the drain. Every single drop! Even the Geoffrey Beene, which no one, of course, wears anymore . . . just for spite."

I was glad, when we saw Dan the next day, that he hadn't been physically harmed in the meantime. He'd seen Robert again that morning.

In fact, Dan looked rather remarkably fit for a man who's just broken up with his lover of three years. He was grave, to be sure, but he was also—well, euphoric. He asked if we thought he should get contact lenses now.

When we left the apartment, William was still in shock.

"But I'd hardly call them the *perfect* couple, William."

"But, Binky! They're the *only* couple we know. What are we going to do now? Where will we turn?"

William released his umbrella from its catch and put it up to shield us from a renewal of the afternoon downpour.

"Turn for what?" I asked peevishly, thinking William really was making too much of it.

"For inspiration! And a couple does so *anchor* things, Binky. They provide such continuity. And they're marvelous for dinner."

"We'll have a perfectly good time tonight anyway," I assured William, trying to avoid having an eye poked out by the tips of his umbrella.

"No, you don't understand," said William, sidestepping a puddle. "In a room with six people, every one of whom is wondering *which* of the others he'll fuck with that night, a couple is such a comfort."

"In some circles," I commented.

"Well," said William, "thank God no one in *our* circle has been so *louche* as to swing or wife-swap or whatever they call it. I *hate* modern life," said William, who was all of twenty-eight.

All the host's worst fears (in a strictly social sense) were fulfilled at William's dinner party that night. The rain had done little to lessen the oppressive humidity and it was, given the circumstances, a rather skittish and sullen group that gathered in William's West 76th Street studio-with-terrace. The vichyssoise was lukewarm. The cold tongue was appropriately unappetizing. The arugula salad was wilted. By the time the soupy ice cream arrived with its garnish of mushy strawberries, conversation was nil and Dan had disappeared, drunk, to the terrace.

"Go out and talk to him, Stanley," I whispered across the table.

"*You* go out and talk to him. I've been on the phone with him all evening. *I* persuaded him to come."

(Robert had declined, not so graciously, William led us to believe.)

Stanley and I tossed a coin. I lost.

Dan had crashed from his euphoria of that afternoon. He missed Robert.

"But, Dan, you'll still be friends, won't you?" I said out on the terrace.

"Oh, no. *That* he's made clear."

"Oh, he'll come around," I said soothingly. "Didn't I?" I added.

"Dear Binky," Dan said, patting my hand rather absentmindedly—who knew how much of our affair he bothered to remember nowadays? "Robert will never come around, sweetie. No, he won't be my friend."

"But it's not as if you'd been living together or something," I pointed out.

"But the companionship, Binky. We might as well have been, don't you see? The *surveillance*. The grip that man had on my life."

"Yes," I said, patting Dan's hand now. "A friendship like yours . . ."

I didn't go on. Dan and Robert had had the most exquisite companionship: private jokes, mutual friends, a shared interest in Deco glass—Robert must have been horribly furious to have broken the

Lalique vase, which he himself picked out for Dan in the springtime of their affair.

"We have to find," I said to Dan after a moment's thought, "some way to salvage your friendship. I'm sure Robert will miss you every bit as much as you miss him. After all, three years . . . "

"Binky . . . " Dan turned a tear-stained face to me. "Do you think you might—*talk* to Robert? Yourself, I mean?"

"Well, I . . . "

"Please, Binky. You know, he's sure you'll *all* desert him now. Talk to him, for my sake?"

"Of course, I'll talk to him," I said. "And in any case, Robert is my friend, too. I'm very fond of Robert."

"That's what *I* am," Dan said, drying his eyes with the back of one hand and staring out across the treetops below William's terrace. "Fond of Robert. Exactly. Oh, Binky, I'd hate to *lose* Robert."

I didn't point out that that was exactly the risk one took when one dropped a lover. Instead, I reassured Dan that I'd talk to Robert on his behalf. And Dan was evidently cheered. After the dinner party, he went off to the baths, his first Saturday night there in three years.

I met Robert for drinks at the Oak Room of the Plaza. Somehow, I felt it best to meet Robert on my own turf. You see, Robert had always rather frightened me, and according to Stanley (who'd heard it from Lars, who'd heard it from Jack), Robert was still furious, all 6'3" of him.

"Robert says," said Stanley, "that contrary to being at all supportive of him and Dan as a couple—which is utter slander, don't you think?—all of us actually worked *against* them. Jack says that when *William* talked to Robert on the phone last night he, Robert, said that contrary to their being an example of some sort to the rest of *us*—which is William's perpetual lament, don't you know—that *we* were a bad example to *Dan*. Robert says all of us are going to drop him."

"We are *not* going to drop you, Robert," I told him in the Oak Room.

"You'll see," fumed Robert. "Stanley broke a lunch date with me just this afternoon."

"Oh, Stanley . . . " I said vaguely, with a wave of the hand, for I knew Stanley had broken lunch to have an impromptu tête-à-tête with Dan over the Spanish boy from last week (whom he'd run into again at the baths that Saturday night). "Stanley will stick by you," I told Robert—thinking that Stanley indeed would, if only for the dish Robert might provide.

"In any case, Binky, I'm glad to see you," Robert said, ordering us gin and tonics. "You're different from the rest."

"Am I?" I asked, feeling myself blush, as one is liable to do when receiving acutely unwarranted praise.

"Yes. I have news for you."

So much *news*, I thought, all in the space of a few days.

"I'm quitting DD&B."

"No!" I said. Robert had seemed so happy at Doyle Dane Bernbach. Dan had secured the job for him in the summer of their affair. "But what will you do?" I said, fearing the predictable answer.

"What else?" said Robert evenly.

"Ah," I said, if not exactly scandalized, then properly impressed. For when Dan met Robert he was a typical Village product quite unlike the Armani-suited young man beside me: He was one of the many to be found sunbathing on the pier on weekday afternoons, one of the many with no visible means of support, with time on their hands, a cultivated affability that is their best asset, a lifestyle somehow more pastoral than urban—in other words, a hustler.

"I *have* to make some money now," Robert said, downing his gin and tonic.

"Not that I see anything intrinsically wrong with—it—Robert," I began.

"Now that Dan has cut me off," Robert said, coloring. "You know that Dan had me on a sort of—allowance."

"But surely, your job at DD&B ... "

"In the *mail room*?" Robert said contemptuously, delivering the most startling news of the day (my dialing finger itched), for Dan had always billed him as a "junior executive" and proudly spoke of Robert's progress. "I'll never get anywhere in advertising. No, let's face it, Binky. Hustling's always what I did best."

"But is advertising so different from—it?" I asked. "Really?"

"I appreciate your trying to cheer me up, Binky, but to tell the truth hustling's the only way to make *real* money nowadays and I have to cash in on the market while I still have the wares," said Robert with rock-hard practicality.

"Well," I said, lifting my glass. "If you've made up your mind, then, there's nothing for me to do but wish you luck, Robert."

"Thank you, Binky. I knew you'd understand," he said, returning my toast.

And somehow, in the midst of all the excitement, I forgot to talk to him about Dan at all.

"Queen Central," answered Stanley with no other preamble.

"Stanley," I said into the receiver, "do I have dish for you."

"Pardon me," said Stanley, "do I have dish for *you*."

"But mine's—"

"No, you absolutely have to listen. As you know, I spent the lion's share of the afternoon with Dan—"

"But Stanley, wait till you hear what Robert—"

"Oh, about hustling, you mean? That's not the half of it. Dan's utterly *devastated* over it. But that's not the dish. The dish is—"

"And about the stock room?" I asked weakly.

"But darling. *All* of us knew about the stock room. Even poor William knew about the stock room. Dan's mouth *fell open* when I told him I'd known for months."

"And about the allowance—"

"Of course. Now listen. I spent the entire afternoon with Dan and— oh, Binky, you won't believe it! He's installed that Spanish boy in his apartment! I saw it with my own eyes. At about four, the boy came up with a duffel bag full of clothes and a briefcase full of tape cassettes—Stevie Wonder and that sort of thing—and he's now in residence at Dan's. He's really very nice. He wants to be a record producer. Dropped out of Brandeis in his junior year. Not at all what Dan thought he was, but divine. They're *very* happy."

The "Spanish boy" 's name was Gregory and he was Italian, born and raised in Forest Hills. His major at Brandeis, I found out over tea with him and Dan the next day, had been English Lit, with a minor in Social Psych. "I did it to please my dad," he said. "He's a teacher at Music and Art High School but he'd never have let *me* go there. Then when Dad died and left me a little money . . . " Well, to make a long story short, Gregory lived on a small annuity from his father's wise investments in the stock market. He was trying to work his way into the recording business. "But there's no real percentage in disco anymore," Gregory said (incidentally making Dan and me, with our charter memberships to Flamingo, feel suddenly very old). "I'm going into soul-salsa . . . "

"What do you think of him?" Dan asked me rather breathlessly in the foyer as I was leaving.

"He's a very sharp kid," I said.

"Isn't he wonderful? Binky, you should have seen where he was living. On the Upper East Side with all those stewards—"

"Male or female?"

"Male, of course. Anyway, he was in this perfectly dreadful little apartment. It was like a dormitory or something. Isn't he wonderful?"

"Yes, yes," I said. "But, Dan, I wanted to tell you about—"

"Oh, yes. Robert. Well? Did you talk to him?"

"That's why I came over today, Dan. I wanted to tell you, Dan . . ." I hesitated.

"Oh, about the hustling, you mean. Stanley told me. I don't think he really means it, do you? I mean, at his age."

"Robert's only thirty-two."

"That's what I mean. He was at a dead end when *I* met him. At least at DD&B—"

"Really, Dan, it was a bit too much of you, wasn't it? Calling him a 'junior executive'?"

"I don't think he'll do it." Dan said placidly, opening the door for me. "I'm sure he'll think twice."

"What I *did* want to tell you, Dan," I said, standing in the doorway now, "was that I just wasn't able to talk to Robert about you two at all. We talked a lot of—business and I just never—"

"Oh, he'll come around, Binky," Dan said, almost pushing me out the door, evidently anxious to return to Gregory, who'd been surveying Dan's elaborate sound system when we left the room. "He'll come around. But it's such a comfort, knowing you're in touch with him. Really. Thanks so much." And, giving me a peck on the cheek, he sent me off.

I thought it was curious, I remember, in the first bloom of Robert's affair with Dan—Robert's notion of fidelity and his attitude toward his work.

"He's madly jealous," Dan had said a few months after they'd begun seeing each other.

"But, Dan, how can he be?" I was rather shocked to find Dan so intensely involved with a hustler in the first place. No one in our circle was so adventurous, preferring, I suppose, to pass this or that young man around ("so incestuous," Stanley'd once pointed out) since we'd long ago worked through each other. "He's a hustler, after all. All those other men."

"Oh, he's wildly jealous if I so much as look at someone else. I tried to explain to him that they only serve as a contrast, of sorts. I mean, highlighting his own beauty. But he won't buy it. And as for hustling, he says he's afraid he'll have to give it up. For me."

"For you?"

"He says he can't put any *love* into it any longer . . . "

And that was how the trade-off came about, though Dan claimed he wasn't jealous in the slightest over Robert's hustling. Robert quit the trade a year into the affair and stipulated that Dan confine his own infidelities to Thursday nights at the baths. Then, eventually, Robert made Dan give up even that.

Stanley was enraged.

"How can he *do* such a thing!" he yelled at me over the phone one day.

"Maybe he's scared of disease," I opined. "I hear you only have to *kiss* someone in the baths nowadays to get amebas . . . " But that had never stopped Stanley, of course.

"It's like slavery, or something," Stanley fumed over the distance of the three floors that separated our apartments. (Stanley and I seldom saw each other face to face now, far preferring the telephone.) "I tell you, it will be the end of *that* relationship. It's only been able to survive this long because Dan is still dazzled by Robert's reputation."

"His reputation?"

"Really, Binky, you're so dense sometimes!" Stanley shouted. "His reputation as a hustler," he explained more calmly. "It *is* heaven, I'll have to admit. But remember when he'd quit and Dan kept insisting he still worked at the dirty bookstore and turned tricks in the back when business was slow? When Robert was actually waiting on tables at Clyde's? So much for romance. Binky. Don't you see? Robert's trying to make a lapdog of Dan and a pussycat of himself. It'll never last."

In spite of Stanley's dire prediction, though, it did last. Until, that is, Dan sneaked off to the baths and met Gregory.

What did Gregory have that Robert didn't? Certainly he was every bit as middle-class as Robert. And hadn't Robert gone to Duke for a semester before San Francisco, Dallas, Chicago, and the Big Apple exerted their irresistible charms and fired his wanderlust? And what was Gregory doing in Dan's apartment? When Dan had so successfully resisted the delights of domesticity Robert himself had so often tempted him with?

I couldn't be so gauche as to ask any of these questions of Dan directly when next we met (without Gregory) for dinner at The Blue Fox, but I was rewarded with some answers in the course of his rhapsodic and rather overblown praise of Gregory throughout.

"He's an utter sweetheart, Binky. Don't you think? *Everyone* seems to like him. You know, I've never, ever, been able to tolerate sharing my space with another human being—though I *did* enjoy having you around, in the beginning, you know—but Gregory. Well, Gregory's like having some dreadfully discreet servant—no, that's not it. Some lovely *object*. Like having some charmingly decorative object around the house. Oh, I know that sounds terrible. But we never *talk*. He's bored to tears with talk about my business and you *know* what I think of any music other than Mozart. (He listens on headphones; he's really so considerate.) But I just sit there and stare at him for hours, curled up there on the couch with his earphones on his head, reading *Jukebox* or whatever it is he reads. I just stare and stare and stare and stare . . . And, Binky, I'm wildly faithful. It hasn't occurred to me *once* to go out to the baths or the bookstore or even to the pier. Not once."

"That's great, Dan," I said as soon as I could get a word in. "But if you broke up with—"

"Oh, I know. It's ironic, isn't it? Gregory's even more insanely jealous than Robert was. That I should exchange one for the other . . . But I don't know. Somehow it's different with Gregory. I'm sure when we finally *do* do it . . . " Thoughtfully, Dan poked at his salad.

"*Do* do it, Dan? You mean you haven't even—had sex yet?"

"Well . . . No, but we *plan* to. Soon. Now, where *is* that waiter," Dan said quickly, once and forevermore dropping a curtain over the subject.

"You see," said Stanley that evening over the phone, "when they met, Gregory had *el clap*. That's why they didn't do it in the baths. And then, later, of course, he had to have all those *shots*. And now—well, it's just too intimate to disclose."

"Stanley," I panted, "have I *ever*—"

"Oh, all right. It seems that Dan has *crabs*."

"Crabs!"

"You know, those little—"

"I know what crabs are, Stanley."

"And that he must have gotten them from *Robert*."

"Robert? But Robert never—"

"Well, who else could Dan have gotten them from? He got rid of them *immediately*, of course. I had to tell him what to ask for at the drugstore as it had been so long since he'd had to buy it. But Gregory, it seems, was incensed. Accused him of all sorts of infidelities and said the thought of having crabs himself just drove him crazy, and was Dan sure he'd killed them all, and he wanted him to see a doctor, and they went around and around about it."

"So they haven't had sex yet?"

"Oh, Binky, really, you *are* dense sometimes! Of course they haven't had sex. I doubt if they ever *will*. That's the secret of it, their connubial bliss: they don't *do* it."

Of all of us, William was most assiduous about keeping in touch with Robert. Perhaps he was able to do so because, working the night shift at the suicide-prevention hotline, he kept much the same hours as Robert, now that Robert had gone back to his call service. (And perhaps they had a lot of notes to compare, so alike were their professions.) It was William who told Robert about Dan's crabs and Dan's allegations.

"Lars says," said Stanley, "that William told him that Robert said he was going over to punch Dan in the nose, that he'd never for one minute been unfaithful to Dan, and that it was the ultimate insult for Dan, having so cruelly thrown him over, to blame the crabs on *him*, of all people, since Dan had refused to have sex with him for weeks anyway . . . "

Robert did go to Dan's, in a murderous frame of mind, according to his own account, but Dan wasn't at home. Instead, he confronted Gregory.

Gregory met him at the door with the earphones still on top of his head, rather cross, Robert thought, about being disturbed at his work.

"I'm screening a demo tape," he said after Robert had identified himself. "La Maricona. She's the hottest new thing in salsa." Gregory invited Robert into the living room to listen.

"I'm not here to listen to music," said Robert frostily, "I'm hear to see Dan."

"He's not here."

"So you said. I'll sit and wait, then."

"Suit yourself," said Gregory, plunking himself down on the sofa and lowering the headphones down over his ears.

So they sat like that for a few minutes, Gregory tapping his foot to the inaudible music and occasionally mouthing the lyrics; Robert in a slow boil only a well-placed fist on Dan's patrician nose would dissipate.

But not even Robert's anger could blind him to the fact that one chestnut-colored testicle hung out of the leg of Gregory's gym shorts, and that he could, with little trouble, see even more than that by moving slightly to one side in his chair. So, slumped there, eyes riveted on Gregory's crotch, Robert experienced his own growing arousal. And an idea came to him, a prospect much more satisfying than socking Dan: seducing his new lover.

"Excuse me," Robert said after a while. "I said, excuse me." He raised his voice for Gregory's benefit.

"Yes?" Gregory said, lifting one earphone.

"May I have a glass of water?"

"Sure." Gregory waved toward the kitchen.

"Actually," Robert said, flashing Gregory what he knew was one of his more wattage-filled smiles, "I'd much rather have a drink. If you'll join me."

"Uh, sure. You know where it is," said Gregory, still under the thrall of "La Maricona."

Robert went to the bar and fixed a light vodka and tonic for himself, a much heavier version of the drink for Gregory. Returning to the couch, he allowed his wrist to graze Gregory's bare shoulder as he dangled the cold glass before his eyes. This time he seated himself at the opposite end of the sofa.

"So refreshing," he commented to Gregory, lifting his glass.

"Umm," replied Gregory, who (for it was sweltering in the apartment) downed half his drink.

Two drinks later, the two of them (fast friends now, and discussing Keith Jarrett to beat the band) reclined on the couch, legs intertwined, heads propped up on Dan's macramé pillows. Robert's toes were busy with the gym shorts.

Then, still enthusing over jazz improvisation, Robert allowed his foot to graze, just barely graze, Gregory's scrotum. He was rewarded with a distension of the tan gym shorts.

"Would you like another drink?" Robert asked. "Or would you

like me to take care of *that* first?'' Giving the bulge a flick with this big toe.

Gregory's eyes had taken on a glazed look. However, he replied: ''Oh, I can't. I'm really sorry. But I'm—dripping.'' He sat up, the ice in his nearly empty glass clinking. ''I've had this—problem—for some time now. Can't seem to get rid of it.''

''Oh,'' Robert said between clenched teeth. He wasn't sure whether he was most keenly disappointed over Dan's not arriving at the apartment to find them *in flagrante* or over not having Gregory in the first place, as Gregory was indeed luscious, as Dan had told us.

''But,'' said Gregory, peeping out between lowered lashes, ''I'll do *you*, if you like . . . '' He smiled. ''If you'll get more ice.''

Robert readily agreed, knowing of course what the ice was for, and it was only a few minutes later that Dan found them, on the floor at his feet, Gregory with Robert's cock in his mouth and savoring it like the Popsicle he'd rendered it.

''And then?'' A pool of water was gathering around my feet on the parquet (he'd gotten me out of the shower) and my hot breath was blowing into the receiver. I pleaded for dish.

''Well, *Robert* wouldn't tell me,'' said Stanley, ''so I had to call up Jack, who'd talked to Kevin in the meantime, who said *William* said— you know Robert tells *William* everything anyway. I don't know why you just didn't call *him*.''

''Stanley,'' I said, ''everyone knows you have the best dish in New York,'' as unctuously as I knew how. ''Go on, *please*.''

''Well, William *allegedly* says that Dan flew into a rage at Gregory and promptly sent him packing, duffel bag and all, and even ripped the cassette out of the tape deck and threw it out the window at Gregory's departing form, screaming something in Spanish after him— where did he learn it, do you suppose? San Juan? Anyway, then Dan just broke down and Robert of course had to comfort him, for friendship's sake alone (though Jack said *Myles* told him Robert was thinking all this time that Dan had never thrown such a scene over *him*, was icy cold—as we knew he was—over the breakup in the first place), and Robert gave him a drink and put him to bed and held his hand until Dan fell asleep.''

''How utterly Greer Garson,'' I said under my breath.

''What? Well, anyway, Robert crept away and *no one's* heard a word from Dan since. He won't answer his phone. The machine's not even on. Of course, as soon as I heard, I went over there immediately—it does seem to help him so, to talk it out with *me*, for some reason—but he didn't answer the bell. He might be dead for all we know.''

"Just licking his wounds," I said. "He really was nuts about Gregory, you know.''

"I don't think I've ever seen him happier," agreed Stanley. "Even when he thought Robert was Cal Culver, Al Parker, and Ronald Colman all wrapped up in one.''

Not a single ray of light penetrated Dan's bedroom as I followed him from the door back into the gloom. He'd pulled the shades and the heavy draperies. The room smelled of stale cigarette smoke and Vicks VapoRub.

"I haven't been well," he whispered, crawling back into bed.

"I'm so glad you let me in," I told him, taking the chair beside the bed, where I imagine Robert had held his vigil. "We're all terribly worried about you. I just thought I'd take a chance on your letting me in.''

"You, Binky? Of course," sighed Dan. I could just make out his features on the pillow. His hand found mine and squeezed it loosely on top of the bedclothes.

"What is it?" I asked discretely. "Influenza?"

"*Douleur de coeur*," Dan said faintly. "Really, Bink, I'm weak as a kitten. That boy took it out of me. Such heartache.''

"Tut-tut," I said. "Why not go to the Island for a few days. Get some sun? You'll feel *so much* better.''

"*Fire* Island, you mean? Why, Bink," he said, "*none* of us has gone there for *years*. So tacky since they ruined it." His hand grasped mine tight, in a spasm of some sort. "It's true that I promised Gregory I'd take him out, just for a day. The dear boy had never seen it. Can you imagine?" Affection had crept into his voice. "I told him, of course, that the Connecticut shore is the thing now, if one *has* to go anywhere. I do love the city in the summer," he said sentimentally, and rather as if all Manhattan had somehow dematerialized. "All empty and silent. So much wiser to vacation in winter, don't you think, when one really *needs* it . . . " He released my hand and sank deeper into the pillows. "But I might have lost him there, too.''

"Who? Where?"

"Gregory," he snapped with sudden vehemence. "Who else? On the Island."

"Oh. I see."

"Ah, we grow older." Dan sighed, lapsing back into his deathbed tone. "We grow older, Binky. Remember *our* affair, those many years ago, on the Island?"

"Yes," I murmured. "But, Dan, dear. It wasn't on the Island. It was East Hampton."

"East Hampton. Yes," he said, as if far into senility and thus not responsible for the slip. "Dear East Hampton."

"But you hated East Hampton, Dan. You said you excoriated East Hampton."

" 'Excoriated'? Did I? Do you suppose he'll come back?"

"Have you tried calling him?"

"He won't answer his phone," Dan said. "Ah, well, I suppose he meant it when he said it was over."

"Maybe if you apologized to him," I suggested. "Gregory's too young to mean half of what he says."

"Gregory?" Dan's eyes opened in the darkness. I could see the whites flash at me. "What do you mean, Gregory? I mean Robert, of course!"

"Robert?"

"Of course!" He sat up in bed. "Blood's thicker than water, you know."

I didn't contradict him or otherwise correct him. Instead, I asked, "You want Robert back *now*? After all this?"

"Of course I do! I've been lying here thinking about him and him alone for the past three—have they been three or four, Binky?"

"Three."

"Three days. How kind of him. How kind he was to have been the—er—instrument of my disillusion. To have revealed Gregory to me for what he was."

"Kind?"

"Of course. He showed me what *true* fidelity is. When that little hustler only wanted the connections I could provide him in the music business—"

"But you have no connections in the music business, Dan."

"Well, I *might have*," Dan said curtly, throwing off the bedclothes. He sat up and blew his nose. "I never got around to it, that's all." He fell back in bed again. "And it took Robert to make the ultimate sacrifice, to take the risk of showing up Gregory for the cheap little chiseler he was."

I didn't reveal to him Robert's obvious motivation in the incident. I was thinking, anyway, what marvelous news I had for Stanley—that Dan was indeed going off the deep end at last and would need our help and care to pull him back . . .

"I know what I'll do!" said Dan, suddenly bolting up out of bed. "I'll *write* him." In a cloud of VapoRub, he crossed the room and threw open the bedroom door. "I'll write him and thank him and make amends for my *awful* behavior. I'll invite him to dinner! Yes!" He flew to his writing desk, bathrobe trailing behind him, and sat down, whisked a piece of paper out of the drawer, and picked up a pen.

"Dan," I said from the doorway. "Don't you think you should get back in bed? Think it over awhile? You're white as a sheet."

"Nonsense," he said, brandishing the pen over the paper. "Where do you think I should take him for dinner? Le Petit Pré? No, that's so public. Four Seasons? *No one* goes there . . . "

"But, Dan," I said gently. "What if he really *doesn't* want to see you anymore? What if he spurns you?"

"Me? The boy's head over heels in love with me. Any fool can see that." And he began to scribble out his apology.

"William? This is Binky."

Stanley paced and fretted behind me, paying one of his entirely infrequent visits to my apartment, a token of how really important the situation had become.

"Oh, Binky. Long time no hear," said William rather languidly over the phone.

"Yes. I've been trying to reach you all afternoon."

"I was sleeping."

"Oh. Well, William, it's about Dan, you see."

"Dan? Oh, Dan. I heard he was—indisposed. Too bad, because I'm having a little dinner party Friday night and I—but didn't you get my invitation?"

"Why, no."

"Oh, the mails are just impossible, aren't they? Well, I'm having a little dinner party Friday night. Just eight of us, it's so hot out, just a light little summer meal . . . "

I remembered the dreadful night of the tongue. "That's great, William,'' I said into the receiver, Stanley now pacing circles around me. ''A dinner party,'' I said for Stanley's edification. ''But I'm really calling to see if you know where *Robert* is. You see, *Dan*—''

''Oh, Robert. Why, he's right here, of course. Shall I put him on the phone?''

''Please do.'' (''*Robert's there*,'' I mouthed to Stanley, who then fell onto the couch in a very passable imitation of cardiac arrest.) ''Yes, please do.''

''Hello.'' It was Robert's deep voice.

Yes, he had received Dan's letter and found it pathetic. The man didn't even know when he was being betrayed and completely humiliated before everyone in New York. No, he wasn't going to dignify such a mercenary reversal by even answering it. Well, he was sorry Dan wasn't feeling well, but didn't I think it was time that *someone else* put up with his fits and childish behavior, he really didn't have the time.

''Besides,'' said Robert. ''We're too busy.''

''We?'' I asked.

''William and I. Planning Friday, for instance. I'm cooking.'' Here he gave a light little laugh. ''Well, you *know*,'' he said, voice somewhat muffled—he was obviously talking to William and not me—''you've never served anything *remotely* to be confused with real food, precious.''

It was the ''precious'' that got to me. I said I'd see them Friday night and hung up.

Stanley was clutching the throat of his shirt and begging for dish the way a drowning man calls for help.

Friday night was a great success, by far the greatest success William had ever had. He'd even rustled up some people we didn't know, two Frenchmen, lovers, he'd met at the Underground and a devastatingly chic Punk Rock girl whose life he'd saved over the phone. The food, under Robert's supervision, was delicious: a marvelous cold salmon soup, a cold roast, celery and mushrooms *à la grecque* (Stanley said it was from Balducci's), a nice raspberry mousse. It was William who lit the candles (dozens of them, in little votive holders) and it was Robert who passed around the joints. It was William who ladled the soup and Robert who poured the cappuccino.

All but throwing a body block on Stanley, I followed William out onto the terrace when he went out to get a breath of fresh air.

"Don't you just love the sky over Manhattan?" he said dreamily, when I joined him at the rail. "Such a violet."

"How'd you do it?" I asked.

"What?" He turned to me and smiled. "The mousse? Why, it's pure Cuisinart. But you'll have to ask Robert."

"Robert," I said. "How'd you do it?"

"Oh, Robert. Isn't he the *end*? And so old-fashioned. Did you see how he lit Yves's cigarette?"

"We all know Robert's the last *man* left on the Eastern Seaboard," I said impatiently. "How'd you do it?"

"It? Oh, I see," said William coquettishly. "Why, I *hired* him, of course. It was the only way to *land* him. I'm surprised *Dan* didn't think of it, aren't you?"

"Dan's too *indisposed* to think of it," I said, quoting William. "But don't you think you should have given him a chance? After all, he's obviously still in love with Robert."

"In love?" William wrinkled up his pug nose. "Really, Binky, when he's been doing everything he possibly could to *get rid* of Robert for the past two years? All that tricking? And then blaming the *crabs* on Robert, on top of everything else. In love?"

"But you said they were the perfect couple, William."

"The psychiatrists have a word for it, Binky, and I have to admit I succumbed: 'projection,' Binky. I simply projected myself into their affair. When all along I should have realized that it was *I* and Robert who would make the perfect couple. And we are. It's a bit early to tell, of course," said William, trailing his fingers in the soot along the railing. "But I *think* it will last. Of course, I *do* have a plan."

"And what might *that* be?" I said, admiring William for the first time, in spite of my feelings for Dan.

"I'll absolutely *insist* that Robert not give up on his—er—career. Pay him myself, if need be. Really, Binky, it's the only thing he's happy doing, and he still has a few good years in him, and by that time, when retirement rolls around, he'll *really* be mine. I'm surprised Dan never thought of that."

"Dan's not as *domestic* as you," I commented rather nastily.

"Don't be cross with me, Binky," he replied, unperturbed. "I mean, the sex angle. No wonder he got tired of Robert. Robert was no longer the hustler he'd met and fallen in love with. We all should have one," William said philosophically, dusting off his hands. "It's such a wonderful device. You see, I can be completely faithful, while he has no choice. And I assure you, Binky, *I* won't stray. Why should I, when I have the most marvelous sexual animal in my bed every night—uh—afternoon? He'll be satisfied, and, I assure you, so will I.''

And with that, William went back to join his guests and his new lover—who was now pouring anisette into little cobalt-blue glasses that looked suspiciously identical to those Dan had given him the Christmas before.

Dan went to the Island after all—"that wonderful Stephen Greco, the designer, who I had a brief fling with pre-Robert?"—and came back with a new haircut (very severe, very short but for a pigtail in the back) and a new lease on life. "I had sex with *everyone*, Binky, I was to be found clawing my way through the meat rack day and night." The day I met him for drinks at Montana Eve, he was wearing a turquoise-and-school-bus-yellow jumpsuit and a huge silver bracelet on one wrist. A brace of fuchsia feathers hung from the pigtail down his back.

"And speaking of," Dan said. "What news of Robert? Anything? Stanley—can you believe it, holding out on me—refused to tell me word one."

"Oh, Robert," I said.

"He never answered my letter, you know."

"He didn't?"

"No. He sent it back, actually. I think, however, he'd steamed it open. I mean, would *you* be able to resist reading a letter from your ex? Under such circumstances? What is he doing?" asked Dan, rather too brightly, I thought, taking a sip of his white wine and pretending to cruise the numbers passing by on the avenue. "Anything interesting?"

"Hustling," I said.

"You know," said Dan, when I didn't provide anything more, "I got the *most* strange invitation from William when I got back . . . "

"Really?" I said, voice breaking a bit.

"Yes. To a *wedding*. At the Little Church Around the Corner. Can you beat that? A wedding invitation. I didn't think people *did* that anymore. Or is it that they're *all* doing it now? I mean now that I've become so madly single suddenly? But who is he marrying?"

Mute, I didn't have the heart to tell him.

"Well, I can see you know," he said kindly. "Just aren't at liberty to tell me. But who will he get to perform the service? I mean, don't they disbar ministers who do such things? Oh, come on, Binky, you always know about these matters. Don't you read *The Advocate* religiously? God knows none of the rest of us do. Well, I thought I'd go, just for a lark, you know, to actually *see* it. A piece of cultural history, I imagine. Do you think it's the wave of the future? I mean, now that I've become so *liberated*? I really *did* love Robert, you know, Binky."

"Yes, I know," I said, signaling the waitress for another round. "I know you did."

"But I wonder," said Dan, staring into his drink, "if *he* knows. Men are so fickle, aren't they?" When I didn't answer, he continued. "Actually, I think at my age I might consider settling down. *After* I sow a few more wild oats. Yes, it very well might be the coming thing . . . "

From *Nights in Aruba*

Andrew Holleran

Nights in Aruba (1983) is Holleran's second novel. Its theme is the way gay men negotiate their relationships to their families, particularly with their mothers. In the following section, part of Chapter 4, the narrator, having been released from the military, settles in New York at a distance from his parents. He meets Mister Friel, a former history professor denied tenure because of his sexuality, when they both are hired to sell encyclopedias door-to-door. The narrator and Mister Friel are joined by their living in the same building, working in the same office, and sharing the same Catholic guilt about their love for young men and the same confusion about how to live their lives.

When I encountered Mister Friel on Sunday mornings going off to Brooklyn for this weekly feast—walking down the same street I was coming home on at ten o'clock after a night of dancing—I said good-bye to him as if he were going to the guillotine. His parents lived next to the Verrazano Narrows Bridge. Whenever I surveyed the harbor on one of my walks to Battery Park, I looked out over the water and imagined Mister Friel—just where the dark span touched Brooklyn—cooking dinner for his parents. He visited them chiefly to prepare meals. That fall Mister Friel and I were proofreaders at the same law firm on Park Avenue. We worked the night shift, read to one another, and shared a taxi home. The taxi was one of the perquisites of the night shift, arranged chiefly because women could not be expected to travel on the subway at that hour. Mister Friel told me the subway was enchanting then, however: You never knew what would be seated in the car when you got on, slumped over, half-asleep on his way home to Brooklyn. So we took the IRT home instead. I got off at Astor

Place, and Mister Friel often stayed on. He got to his parents' place around five in the morning and prepared their breakfast. Or he went directly from the baths. His father liked to walk, but in recent years the esplanade along the Narrows had become dangerous for an elderly man because of teenage thieves; so Mister Friel escorted him on a promenade after breakfast, while his mother (who went in and out of lucidity like a country radio station) watched *Donahue*. After they returned home Mister Friel prepared lunch and dinner, put them in Tupperware containers in the refrigerator, and came back to Manhattan.

It was the sort of double like I never had to think about while I was in New York, a city which, if it held for me all the possibilities of a tale from *A Thousand and One Nights*, was nevertheless anchored in a sea of brick houses whose walls contained families just like the one I was separated from. My New York held no families. My New York was a late-night city, its streets occupied by prostitutes, taxicabs, roaming homosexuals, its parks trysting places, its ruined neighborhoods mere stage sets on which isolated figures appeared to fulfill my romantic dreams. That these figures all came from families enclosed by the walls of the numberless houses that stretched in all directions around Manhattan was not a fact I dwelled on.

One never met the family—that was the moment which didn't occur in these relationships. One heard tales of families whose members you would never lay eyes on. When I met some stranger we eventually spoke about our origins—like the warriors in the *Iliad* who describe their family trees to one another in the midst of battle—in the aftermath of erotic love, his white limbs glowing in the pale radiance reflected on the brick wall outside my window, or when, nearly hidden in the gloom of a rainy night whose drops zigzagged down the windowpane as he talked, he spoke of his family, it was like hearing the description of a puzzle that possessed endless variations. Each word only endowed his body with more interest. Like the young men I saw at Mass in Pennsylvania, flanked by their families, the stranger's beauty was enhanced.

From the lips of these somnolent refugees I heard about families very different from my own: a cold mother so sarcastic to her son that he still twitched twenty years later; of a four-hundred-pound woman who sat on her children when they misbehaved, who locked them in closets and threw them down the laundry chute. I heard of the mother who—in a provincial city in Brazil—convinced her perfectly healthy, handsome son that he was dying of cancer and so should not leave home. I heard of a woman so unhappy on learning her son desired men that—after inviting beautiful young women to her house, one of whom ran off with her husband—she slept with him herself. I also heard of a mother who took her son to house parties in Capri and fell asleep beside him discussing which men at dinner were the most attractive. I met young men who were to their mothers as curators to a museum collection—who served as hairstylist, confidant, dresser, hailer of taxis, escort in restaurants; and others who were grateful when theirs went to Florida at Christmas because it meant they would not have to see her for their annual dinner. A visitor from San Francisco remarked to me that his mother lived in a town across the bay beside which we lay taking the sun on Fire Island one afternoon; he could see the roof of her house amongst the trees on the Long Island shore. She did not know he was in the East, however, much less a boat-ride away across Great South Bay. He called her that evening and pretended he was still in San Francisco, "because," he said, "if I tell her I'm here, she'll be hurt if I only have dinner with her and don't stay the week." So he went back west without even seeing her. One man told me he fought bitterly with his mother until he told her he was homosexual; now they were friends, and she came with his father to the party he threw every New Year's Eve and bantered with the weight lifters and the boys from Yale. I loved stories of families—at a distance.

One weekend Mister Friel and I had to work overtime because a loan agreement between Citibank and the Republic of Nigeria was being prepared on New Year's Day. I went home with him because the documents we had to compare were so long we decided Mister Friel could not take time out to attend his parents. He would have to do both at once.

We did not leave the office until four in the morning—the lawyer finally went home himself—and we emerged from the subway in Brooklyn behind two young men on their way home from a party in Manhattan. The streets were lined with redbrick row houses in every direction. There was an air of quiet and repose which one felt whenever one left Manhattan. We went up the stairs of a house like all the others, four blocks from the subway. "Welcome," Mister Friel said as he turned the key and opened the door, "to Nightmare Abbey." We went into the kitchen and unpacked the food Mister Friel had purchased earlier that evening. "Come," he said. We walked through a small living room and went upstairs. Mister Friel paused in a doorway—beyond him I saw his parents sleeping still in their beds—took me by the arm and whispered, "One day I tell myself I will find them not breathing. I will have to act. Go to the telephone, phone whom? The ambulance, a funeral home? I dread it more than my own death. I will have to invite people to the funeral, choose the dress in which Mother is to be laid out. Doesn't life stink?" he whispered, and led me downstairs. "Even if everything goes *well*, it stinks." We set our documents out on the dining-room table and then Mister Friel began to prepare breakfast. He unpacked the bag from Balducci's: the kippers, sour cream, croissants. "My mother loves starch. She's in ecstasy eating rolls that cost a dollar nineteen a dozen at Daitch, but I bring her these extremely expensive croissants anyway." He set these on a plain white plate with fluted edges and a blue border, and put them on a tray. He waved his hand toward a cabinet in the hall and said, "They have all this Rosenthal china she refused to use all her life. But what am *I* going to do with it? Serve hustlers tea? Look what I got," he said, producing a cluster of irises which he put in a glass vase and placed on the tray. He turned to me and said, "Remind me to ask Mother about her soap opera. I watch it with her from time to time—so we have a topic in common." He put a jar of Fortnum & Mason's apricot preserves on the tray, a silk scarf he had bought his mother at a discount-designer store, and then prepared his father's tray with a neatly folded copy of the *Irish Echo*. We took them upstairs. I waited in the hall. Mister Friel took both trays into the bedroom. I heard his father say, "Well, good morning, son, and Happy New Year. Your mother and I were in bed last night at ten o'clock."

"You and the Lindsays!" said Mister Friel.

"And the what?" said his father.

"The Lindsays—the former mayor and his wife," said Mister Friel. "The *Times* did a piece on how people spend New Year's Eve. Most of them said they liked to stay home. Mayor Lindsay said he and his wife are always in bed sleeping when the New Year comes in." Then he said: "Good morning, Mother. What happened to Ned yesterday?"

"Oh, Ned," she said. "He's still being poisoned by Vanessa and doesn't know it."

"And is Sheila going to tell him then?" said Mister Friel.

"She's tried, but everyone knows how she hates Vanessa, so no one will believe her when she's telling the truth," she said. "But Elaine was told off, at least, and I'm glad for that."

"Was she the one dealing dope?" said Mister Friel politely as he stood, his back to me, between their beds, while a white curtain at the window bathed the room in a pearl-gray light.

"Yes. You've never tried any of those things, have you? Dope?" she said.

"Of course not," said Mister Friel, turning now to leave the room. "As James said, 'Consciousness is everything.' I'll be up in a few minutes with your omelettes."

We went downstairs, into the kitchen, and he began chopping up a large mushroom and a small onion on a cutting board. "I can't bear to watch soap operas," he said. "I would much rather sleep with the actors, half of whom I see at the baths. I don't see how I can tell Mother that the man who plays the chief surgeon in *Gull City* is a man who always has his boyfriend stand in the street beneath the window of his apartment before he comes inside, so he can massage his crotch and then hold up a piece of paper with his apartment number written on it. As if the boyfriend were a perfect stranger being picked up on the street! Much more interesting than the scenes he has to play as Doctor Ramsey," said Mister Friel. He broke two eggs in a bowl and stirred them with a whisk. "On the other hand I'm quite shocked by what does go on in these shows. *We* may live for sex, but I don't like to think the rest of the country does! I would *never* allow children of mine to watch television," he said. "I would raise them abroad. In rural Japan." He poured the eggs into the warm skillet and shook it back and forth to prevent the eggs' sticking. "I do so long to travel," he said to me, looking over his shoulder. "But how can I go to São Paulo when my parents can hardly make it to the icebox?" And he went upstairs with two plates of eggs.

At ten o'clock we went to church—his parents in black coats, his mother with a small black hat, arm in arm with Mister Friel. His father, a few paces ahead of us, looked up at the sky, remarking what a fine day it was. The church was only two blocks away: one of those immense, grimy edifices whose interiors are far more magnificent than anything a modern church possesses. If New York was a city full of fountains that were never turned on, it was also a town full of churches that were empty. In the afternoon on Fifth Avenue I went into them to rest and get away from the crowds. Here the church held far fewer people than it might have and those were chiefly families from Central and Latin America. The paint on the wall just beneath the gilded ceiling was peeling off in patches, but the service was modern. The priest

Above: Edmund White photographed by Robert Giard at David Kalstone's apartment in 1985. *Right:* Andrew Holleran photographed at his apartment by Robert Giard in 1985.

Left: George Whitmore photographed at his apartment by Robert Giard in 1987. *Below:* Michael Grumley (*left*) and Robert Ferro (*right*) photographed in their home by Robert Giard in 1984.

Right: Christopher Cox photographed at home by Robert Giard in 1989. *Below:* Felice Picano photographed by Robert Giard in 1985 at the Amagansett home of Michael Hampton and George Stambolian.

The Gay Writers Group in the 1982 Heritage of Pride Parade. Michael Grumley and Robert Ferro in the foreground. (*Photo by Lee Snider. Copyright Lee Snider/ Photo Images.*)

Top: David Rothenberg, Robert Ferro, and Larry Kramer at the 1981 Gay Pride March. (*Photo courtesy of Ferro-Grumley estate.*) *Above:* Robert Ferro and Andrew Holleran at the 1981 Gay Pride March. (*Photo courtesy of Ferro-Grumley estate.*)

Left: Bill Whitehead
and Michael Grumley at
rally in Central Park
following the 1981 Gay
Pride March. (*Photo
courtesy of Ferro-
Grumley estate.*) *Below:*
Charles Ortleb of
Christopher Street and
Christopher Cox at the
Central Park rally,
1981. (*Photo courtesy
of Ferro-Grumley
estate.*)

Top: From left to right: Marcia Pally, George Stambolian, James Saslow, Robert Ferro, Michael Grumley, Stephen Greco, Lawrence Mass, unknown woman, and Arnie Kantrowitz at the Central Park rally, 1981. (*Photo courtesy of Ferro-Grumley estate.*) *Above:* From left to right: Robert Ferro, Vito Russo, Michael Grumley, and George Stambolian at the 1981 Gay Pride rally. (*Photo courtesy of Ferro-Grumley estate.*)

began the service by turning to us as he reached the altar and saying, "Good morning." The congregation shouted, "Good morning, Father!" Mister Friel leaned toward me and hissed in my ear: "And now what, calisthenics?"

The priest began to talk about the fine weather and his hope that everyone had celebrated the New Year in moderation—while Mister Friel continued to whisper to me: "Look who's around us—Latinos! White people have no more religion. They're too busy examining their biorhythms!" He fell silent when the Mass began, following it in his old, faded missal, whose pages were clogged with tiny prayer cards which he would turn over from time to time, revealing on the back the name of some deceased person beneath a small black cross. His mother said the Rosary and his father stared straight ahead with an alert expression, trying to follow a Mass he could not hear. The words, amplified by a microphone whose effect was considerably diminished by the echoing spaces of this once-rich and once-crowded church, came to us in fits and snatches during the sermon. At one point the priest warned against "fictitional beliefs that lure us to the desert of self-satisfaction."

"Fictional!" Mister Friel hissed beside me. "It is either fictional or fictitious. There is no such word as *fictitional*." He sat beside me, swept with thundering sermons only he himself heard, jolted out of his daydreams by occasional crimes against syntax on the part of the priest. "When will people understand," he said, leaning toward me and speaking in a whisper, "that there is no such thing as 'most perfect.' Something is either perfect or it is not. There are no degrees of perfection." Mister Friel sat back and frowned as the sermon continued: rambling, discursive, and metallic in sound.

At the Communion his parents went up to the altar, slowly, his mother already hunched over with the pinched posture that comes to women in old age. Mister Friel turned to me in the freedom their departure allowed and said, "*E*veryone goes these days. There are no standards anymore, whatsoever. It's impossible to find a good cotton lisle polo shirt, or a Catholic who does not go to Communion. A Jesuit I know who lives on Eighty-first Street told me not to worry about going to Confession. He told me that if I wanted to go, I should walk into Central Park and confess to a *tree*! Can you imagine?" he said. "This encouraging advice only confirmed my belief that the Church is on its way toward oblivion. I wouldn't *dare* go to Communion without having confessed," he said.

"Why don't you confess, then?" I whispered.

"Because the Church considers *it* a sin, and I don't," he said. "Or rather, they consider homosexual acts a sin, and homosexual acts saved my life! Whoops, it looks like Dad has lost his way," he said, and stood up. Mister Friel left the pew and walked up the long aisle to his father, who stood on the tiled floor with hands joined, looking around at the sea of strange faces and empty pews, unable to remember where we were sitting. Mister Friel led him back down the aisle and went up again to retrieve his mother.

Within a few moments the priest turned to us and gave the final blessing, which Mister Friel took with the eagerness of one who was glad to receive anything—from invitations to costume parties to the blessing of God—free. By the time we left the church he was much calmer, almost reluctant to leave, and he lingered in the foyer, dipping his hand in the font of holy water, turning to look back at the altar and kneel once more.

"Can't hear a word the man says," his father remarked as we walked home.

"You didn't miss much," said Mister Friel. "There should be a school for men who must deliver sermons. Surely these poor people deserve to have the full splendor of the Catholic Church break upon them! One does not take as one's text *Raiders of the Lost Ark* even if you want to suggest that Christianity is also a treasure hunt. That concedes too much to the enemy. It makes you think of the scene in which she kisses Harrison Ford on his wounds."

"Oh, what a lovely day. The New Year! So much to look forward to! The Masseys are already in Florida," his mother said, looking at a house across the street, and then we went inside.

The remainder of the day passed quietly. Mister Friel and I worked on a big round table in the kitchen. Across the hall from us we could see his father in the den constructing on a card table a model of Rockefeller Center made entirely out of toothpicks. His mother read the newspaper until *Gull City* began on television, and then she closed the door and watched this show for an hour. At five o'clock Mister Friel's father rose and put his toothpicks away and came into the kitchen to mix cocktails for himself and his wife, while we searched the minutes of a United Nations conference on rubber for data the lawyer we were working for needed. By the time we went into the den with the dinner Mister Friel had prepared, his parents were voluble and excited by their cocktails. His father played with his false teeth as he watched the evening news, lifting them up with his tongue and pushing them forward and backward.

"Well, who threw her baby onto the subway tracks today!" said Mister Friel as he set up the television tables and made sure they were secure.

"Some Rastafarian! There are no Americans left in this country," his mother said as the tenants of a building in the Bronx were interviewed about the murder that had just occurred in a hall on the fifth floor. "None!" She said grace and we began to eat our dinners.

Just before the local news ended, I saw Mister Friel begin to stare at his father; he frowned as he watched his father bring his plate close to his face, mashing the remaining bits of food together with a frantic thoroughness. At one point it seemed he would begin to lick the plate, it was so near his lips. His chin jutted forward so that in profile he resembled Popeye. I saw Mister Friel, still frowning, glance over at his mother as if to see if she was not horrified by the sight of his father nearly kissing his plate, as the mad fork went on pressing, scraping, mashing, rubbing the surface to get every last morsel. We were both astonished when his father sat up suddenly, put the plate down, turned to my friend and said in a normal voice, "That was very good, son. Thank you." Until that moment we were staring at a drawing by Goya of Saturn devouring his children; suddenly we faced his father, composing himself and turning his attention to the "CBS Evening News."

"Mark my words," his mother said, turning to us with a roll in one hand and a knife smeared with butter in the other, "when I am dead and gone, you'll see—Walter Cronkite is a Communist."

"Oh, Mother," said Mister Friel. "He lives in Westchester."

"And where else do the Communists live?" she said. She held up the knife, and then turned to watch the television. News of the French takeover of a contract, which an American company withdrew when the President imposed sanctions against Russia, elicited from her an impassioned denunciation of the French. Coverage of an AFL-CIO convention increased her ire. "The unions have destroyed this country and no one has the guts to stop them!" she said.

Mister Friel said, "Now calm down, Mother," and served the chocolate mousse.

After the news a game show began which his mother asked us to watch because she liked to hear Mister Friel answer the questions. When the master of ceremonies of "Tic Tac Dough" said, "On what play was the famous opera *La Traviata* by Verdi based?" Mister Friel called out: "*The Lady of the Camellias* by Dumas!" and his mother turned to him with an ecstatic expression. "Why don't *you* get on these shows?" she said.

Mister Friel smiled, and began clearing the tables during the commercial. "Because a bachelor of forty-six is not what America is comfortable with on its game shows," he said in the kitchen. "The unmarried have always occupied a place in human society similar to that of the undead," he said.

Suddenly the sound of the television stopped. A voice came to us from the den: "*Aren't* you going to watch this with us?" his mother called in a tone so plaintive it froze Mister Friel in the act of putting the leftover broccoli into a Tupperware bowl. "We have so few moments together as a family," she said.

Mister Friel resumed his work and called, "I'll be right in." The television burst out afresh as she released the Mute button on the remote control, and Mister Friel turned to me with moist eyes and said, "Of all the words in the New Testament, the saddest ones I've always thought were those Christ addresses to his slumbering apostles. And now my own mother has asked the same question. 'Could you not watch an hour with me?' " He took down the cups and said in a sharper tone, "Only in this case it is not to make sure the priests of the Sanhedrin do not arrest the Messiah; it is merely to watch a housewife from Yuba City win a week in Acapulco."

We returned to the den with coffee just as the organ began the wild, hysterical theme of "Tic Tac Dough" while a new contestant came out onstage: a sales promoter from Redondo Beach so handsome that Mister Friel glanced at me with an alarmed expression. Mister Friel and I remained for the rest of the show. He missed only one question, about the Sargasso Sea, an exotic name that made Mister Friel think it was located off the coast of Indonesia, when it was in fact in the Atlantic.

After the show we left to work; and the sound of the television went on and off as his mother muted the commercials with the button on her remote control. During one of these silences, I heard her say in a quiet voice, "Where are we going to be buried, John? Here or in Rhode Island? We've got to decide. It's not fair to the kids."

"Mother!" Mister Friel said, raising his head from the document on the table. He frowned, stood up and went across the hall to the den.

"It's nothing to be afraid of," I heard his mother say. "We're going to die someday."

"Mother!" he said, louder and more frightened this time.

"Well, don't be silly," she said. "I *am* going to die. And you'll have to choose the dress they lay me out in. I think the navy-blue dotted Swiss."

"Is this what you think of during the commercials?" he said. "Perhaps it would be better if you didn't mute them, then."

"Or should we be cremated?" she said.

"If I had my way," said Mister Friel, his voice rising and turning colder, "I'd bury you in the backyard on a moonless night. Between the garbage cans and the clothesline. I *loathe* funerals! Cremation is simplest. Mother, the show is back on. Press the button!" he said. She did, and the television erupted into laughter. "Would you like some ice cream?" he said. Mister Friel passed me on the way to the refrigerator. "Thank God for television," he said as he scooped the ice cream into a bowl. "It is what Allen Tate said about civilization—the agreement to ignore the abyss." He sighed and returned to the den with a bowl of Sealtest Heavenly Hash.

At eight o'clock his father bid us good night and went upstairs. At eleven o'clock his mother rose and Mister Friel helped her up. As she passed the kitchen door, leaning on Mister Friel's arm, she said in a gentle voice, "I love you, you know, not for what you're doing to help us, but because you're you." And Mister Friel—who had turned so cold when his mother referred to her own death—looked stricken and bit his lip.

At midnight—after Mister Friel had opened all the Tupperware bowls and made sure that what he thought was in them was in fact there, like a man making sure his children are safely in bed—we left the house ourselves. The moment we stepped outside, the lights of the bridge, the cold, brisk wind, the distant figures of young men walking toward us in jeans, tennis sneakers, and blue bomber jackets, made Mister Friel put his hands over his mouth and shriek. "I'm going directly to the baths! The fact that we are young—well, *you* are young," he said, "and they are not, is so radical, I sometimes feel when I finally shut this door behind me that I have been born again. A born-again *flâneur!*" he said with a laugh as we went down the stairs. "And yet is it not totally unfair, as unfair as life itself, that they should be lying there facing Death when *I* am on my way to the Everard? I tell you, life stinks, it stinks, it stinks!" He turned to me as we went down into the subway. "You will come again, I hope, to Nightmare Abbey, when we do not have to spend the entire time working, when I can show you some of my scrapbooks, my first editions of all Donald Wyndham's novels and my back issues of *Horizon* magazine.''

But I had no intention of ever returning to that house—because I had no intention of leaving Manhattan at all. I always inquired after Mister Friel's parents, a courtesy he appreciated, even if it only allowed him to pass a hand over his forehead, sigh, and say: ''Oh, they're fine. As well as can be expected of a family which reminds me more and more of 'The Fall of the House of Usher!' '' That every one of those brick houses facing the Verrazano Narrows had behind its neat façade a tale by Poe I had no doubt. And while I loved to hear them told by some lover in the still of night, it was as a refugee that he lay there beside me—tied by these elastic teguments that stretched indefinitely over time and space, but momentarily free.

Vittorio refused to go to Mister Friel's for lunch on Sunday; he refused to go home himself that year except at Christmas and then only to recuperate from hepatitis. One evening not long after New Year's Day, Mister Friel met a young man who drove him home to a town in northwestern New Jersey. In the morning he awoke beside his host. There was a knock on the door. His host called, ''Come in!'' as he lifted his head from the pillow, and a middle-aged woman in a white apron carrying a tray with two bowls of cornflakes and peaches, two glasses of orange juice, *The New York Times*, and a daisy in a vase walked in.

''Good morning,'' she said, and put the tray across their laps.

''Good morning, Mother,'' said his host. ''Mother, I'd like you to meet William Friel.''

''How do you do, William,'' she said, extending her hand.

Mister Friel—who was at his best making new friends, who always had something charming to say to a stranger—found himself unable to speak. After a brief conversation about the family car, she left the room. ''You know how mothers are,'' his host said. ''She always likes to meet the people I bring home. Sugar?'' he said, turning to his guest.

But there was no answer. Mister Friel had fainted.

From *The Blue Star*

Robert Ferro

Although parts of The Blue Star *depart completely from Robert Ferro's life, the opening section of the novel is highly autobiographical. For long periods Ferro lived in Italy, and Italy appears in all his mature novels. Rome brings together in his work the spiritual, the erotic, and the aesthetic, as this chapter amply shows.*

In June of 1963, when I arrived in Florence, the Pensione Bardolini was in its ninth decade. Seasoned boarders invariably made the claim that E. M. Forster had written there all or part of *A Room With a View*, calling it the Bertolini. I had heard the name on the train from Rome. Ease of travel in those days, before the tourist boom, coupled with the confidence of a twenty-one-year-old whom life had scarcely noticed, seemed to lead me to it naturally. At the tourist agency in the train station they spoke to the Signora by phone, and a very low price was quoted: 1,900 lire a day, meals included, which then was just over three dollars. The taxi left me at the *portone* of a red palazzo on the river. The room I was given looked up and down the Arno, at the Ponte Vecchio in the morning mist, at pink, atrocious sunsets in the evening. For symmetry's sake within the frame of the window—and in an otherwise perfect situation—the Duomo might have been moved a foot or two to the left.

Signora Zá-zá was an attractive, childless widow inclined to show affection for those she liked. She always used the formal *Lei*, but with varying degrees of intimacy, from friendly to cold and abrupt. As a result I think she seemed slightly different to all her guests, like a team of sisters who greatly resemble each other. She was a small woman, probably only about forty-five at the time, who did nothing to glam-

225

orize herself. She wore housecoats and flats that slapped the bottoms of her feet down the long corridors; this sound of her arrival preceded her, giving us a moment to collect ourselves for the *padrona* and precluding surprise, which is anathema in a hotel.

It was not apparent at first but the clientele of the Bardolini was hardly orthodox sexually. I recall one or two elderly English couples, but everyone else was younger and single; not surprisingly, since Zá-zá did not bother with transients and preferred long-term boarders, and who else but young loners would be abroad for months at a time? When someone new rang the bell unannounced, which was common, Zá-zá would size him or her up according to some inner hosteler's instinct that had nothing to do with the availability of rooms. In the year I was there a few troublemakers slipped through her net but these, when they declared themselves—a theft, rudeness, a pregnancy—were sent packing without a qualm. I wonder now if this instinct of hers wasn't basically sexual. I once asked how she had made up her mind about me, by telephone, and she said she had asked the agency at the station to describe my footwear. She said she always looked at the feet. But I think she looked into our eyes and judged us by the degree to which we knew what we longed for.

In the dining room she always seated a new arrival at a table alone, at least for the first few nights. Then a group table was selected according to her choice. This period of adjustment, as if the new people were divers coming to the surface in stages, might last days or weeks.

The June nights, like the days, were hot, even excruciating. This and something else drew me into the streets around midnight. It seemed I was too excited for sleep, too warm, too young. After a few hours of writing in my room, I told myself a walk would calm me, and that Florence was beautiful at night. But the walking was like the writing. I didn't understand the purpose of either—only the mechanics. Putting the words down on paper was the same as putting one foot in front of the other in the empty streets.

These night walks were soon ritualized. After a few hours of work, on countless beginnings and fragments, I would go out. It wasn't clear to me that the writing was a preamble to the walks, an excuse, rather than the walks being a decompressing coda to the writing. Gradually the work interval was shortened. The moment of departure, like a decree, came earlier, and the walks lasted later into the night. By the beginning of July, I no longer wrote after dinner, and only prepared for the night.

* * *

The fifteen-foot portone downstairs, which lay open all day, was closed and locked at night. Beside it a stone lion face gradually smiled as the sun went down. The sound of the heavy door closing behind me, with its stony reverberations, meant freedom. Each time I felt I was turning suddenly to face a new life—all at once, a fresh, different existence in a new place nearly out of time.

At that hour you would have thought the years had flown away. Except for the streets along the river, or perhaps in Piazza Repubblica, no cars went by, and scarcely a carriage. In the narrow, cobbled streets of the perpetual past, in the shadows down a long, unlighted *vicolo*, it seemed whole centuries melted away in dark theatrical gloom. I was as if transported to a vague, operatic past, within elaborate tableaux— lifelike but unreal. And my impulse was to picture a role for myself within the spectacle in which these convincing street sets and cleverly lit night skies might have some personal use. Florence and me. It seemed that at night the place was abandoned to sensation and a whole new set of inchoate longings I scarcely recognized. Nothing was clear; nor did I suspect any motive behind the walks other than appreciation for the city and the formation of a new, unorthodox but sophisticated pattern—so different from life at school—that now suddenly was open to me. I felt some compunction to be in bed by dawn—when anyway the magic stopped—or at least before breakfast was brought in; but sleep was a matter of indifference, while the exquisite disregard of all previous patterns and rules gave me for the first time the impression of an inner life; as if, each night, as I slipped silently down the dark- ened stairs and through the vaulted hall, counter to all of life's currents, I was hurrying to a meeting with a new self—someone like me, but different.

This naïveté as to what I was doing lasted about a week. I remember the exact moment when the balance was tipped. It came in my second week there, as a kind of retrospective revelation that swept everything away. I had been looking at the river from the Ponte Vecchio. It was very late. A man walked toward me across the length of the bridge. He approached and in Italian asked the hour. I wasn't wearing a watch, and realized, as I looked at him, that he was not interested in the time. He had stopped in the light, and I saw in his luminous eyes, or thought I did, the two of us embracing—two sets of figures so tiny that only he and I would have recognized them as ourselves. He smiled, with what I understand now was a smile of self-congratulation: his instinct, even at fifty feet and in the dark, had not failed him. He had seen at a distance what I had not yet perceived within myself.

He might as well have struck me. Instead he said, "Thank you just the same, and good night," and walked on down Por Santa Maria. I pretended to look again at the river, the while listening to the sound of his receding footsteps.

Wandering at random through the streets, one after another, I think I wanted to walk until something happened. I walked along the Arno and into the park. I approached the train station as if to leave the city, or as if meeting a lover's train. I took a bus to the outskirts up the valley and walked back. At other times on other nights, I set up a circuit of visits to cafés in order to see the faces of men well lighted and close at hand. In these places I would try to blend in, to speak minimally but convincingly as a Florentine. I bought other clothes and cut my hair, fitting myself out in the manner, perhaps, of a young Italian student. This meant looking less American, less middle-class, less white, less male, less of everything I was—and more of this other thing.

A few weeks after I arrived, a Moroccan homosexual checked into the Bardolini, exotic and effeminate, the first such person I had seen at close range. In the evenings Rashid appeared at dinner wearing kohl on his eyes, discreet but discernible, and belladonna in them, he subsequently explained, which gave them a bright, bluish, myopic, doll-like gleam that was quite unnatural and mystifying. He wore also scent, and the kind of fine silk tops one's mother would wear in the 1970s. Rashid too was seated at a table alone but came over to mine at the first opportunity, choosing me out of all the others naturally and automatically, as though attracted I feared by a spoor, a sign, a physical invitation. This was embarrassing. What had he seen, I wondered, to choose me? What did it mean to the other diners that we sat, nightclub fashion, as in the whirling vortex of scandal?

I knew I was not like Rashid, but I knew I was not completely unlike him. I knew I would never wear eye makeup, but I was already conscious of the fact that I had appealing eyes, meaning they were a sexual tool I might use, if not to the same exaggerated degree.

Rashid's faulty English provided a screen behind which I managed to hide. When he asked what one did of an evening in Florence, I suggested the opera. When he asked if there weren't *certi posti*—certain places—where one could find *da fare*—things to do—I gazed blankly into his crystalline eyes. But the next night we encountered each other in the street. Rashid looked at me strangely and said, "Are you drugged?"

"No," I said firmly.

Then what was it, Rashid wanted to know. "Are you in love? Are you with child? I can always tell."

"I'm free," I said rather simply.

"Well, you have the strangest look in your eyes," Rashid said. "I suppose it might be freeness."

"Freedom," I corrected.

"You mean, of course, freedom to chase men," he went on, with a great cheap wryness. He looked at me and raised his chin. Regarding me speculatively, he said, "In Morocco they would take you like a ripe melon. Wait . . . they will come to you."

As late as the nights were, I would rise when Zá-zá or her niece Rosa brought in the breakfast tray. One or the other of them would knock briefly and come in, setting the tray down on the desk. Zá-zá always said something when she opened the shutters—*"Che bella giornata!"* or, as the days wore on, *"Che bel caldo!"* She would take the desk chair by its back, set it beside the bed, seat first, and remove the tray from the desk to the chair. I lay back against the pillows and looked through the open window at the sky. You could hear the city outside, and the pensione through the door.

Zá-zá's niece Rosa was a big-breasted, short girl with a beautiful face obscured and distorted by thick glasses. It was impossible to tell if she was eighteen or twenty-eight. Occasionally she released the bun of dark hair behind her neck and removed the eyeglasses, and, like a lovely blind girl at home, would deftly navigate the halls, avoiding the furniture by memory.

Alvaro, the houseboy, was someone's cousin. He was also short, but slight and birdlike. From his manner with everyone he seemed to maintain a strangely low opinion of himself and was given to little fits of subservience. He cocked his head to one side to make himself shorter, kept silent, did his work; and two nights a week drank himself to sleep, so that on the following mornings he looked green and ill and miserable.

Beside these three—Zá-zá, Rosa and Alvaro—four others made up the Bardolini household. Babbo, Zá-zá's father, was old, rheumy, obese, but still quick and humorous, and was cared for in the kitchen and treasured like a rare, dear pet. Rosa-mama, who was in fact Rosa's mother, was Zá-zá's sister-in-law. Orazio, Zá-zá's brother, was a laborer, a dark, thick man seldom seen, and then only in the kitchen like Babbo at mealtime, when you came in after lunch to say you would or would not be in for dinner. Their son Lorenzo was fifteen and had, through some trick of fate or ecstatic pact between Rosa-mama and her saints, been lifted from Caravaggio's erotic dreams and given to them all to worship. His beauty, of the heart-stopping variety, was something even the family could not get used to. Under its cover Lorenzo came and went unfathomed, unknown, but like visiting royalty indulged to the edge of belief.

Zá-zá's husband had been killed in the war. One afternoon as lunch was ending and a few of us sat at a table by the open window over the river, someone asked her what it had been like during the war, when the city was spared but many of the bridges were blown out of the water by the retreating Germans.

"Ah, *cari miei*..." she began, waving away the memories, the experience, the shattered windows and bullet-riddled walls. At the window she leaned pensively against the railing. "They fired from Fiesole," she said and pointed across the city to the hills beyond. "We were serving lunch. What did we know? These little popping sounds in the distance, and the window glass broke, the chandelier shattered and my poor husband fell, there..." She indicated a spot beside me on the floor. "After that we had terrible times, *tempi duri*..."

In the late morning, having carefully shaved and dressed, I rushed down the hundred steps to the street, carrying my notebook of fragments. I had formally asked the owners of various cafés if I could sit at their tables by the hour, writing. Some refused, some thought me eccentric and possibly dangerous, some claimed to be honored. One owner near the pensione thought me an improvement over his regular trade, which included an unusual number of amputees from the war, cripples and deficients. There being no social programs for them, these types had chosen the bar as a place where, as a group, they would not be interfered with. I did not understand this until one morning, while at a table in the corner, I was seized by a feeling of anxiety and looked around to see a quartet of deaf-mutes engaged in a vicious but silent argument. Red-faced and gesticulating, they cursed each other with swooping hands and enraged looks. The bartender was required to calm them. It was then I noticed the man with no legs in the makeshift wheelchair, the man with the bandage covering what had been his nose, the woman with two eyes on the one side of her face, the blind man with the tiny, white, vigilant dog, the little men shorter than the backs of chairs who held up their coffee cups for sugar from the bar.

In the afternoons I took naps, as did the rest of the population except the tourists, if for different reasons. Wandering all night, with only a few hours' sleep in the early morning, the day's felling heat gave me an excuse to sleep from after lunch until just before dinner at eight. I felt this new schedule qualified me for the life I knew must exist in Florence, as I imagined it existed in cities everywhere: an underworld, the back half, the obverse, the hidden part of life. My writing attempts during the day—intended as cover as much as an occupation or self-expression—were miserable little failures that went nowhere. You would have thought from these fragments that I was luxuriating in some nineteenth-century way in the glories of Florence and the free-dom of youth unfettered, youth released. Perhaps I was, or was at times. But inside I was crazed by a dilemma I was at last allowing myself to face. At the same time, as I sat staring in the cafés, I realized how dull and uneventful, how banal life had been until then; or at least how usual and common. It seemed to me, suddenly, that the only aspect of my nature worth pursuing was this new, horrifying urge. Poverty of experience—so galling, so embarrassing to the young writer—caused me to change my mind, again in an instant, about all of it.

I was sitting on a marble bench in Piazza della Signoria. It was well after midnight. The little cars came along one edge of the piazza, outlining the square with bright red dashes of light. I felt certain—in the way you are sometimes certain of the inevitability of the next move, as if you had already taken it—that now was the moment, the end of avoiding the issue, and that the next man who presented himself would, within reason, as in a kind of lottery, be accepted.

I looked across the square and saw a figure leaning against the railing of the fountain of Tritone, which the Florentines call *Il Brutto,* for Neptune's ugly face. The body however is glorious and the face only streaked by weather. The man leaning against the railing with his arms crossed over his chest was watching me, as well he might, since for the moment we were the only two people in the piazza.

I stood up, with the same sudden deliberateness with which one leaps from a great height, and started toward him across the cobbles. It seemed, in this walk of perhaps fifty yards, that the whole piazza was tipped in his direction and that I fell toward him lightly, according to a natural gravity.

As I drew near him he smiled a little smile, without which, who knows, I might have faltered and changed directions, and on account of which I give him credit for the seduction, such as it was. I find it ironic to think I didn't recognize him, having searched for his eyes in each passing face for two weeks: the man from the Ponte Vecchio.

But he remembered me, and with a kindly, a sweet, indulgent smile, he said, "*Sa l'ora?*" Do you know the time? This in spite of the thirty-foot clock face just over our heads in the Arnati tower.

"It's you," I said, blushing and wondering at the coincidence.

"It's been me a few times," he replied. "It seemed to me you knew that, no?"

By which he meant, he later said, that several times he had been just across the street, or on the other side of the nave of a church, or passing the door of a café in which I sat gazing distractedly into the street.

I do not now remember his name. He was perhaps thirty-five, which then I considered middle-aged but which, now that I am myself past forty, seems simply mature. I was fortunate in choosing him, for he was gentle; he less so in accepting me, because I didn't know how to act. In the end, after two confusing weeks, we both gave up, as two people do who face each other over a torrent that would sweep them both away. He was an artist; all of this was beyond me. My Italian was rudimentary and dim; my expectations, as I followed him home that first night and the nights thereafter, were based on the tribal nonsense of high-school and college sweethearts, and on the marital confusions and humiliations of my parents. His antidote for this was minimal conversation, with nothing beyond pleasantries, and the simple directives and questions necessary for logistics. His eyes soon mocked me, or so I thought.

But all that came later. The first night was magical, a delicate, polite dance; he treating me like the alien species I was—young, wild and liable to bolt—and I regarding him with devotional awe, as teacher, expert and master of these new mysteries and sensations.

I see him differently now—now that I have become him, and have again become what I was. He is demystified. Even the fact that he lived nearby, in a street just behind the piazza, reduces him somewhat, to a kind of provincial boy-chaser preying on tourists just outside his door. This maybe was cheap and easy. The conflict that developed between us came out of my need for some real connection—which, from his point of view, would only have served to complicate the purpose of our meeting: sex. I see now how right he was. But I remember standing in the doorway of his bedroom saying loudly that I was not an animal, nor yet a piece of meat, but an artist too, like him.

The patience he showed in his lovemaking easily carried over to handle these outbursts; but it was in turn this stoicism that drove me away. I raged at the spongy depths of his dark, eloquent eyes. After several scenes, he made no effort to stop me from leaving, and I left.

But that first night he gently took me to bed and caressed and kissed me—not the approximation or imitation of lovemaking, but the real thing, ending in a physical connection that I had had no inkling was possible between men.

I left his bed with the palpable feeling of pride and discovery, and the next day could not wait to tell Rashid, who listened raptly, a knowing half-smile on his lips.

"Che debutto!" he kept saying. What a debut. And *"Troppo puro"*—too pure, too pure. Rashid's doctored eyes glistened with envy, I saw, and quickly I was asked a succession of questions—How old? How tall? How big? Who was he? Did he have money? Did he have hair?—which made me realize that after a full night together I could not remember the man's face. It was gone.

"But, Rashid," I said, whispering unnecessarily in the dining-room din, "I had no idea that . . . you could . . . "

"Could what?" Rashid asked, fascinated.

" . . . that men could fuck each other," I whispered.

Rashid said nothing and only stared at me with something like distrust, not believing me. Then looking again and deciding I meant it, he said, "Ah, this is excellent." He leaned closer, across the table, pausing for me to lean in as well. "It is the wonder of Europe," he said, "that American boys can all be so stupid, and so good with their mouths."

The night after the artist affair ended, like a jockey under different colors, I was out on the street looking for another mount. This new and powerful mode of expression—cruising with intent—which seems now to be nothing like it was, distracted me completely, like a rich, jaded gambler in the *salle privée,* so that my feelings for the artist— my indignation, confusion and frustration, all of which obscured the deeper, larger issue of coming out—were themselves replaced by a sense of excitement tinged with danger, glamour, romance, sexual longing. Before I knew it the artist had been replaced by a man who stopped his car by the river to ask directions with his fly open and his cock out. You did not resist such directness, for why then have put yourself in front of it in the first place? Why walk along the river at night unless you were a whore or wanting to act like one? Why say no to anything that was not plainly repulsive? By whose standards did it attract or repel?

I roamed the streets and parks, as far removed from the idea of art and pretense as I could take myself, discovering there the kind of truth I was supposed to be setting down on paper; and setting down on paper a rendition of life in Florence that might please professors and critics; and in the end not even that.

From *Nebraska*

George Whitmore

Nebraska *(1987) was George Whitmore's second novel, published two years before his death. In his obituary,* The New York Times *described his fiction as "gay literature set against the broader background of traditional American taboos and denial."* Nebraska *portrays the literal dismemberment of gay men against the background of alcoholism, divorce, teen pregnancy, and economic oppression.*

"You would never listen to me and now look what's happened!" Mama fainted dead away. The next thing I knew, I woke up with my leg gone.

She meant I would refuse to walk when I could run. I would not look both ways before I crossed the street. I would forget and have to be sent back to the store when it was already dark.

I felt sorry for the man who hit me. When they put me in the ambulance, he was sitting there on the curb, an honest workingman in coveralls.

I would run. I ran blind—I was twelve years old but more a baby. In my imagination, there were worse things along that stretch of road than getting hit.

"What is wrong with you?"

I was a case, that's for sure. My arm was broke. The skin was off whole parts of me. I had stitches I didn't even know about. When my sisters came to see me they both cried out.

I had two doctors. The first one said, "That child keeps wetting the bed his stump will never heal." The other said, "Sure you can take him home but how will you take care of him?"

Mama said "We will take good care of him. He is the only one we have."

I was in and out. I lost whole days. I heard Mama saying "We're going to be paying off the bills for the rest of our lives."

I tried to think how I could help. I heard her say "Now I guess we won't have to buy that bike." I cried because I could not have my paper route now.

When I was in the hospital, I was like the lady in the magician's box, who must smile and smile as the blades get slipped into her. When I came home, Mama tried to keep this torture up as they had told her to. However I begged, Mama would poke and prod. Mama would flip-flop me morning and night. Mama wore herself clean out with tormenting.

When I was in the hospital, I heard the nurses say about a little girl who died "Do you know what they said? They opened up that little tyke and found such a tumor there she must have been in terrible pain all her life. But you see she didn't never know it. She must of thought This is just life."

I lay there thinking To be in terrible pain and not know it because it was all you ever knew. And maybe this is true. Maybe you just don't know it. Maybe if you're lucky you get numb, for all I know is, after a while that chawed up lost leg was all I felt—even if it was buried somewhere in some city dump, that lost leg was more real than my real body. Answer when I'm talking! Mama yelled at me but I was deaf and dumb. At night I turned that lost leg over and over and over like a new limb held in my hands and after a while there wasn't anything they could do to me that hurt anymore.

Mama was wore out. She worked all day at Monkey Wards. She waited on tables on the top floor. I liked it there because you could sit on that balcony and watch all the shoppers far below crowding up against the counters.

I lived with Mama, Betty and Dolores in a half house—each step on the stairway there was supposedly the same as the one next door. We rented our half longer than anyone else.

When I came home from the hospital it was summer already. Mama had a real hospital bed waiting for me out on the sleeping porch—they could not get it up the stairs. She made Betty and Dolores wait on me. I thought Mama was so wonderful.

This sleeping porch was on the side of the house and lilac bushes screened it from the street. In early summer those blossoms hung off every branch like big bunches of grapes but through the chinks in the bushes I could see people passing by.

Most days the only sign of life all day was a sprinkler on the lawn across the street but every day at four the paperboy who got my route would come whooshing by, pumping hard.

I watched TV and did my puzzle books—I was a puzzle freak and went through dozens of those books each week. I even had made up puzzles myself. This was my only talent and had once got me in the paper.

They came out and took my picture. They printed it in the paper over the caption

Boy Puzzle Whiz

But now the neighbors did not go by our house and say as I hoped they would "That's the house where the puzzle whiz lives." They said "Look at that yard, it's disgraceful, it's all dirt."

When I got my cast off, they told Mama I was not yet to go to physical therapy in spite of all they had promised. Sometimes my pee was still pink. I lived in fear.

"Get ready to die," Dolores said setting down my lunch.

One day in the middle of that summer, Mama came to me with something in her hand. She sat down on the edge of the bed.

"I found this in the hamper when I was sorting the wash," Mama said, letting my handkerchief uncrumple. "I know boys have urges," she said, "that are mostly natural."

I thought of lying and saying I just blew my nose in it.

She held the handkerchief up. "I don't want to see this ever again, understand?"

I did. I nodded. But a door closed in me. Mama had shut it.

I was, you see, the only male in that household until Uncle Wayne came home.

For all my childhood it seemed Uncle Wayne was a sailor. He was away in the navy so long I didn't know what he looked like anymore.

We all worshipped Uncle Wayne the way you worship movie stars. A postcard from Uncle Wayne was a holy relic. We all awaited news from him.

When I had my accident, a package arrived for me from Honolulu. In it was a plastic ukulele. You could strum on the strings or play it with a crank. It played Lovely Hula Hands.

So all my childhood Uncle Wayne was sailing around the world from one dangerous port to another. I found out later of course he had not been so close to combat, only dispatched some fighters into the war zone, but when Uncle Wayne came home he might as well have been the greatest hero.

When Uncle Wayne came home he came up to my bed and stood there grinning and said "What the hell happened to you, Skeezix?"

The first thing you noticed was the ring on his little finger. It was a diamond engagement ring. Betty perched on the arm of his chair and picked up his hand.

"What's this, Uncle Wayne?"

"This here, Betty, was recently returned to me by a young lady in San Diego."

"Oh Uncle Wayne, you mean you was engaged?"

"For a brief while there I was, kiddo."

But when he came downstairs later it was gone.

Women made a terrible fuss over him. Aunt Eileen almost peed her pants to see her baby brother when he walked in the door. He tossed down his white duffel bag and the girls were jumping up and down but Mama stayed in the kitchen frying chicken and he had to go in after her. She was crying too.

That night we had a picnic in our back yard. Wayne carried me out and laid me on the air mattress to Dad's old sleeping bag. We ate chicken and potato salad and watermelon. By the time we finished eating it was dark. But we stayed out there talking and laughing at Uncle Wayne's jokes—I thought he was so funny. There was just the sink light on in the house and a blue glow from the TV next door where you could hear the sound of laughter from New York.

It was so hot. Everyone agreed it was a real Nebraska summer to welcome Wayne home.

Everyone was amazed how fast the plane had brought him home.

"I bet you ain't even lost your sea-legs," Uncle Sparky said. "Those ships are just like floating cities, ain't they?" he said.

"Sure are," said Uncle Wayne.

"What was your ship called, Uncle Wayne?"

"My ship was the Alameda."

"Will you miss the Alameda, Uncle Wayne?"

"Why, hell's bells, honey. The Alameda was my whole life."

But now he announced he was going away again soon to open up his new garage in California. He was going to be a partner with his shipboard pal the Chief. We all yelled No, but he held his hands up and said California is the place.

Then at that very moment the phone rang long distance. Uncle Wayne bounded up the stairs.

It was so hot the birds hung like they were dead in the trees. We were all silent. We didn't have anything to say to each other. We could hear Uncle Wayne on the phone.

"No, I'm sorry, Miss," he said, "Mr. Wayne Smith is not here."

Then he came out back and said that was all arranged ahead of time so the Chief could call person to person and know he was home safe but not have to pay for the call.

By the time Eileen stood up and dusted off her skirt telling Sparky they must go home, so many empty beer bottles lined those back steps it looked like you could walk up into the house on them.

Mama went inside and washed up the pots and pans Betty and Dolores had conveniently forgot. Dolores went up to set her hair. Betty sat there next to Uncle Wayne on the blanket with her head on his shoulder like he was her drive-in dream date.

"Why can't you stay in Nebraska forever, Uncle Wayne?"

"Well soon as you can visit me, can't you? Wouldn't you like to take a bus all the way across the U.S.?"

"Only if it was to see you."

"She gets car sick," I said.

Uncle Wayne stroked her cheek.

The porch light came on and Mama, moths around her head, said it was time for bed. So Uncle Wayne picked me up in his arms and carried me inside.

Uncle Wayne smelled of sweat and whiskey and beers and Camels—Grandma once said How bad Grandpa's long-johns stink from his chewing tobacco when I put them through the mangle!

Before I went to sleep, Mama gave me a sponge bath and bandaged the stump as you must do.

"Will Uncle Wayne live in his own house in California?" I asked her.

"Where else would he live?"

"Will he own a convertible?"

"He'd like to, I bet."

"Will he have a swimming pool?"

We learned about the Chief. First of all he was Uncle Wayne's best friend and also his chief petty officer. Second, the nickname Uncle Wayne gave him on the Alameda, the Shadow, was given him for being a great practical joker. The Chief came from Chula Vista, a town near Mexico, and had a legendary capacity for booze. According to Uncle Wayne, the Chief was going to borrow money from his brother-in-law to open up that garage.

Uncle Wayne spoke of his plans at the breakfast table. Mama was upset for he was her nearest and dearest and had been away so long. "This is so fast," she said. "Why can't you boys open up a garage here in Lincoln?"

"Because the Chief's out on the Coast, Sis."

"But why can't he come here?"

"Because all his connections is out there, you see."

Mama shook her head. "You go out there and I'm afraid you will never come back home."

"Sure I will."

"And what about our Dad?"

She did not mention Grandma. Uncle Wayne had really come home to Mama because she was the only one who was once a real mother to him.

Grandpa had a handsome Studebaker but he liked it too much to drive it. So when Uncle Wayne arrived in Lincoln Grandpa said Let Mohammed come to the Mountain. But Uncle Wayne didn't go. He hated his old family home. After lots of phone calls Grandpa and Grandma came to Lincoln after all only because Sparky went and drove them.

And after all when they met after such a long time, Grandpa kissed Uncle Wayne on the ear and held him like he would like to dance with him—Grandpa dance! Grandpa was so big around it would take two girls to hold him in their arms.

All of us were scared of Grandpa but not Uncle Wayne. All of us knew the story of how Uncle Wayne would never let Grandpa whip him—not since Grandpa cornered him in the cellar one time and Wayne tried to slice him with a knife.

I myself had a first memory of Grandpa. It was him bouncing me on his knee and making me so sick because I was only two and afraid he would not stop—he might bounce me until my eyes popped out of my head and I bit off my poor tongue.

When Uncle Wayne told Grandpa his plans about California, Grandpa was mystified. He had just figured all that time Wayne would work on the railroad when he got out.

"But I told Ed the other day."

"Dad, I never said a thing about working on no damned railroad."

"I told him you'd call."

"I'm just here for a brief visit's all."

"You'll never get the benefits they got!"

This meant a great deal to Grandpa. Grandma was going to have a pension equal to one-third his current wage.

Uncle Wayne just laughed, covering his bad teeth—he forgot the navy fixed them for him free.

"Why the hell did you get yourself discharged then?" roared Grandpa. He was shaking. This was their life-long battle and Grandpa sensed he was losing again. He looked around for someone to yell at and decided to pick on Mama for the spoons—Grandma always had to keep spoons on the table for him in a cut-glass jar but Mama didn't.

"Why the hell can't you keep a proper house, Janice!"

"I am not going to work on no goddamned railroad."

"Well why the hell then did you get out of the navy?"

Grandma was twitching with nerves by now. Her fingers ran like spiders over the buttons on her dress.

"Wayne will make up his own mind," Mama was so bold as to say.

Then a tear formed in the corner of one of Grandpa's old yellow eyes—he figured maybe he could weep his way out of this. He said "This'll about kill your poor mother."

Grandma sat up in her chair.

Grandpa turned to Grandma and said "Now won't it!"

Grandma just about jumped out of her chair.

Wayne lit a Camel.

"I would like it," Grandma kind of squeaked, "if Wayne could move closer."

"Course you would!"

Uncle Wayne shrugged Grandpa off as if to say China was not far enough away from Nebraska to suit him but California would do.

That next week when he got a letter from the Chief he sat there in the living room on the sofa and snickered away at it.

"This man is such a card."

"Does he say anything about the loan from his brother-in-law, Uncle Wayne?"

Uncle Wayne flipped over the paper and kept on reading.

"I bet you miss the Chief, Uncle Wayne."

"I was with the man almost twenty-four hours a day, Skeezix, three whole years you know."

"I wish the Shadow would come here."

"Well, Betty, you will get to meet him, won't you, when you come to California."

When I was in the hospital my class made me a big get-well card out of construction paper and everyone signed it, but after I came home nobody visited but Wesley.

Wesley said all the kids were not taking the Red Cross water safety class learning how to swim. He showed me the crawl moving his arms like a windmill and kicking one leg into thin air.

That summer Wesley got to go Summer Baptist Bible too—Wesley had about the best life of any boy in Lincoln, Nebraska. He was an only child. He lived in a big house with trees in front and a two-car garage. He had a room full of toys like an ant farm, a chemistry set and a Prince Valiant castle with rubber men.

When Wesley came over to see me when I was laid up he would bring his used comic books—Superman, Terry and the Pirates, and horror comics where people got chopped up or melted or burned or slashed to ribbons. Wesley and me would argue over things like How much of you would blow up if a hand-grenade went off when you were holding it? I said all of you while Wesley said just the middle.

Pretty soon that summer Wesley was talking about the Scouts most of the time. He belonged to the Cubs—his den made a big Indian drum out of an old oil can and innertubes. But in the fall Wesley was going to become a real Boy Scout. He already had his Tenderfoot knots down perfect.

"This is the best troop in the whole world," he informed me.

"Well, my Uncle Wayne says in California they have the greatest troops."

"This troop won all the awards."

I pretended I wasn't so interested anymore but I wanted to be a Scout so bad I could taste it.

"You could be a Scout," Wesley said. "I bet you anything you could. They don't turn down anybody I bet."

But I could tell Wesley didn't believe that any more than I did. Probably for the only time in his life he was listening to his mama say Be nice.

"When you have your artificial limb," said Wesley who was afraid to look at the empty place on my bed, "you can even go on some hikes. You couldn't be an Eagle but you could be a Scout."

I had it in my head, however, that you needed a dad to join.

All that summer they called the hottest summer in human memory I lay on that porch still sick with sweat dripping off me. The County sent me back to the hospital to break my arm again. Parts of me were now yellow.

Uncle Wayne bided his time. Every week like clockwork for a while a letter came from the Chief but he still didn't, we guessed, have the money.

Uncle Wayne bought a second-hand Chevy for his drive to California. For a while there you could hear him out in the garage working on that old car. Next he took the Chevy to a body shop and had it painted Candy Apple Red.

Uncle Wayne involved himself in my rehabilitation. He gave me backrubs and saw to it I moved my limbs. He gave me a little rubber ball to squeeze because that developed your arm muscles. I squeezed that rubber ball until it popped apart along the seam.

Uncle Wayne also worked hard at keeping his own body in shape. He did sit-ups and push-ups. He had a pipe in the doorway for chin-ups. He was an inspiration to me.

Weekends Uncle Wayne would go out drinking with his friends Butchy, Martin and Harold. Harold and him would drive over to Warren to the Big Top or Butchy and Martin, because they lived in Warren, would come into Lincoln to the Blue Bird.

All these men were cutups together since they were boys, but for Uncle Wayne I saw it was not just like old times. He complained to Mama ''We grew apart, they ain't never been nowhere and never will.''

''I ain't been nowhere either,'' Mama replied.

Mama didn't understand but I did. Since I could no longer be a sailor maybe I would be a merchant marine.

''With a peg leg?'' Uncle Wayne said giving me a sponge bath. ''Like Cap'n Hook?'' he said. ''I don't know why not.''

I told Dolores I was going to sail around the world as Uncle Wayne had.

''The only place you're going to,'' she said, ''is H-E-double-toothpicks.''

''You're the one's going to hell,'' I said, ''for all your manifold sins.''

Dolores turned on me with her mouth hanging open. ''What do you mean?''

''I saw you,'' I said from the fastness of my bed.

Dolores hit the ceiling. ''Look here,'' she hissed at me, leaning across the sheets with hands clenched like claws—Mama was in the kitchen. ''You ever tell anyone anything and I'll kill your guts.''

Dolores was telling Mama she was going off babysitting or out to a movie or for a spin in a car with her girlfriends but those were just lies. She was sneaking off to meet someone and I found out who.

No wonder Mama wondered why Dolores was even lazier than usual. No wonder if Dolores was doing all this babysitting, she never had spending money.

Two nights that I knew of Dolores went up to bed and you heard her go to the bathroom and brush her teeth. Then you heard the springs cry out when she fell onto the bed. But after Mama turned out the lights and went to bed herself, down came Dolores carrying her shoes in one hand.

From my bed out on the sleeping porch with one eye squinted shut, I watched Dolores cross the living room and sneak into the kitchen— she didn't dare go out the front way because Mama's bedroom was over the door.

The second time I saw Dolores sneak out I turned over on my belly and watched through the lilacs as she tiptoed down the driveway to the sidewalk and down the street to the corner, then she gave a little Eek when someone said Boo and stepped out of the bushes. It was Uncle Wayne's old pal Harold and here Dolores was only sixteen.

On the first of the month Uncle Wayne called the Chief long distance. He took the phone over to the stairs and spoke low into it.

"Well I was wondering," he said.

"That's just what I was thinking," he said.

"I can see that," he said.

"I guess we'll just have to," he said.

"Me too," he said.

"Do you?" he asked.

"This town is the asshole of creation," he said.

"You too," he said.

Then he hung up and went into the kitchen. When he came out with a beer in his hand I asked How is the Shadow?

Uncle Wayne looked at me like he had forgot I was alive. Then he looked at me almost with hatred.

"I mean the Chief," I said.

"Ain't you supposed to be asleep?"

"It's only nine."

"Little pitchers have big ears, don't they," he said and left the house. I heard a car door slam in the garage. Then I heard his radio playing

> *Whenever we kiss*
> *I worry and wonder*
> *You're here in my arms*
> *But where is your heart?*

and sadness stabbed me. I wanted to be sitting next to Uncle Wayne in his car listening to the radio but Uncle Wayne never even offered to carry me out to see that Chevy.

Grandpa would not let up. Grandpa was like a leaky faucet in a rusty sink. If he could not talk Uncle Wayne into the railroad anymore, he thought now Uncle Wayne should aspire to work at Chicks with Sparky.

"But I have spoken to him at every opportunity," Sparky told Grandpa.

"You sure have, honey," said Aunt Eileen.

"I ran into him the other night when I just happened to stop off for a drink at the Blue Bird and we had quite a long talk," said Sparky.

"You done your best."

"Now this California feller," said Grandpa, "is like the pot at the end of the rainbow if you ask me."

"Chicks," said Sparky, "has been damned good to me."

Mama did what they asked. She brought up the subject. She was ironing his shirts. He was finishing supper.

Mama said "You know if things wasn't to work out in California— I mean they almost closed down Chicks two years ago, I don't know if I wrote you, but now it seems they're going great guns."

"Maybe next time they will wise up and close it down for good," Uncle Wayne said.

"What I mean to say."

"Fuck Chicks."

Mama hated profanity but she just grit her teeth and said "It doesn't strike me, Wayne, that things are going too well at the other end out there."

"They are going fine," Wayne said.

Then he slapped his palm hard on the table and said "Jesus! Why why why!" Uncle Wayne yelled. "Why can't anybody in the world let me live?"

Mama said "Well, excuse me for living."

There was a silence then. I could hear the iron thump on the ironing board. Mama muttered You can live, but Uncle Wayne said No this is the way it always is, this is why I joined the navy lying about my age in the first place, and stormed out of the room.

He went upstairs. A few minutes later he stomped down the stairs and slammed the door. You could hear the garage door smack the fence post then that Chevy tore out of the driveway and laid rubber down the street.

Mama said Uncle Wayne almost killed Grandma and because she was so sick after she had him Mama had to take over.

Aunt Mona was gone. Uncle Walter was but a boy himself. Aunt Eileen was just like Dolores.

Mama was the one who got up in the night and changed Uncle

Wayne. She gave him his bottle. She changed him and fed him breakfast before she went to school. When Mama came home for lunch she had to attend to Wayne. She took care of him in the night too. She was the one who gave him his dinner and put him to bed then she tried hard to do her homework. If he ever cried Mama was the one who must be there.

When Uncle Wayne was little he would not go to sleep without Mama—she had to be with him on the bed. Children would be playing outdoors. Mama would hear their cries in the twilight outside the window. They were playing Kick the Can and Blindman's Buff and It but Mama had to stay inside and very still on the bed because Uncle Wayne would lay on her arm so if she moved he would wake up and start crying again.

This is why Mama said in the hospital after my accident "You are not ever going to be robbed of your precious childhood."

"Course he won't," the doctor said, smiling.

Late that night after their fight Uncle Wayne woke me up standing by my bed. He was pretty drunk.

"Didn't mean to wake you," he whispered, grinning from ear to ear down at me.

"That's all right," I said.

"Look at your sheet," he said like he just noticed though my bed was soaked with sweat every night. "Let's change that sheet," he said, switching on the lamp.

"That's all right," I said—he was teetering and I was afraid he would fall on me, but Uncle Wayne was already pulling the sheet out from under me and rolling me over to the other side. He knew how. He had changed my sheets lots of times because he loved me and wanted to take care of me. I was his only nephew.

He said in a whisper "Your mama didn't change your p.j.s either, did she, Skeezix?" He slid the sheet away. Quickly and efficiently as you would expect a serviceman to do Uncle Wayne changed the bed. He got me fresh p.j.s. He helped me off with the bottoms then when I was pulling the top off my head I felt Uncle Wayne's hand on my nuts.

"You're getting hair down there, Skeezix."

That's all. Then his hand was gone.

Inside my p.j. top I gulped. It smelled in there. I heard some old dog bark down the street.

When Uncle Wayne went upstairs, I lay back against the moonlight on my pillow. The new p.j.s felt good, almost cool. I felt my nuts. I felt the fuzz on them.

Sparky was always trying to get Uncle Wayne to consider Chicks not just because Grandpa said to but because he was devoted to Chicks. Sparky talked like he ran Chicks when he never held a hammer or a wrench in his hand all his life. Sparky thought he was such a big shot. And Uncle Wayne would just laugh in his face.

So naturally Sparky was fit to be tied when one night Uncle Wayne called him up out of the blue and asked Do you think Chicks might be able to use someone on a temporary basis?

Sparky was in ecstasy. "Jesus, didn't I tell you they's dying over there for men with your expertise? I'll take this up with Mr. Chickowskowitz first thing in the morning!"

But what about California?
"Things has hit a snag."
But when was he going then?
"That isn't definite now."
But what does the Chief say?
Poor Uncle Wayne. You could feel his chagrin. He had to ask Mama if it was all right to stay. He had to ask Sparky about a job at Chicks. He'd spent all his money on that Chevy.

That night I heard Uncle Wayne pacing back and forth. I heard him kick my baseball bat across the room. I heard Mama call out to him from her bed. I heard him pacing.

When he came down in the morning I asked him why he couldn't just go to California now anyway and get a job out there, why couldn't he just stay with the Chief?

"Well that just don't happen to be the kind of arrangement I have with the man," Uncle Wayne said to me in a sarcastic singsong voice.

"Don't you even want to go to California anymore, Uncle Wayne?"
He sneered at me like I was a moron.

"Course I do. Not that it's any of your-type business."
Then he ambled away into the other room.

* * *

The first day on the job at Chicks, Sparky took Uncle Wayne all over the place one hand glued to his back so everyone could see who got Wayne the job.

"Course neptunism isn't company policy here, howsomever," Sparky hee-hawed to the men at every work station.

At Chicks they put Uncle Wayne in charge of three machines on the line. His foreman was named Rodney and Rodney was greatly admired. When Sparky took Wayne up to meet Rodney, Rodney said "You mean he ain't seven foot tall with ten arms? Well maybe he's got Einstein's brain in there anyway as you say he does, Sparky."

Rodney told Uncle Wayne that first day "A man should know his machine so he can do one thing superbly so I would like you to just take your time here getting acquainted."

Uncle Wayne learned fast. Soon he knew his job backwards and forward. He buckled down for he was saving up to buy that garage with the Chief. Soon he was promoted to troubleshooter.

But this didn't seem to be enough for Uncle Wayne. He worked a forty-hour week at Chicks then got him a moonlighting job pumping gas too. We just figured he was waiting for that snag in California to come undone.

Every night Uncle Wayne came home so beat. He ate his dinner and went to his other job or upstairs to his bed. He yelled at the girls. He did not horse around anymore or joke with me.

When he saw that letter his eyebrows shot up. He held that letter between two fingers.

Uncle Wayne's hands were black under the nails. His fingerprints could be read from the ground-in grease. His nose was flecked with blackheads. He was getting like his machines, greasy and dark. Uncle Wayne was powerful. His body was well-honed. He could lift up a car by the bumper. For a small man his shoulders were broad. His arms were ropey. His wrists worked like ball bearings. He had that AIR MAIL letter in his hand then he put it in his breast pocket and sat down to dinner.

He ate pinto beans with cornbread. The only time he said a word was to ask for more. Feeding Uncle Wayne was like throwing gasoline onto a fire—Mama piled up the cornbread and the beans. Uncle Wayne took three helpings with lots of ketchup. Then he ate two dishes of cling peaches. Meanwhile he drank two bottles of beer.

He belched and pushed back his chair. He stretched and touched that letter in his breast pocket then he went upstairs to read it.

At three A.M. the Highway Patrol brought Uncle Wayne to our door the way they used to bring Dad.

They told Mama he was lucky they didn't put him in jail. They told her the location of his Chevy.

He had thrown up the beans all over himself. Mama made him take off his clothes at the front door.

"They have got me," Uncle Wayne said. "They have got me again."

"No, they do not," Mama said. "They let you go this time."

"No, they have got me."

The next day Uncle Wayne went to work late and shook so bad Rodney took him off the line. He was so sick Rodney sent him home. When Sparky saw Uncle Wayne walking across the parking lot through the office window, he ran outside like a shot.

Uncle Wayne was struggling to get into his car.

"Got the bug, huh?" said Sparky through the window.

Uncle Wayne just drove off.

When I was little Dad used to sit in his chair and let me climb on him. I used to climb up on Dad's shoe and hold onto his leg. I used to flop over his knee and walk all over him. I used to sit on Dad's shoulders and hold onto his ears. I used to play Mountain on Dad.

But when Dad got tired of Mountain he would give me his beer to drink. He would put his hat on my head. I would stagger around the room until I fell down.

Then Dad would cry What have I done? and bawl. Dad would grab me and squeeze the wind out of me. He would beg forgiveness.

Mama would come home and I would be asleep drunk on the living room floor. Dolores told me this.

Uncle Wayne's friends did not notice the change after he got that letter. Uncle Wayne's friends thought he was the same old Wayne. They thought he was funny. It was just like old times to them.

One night at the Big Top he got beat up by some lady's boyfriend. One other night his friends brought Uncle Wayne home with panties on his head.

"I really got to apologize," said Harold to Mama when they had got Wayne upstairs. "They's quite adolescent."

So Uncle Wayne went downhill like a monkey on a greased pole and I watching from my bed saw him crawl up the stairs like Dad used to on his hands and knees nights and I decided I must hate him.

I was pleading with Mama to let me have Wesley sleep over as we used to before my accident.

"That was then," she always said.

"But this is a big enough bed, Mama."

"I know it is."

"Why was it then then?"

"Because it was."

But finally Mama said we could. "No, he don't have something," I heard her say over the phone. "He's perfectly okay. He's like any boy too, you know."

So Wesley got to come over one night with his p.j.s in a paper bag and his toothbrush. He brought his mess kit from the Scouts as well—this mess kit came in an olive-drab slipcover and contained a frying pan and a plate, a collapsible cup, knife, fork and spoon, all out of aluminium.

Wesley regaled me with tales of scouting. He told me about his first overnight hike. They cooked a meal, he said, and ate it out of their mess kits. They cooked the potatoes in foil in the fire and the beans in the can so you wondered why people even bothered to take them out and put them in a pan.

> *Beans, beans the musical fruit*
> *The more you eat the more you toot*
> *The more you toot the better you feel*
> *So eat your beans at every meal*

They waded in a crick and studied underwater life. They hiked at least fifty miles.

This gave us the idea for the tent. So Mama let us string up a rope from one nail to the window and hang two sheets over it with clothes pins. Then we needed a flashlight. What do you need that for, said Mama, if you got on the TV? For late at night, I said. In case any of us needs to take a whiz-bang in the bushes, whispered Wesley.

We watched TV till Mama made us turn it off and said Go asleep.

Then Wesley told me more about scouting. You had to learn the Morris code—he tapped some on the rail for me with his knife until Mama yelled downstairs.

The knots held up a lot of boys, Wesley said, though not him since he was so proficient at knots because his dad helped him every Sunday after church. In scouting you have to promise to do your best to do your duty and dig a latrine to do it in, Wesley said. That cracked me up. Everything Wesley said that night cracked me up.

I was so happy. It was Indian summer. The windows were open and our tent was cozy with the glow of the flashlight so weak Wesley had to keep shaking the batteries inside to keep it going.

In scouting after dinner after everyone scrubbed out his mess kit with sand and rinsed it in the crick, you sang songs and told ghost stories "But they're such baby stuff I won't tell you any" then you went into your tent and slept in a sleeping bag.

"Here we are in our tent!"

"Yes," Wesley said, "but it's soooooo dark out there camping out. Bats and bears. Every little noise. Some kids can't even go asleep their first night. You think they'd never been camping."

"Yeah," I said.

" . . . So the salesman comes back five years later and there's this little kid out in the yard. He's real skinny. And the salesman says Boy, are you skinny, and the little kid says You'd be skinny too if you was strained through a sheet."

"I guess we ought to go asleep," Wesley said at length. "I guess it's getting pretty late."

"Tell another one, Wesley."

"I can't remember any more."

We lay quiet at the end of the night I never wanted to end. The bed was like a raft afloat on the dark sea—the batteries in the flashlight were dead for good. It started raining outside our tent, breaking out like goose bumps, falling on the fallen leaves in the yard.

Wesley's voice was small in the dark. When I turned to him I could see the whites of his eyes over there on the pillow.

"Could I feel your leg?"

I was surprised. All that night long Wesley had still looked away when he was liable to catch a glimpse of even my empty p.j. leg.

I said, "If you want to."

"I won't hurt it."

"I know that."

"I just want to see what it feels like."

So I rolled my p.j. leg up over the stump and let him feel the bandage.

"Does it hurt?"

"Uh-uh."

He felt around a bit more. "What's it really like?"

So I took down my p.j.s in the dark and unwound the bandage, which I was not supposed to do. I lay back. Wesley patted around on the mattress until he hit it then his hand shot away. I heard him swallow. His hand then floated back over here and rested on the stump.

"It's like anything," he said.

"It's just flesh and blood."

"It's bumpy."

He felt it.

"It's a little soft but for these lines, like a baby's head."

"I never thought of that," I said, feeling myself. "It is somewhat."

Wesley lay back on his pillow. I wrapped up my stump as best I could. I pulled on my pants.

"I just wanted to see," he said.

"I know."

"That didn't hurt?"

We lay there. My heart started beating. There came a singing in my head. I could feel the heat from Wesley next to me. My dick was standing up against my p.j. pants.

Wesley must have thought I was ashamed of my stump, I was so quiet. Maybe he regretted asking. But all of a sudden he turned over on his side with his back to me and pulled his knees up against his chest.

I listened to the rain outside our tent.

"Wesley?"

When he answered it was like I was rousing him but I could tell he was still wide awake.

"Wesley, you think I can feel your dick?"

After considering, I guess, he said yes. His voice was breathy. He turned over on his back. He pulled down his pants and turned to me. He pointed it at me. I stroked the top with my fingers and watched it get hard.

"Me too."

But Wesley jerked up in bed and shushed me.

We froze, listening hard. We listened.

"She's asleep," I whispered. "Honest."

Wesley hunched back down. His dick was now limp again but mine was poking out through the slit in my p.j.s.

Wesley then said I don't think we should and pulled up his pants.

"Come on." The skin on mine felt like it would bust.

"It isn't right."

"Sure it is."

"Not for a Baptist."

"Didn't you do it, Wesley? Didn't you do it once with me?"

"Once I did it with you."

"Well, I bet other boys do it in the Scouts."

"I bet they don't!"

"I bet they do."

Wesley must have known that was true for he could only repeat It isn't right.

"Sure it is."

"No it isn't."

Then I was inspired to say "They even do it in the navy. My Uncle Wayne told me. You don't think they have girls on ships, do you? They have to get rid of their jizz on ships too. If they don't it impairs performance." I was talking so fast I was almost out of breath. I wanted to roll over on top of Wesley. "Let me do it to you first then," I said. "If you don't like it, well you don't have to do it to me."

"I don't believe that ship stuff," Wesley said.

"My Uncle Wayne told me, Wesley. He even showed me how."

"Liar."

"He did. Lots and lots of times."

"Liar."

"He showed me the best way. Wanna see?"

"You're lying and they don't do that in Scouts either."

I couldn't get Wesley to. I even reached over and felt around there but he let me for only a minute then pushed my hand away. He turned over on his side again. I said "Mama's fast asleep, Wesley, she never wakes up" but he would not answer. He pretended to go to asleep.

Of course I had been doing this to myself all along—Mama didn't know that because I'd learned to hold it in.

I thought that night about doing it to myself in spite of Wesley being there. I thought about asking him if he minded but I didn't. What I really wanted more, I knew, was to feel Wesley's hand on it the way I had before.

Late, late I heard Uncle Wayne come in but I couldn't see how drunk he was that night on account of our tent. Wesley stirred in his sleep when the door slammed shut.

I felt ashamed for telling those lies about the navy and Uncle Wayne. Shame burned on my face. Then I remembered I was supposed to hate Uncle Wayne now.

Dolores and Harold were so happy in their little trailer. They almost forgot they were going to have a baby—they were so pleased not to have to sneak around anymore it was like they were going steady for the first time.

Dolores liked being able to come and go when she wanted without answering to anyone but her beloved. She could go down the road to the store for a Coke at any time. She liked being Harold's wife, she told us, for now it seemed he cherished her more. Now that he was responsible for both of them totally, she said, he acted more like a man. Oh, he would clown around—when she did something stupid he would pretend to strangle her to death and they would both laugh.

At first she made a few stabs at fixing up the trailer, but soon she gave up. It was a lost cause, and anyway they would soon be in their house. For now Dolores and Harold could be as slobby as they wanted so there were clothes and magazines laying all over the place and the ashtrays overflowed. It got worse when Dolores got bigger and bigger. Even just mopping the little strip of linoleum in front of her sink seemed too much for her. Harold would come home and say "Dee, what did I marry you for anyway?"

But their passion for each other did not cool and this is what they were doing when the phone rang that night. It rang six or seven times before Harold picked it up.

So at ten the next morning Harold was down at the jail when they brought Uncle Wayne back from court. Harold had to wait an hour or so before Wayne could come out into the hall.

"You got a cigarette?"

Harold shook one out for him. Wayne looked bad. That night before

Harold had asked over the phone What's the matter, Spike, you drunk again? but Wayne did not chuckle, only said I wish to hell I was.

Wayne walked right through the revolving doors. Outside on the steps Harold asked "What's up?" but Wayne didn't answer.

When Harold unlocked the passenger side Wayne slipped into the car. He was holding his hands as prisoners do to show you how harmless they are. He sat with his hands in his lap while Harold walked around the car. He took a long drag on the cigarette and the smoke spread out on the windshield.

Harold got in behind the wheel. He'd thought all this would be jocular but now he was worried.

"This thing out of gas?" Wayne said.

Harold turned the key. The car rattled in the cold then started.

"You didn't say where to."

Wayne just sneered and looked out the side window.

So Harold started out for our house. They drove in silence down the icy streets. Harold wondered if it was aggravated assault—it must be something bad. But Wayne didn't look like he'd been in a fight. His clothes were clean and his face unmarked. He just looked like shit.

"What was it, Spike?"

"Huh?"

Harold pulled over to the curb and stopped the car. He turned off the motor. They were not halfway to our house. Wayne looked around.

"Listen, buddy, I just shelled out one-hundred dollars up there. What the fuck's going on?" Harold's voice sounded weak and frightened to him.

Wayne then spoke to Harold like he was some snot-nosed kid. "Harold, just drive me home, I ain't slept a wink, you hear?"

That night when Harold saw Wayne's name in the paper he laughed his ass off.

What a colossal error, he said to himself.

Nevertheless he remembered Wayne had not seen any humor in what happened to him. If he had, he would have told Harold all about it, wouldn't he? Harold did not show the item to his precious Dolores.

Perhaps if he had not found out about it the way he did Sparky would not have made it worse. But when he came into work that morning Denning motioned him into his office.

"You better sit down," Denning said.

Alarmed, Sparky did—Denning never had him in his office, preferring handwritten notes.

Denning took a newspaper clipping out of his shirt pocket.

Now Denning didn't like Wayne. Sparky knew this. Denning called Wayne a fuck-up in front of Mr. Chickowskowitz. He did because one of Wayne's machines down on the floor was sending up clouds of smoke so Sparky could not very well contradict Denning at the time but later he took him aside.

"Jesus, Bob, can't you let up in front of Mr. Chick? This guy's my brother-in-law and I brought him in here, you know."

"Yeah?" Denning said. "You seem to forget from time to time, I'm the personnel man here. So I suppose that makes you the monkey's uncle, don't it?"

Now Sparky read the newspaper clipping all the way through but he didn't get it. It made him a little sick to his stomach but he didn't get it.

"So?"

Denning was perched on his desk. He smiled.

Sparky started to read it all the way through again then his eyes darted down to the line

W. Smith, Resident of Lincoln

and the hairs stood up on his neck. He read the first two or three paragraphs again. He wiped his mouth with the back of his hand and glanced up at Denning. Then he handed the clipping back.

"Can't be," Sparky croaked.

"Tis."

"Can't be."

Denning seemed to sigh and picked up a file folder with Wayne's name neatly inked on it. Sparky was sitting back in the leather chair like a jet pilot in a plane taking off. Denning reached into the file and pulled out a piece of paper with a printed seal on the top. He held it before Sparky's eyes.

Sparky read this too. He read this twice too. It was confirmation of Uncle Wayne's discharge from the navy. It said

DISHONORABLE

"Son of a bitch." Sparky could not think how to save himself from this. Wayne had lied to him and to everybody. He must have been forcibly separated from the navy, not just decided he wasn't going to sign up again. "Holy jumping shit."

"And now," said Denning from a certain distance, "I'd like you to tell me what it says in this little box down here," pointing.

Sparky read the box then he looked up at Denning with baby-blue eyes.

"Why?" Sparky said when Denning didn't answer.

"So?" Sparky said.

"Not being the personnel officer around here," said Denning, "you did not send for this confirmation form, did you? Being the personnel officer who is acquainted with such matters I did. And not being the personnel officer why would you have any reason to know this is a code?" Only then did Denning raise his voice. "I never would of hired that fuck-up of a brother-in-law of yours in the first place and not just because he's a drunkard. You know why in addition?"

Goddamnit, Sparky thought.

"Now look here, Bob, this man here's been a damned good worker."

"Cocksucker," Denning said.

At first Sparky thought Denning meant him.

"This code means the man's a cocksucker," said Denning, pointing to it like he held the patent on it. "That's what this code means, chum."

"It could be any Smith, see?"

"But it ain't."

"Honey, it could be any Smith. Lincoln is full of Smiths, see? There's two pages of Smiths in the phone book, Honey. There's lots of Smiths here. Wallace Smith, Wilbert Smith, two William Smiths. Look!"

"Can't."

Sparky lay on the bed. His shoes were still on his feet. The ice-bag over his eye was almost water.

"Well what did he say, honey?"

"He wasn't caught up in no dragnet if that's what you mean."

"But what was he doing there?"

"He was in there with the rest of em."

Aunt Eileen was still in her robe—she'd hardly expected Sparky back home in the middle of the day.

* * *

It traveled like wildfire around the factory but Wayne turned his back and went on working. He didn't know what else to do. Then Sparky got hysterical when he wouldn't leave so he had to hit him.

They will have to fire me proper, Wayne said to himself. No one fires me from a job just like that—though in truth he had been fired from the navy just like that and his commanding officer was not able to restrain himself from yelling at him after the court-martial.

So at three o'clock Rodney finally walks up and hands Wayne his pink slip and says It would be a good idea if you leave now before the end of the shift.

They stood amidst the whir and pounding of the machines.

Wayne had to shout. "And what if I don't?" But Rodney's face was filled with hatred and that as much as anything else prompted Wayne to turn and go.

Aunt Eileen lay on the bed with Sparky. "Not my baby brother," she said. "No."

Sparky had explained the evidence to her three times at least.

"No no no."

Then Sparky was up, putting on his jacket.

"Where you going? Don't go out asking for more trouble, Honey!"

Sparky kissed her on the hair.

"I am not going out asking for any trouble."

Sparky looked almost jaunty with that eye.

"Then where are you going?"

"To Monkey Wards before your sister gets off work."

Wayne went right to the nearest bar. After a couple of shots he felt better. He said to himself he would assess his situation calmly. He said to himself he would stand back and take the measure of it. Problem was, his damned hand was shaking so bad he could barely light a cigarette. Well, the worst had happened. Ha! The worst just kept on.

When Mama came out of work there was Sparky at the elevator.

"Thought I'd drive you home," he said taking her by the arm. He punched the button for the elevator.

"You get the day off?" was the first thing she thought of saying. Mama imagined Sparky downtown all day looking in all the shop windows, buying himself underwear. "What happened to your eye?"

He didn't answer. They went down in the elevator. He still had her arm.

"What's wrong? Is it Craig?"

For Sparky he was being downright breezy. Whistling a tune softly he walked her out of the building. He held open his car door for her.

When he got in the other side she asked "Is this some kind of surprise?" She was briefly flustered, like a Queen for a Day.

But Sparky would not answer. He drove them to the city park. He stopped next to the duck pond and turned to her. By this time Mama was hopping mad.

He never once thought about not telling her.

> *Lincoln police today reported that 7 men were apprehended last night for lewd and lascivious behavior at the municipal bus depot.*
>
> *District Attorney Madison Schultz affirmed that the bust was in response to numerous complaints to his office that the men's rest room at the station was the scene of vice.*
>
> *Decent citizens and travelers could not use the facility due to this other element, said the D.A. Police and his office worked together, he said.*
>
> *D.A. Schultz released the men's names to the press in hopes, he said, that "it will serve warning on others of their kind."*
>
> *Apprehended in the raid were:*
> *P. Codd, Resident of Lincoln*
> *F. David, Resident of Chicago, Ill.*
> *S. Galvin, Resident of Lincoln*
> *K. Notes, No Address*
> *W. Olmstead, Resident of Cedar Bluffs*
> *W. Smith, Resident of Lincoln*
> *J. M. Yelland, Resident of Lincoln*

The Chief's letter warned him

> *They have some way of knowing. It has not just been my imagination.*

Now Wayne knew he was right. It was not just the DISHONORABLE on his discharge or else even with the whole fucking world knowing he could go out and find another job where there wasn't a Denning to give a shit.

He knew on account of Sparky the Chief was right, there is something on their forms.

This made him despair in a way he had not yet even when the Chief wrote the letter which cast him off.

> *We would both be hounded across the face of the earth by this.*

They had not just bored holes in the wall at the bus station, they had bored right into his life.

Wayne knew now he was one. He'd gone ahead and been it on his own without the Chief. Before, as long as he was on the Alameda, he never did have to think it was anything but the Chief, like by accident. When he got flown off the ship all alone he thought That's that.

Oh, if he had only never been driven to go to the bus station. If he had not given in. If he was ever able now to shut such thoughts out of his head.

When he was still waiting to go to California, even then he did not dare ask himself why. He could not then say to himself the word Love until he was discarded by the Chief. Now he hoped he hated the man more than he loved him.

> *I got you into this. You were right in Honolulu, I am poison. If you came here there is no chance. You will be lost as I am, at least this way there is a chance.*

He had let himself trust the Chief. He had surrendered on the Alameda to him and later. He had let himself believe him in Honolulu when he begged and said We can lick this together. He then went to San Diego and got back his ring. He burned all his bridges.

When Wayne got home, Mr. Burrows was there with Mama in the living room so he knew Sparky had already got to her. At first he tried to lie. He said he was damned glad Mr. Burrows was there for he was going to fight this thing to the top. They let him gas on like this for a while. Mama cried softly. Then Mr. Burrows cleared his throat.

"I would advise you, this is my opinion, to plead guilty and take your medicine. The harm is done. You cannot fight this. You will only get in deeper's all."

"Oh yes," Mama said, twisting the handkerchief in her hands. "Listen to William."

"And then," Mr. Burrows said, "you must move to another state."

Wayne sat in the chair.

"It is the only way."

Mama busted into fresh tears.

"Well I will not," Wayne said rising and standing in the middle of the room, "inflict my presence on you people any longer. I'll go tonight."

"But where?" Mama was not trying to stop him. "Please don't jump your bail!"

"To a hotel. Somewhere."

Already Wayne was thinking he had that ring upstairs to pawn and tomorrow was Friday. He thought wildly he would make the Chief take him back no matter what or now he would kill him.

But the next day who was waiting for him when he came back to his hotel from the pawn shop but Harold.

In the hallway then Harold, who always got laughed at, worked Wayne over. Harold started with the head and ended up kicking him where he lay curled up on the floor. Wayne did not cry out or try to defend himself in any way. He crawled into his hotel room and crawled up onto the bed.

Wayne went to court with Mr. Burrows and lodged his guilty plea as did all those apprehended that night. They received a fine and a good talking to. The evening newspaper didn't print any names. "Thank God," Mama said. "Oh, thank the lord." But the next day Wesley's dad came forward.

JUDGE KRAMER: Now, son, just sit down there. No, that one. This is the court stenographer, Mrs. Vesey. She is keeping a record of what we say.

WITNESS: Hi.

JUDGE KRAMER: Do you need help?

WITNESS: No.

JUDGE KRAMER: Are you comfortable?

WITNESS: I guess.

JUDGE KRAMER: How did you get down here? Did you come down in a car?

WITNESS: Uh-huh. My—we came in a car.

JUDGE KRAMER: There is nothing to be nervous about. Is there, Mrs. Vesey? Mrs. Vesey is an old hand, aren't you? Mrs. Vesey has worked in my court for almost twenty years. We do this all the time. Now. Are you quite comfortable?

WITNESS: Uh-huh.

JUDGE KRAMER: Would you like a glass of water?

WITNESS: No thanks.

JUDGE KRAMER: Okay. Let me just—look—yes. Well. The first question I have to ask you—you got sworn in, didn't you?

WITNESS: Sorry?

JUDGE KRAMER: The bailiff swore you in on the Bible.

WITNESS: Oh, uh-huh, yes.

JUDGE KRAMER: Good. Then the first thing I have to ask you, son, is do you know what a lie is?

WITNESS: Yes, sir, I do.

JUDGE KRAMER: You are—twelve years old.

WITNESS: Almost thirteen.

JUDGE KRAMER: Yes. Well, you are certainly old enough to know what a lie is, aren't you?

WITNESS: I guess so.

JUDGE KRAMER: A lie is not the truth.

WITNESS: Uh-huh.

JUDGE KRAMER: Do you know what you swore on the Bible?

WITNESS: I swore I was going to tell the truth and nothing but the truth.

JUDGE KRAMER: Very good. Now. You have an uncle.

WITNESS: Uh-huh.

JUDGE KRAMER: By the name of Wayne Smith.

WITNESS: He is one.

JUDGE KRAMER: He is one of your uncles? Yes. Do you know your uncle—he has been brought to this court's attention?

WITNESS: Mama said he is in trouble.

JUDGE KRAMER: Would you like to scoot over here closer, Mrs. Vesey? Well, son, he might be and he might not, you see.

WITNESS: Oh.

JUDGE KRAMER: Speak up, son

WITNESS: I said oh.

JUDGE KRAMER: Do you know a man Wesley Gordon Senior?

WITNESS: That is Wesley's father.

JUDGE KRAMER: Yes? Now just sit back. Who is Wesley?

WITNESS: Wesley is my friend. His son. Wesley is the son. His father is Wesley Gordon too.

JUDGE KRAMER: Yes. Wesley Gordon Junior is your friend? He is your age?

WITNESS: Yes. He is in junior high. I'm not but I got held back.

JUDGE KRAMER: Yes, I see. Now.

WITNESS: I was sick.

JUDGE KRAMER: Yes. You had an accident, didn't you?

WITNESS: I got run over by a truck.

JUDGE KRAMER: I think I knew that. I was told that. You were in bed some time.

WITNESS: Uh-huh.

JUDGE KRAMER: You were confined to bed. And. This Wesley is your friend.

WITNESS: He is probably my best friend.

JUDGE KRAMER: I see. So you must spend a lot of time together.

WITNESS: I don't know if I'm his.

JUDGE KRAMER: I see. You were sick. And Wesley must have come to visit you when you were sick.

WITNESS: Yes.

JUDGE KRAMER: Did he often visit you when you were sick?

WITNESS: Sometimes.

JUDGE KRAMER: When did he visit?

WITNESS: Sometimes.

JUDGE KRAMER: Yes. Did Wesley ever spend the night with you?

WITNESS: I guess.

JUDGE KRAMER: Do you remember Wesley spending the night with you?

WITNESS: I think he did.

JUDGE KRAMER: I see. Do you know we have talked to Wesley? Wesley was here.

WITNESS: Here? In this room?

JUDGE KRAMER: Yes.

WITNESS: Oh.

JUDGE KRAMER: So I know Wesley, too.

WITNESS: He did spend the night with me once.

JUDGE KRAMER: You seem—do you know why you are here, son?

WITNESS: I think.

JUDGE KRAMER: Yes?

WITNESS: Wesley said something.

JUDGE KRAMER: What was that?

WITNESS: Something. I don't know.

JUDGE KRAMER: You don't?

WITNESS: I know a little.

JUDGE KRAMER: What is that?

WITNESS: Something about—I don't know.

JUDGE KRAMER: Do you love your uncle?

WITNESS: Uncle Wayne?

JUDGE KRAMER: You will have to speak up for Mrs. Vesey, son. You will have to speak loud and clear.

WITNESS: Yes, sir.

JUDGE KRAMER: You love him.

WITNESS: Yes, he is my uncle. Sure.

JUDGE KRAMER: And you love your mother.

WITNESS: Sure. Yes I do.

JUDGE KRAMER: We often want to protect those we love, don't we?

WITNESS: I suppose.

JUDGE KRAMER: Keep them safe from harm.

WITNESS: Yes, sir.

JUDGE KRAMER: I bet you would like everyone you love to be happy.

WITNESS: I guess.

JUDGE KRAMER: All of us feel that way. I know I do. Now, son—your friend Wesley had said—do you remember the night Wesley spent with you last fall?

WITNESS: The night.

JUDGE KRAMER: Wesley came over and spent the night with you?

WITNESS: I guess.

JUDGE KRAMER: Wesley said—you made a tent over the bed with bed sheets?

WITNESS: That night?

JUDGE KRAMER: Did you make a tent over the bed when he stayed overnight with you?

WITNESS: Yes.

JUDGE KRAMER: You told Wesley something about your uncle that night. He says. Do you remember? Excuse me.

* * *

UNRELATED MATTER NOT TRANSCRIBED

Excuse me. I had told them not to—now—we have all the time in the world. I was asking—do you remember when Wesley was over that night—do you remember telling Wesley something about your uncle?

WITNESS: What?

JUDGE KRAMER: That's why I'm asking. That's what I'm asking. What.

WITNESS: About my Uncle Wayne?

JUDGE KRAMER: Yes.

WITNESS: I don't know.

JUDGE KRAMER: We are just trying to get at the bottom—the truth is very important here. I am here to find the truth. Would you like to help me find out the truth?

WITNESS: I guess. Yes.

JUDGE KRAMER: Good. Good. Well—Wesley told us you told him something about your uncle that night. Is that true?

WITNESS: I might have I guess.

JUDGE KRAMER: Your uncle was living with you?

WITNESS: Then?

JUDGE KRAMER: Yes. He was living with you, in the house with you and your sisters and your mother.

WITNESS: Both of them?

JUDGE KRAMER: Pardon?

WITNESS: Dolores is married now.

JUDGE KRAMER: I see. Yes. Getting back to Wesley.

WITNESS: Uncle Wayne lived upstairs. He slept in my room. He was at work all day.

JUDGE KRAMER: Yes. Wesley told us you told him something about your Uncle Wayne. Do you remember?

WITNESS: I guess.

JUDGE KRAMER: We are just trying to get at the truth.

WITNESS: I know.

JUDGE KRAMER: Well, did he—has your mother said anything to you about this, son?

WITNESS: About this?

JUDGE KRAMER: Has your mother said anything about what Wesley's father, for instance—did Wesley's father visit your home?

WITNESS: Yes, sir.

JUDGE KRAMER: Did he make—what did he say?

WITNESS: He said—I was not in there so long. He said. I don't feel so good.

JUDGE KRAMER: Have a glass—maybe you'd like that glass of water.

WITNESS: I just don't feel so good. My.

JUDGE KRAMER: I understand. Do you have to go to the bathroom?

WITNESS: No.

JUDGE KRAMER: Good. But if you want to you can go. We have all the time in the world here.

WITNESS: I know.

JUDGE KRAMER: It's a bit hot in here, isn't it?

WITNESS: Yes, sir.

JUDGE KRAMER: In my opinion, they keep these chambers overheated. Now. You were going to tell me what Wesley's father said when he visited your home.

WITNESS: Well. He said. He said Uncle Wayne was—inter—interfering with me.

JUDGE KRAMER: Interfering. Good. Wesley's father came over and he said—do you know what he meant by that?

WITNESS: I guess.

JUDGE KRAMER: Now we are getting to the—I want you to tell only the truth now. Did you tell Wesley that?

WITNESS: What?

JUDGE KRAMER: That there were certain—about this interfering.

WITNESS: Do I?

JUDGE KRAMER: Speak up, son.

WITNESS: Okay.

JUDGE KRAMER: Do you know what that means?

WITNESS: What?

JUDGE KRAMER: All right. Now son. Now I am going to—I am going to ask you directly. Did your uncle ever touch you in places—did he touch you?

WITNESS: He gave me a sponge bath.

JUDGE KRAMER: He gave you your bath? When you were sick?

WITNESS: He gave me a sponge bath. He gave me backrubs. He was nice to me.

JUDGE KRAMER: Now we're—he bathed you.

WITNESS: Yes.

JUDGE KRAMER: And when he bathed you, did he ever touch you?

WITNESS: He gave me sponge baths. I could not take real baths. I could have but we didn't know that. I could not go upstairs on my own. Anyway, they did not know if I could. The County.

JUDGE KRAMER: I see. Your uncle gave you sponge baths.

WITNESS: Yes.

JUDGE KRAMER: And when he gave you these baths, did he ever touch you down—down there?

WITNESS: There?

JUDGE KRAMER: Do you know what your genitals are, son?

WITNESS: I guess.

JUDGE KRAMER: They are—ignore Mrs. Vesey, son. She's heard everything, haven't you, Mrs. Vesey? They are your sex organs, between your legs.

WITNESS: Yes.

JUDGE KRAMER: Did your uncle ever touch you there? Just answer the question directly, son. Just answer yes or no. We only want the truth here. We are trying to get to the bottom of things. After all, I often say, if it looks as if there is black everywhere, that doesn't mean there is no white anywhere. We are trying to find the black and white truth for these purposes. We want to do the right thing. So you just tell us the truth here. All right?

WITNESS: All right.

JUDGE KRAMER: Did he?

WITNESS: Touch.

JUDGE KRAMER: Did your uncle ever touch you on the genitals?

WITNESS: I think he may have.

JUDGE KRAMER: Good. That's right. That's just what we—just answer my questions.

WITNESS: Is that what inter—interfere means?

JUDGE KRAMER: Well, it can mean that, son. Yes it can.

WITNESS: Then.

The Last Diary

Michael Grumley

Like Felice Picano, Michael Grumley kept a diary. Grumley's filled more than twenty volumes at the time of his death. But in many ways Grumley's is a far more personal statement than Picano's, for Grumley is more interested in the smells and colors of the day, the arrangement of objects, than in who came to dinner and what they said. However, in the last year of his life, as he grew sicker, this sensitivity to the changes of light takes on a certain urgency, and he more diligently recorded the mundane comings and goings of people and events. The following are extracts from the last volume of his diary.

July 24, 1987—Amagansett, N.Y.

The asphalt melting in the city, we arrive here early afternoon and are relieved to find cool breezes by the pool. Tour the garden down below, amazed by the beauty of the cucumber vines, the tartness of the strawberries. I swim a few laps. These old unused muscles—a welcome strain. Robert pores over the plans for George and Michael's new flat on 14th Street.* George a little tired, but Michael quite snappy.

July 25—Amagansett

Garden tours today, with the Hamptons flower club—the first garden is memorable for its small white "gooseneck" blossoms, and some

---

*George Stambolian (1938–91) and Michael Hampton were lovers. George Stambolian was a professor of French literature at Wellesley College and the editor of, among other books, *Men on Men*. Michael Hampton is an advertising executive. Together they owned a summer house in Amagansett, Long Island.

fine Shastas. The second is enormous and costly and winds all along the property; first, a cutting garden with fifteen-foot hollyhocks and brilliant dahlias and zinnias—then roses upon roses. Through a hedge the roses and dahlias give way to an all-white garden. The gardener who leads us through has seven assistants. A woman in shorts lies on the grass in the white garden, communing with the garden ''spirit''— George and Michael say she does so at every tour, a prone and eccentric presence among the gentry. Would anyone mistake *us* for gentry, in our white hats?

I hear that George has—perhaps, he can't quite remember—let Holleran know that I am ill, too. I'm sure Robert didn't suggest that knowing about one of us was the same as knowing about us both. I am not angry, but I don't much like it. Talk of peonies and the Duchess of Windsor.

July 26—Amagansett

Swimming. Reading bits and pieces of Ned Rorem.* How he idolizes Paul Goodman after all, and after all these years.

Flap into town and buy scones and gym shorts, an ice-cream cone for Robert. After Michael leaves, George sits us down in front of the VCR, and we watch 2½ hours of him speaking to a gay group in Madison, Wisc. Alternately numbing and chilling. Robert and he talk about apprehensions and misapprehensions concerning novels, and being a novelist. Robert feels better after, clearing the air somewhat regarding Felice Picano, and the remarks George has made in Madison. But George's ''positive aspects of AIDS'' section, particularly, sticks in my craw. The AIDS remarks *have* been trivializing, and when he's mentioned, briefly, *Second Son*, he's said it's about someone dying of it, when of course it's about someone living through it, surviving.

July 28—N.Y.C.

Walter [Clemons]† comes for tea at 4:30—then Woolley for a drive at 7:30. We learn his mother-in-law will be putting in $800 a month

---

*Ned Rorem (b. 1923), one of the best American composers and the winner of the Pulitzer Prize for music, was a friend of the Ferro-Grumleys. For many years Rorem was the lover of Paul Goodman (1911–72), the American novelist, poet, playwright, and social critic.

†Walter Clemons (b. 1933), the book critic for *Newsweek*, was a close friend of Robert Ferro and Michael Grumley's.

for the rest of his life, "paying J's half of the rent." He's resilient, and strong, but sometimes tonight, here, the weight of what he's saying makes him stop, pause as if lost. As lost he is.

My father's birthday today; burn a candle at the Japanese altar.

July 31—N.Y.C.

Dinner tonight at the Chelsea Hotel—up on the tenth floor with Bill Whitehead and Tony. Bill Whitehead* has been to his eye doctor, who is alarmed over the advance of CMV in his left eye. Bill Whitehead, too, is alarmed—he sees dark shadows on objects now. His own M.D. wants him to consider DHPG treatments, but they involve going to the hospital and getting a catheter put in his neck. (Barry has just had his put back in yesterday, and his fever is back, Stephen tells us today.)[†] Another problem is whether he'd be able to continue his AZT protocol, with the new quite potent drug working in him.

Robert has been depressed today—we discover a $500 misunderstanding in our bank account—the money that was meant for Massachusetts. His father says he can't give him any more just now—there are intimations of having to sell the shore house to pay for the medical expenses, AZT. This seems unfair, as the expenses thus far have been covered by the insurance company.

August 3—N.Y.C.

Straining to get out of town tonight. First we had to wait for Robert's manuscript, then we had to wait for money, and today we had to wait on a car with a dead battery, smoking wires.

---

*Bill Whitehead, the celebrated editor, worked with Robert Ferro and Edmund White. Christopher Cox was his assistant. Whitehead died of AIDS.
†Barry Laine (1951–87) and Stephen Greco were lovers and close friends of Michael Grumley and Robert Ferro's. Barry Laine was a dance critic and founder of the Glines, an important venue for gay theater. He died of AIDS. Stephen Greco is a writer and journalist, an editor for *Interview*. A portion of his diary concerning Barry Laine's final illness is printed in John Preston's *Personal Dispatches: Writers Confront AIDS*.

August 7—Tully Pond, Mass.

Reading Sylvia Bedford down at the water's edge, quite peaceful just after the sun goes down and everything is still. Even the children's voices from the church camp across the lake blend in. Today a young woman named Amy, from two cabins down, comes to say hello— she's an illuminator of manuscripts, and sometime botanist, living with a builder named Wayne. She gives us tips on the local cultural scene. The welcome wagon.

Run into Allen [Young]* at the post office. He settled us in yesterday.

August 8—Tully Pond

Back to weeping in the afternoon. Robert props me up and I am better by evening. And sitting in the dark by the edge of the water after dinner, I feel a rub on my legs and it's a black cat (with a white throat patch) come to call. When Robert sees (feels) him, he brings out milk. We take it as a most reassuring sign.

Work just a little on the novel.

August 9—Tully Pond

I do one drawing—of a sprite or a little pea-angel—and then this evening begin on another.

I've brought up Bruce Cratsley's† photo of the Elgin Marbles—the centaur—and it sits quite regally on the mantel; on the other side, the Dalai Lama. Robert has rearranged all the furniture, and it's got quite cozy.

Last night a dream of Lulu (the original), and then of Madonna. I'm engaged by her to make little devices that, when thrown to the crowd, release little puffs of scent. Her scent, presumably. Robert asks, in the

---

*Allen Young (b. 1941), writer, editor, and gay activist, was the person who introduced Ferro and Grumley to Tully Pond. With Karla Jay, he edited two important early gay books, *Out of the Closet: Voices of Gay Liberation* and *Lavender Culture*.

†Bruce Cratsley (b. 1944) is a photographer. Robert Ferro wrote the introduction to the catalog of Cratsley's 1987 show at the Witkin Gallery; the catalog contains a portrait of Ferro and the photograph described here.

dream, "But won't some people find them—offensive?" *"Offensive?"* screams Madonna, "Of *course* they're offensive!" She and I exchange a look of complicity.

August 10—Tully Pond

Car won't start again this A.M.—neighbors to the right and left help Robert get it jump-started; then, there's a service station in town—finally, about 5, the cables or whatever are spliced, the battery's restored. Allen comes for a cup of tea, bearing gladiolas and asters, wax beans, basil, and giant zucchini. We plan to take him out to dine tomorrow night.

Robert has started a fire while I've slept—the workroom is thus so inviting I slip behind my desk and work all day on Rome. Still re-reading now, at midnight, after dinner and various walks down to the water's edge. Later this afternoon, while R's talking to the telephone company (our bell doesn't sound today—we can't get calls), I hear children below and come down to see two terrified teenagers of color jumping out of a rowboat into the water, surrounded by a swarm of angry bees. They are crying, batting at them. Someone from across the lake at their camp is yelling for them to get under the water to get away from them. They do and, gasping, swim to our magic rock and crawl up on it. I tell them to be calm, that it's all over, but they are in such anguish from the bites—I learn later one has been bitten eight times—that I can't help at all. Their rowboat is stuck in some limbs just a few feet from my reading chair—and it's there that a great mad cloud of insects is buzzing. A counselor appears in another boat and pulls them in, takes them back across the pond.

Robert talks with Felice Picano. No visit this coming weekend, thank goodness. Something about minding someone else's cat. When pressed, he says he *has* read *Life Drawing*, passed it on to Larry Mitchell*—says of course he hasn't changed his mind (his delay this week makes me paranoid) and still means to publish it, but thinks it needs *some work*. What heinous words, what a maddening prospect. I rail at Robert, whose fault it's not.

---

*Larry Mitchell (b. 1938) was one of Felice Picano's partners in the Gay Presses of New York.

August 13—Tully Pond

Strident hymns from the church camps float across the water. Yesterday, we went out in the canoe and took a turn all the way round. What we looked in vain for all last August presented itself at the eastern end: the blue heron. Still, glass-smooth waters, great clumps of water lilies blooming.

It was beautiful on the lake yesterday, but these muscles are weaker than last year, and today we must paddle less strenuously. Head fatigue, eyes unfocused. Stephen's called, to say Barry really may be home tomorrow, or Monday.

August 14—Tully Pond

Call Mario Sartori at Lyle Stuart, tell him Joy Harris and Paul Reed have suggested I show him *Life Drawing* and would he like to see it? He asks what it's about. I none-too-imaginatively say, About growing up in the Midwest (Robert groans in the living room), but add, A piece of it was in the gay anthology *Men on Men* and got good reviews. He says, Of course, send it along. I've thought to replace the three-part division of it with six smaller chapters, but after going through it and talking with Robert, it's decided no divisions at all might be best . . . no parts, no chapters. Write a cover letter, pack it up—I'm now about to drive it to the P.O. to mail it.

Robert talks to George's friend Richard, who's in the Beta Interferon project at Roosevelt Hospital, asks him several questions about it under cover of a pseudonym. Richard was ARC-diagnosed 5 years ago, says his lesions have been flattening out in the 8 weeks he's been getting the injections. It's injections, not IV. On Mon, Wed, and Fri—they stick you, then you stay for an hour while they check your vital signs. Every other Monday you have to stay for 3 hours because the dosage is upped. Headaches before, which now they're giving Tylenol-Codeine for, and ameliorating. He has Dr. Wernz, too, as well as the Roosevelt doctor.

8/14—P.M.

At the public library we find on the shelves not only *Max Desir* but the Atlantis book as well, and my own *Giants*. *Atlantis* is *very* well thumbed, card after card pasted in over the years. We sign them for the gracious librarian, and I get a library card—it's really such a bracing thing, to find oneself in the odd little out-of-the-way places of the world.

Bill Whitehead calls, his fever's abated—on AZT for 2 weeks now. He's heard from Louise Erdrich, who's just starting *Second Son*—expects to hear from Doris Grumbach any day. He says the *Native* is pooh-poohing AZT.

August 17—Tully Pond

Yesterday the Harmonic Convergence. We are out while the mist is still on the water; we paddle the canoe down to the blue heron's cove, light our candles, and chant. It's still, and quite beautiful—the sun pokes out at 8—two crows fly overhead.

Stephen calls, quite depressed—we listen, and try to make the right sounds.

The Royalton Fair on Saturday. Mrs. Boulton, a fragile widow under a wide-brimmed hat with a Blanche DuBois air, tries to induce me to try her peanut-butter fudge. I admire a Deco dish, telling someone named Myrtle that I have one at home just like it. "Now you have two," she says, and thrusts it upon me. I try to pay something, but she won't have it, says she doesn't want to cart it back home.

August 18—Tully Pond

A cool breeze this morning: Robert typing a plot résumé for the publicity department at Crown. Yesterday he was tired all day, depressed, concerned about the lesions' size—but today, the air is cleaner, and he's back in good spirits.

August 20—Tully Pond

This morning we see the blue heron again, coming around the bend from the little island house where we've gone ashore. We are able to approach it more closely than previously, and I am able to get a sketch.

Last night, we joined Allen, Felice Picano, and their mutual friend Scott [Facon] for dinner in Ashburnham, at the Victorian House.

Felice is subdued, Scott personable, and Allen well behaved as ever.

We've yelled at Felice the night before for being horrid and manipulative, and gotten it off our chests.

Two days ago, *lots* of work done on my novel.

August 22—Tully Pond

Robert finds an ancient four-leaf clover among the pages of the songbook tonight. He's heard via Bill Whitehead that Doris Grumbach has liked *Second Son* and is writing a blurb, and his relief and pleasure at this are considerable.

Last night, dinner at the Octagon house (Allen Young's)—one guest, Felice Picano's friend, doesn't make it back until we've eaten Robert's pasta and are midway through Allen's chicken. Out looking under every bush, the victim apparently of an ongoing sexual compulsion. Rather distasteful, in these times. Allen, as host, none too charmed.

Stephen calls—his and Barry's cat, Farquar, has died yesterday, with Barry finally due home on Monday. It seems so unfair, it *is* so unfair—Stephen has had to tell Barry at the hospital tonight.

August 25—Tully Pond

We've sent flowers to Brooklyn last night—welcome-home blooms for Barry—but have heard nothing from Stephen. We're afraid this morning that he's still in Beth Israel.

Still, not a peep about *Life Drawing* from anyone at GPNY. And Joy tells Robert she in fact hasn't suggested Sartori to me, when I was sure she had. Even got it written down. Hmmmm—who did?

August 27—Tully Pond

Bob Bontelle, the Petersham realtor and civic booster, has driven us all through Petersham Tuesday afternoon, starting at a beautiful site—a hilltop with a view of Mt. Monadnock to the north. But a brutally ugly house sits on it, and the driver's pallet business has left pallets and bits of pallets strewn all across the property. The house, even worked on, is unthinkable.

Yesterday, Stephen calls to say Barry *is* home, disoriented but happy to be there. Stephen unable to sleep the first 2 nights—a full-time nurse in attendance by day.

Raining all night here—yesterday we took the canoe all the way round, and came upon the blue heron out on the water standing amid stumps—a few quick sketches before he flees.

August 28—Tully Pond

Work from 2 to 5 on a drawing of the Spirit of the Lake—freeing myself a bit. Robert at the downstairs table when I'm not, doing his house drawings; designing, designing. . . .

Stephen calls to say Barry is really very improved, eating and talking and making sense. Bill Whitehead is not doing so well, goes into the hospital Tuesday for 10 days of DHPG for his CMV. His vision now quite bad.

September 1, 1987—N.Y.C.

Back to Manhattan. Today, appointments with Dr. Wernz—he says we're both doing splendidly. Robert, though, is apprehensive about tomorrow's meeting with the doctor administering the Beta Interferon program.

I have gained nearly 6 pounds in the wilds of Massachusetts, which is good. But the insurance company is giving me trouble about reimbursement for the AZT—nearly three thousand dollars as of today! I speak to them again at N.Y.U. pharmacy, get them to sign the claim.

Ryan White out in Indiana, so ill a few weeks ago, is taking AZT and is recovered enough to start school this week.

September 4—N.Y.C.

Robert concerned about his face—particularly his right temple, and under his right eye.

Robert gives George a pep talk about his fiction writing. Yesterday, Robert hears from Felice Picano that Larry Mitchell is still out of town, with *Life Drawing* in his suitcase. Felice Picano wants him to be the editor on it.

September 6—N.Y.C.

We're meant to go out in the evening but Robert feeling nauseous. He rallies. Tonight, piano. Work a little on the book.

September 8—N.Y.C.

Yesterday, Robert called on Bill Whitehead at the Harkness Pavilion. Bill is very low, thinking he's a burden to all. Barry is acting up in Brooklyn, throwing himself out of bed—a 24-hour nurse is now thought necessary. Stephen upset, depressed.

Try to help keep Robert in a positive mood. My efforts abetted by B[arbara] Grossman calling to say Doris Grumbach *has* come through with a blurb, saying she "loves" the book. Upbeat, too, like Ozick's.

September 12—Sea Girt

Felice Picano tells me on Thursday that he doesn't want to publish *Life Drawing* after all, that our agreement wasn't really binding since there was nothing on paper! Says the book is "a mess"—a collection of notes, a short story, and a sketch. It is all too opaque, and isn't interesting in any way. More nastiness of this nature—an ugly, ugly exercise—he is extremely combative, sarcastic. I say little, wait till he's done.

Robert as upset by this treachery as I. What to do?

September 16—N.Y.C.

Robert has started the Beta Interferon program on Monday—he has a slight—99 to 100—fever in the afternoon, and his joints, particularly his knees, ache. Today, he goes in and is back by 10:30 and gets only a slight headache. There is some depression, both days, but we think it may be because none of his family has called to find out how it's gone. Camille finally checks in today; Beth and Aunt Mame called yesterday. Tonight his father calls him from Portugal. George [Stambolian], too, calls, to say how much he's enjoying *Second Son*. I've got a very sustaining call yesterday from Stephen, saying the same about *Life Drawing*—haven't told him about publication falling through; I'll wait until he's done.

The Pope is in California, trying to hold back the sea—tomorrow there are demonstrations planned in San Francisco. For our part, we're going down to Washington next month, to protest at the White House—Robert has gotten enthusiastic about it, too.

September 26—Sea Girt

A flyer from Ned [Rorem] in the mail, about his new Diary. Robert decides to apply for the Guggenheim again. I've got him a catalog for the N.Y. School of Interior Design, and he thinks he might do a course or two.

Robert has given me what may be some rather good advice about *Life Drawing* at dinner two nights ago—some reshuffling needed. I am receptive enough to the idea, initially, to think it just might be valid.

Watching Judge Bork in the hearings today—with such a face, how could goodness prevail? A man who wraps himself in the theoretical is surely no less a threat than a man who's a foulmouthed spitting bigot.

Sea Girt

Dear Stephen calls to say he thinks Barry is near the end. When he climbs into bed with him last night to talk about mortality, Barry says I want to stay here.

Robert working on the copy reader's pages, feeling quite good about *Second Son*, I think. And so am I. And today, rehandling, reshaping *Life Drawing*.

September 22—N.Y.C

Yesterday afternoon, at the Riverside Chapel, a service for Barry, who has died on Sunday night. Stephen has called us in N.J. just afterward—he has been so brave, giving it all a dignity. Saslova* leads the service—there are over 200 people, standing in the aisles, weeping, hugging each other after. Victor Bumbalo† reading scripture—the "love is stronger than death" passage from David and Jonathan. Victor, especially, evoking the pain of losing Barry. Robert has had his Beta Interferon in the morning, and the super has been knocking down our bedroom-bathroom wall through the day—but we manage to appear, for Barry's sake.

---

*James M. Saslow, a Renaissance scholar and the author of *Ganymede in the Renaissance*, among other works.
†Victor Bumbalo (b. 1940) is a playwright.

September 26—Sea Girt

We bring Stephen down yesterday afternoon, to get him out of the apartment. A long walk along the strand, talking about B.

Doris Grumbach has called Robert two days ago—talk of the book, and Bill Whitehead. Edmund [White] calls later the same day, on his way back to Paris, wanting to do a duo reading with Robert this spring. His book has been delayed until March.

September 29—N.Y.C.

Go with Stephen last night to hear His Holiness the Dalai Lama in Brooklyn Heights. He looks just the same as three years ago, speaks again of compassion and loving-kindness, how the next century will be better, more enlightened. The Presbyterians who precede him lack eloquence.

Yesterday, work rearranging *Life Drawing*. Tony calls to say Bill Whitehead is resigned to losing the sight in his eye, is back at the Chelsea. His parents not wonderful as visitors, consolants.

October 1—N.Y.C.

George Stambolian has told Robert about [Michael] Denneny, [Eric] Ashworth, etc., getting another book on It,* *Valley of the Shadow*, moved up at St. Martin's, so that it will come out before Robert's in April. After Robert tells Barbara [Grossman] this, she calls back an hour later to say that now Robert's will be moved ahead, too! This means books will be available the latter part of *January*, with a March 1 official pub date. I make him promise not to tell George.

The doctor's appointment on Tuesday went well enough. Weight stabilized. Dr. W. says we're not to worry unless my fever goes up to 101—that 99 is okay. In fact, the temperature does go down. He gives me the name of a doctor at Sloan-Kettering who's doing an aerosol pentamidine study.

---

*Neither Grumley nor Ferro liked to refer to AIDS by name. They often referred to "It." Indeed, *Second Son*, which Ferro wanted to be the first novel about AIDS, never refers to the disease explicitly.

Dinner with Richard de Combray* pleasant—we laugh as of old. He tells Robert that he's going to finish *Second Son* as soon as he gets back to Paris, that the death of another friend last month has brought him face-to-face with It again.

After a nice chat with CW last evening, he tells me just at the end that he's "shared" my illness with a friend of his. This hurts me terribly. I remember the pain of finding out about Fred B's indiscretion—how like a betrayal it seemed. After entrusting C with this personal thing, after being so careful, for so many reasons—that a stranger should know now what most of my closest friends don't is so upsetting. I don't know what happens now with C; I suspect very little. An old friendship restarting up, now stalled—needless pain.

October 4—Sea Girt

Geese flying overhead—sandpaper against the sky—run out and take a snap just as they pass the lighthouse. Glorious days down here—the sea is tense and beautiful, goldenrod filling the view. Today we plant a large yucca in the garden, and two great fat mums elsewhere.

October 7—N.Y.C.

We go down this morning, after Robert's session at Roosevelt Hospital, to see Bill at the Chelsea. He's unable to talk, and is heavily drugged—a slight widening of the eyes our only encouragement. He isn't able to swallow easily—Tony is grinding up his AZT and giving it to him in applesauce.

After the Chelsea, I go over to the U.N. on 44th St. to see if I can lend support to the Tibetans—but they've been, yesterday, about 100 strong, protesting. More horror stories out of Lhasa today.

October 9—N.Y.C.

Tony calls this morning—Bill has died a little after 9 A.M. Robert, now, is at Jory's office, and with her coordinating an obituary notice for the newspapers. Robert has woken up from a dream of Bill this morning—there won't be any service here till February, and his ashes

---

*Richard de Combray, a writer and photographer, and an old friend of Ferro's and Grumley's.

will go to his family in Virginia, for a service there. Robert calls Edmund; I tell Stephen. Now, Tony has just called again—he tells me about how good Ram Dass has been, and a therapist says Ram Dass has told him to light a candle and talk to Bill each day.

October 10—Washington, at the Watergate

So far, so good. Came down on the Metroliner in a great clique—Hampton and Stambolian behind us, Stephen and Saslova next to us—Vito Russo hovering, the Mass-Kantrowitzes close at hand.* Brioche and tea and a game of Bali just before Baltimore.

When we check in at the hotel desk, they suggest that since they're *so* full, we might like to double up (Stephen and us) in the Presidential Suite! And here we are. A thousand-dollar-a-night pile with big white terry-cloth Watergate robes to put on, two bedrooms, living room, dining room, two baths, kitchen, and a terrace as long as Constitution Avenue. Beneath us, now, in the sunlight, they're sculling on the Potomac, and we can watch the visitors peeking over the balcony of the Kennedy Center. Lunch is on its way up, and we've called the bookstore to make sure we'll be welcome (after our nap). Robert calls Tony in N.Y.—the bit has been in the paper today. Tony says we're in the suite Balanchine was always given when the dance company was here.

We decide it's Barry Laine looking down on us and arranging this glory. Tonight, dinner planned at the Potomac Restaurant.

October 11—Washington

The day begins with breakfast here for 8—David Mossler, George and Michael, Stephen and us, and two friends of Stephen—a newly married couple. Lovely eating eggs and sausage, looking out on the Potomac as three hundred thousand compatriots are assembling in the streets. We find a taxi to take us to H Street, but the N.Y. contingent has got anxious and gone on ahead to the Ellipse—Saslova waiting for us to show the way. It's quite amazing to see the streets so thronged—the impression is of mostly staid middle-class types (like ourselves) pro-

---

*Vito Russo (1946–90), the author of *The Celluloid Closet* (1981), an important study of homosexuality and the cinema—an early gay activist, he died from AIDS; Dr. Lawrence Mass, one of the first physicians to write extensively about AIDS; his lover, Arnie Kantrowitz, the author of *Under the Rainbow* (1977).

ceeding two by two. But, later, in the march itself, so many colleges are represented that no generalities prevail. All ages, all types.

We muster on the grass; Vito has brought two Quilt panels for the Names Project and stands by them. But there are so many people that the pace is slow—we wait there from 11:30 to 2 and then decide to be unaffiliated and make our way along Constitution Avenue toward the Mall, and the Quilt there. Get a hug at the ACT UP table, buy an AIDSgate T-shirt. Sign petitions for an AIDS funding project to be presented to the White House, get photographed, grin at strangers.

The Quilt is beautiful, the experience of wandering through the little coffin-sized patches of color with hundred and hundreds of names stitched and painted and sewed on them is very moving—the Capitol looming over the spread of motley. See Michael Bennett's square, and Tom Waddell's. Then march along for a while, get out of the flow as the line turns toward the Capitol, watch as group after group strides by. Stephen is cast down by it, now and again—especially at the Quilt—but rallies, and is brave. Good to have my old chum David there—and George and Michael.

We hear the speeches floating on the gray air—but must leave to catch our train before Jesse Jackson appears—we've been swayed by gospel group Lavender Light at the pre-march muster. A group of gay swimmers called Different Strokes throw themselves to the pavement to demonstrate precision swimming, in sixes and sevens—a man carries a sign saying "It's *Mister* Fag to You!" Idaho marchers chant "Idaho-mo!" And a church group sings "Ho-Mo, Ho-Mo, It's on to Church We Go!"

Gerry Studds and Barney Frank and Whoopi Goldberg have spoken. We've come and been counted—and that's the thing.

October 13—N.Y.C.

Down in D.C., hundreds of gay men and lesbians today arrested on the steps of the Supreme Court—the demonstrators (all passive resisters) closing the Court for the first time in its history—all to protest last year's *Hardwick* decision. Hardwick himself is arrested with the group. The estimates now coming out on Sunday's march get higher—between 500,000 and 600,000—a figure from the Parks Department.

Earlier, I've had a blood test at N.Y.U. Hospital, run into L.R. outside—neither of us acknowledging to the other that we are there, chatting about the Quilt—about how we've come back resolved to make and donate panels.

He's heard from B[arbara] Grossman today that Anne Rice wants to give *Second Son* a blurb. From Doris Grumbach that she'd called the Watergate Saturday to ask us for a drink, but couldn't reach us. From Tony that he's going to try to keep Bill Whitehead's apartment.

Robert's dosage upped yesterday at St. Luke's–Roosevelt—a little headache, but no fever.

October 14—N.Y.C.

Richard Howard calls from Texas; David Alexander hasn't told him about Bill Whitehead till today.* He's hard at work, has got an ameliorative call from Edmund [White] in Paris—the first time they've spoken since *Caracole*.

George has had lunch with NAL and says they do want to see *Life Drawing* again.

October 15—N.Y.C.

Edmund calls again from Paris, talking about a *PW* [*Publishers Weekly*] piece that five of Bill Whitehead's authors will write.

The typist Rodd has brought his chum in to say hello as he drops off *Life Drawing*. Now, at 1:24 A.M., I'm trying to pull myself away from the fresh lovely pages.

October 19—N.Y.C.

Feeling a little disconcerted. Only because the agent I called today (on Vito's suggestion) didn't make me feel particularly famous. Also a voice like a squeegee.

Robert talks to Doris Grumbach and Stanley Elkin over the weekend about a memorial piece for Bill Whitehead. The stock market took a plunge today. It seems very remote.

---

*Richard Howard (b. 1929), the distinguished translator and Pulitzer Prize–winning poet, was a friend of Ferro and Grumley's. His lover, David Alexander (b. 1952), is a painter.

October 21—N.Y.C.

Robert's birthday so far not so festive. He's come home from St. Luke's with a bad headache, and I've put him straight to bed. The dosage, 180, is apparently the maximum for him.

A man from Oberlin College wants him to come out and speak to them next month.

My old pal Quentin, who after not a lot of hesitation—just right— really well done—tells me he's been taking AZT, and that no one knows. He's been diagnosed since August. I let two or three sentences pass, then tell him, Me too. His trust in my confidence is enough to bring out my own in his—we compare stories and symptoms (I don't tell him about Robert—and later, don't tell Robert about him) and it is strangely settling. He's such a good soul. He tells me he was very sick before the doctor gave him AZT—now he's back to himself— although the five flights of steps up to his apartment are still difficult. His T cells right now are at 200. We bring to each other optimistic voices. He says, in fact, that when he saw me on the street this spring, he did worry about the way I looked.

He was in D.C. with the N.Y. Chorus, singing up the Mall—he hasn't told his family, or fellow workers.

At Richard de Combray's the other night, we marveled at the refurbishing, and spent the last hour upstairs, singing our *Dodsworth* songs for him, singing along with him playing Noël Coward tunes, all of us misty-eyed and beaming.*

October 26—N.Y.C.

A week after the crash, Wall Street still feeling the heat. Apparently Tokyo and Europe are going through the same panic, and everyone is selling everything. We leave the beach—a great waxy red rose blooming in the garden—and drive back here. Robert gives his doctor a copy of *The Magic Mountain* today.

The phone rings as I write this, and it's Stanley Elkin.

---

*Ferro and Grumley worked for many years on a musical version of Sinclair Lewis's novel *Dodsworth*.

October 27—N.Y.C.

Yesterday, the publishers phone to say Anne Rice has given *Second Son* a glowing blurb—Robert fears it is too hyperbolic for use.... When we get home, the publishers call to say galleys have been speeded up, and are arriving here by messenger *tomorrow*!

I call Quentin, want to give him a pill-timer like mine. Shall I start Elkin's new book?

October 29—N.Y.C.

Last night, step out with Susan—dancing and a rather lavish buffet at the Puck Building down on Lafayette Street: Geoffrey Holder, Carmen de Lavallade, Jerzy Kozinski, Shirley Stoler. I'm in black tie and Robert's green velvet jacket—we get photographed twice.

October 31—Sea Girt—Halloween

Meet Robert at N.Y.U. Hospital for our appointment with Dr. W.— I've gained another 6½ pounds—and he says I'm doing extremely well, no bone-marrow or blood-cell depletion, and no swelling of glands, etc. Robert, too, gets a good report. It is decided that starting him on AZT might jeopardize the Beta Interferon treatments, so it's better to wait.

Bring down the *Second Son* galleys, begin reading them last night— what a fine beginning it is.

No tree-man appears today; Robert being philosophic, working on his paper for Oberlin College.

November 2—N.Y.C.

Read through Robert's galleys—find thirteen more mistakes/typos in addition to what he's found. Talk to Quentin on the phone—his doctor's opinion is that he oughtn't to start pentamidine. The new bed is delivered tonight—and it's a whole new continent beneath us now. Higher and firmer and infinitely more stable than the one we've inhabited up till now, a Beautyrest then.

November 4—N.Y.C.

Gave the pill-timer to Quentin last night—he seems quite pleased to have it—it seems rather like a fraternity we're in, now, and all we can do to help each other, or simply support each other, we ought to do.

November 7—Sea Girt

The moon due at any moment—last night it pulled itself up out of the sea, orange and full, quite magical. The fire is laid, the tea is ready—waiting for Robert to come down from his nap.

November 8—Sea Girt

The air thick and smoky today—quite extraordinary. It's the result of forest fires in Kentucky and West Virginia, brought up along the coast-line. Robert working on his paper, reads it to me—a bit of it—before tea. Nice work about the death of the novel being the death of the narrator, and gay literature revivifying the form.

November 10—N.Y.C.

Yesterday A.M. sideswiped by another car on Central Park West—the driver so incensed, he jumps on my hood!

Find a review of *The Blue Star* in an Irish gay magazine, bring it home for Robert.

Cynthia Ozick and he have a chat this morning—she's still working on her memorial piece about Bill Whitehead. She's so complimentary about Robert and his work—bless her.

Still nothing from N.Y.U. about the pentamidine inhalation protocol.

Quentin calls last night—making sure I've seen the *Village Voice* article on new drug therapies—very optimistic.

November 11—Vets' Day—N.Y.C.

The galleys (bound) arrive this morning—a baby-blue jacket, with Cynthia's and Doris's lovely blurbs on the back!

PWA newsletter arrives—new good things about ampligen and other drugs.

November 14—Sea Girt

Quite a lot of work done yesterday—working from 5 to 11, with a quick dinner break. Perhaps Salvatori Santagati the other day at tea, asking me for 20 pp. of it for the *European Gay Review* (Renaissance issue), has had an effect. (He is charming, talking to Robert about all manner of things, asking Robert to be on the advisory board.)

Robert now on the phone with Stephen, talking out some problems with his Oberlin paper.

November 16—N.Y.C.

He's working so hard on this Gay Literature talk—good to have something to concentrate on, though.

November 20—N.Y.C.

Waiting for Robert to come in from St. Luke's, now—his subcutaneous is to start today. Yesterday, he got back from Oberlin midday, just as I'm shooing out the last of the window-installers here. On Wednesday, the car won't start, and I get a ticket, and at midnight, in Times Square, a desperate character hurls himself across the sidewalk as I'm buying a *Times*, thrusts his hand into my right front pocket, clutches the bills he's found there ($11), and catapults back across the sidewalk, into the crowd. All in broad nightlight, with half a dozen idlers witnessing it. They say, Go after him, Chase him, etc. But I come home instead, glad all he's got is the few bills and change, not the wallet or pills or keys I carry inside in my jacket pocket.

November 22—Sea Girt

What bad days I'm having. Friday morning, a bad headache, made worse by the news that Crown isn't going to credit my jacket image. Too "political" a situation, apparently, with the art director pitted against the editor, etc. Also, now it's too late. I tell Robert I'll never forget this—and I won't. The idea is I should be so thrilled to have contributed the image, the photo for the painting, that any credit would be superfluous.

In bad shape, physically and emotionally. Then yesterday, discover we haven't packed my weekend supply of AZT. Spent all day trying to track down a supplier down here—a pharmacy, a hospital. Finally get the Burroughs Wellcome representative to call back—and the doctor who's covering for Wernz—and find 100 capsules at the Shop Rite Pharmacy out on 35.

The N.Y.C. window marathon, the mugging, the cover, all of it making me feel taken advantage of—and of course the lack of response on *Life Drawing* coloring it all. Robert wants me, either through ICM [Grumley's agent] or on my own, to submit it to [Editor] David Groff at Crown, but after this photo-cover fiasco, I'm not feeling very positive about them. No work done here. Whine, whine, whine.

November 28—Sea Girt

The last few days, Robert feeling the exhaustion of his new everyday Beta injections. Thanksgiving very taxing—I do all the driving, etc., but he's still so tired. Yesterday, he perks up after his nap, but this A.M. it seems like fatigue, again. It's 90, every day, and he is injecting himself—in the thigh.

I talk to my mother in Racine—she has lost a tooth and the dentist says it's because when she sleeps she grinds her teeth. She's a little weepy when she talks about not seeing me for so long—but I quickly put in that if Robert comes to Chicago for *Second Son* publicity, that I'll come, too, and she can scoot down. This brightens the mood.

December 1—N.Y.C.

Tony Blum's just come and gone, for tea. Tony is rather amazing, really—at the end, when it's just the 3 of us, he tells about his last dance—the six shots of Novocain they gave him in the spine to keep dancing in *Goldberg Variations*, in Paris. Jerome Robbins the villain of the piece. James Baldwin dies today. What a loss—Robert just talking about his influence, in Oberlin, last month.

December 2—N.Y.C.

I do two drawings today—one of them a poster: Don't Forget Your Rubbers! which I'm going to give to GMHC to do with what they will.

Call from Christie's to say the Gauguin I'm trading sold for $5,000 at auction last month—not a lot, really, considering the many millions

Van Gogh is lately fetching. It would be perfect for the *Life Drawing* jacket. Perhaps too grand to use Gauguin? A letter from Andrew yesterday, apologizing for being hurtful, *but* saying we've judged Felice Picano too harshly! This prompts a Lady Bracknell note from me, but I keep it overnight instead of sending it, and then don't send it today.

Soaking my toe morning and night—the infection still there after a week of medication.

December 7—Sea Girt

I'm upset with Beth for turning me down *again* about the altogether cake I've asked her to make for R. One has to be careful not to ask too much of people—but who'd have thought a cake pan full of raisins and flour and molasses would be too much?

Robert's talked with Stephen and cleared the air about his reaction (or lack of reaction) to *Second Son*. They've assigned the James Baldwin piece to someone else, so I won't be doing it. Pity. I found I had a few things to say. About the integration of the gay character into the weave of *Another Country* particularly.

December 15—N.Y.C.

Michael Ossias has died—the service today, downtown—one of those good stalwart editors so seldom encountered—only 38.

The rain comes down—but we need a little Christmas, and schlep over to Broadway and buy a tree on 99th. $50, and a beauty. I put on the lights and all the antique ornaments through the afternoon while he goes up to Columbia-Presbyterian for his first radiation treatment.

December 19—Sea Girt

Bill's memorial service on Thursday rather beautiful—especially Robert's and Doris's tributes. Stanley Elkin is the first speaker, reading his *PW* piece, an impressive display of infirmity as he is helped to the steps. Between 200 and 300 people showing up—a large crowd perhaps as a result of the *PW* piece listing time and place the day before. After Stanley, Robert reads his piece—something quite moving about soldiers in a war. He also mentions Tony, the sustenance of a dear friend. Doris is clean and eloquent, speaking of the editor who is the writer's knight and protector. Maxine Groffsky reads words from Ed

[White]. Many people weep—Bill Whitehead's parents sit in the front row, obviously moved by all the love in the room.

Now Stephen and Saslow are having breakfast with Robert downstairs, and I'm hiding out up here. St. has brought down the *Advocate* review of *Second Son* by Paul Reed, and [Barbara] Grossman has called with the *PW* review—both quite good. Robert is immensely relieved. And most important, an article in yesterday's *Times.*

December 23—N.Y.C.

Take *Life Drawing* into Crown two days ago—though D.G. [editor David Groff] won't get to it until after the New Year.

Yesterday, meet for our doctor's appointment at N.Y.U. at 5—Dr. W. tries to dispel Robert's incipient depression about the Beta Interferon program not really having an effect on him, on his lesions. He says we're both doing well—not much in the way of specifics this month.

After the hospital, have a sandwich at the Stage Deli on 7th Avenue, then see Mary Beth [Hurt] in *The Day Room,* Don DeLillo's play, at Manhattan Theatre Club's City Center Theatre.

We go backstage to see her, then share a taxi uptown together—she tells me about Paul and brother Lenny's falling-out, about Paul's play. Nice to brag about Robert's book to her (just a little)—nice to have successes in one's life. She's actually very good with comedy, always has been.

December 31—N.Y.C.

Last night, a tough night to be a dancer—Patrick Bissell of ABT is found dead in his apt., in Hoboken. Drug-related, they say—a brilliant dancer, on his way up, at the age of 30. But the Joffrey dancers dance on—in a really beautiful *Nutcracker* at City Center. The snow scene is heavenly—a sort of magic one wants to go on and on—blue- and purple- and mustard-colored flakes against the white tree limbs of the set, the whirling bodies. The scene when the full-sized Nutcracker appears seemingly out of thin air next to old Drosselmeier also thrilling. Terrific dancing throughout—Joffrey himself comes on stage afterwards, faltering steps but a broad smile.

January 12—N.Y.C.

Last night down at P.S. 122, the memorial dance program for Barry goes very well. Stephen introduces and welcomes, warmly and articulately. Arnie Zane presents his partner Bill T. Jones, who dances "Red Room." Bill is so glorious under light—Arnie's intro moving, as he speaks of being ill himself, Barry's words to him about their shared illness. Stephanie Skura presents an amusing Jeff McMahon in his work in progress of the moment—tight and witty. Then, David White speaks before Laura Dean's indefatigable trio whirls through "Magnetic."

At the interval, much sociability—George Whitmore, Victor Bumbalo and friend Tom, Seymour Kleinberg, Allen Barnett, Saslova. Half a dozen gents congratulate Robert on the Baldwin letter he wrote that appeared in the *Times Book Review* on Sunday.

On the news tonight, the total number of AIDS cases is now 50,000. Twenty-eight thousand of these men and women have died.

January 18—Sea Girt

Fevers this afternoon and evening—the back worse, the stomach better. Robert's rash on his thigh perhaps a little less uncomfortable. George [Stambolian] calls, back from Calif.—he says one Christopher Coe is going to review *Second Son* for the *SF Chronicle*.

Robert feeling fairly good about the NAL floor bid of $20,000—and also about the English hard-and-soft offer (twenty-five hundred pounds).

January 21—N.Y.C.

The first copy of *Second Son* arrives by messenger—to great sighs of relief—until it's a book it's not a book.

Robert gets a sweet note from Ned [Rorem] about his Baldwin letter, and Richard Howard calls from Ohio with his own brand of praise (calls Robert "noble").

Now we're going out the door to our doctor appts—Robert wants to go off his Beta shots—and I must find out if my stomach pains mean I'll have to cut back on my AZT dosage. In the PWA newsletter today, a piece by Vito Russo about finally telling his parents.

January 23—Mohouk House—New Paltz, N.Y.

Robert buys me a stone Russian rabbit, in the gift shop, and gives it to me after dinner. On my own, earlier today, I've given it a fond look—the only item in the whole display that inspires one. What a sense of well-being is engendered by him picking it out.

January 30—N.Y.C.

Unremarked in here, for the last month and a half, the various notes and telephone calls and general gnashing of teeth leading up to yesterday's decision by Crown Publishers that they'd be pleased to publish *Life Drawing*. David Groff is the editor—we meet on Wednesday for lunch at Claire [Restaurant] to discuss details, and what work seems still necessary. Robert collapses in happy tears yesterday afternoon when he comes from his medical marathon and I tell him. D.G. has called me once 3 weeks back saying he was gathering support. D.G. thinks it needs a bit more bulk, especially in the California pages—I think some of the dark encounters that I trimmed may go back in. It's been 13 years since I've signed a contract—I won't let *all* my defenses down till after Wednesday, but did I sing yesterday! Now we can go through *Second Son* publication without me grumbling in a corner, kicking the dust. But isn't it odd, really, that with our nine books only four publishers are involved—we've always shared, as it happens.

February 6—Sea Girt

Fevers the last few days—a little better this morning. Robert feeling vulnerable—the rash hasn't abated on his flanks, and he's feeling that all his therapies are pointless.

Wednesday lunch with David Groff goes well. David wants a letter of intention from me—and would like to see pages immediately, but I believe I'll work them up first. He says he doesn't think I realize how good the writing is in the book! How sweet is praise.

February 10—N.Y.C.

Fever yesterday, up to 100, almost 101—worst in the evening. Robert feeling depressed about the rash; now it's infected, and I get him to take some penicillin pills. He's at Dr. Hatcher's as I write this—it's getting worse and worse, and the pain is quite severe.

Filthy smirking Pat Robertson has come in second in the Iowa Republican caucuses—but good old liberal Paul Simon is 2nd for the Democrats. Bush knocked rather flat. Thank goodness that's over at least, Iowa day and night on television.

February 12—N.Y.C.

Too busy yesterday. Light incense at the Shrine of the 100 Buddhas, on Mott Street, and buy a Dragon poster for the New Year, and little red envelopes to put N.Y. cheer in—get cookies and baba au rhum at Ferraro's on Mulberry Street. All this, after buying salmon at Balducci's and being kept waiting nearly an hour at my inept dentists!

Robert's books have arrived, so I bring one in along with the novels previously bound to Ginesta the bookbinder on West 27th. Dear old soft thing, surrounded by cats, he agrees to narrow the margins as Robert has requested—we pore over marbleized endpapers, finally I find the right ones. Put down 150; don't know how much it will all be.

Run into Quentin on the K train—he's being taken to London today by his Irish lover. The first time he's ever been abroad—he looks so good, and he says his T cells are *up*. His friend is taking AL721, and Virgin Airways has agreed to freeze it for him during the flight.

Robert gets a magical letter from Jacques Barzun, enclosing his Guggenheim recommendation. Stressing the "classic" nature of his prose.

I get a tape, from brother Tim, of Dad singing some of his old songs! Now, to get a machine to play it on.

Walter [Clemons] calls—he's doing something on the emergence of gay writing in mainstream publishing—for *Newsweek*. I give him names of eminent lesbians—Robert gives him his slant.

February 18—N.Y.C.

The reading goes beautifully—50 or 60 souls, 40 minutes' worth of intelligent questions afterward. He wears his new plum-colored jacket and black shirt and slacks—extremely luxe—even under their horrid neon.

February 19—N.Y.C.

Yesterday, pick up my drawing at GMHC. Then, N.Y.U. and Doctor Wernz—he tells Robert his glands are no longer swollen, and that the lesions on his feet have improved considerably. But Robert for some reason doesn't want to hear it.

My toe is infected again—penicillin prescribed. And I have an X ray of my chest taken, as it's been quite a few months now. Robert tells him I'm having fevers every other day, which I think is an exaggeration and upsets me.

February 20—Sea Girt

Talk to Dr. W. Robert buys me a little Walkman so I can listen to my father's singing—not so sad as I'd feared; his voice so light and joyful that I'm elated by it. But oh how Irish he sounds—a classic Irish tenor—"September Song," "You'd Be So Nice to Come Home To" singing along with the radio—the "Ivan Skivinsky Skavar" and "Billy Johnson, the Monkey," etc., and "The Lonesome Hobo's Lament." Have I stolen the intro for "Baby Me" from the latter? Not *exactly.*

February 21—Sea Girt

Robert gives everyone in his family a copy of *Second Son.* All are thrilled. Now to *read* it and still be thrilled.

February 26—N.Y.C.

Yesterday, anniversary number 21: I get a dozen red roses and my refurbished robe back—Robert gets the leather-bound copy of *Second Son* a few days early—we can't wait till pub day on Monday. He appears to be thrilled with it—the endpapers do look smashing, and the binder *has* cut the pages down, almost to the size of the other 3 novels.

Call from Chris Cox with superlatives for *Second Son.* Letters from Andrew, praising the book, too, rather thrilled by the Matthew character.

I've had a fever Tuesday and Wednesday, and haven't been able to call on my avian friend. Legs aching—up to almost 101. I've had the radio isotope put in me on Monday, must go down this afternoon to have it "read."

March 4—Boston

Yesterday, before flying up here on the shuttle, we hear from Dr. W. that he wants me to come in for a bronchoscopy on Sunday night. This to be followed by a treatment program of pentamidine—but administered intravenously rather than by aerosol. Which means, we learn today, 2 to 3 days in the hospital. Hard to accept. It means Robert being my co-op care partner and therefore having to cancel all the readings and interviews in California, the whole trip—not seeing my mother and taking her to lunch at the Pump Room in Chicago. Dr. W. says there's no way I can go, and Robert can't come and go—and won't, anyway—so all we've been looking so forward to is dashed.

March 11—N.Y.C.

The good news is that after 5 days of tests and queries and endless bloodletting, and the bronchoscopy itself on Tuesday, they have found no traces whatever of PCP. The bad news, and it's not so very bad, is that what they did finally find, yesterday, via Dr. Luiz in Infectious Diseases, is TB.

So Robert is going on to California alone tomorrow, and I'm lying low. At first he said only S.F. but now it's L.A., too—so I'll manage on my own for 5 days.

Easter Sunday April 3—N.Y.C.

We've just sung the Holy City, and my lungs sound not so bad. I'm sitting up in the living room, and been able to walk unaided to where I sit.

What's been happening is this—they still don't know what's going on! Now Dr. L says I've MTB, which is a rarification, but none of the pills prescribed—and there have been many—have had an effect against it. The result is I've been in bed for 3 weeks, sometimes unable to eat, always with fevers at night up to 105—no sleep but in 10-minute spurts, convinced I have to lie a certain way. And sweating, changing my shirt at dawn—more and more pills, and deep deep depressions. Not to hold this pen for a month—! Today, Mame comes in with Easter eggs, and Shannon's baby has arrived yes—today (Alison Camille) and I must go on.

We've told [a close friend] about us being ill, one day at a time. Predictably, he's a brick and suggests a fine bright woman named Charlene to come in when Robert's out—a muse. Arnie Zane has died on Wednesday, Robert Joffrey on Friday [of AIDS]. God bless them.

From *Second Son*

Robert Ferro

Following is the opening chapter of Second Son *(1988), published the year Robert Ferro died. This section of the novel is highly autobiographical. The Ferro family owned the beach house, which plays a principal role in* The Family of Max Desir, *and was known to Robert's friends as Gaywyck. Andrew Holleran's memorial to Ferro and Grumley (later in this book) discusses the importance of that house for Robert. After Ferro's mother's death, the family considered selling the property, and Robert stubbornly fought the decision. The house is still in the possession of the Ferro family.*

After some time he realized the house was speaking to whoever might be listening: this was Mark. He heard it in the wind through the porch, in the boom at the end when a door slammed, in the whine of the furnace when first engaged; sounds that held images the house reminded him not to forget, images of moments fractured in air as when, turning at the banister at the top of the stairs, he saw his young niece tilt her head to listen to her vanity and adjust a gypsy earring—a languorous, emblematic moment of her magic childhood, in an older safer world. The house made this possible. He could see it still in the air.

Images also, besides his family, of the two strangers who long ago had built the house and lived in it and died upstairs: the Birds. Captain Bird, it appeared. The childless Birds had never struck such chords, while the numerous Valerians, occupying every room, adding others, had changed the house into something alive and hovering, a huge pet that loved them, vitally interested in the goings-on. Captain Bird however had seen to it that everything about the place was nautically and astronomically sound. It faced exactly east, on a line drawn up the middle, like a keel, that passed through the center of the hearth and out the bay window into the heart of the sea with the sudden precision of the speed of light. The sea, visible from every room, was in some rooms a wall; in others a picture on the wall. From the upper windows it seemed you were on a riverboat, and in winter, with the furnace, as if the whole place were under way, moving through a delta; approximately. From the long deck over the porch, leaning into the wind, he could see the sharp edge of the planet he was on.

Mark was ill, dying perhaps. He stood at the window downstairs— the window toward the pond, as opposed to the one toward the ocean, or toward the lighthouse. Its view contained a wedge of sea on the right, high after a storm and figuratively rushing across a bight of beach as if to flood the house. A man with a metal detector was weaving an invisible herringbone pattern across the sand, feathering back and forth along the beach, now and then scooping up small amounts of sand with a long-armed basket. Within the ranging intimacy of his binoculars Mark could almost hear the electronic *ping* of the metal detector as the man suddenly stopped.

This small drama: the man drops to a crouch. After two or three diggings in the sand, the little metal scoop proves inadequate. Only the human hand will do. The man is young, distantly handsome. Through his binoculars Mark can see the cold, downlike glow on his cheek. Fingers touch something that then is held up. It glints. Again the young man takes up the scoop and detector, glances for an instant up at the house, perhaps sees Mark in the window, and resumes the inferred pattern along the beach.

Mark's heart is thumping. What had he seen? Someone searching for valuables on the beach. His beach. Taking a deep breath he calmed himself. His sister Vita, had she been present, would have an explanation. An obvious metaphor, she would say, considering his illness, but useful. Mark might feel that much of his life lay buried on the beach—to be found and pocketed indifferently. This could be it, he thought. Or was it that the man with the metal detector was handsome? Perhaps Mark, being alone and frightened, merely wanted company— to talk—but wanted it as a pale vestige, in all its dimmer configurations, of desire.

Like the Birds before her, Mark's mother had died upstairs, eclipsing those two earlier, less-felt deaths, and claiming the house at last and utterly from its builders. Their two transparent shades faded further and Mrs. Valerian's presence took over, as had been her intention. Her dying one year before, from a series of hemorrhagic strokes, had overlapped in an ironic but intentional way with an extensive restoration of the house—two processes sharing themes and schedules along similar though reversed lines: an Egyptian way of death, in which a place for the abiding comfort of the spirit is prepared. Mrs. Valerian had theorized that the house would bind its occupants—her family—to her after she was gone. She had concluded that she herself would also be bound, an intention to be evoked with her name and memory by whoever entered the house.

Restoration had required a lot of money, thousands every week for months. This was regarded as a medical expense by Mr. Valerian, who on the surface appeared to be rich, and who on the surface was, and he willingly gave whatever was needed because doing so assuaged his helplessness and grief. You could do nothing about a stroke, but the roof could be changed, and even the roof-line. On the ocean side windows could be cut to improve the views and lighten the interiors, with the immediate effect of liberation, as if something trapped inside the house, the Birds themselves, was at last released. Ten rooms of curtains, a dozen new rugs, every stick of furniture restored—the house emptied into a huge van and hauled to a penitentiary in Pennsylvania for refinishing. This had been arranged by Mr. Valerian, a person not averse to pursuing a bargain across state lines. Mark had asked if this meant their furniture would be stripped by convicts with guns held at their backs—the sort of question his father found surprising. Outside, the garden was reconsidered, with spaces around the house pushed back so that new sweeps of lawn were created where sea rose and masses of creeper and honeysuckle had stolen up over the years nearly to the porch. A different curve was cut for the drive, as if Margaret Valerian, in her imagination, had flown up above the house and looked down to select the ideal line. These improvements went on all at once with a number of different crews and loud machines. After the broad measures came the smaller, meaningful ones—with outside the new garden, a dozen trees, a fence—all corresponding to the different phases of Mrs. Valerian's decline, in which every day some new deficiency appeared or matured. As she deteriorated she rested her ruined mind on the new stability of the house, its lovely air of completion and bounty. Each day she went in a wheelchair room to room to see everything in its place, fixed by rules of association and design. Beyond regular use of the wheelchair, she lay propped on pillows, regarding the sea through the big window in her room. On the best and dwindling days Mark read to her from a pile of cookbooks—recipes like short plotted stories, with twists, nuance, surprises and uncertain endings, success by no means assured. To these details she listened closely, as to a chronicle of mysterious events. And when finally she died, it was with everyone around her, after a long and decorous farewell commensurate with the many months of the other sort of preparation. Light played over her face. Mark kissed her cheek and felt her spirit swirl into an angle of the ceiling, like perfume seeping through the house, a faintness of scent relative to its distance from her room—all of it lingering behind as planned.

He could not then agree, precipitously, to a plan to sell the house. Odd that all her labors and intentions, her clearly expressed wishes, should now be used against her. For no one could bear the accomplishment: that she permeated the place. For months everyone but Mark avoided it. And the upkeep, coupled with an obvious enhancement of the site, made its sale an ongoing temptation that grew. Why keep it when no one but Mark cared to use it? Someone had approached Mr. Valerian with a blank check, willing to pay anything, anything at all. Here would be life's financial truncation of the dilemma. To discuss the matter, and since Margaret had left the house in their names, Mr. Valerian invited the children to his house in a Philadelphia suburb.

None of them had been there in a year. Not a thing, not a stick, had been changed since the onset of Margaret's illness three years before. In his grief Mr. Valerian was reassured by the certainty of things as they were, like a blind person who has memorized the layout. In a state of only slightly diminished mourning, now ritualized, he relied on the illusion of permanence, of repetition and changelessness. The legs of chairs sat in invariable indentations in the thick rugs, so that if moved they could be put back exactly, with the precision of landmarks. They *were* landmarks. Everything in the house referred to something else—something absent.

The fact that it was their first gathering in this house since the funeral brought back all the same feelings, so that Mark at first sat in a daze in the huge den while Mr. Valerian outlined the situation.

"This came in the mail," he said, holding up the check. "Some people have too much money, and rocks in their head." He handed the check to his older son, George, who held it with both hands, a live delicate thing, and shook his head in wonder. George handed it over to Vita, sitting on the couch beside Mark. Together they examined it for clues to such extravagant behavior.

George said, "We could get as much as a million dollars . . . "

"It's worth much more than that," Mark dropped in. He knew something about real estate since he had chosen to spend his time landscaping gardens professionally; with some success, since there were so many gardens, and people with so much money they mailed out blank checks to buy whatever caught their eye. Mark thought he overvalued the beach house because of its associations and his outright love for it; but its location directly on the sea, surrounded by empty buildable lots, the last in the area, had made the place more valuable than even he imagined. His younger sister, Tessa, came over and took the check from Vita. "Oh my god." She covered her mouth.

"So let's write in two million," her husband, Neil, said.

"Two million dollars?" Tessa exclaimed. "Are you kidding?"

"Four lots at five hundred thousand each," Neil said calmly. "Forget the house. They could bulldoze it and put up condominiums."

Mr. Valerian's eyes, and those of his son George, glittered. "Is it zoned for that?" George asked. And Mr. Valerian said Find out.

"What is this?" Mark demanded. "Aren't you all rushing things? I want you to know I will never agree to sell. You know Mom never would have . . . That house is neutral ground, for all of us. We're supposed to be together there."

"Mark." George turned to his brother from between the wings of a tall chair, the mate to one Mr. Valerian invariably occupied. "Two million dollars," he repeated slowly.

"I don't care. It's been . . . It's too soon. You just can't do it. Besides, it's worth more and more each year . . . If you're just thinking of the money . . . "

"I say sell it," his sister Vita declared suddenly, hers for various reasons the pivotal vote. Mark turned to her as if struck.

"But, Vita . . . "

She gave him a look she sometimes felt it necessary to give, a look of baleful seriousness that meant it was time to absorb something difficult but real, and which she felt would not go away on its own.

"But it can't be a question of money," he insisted. "It's too important for that. The *house* is the legacy, not the money . . . She wanted us to be there together," he repeated. "I know she did. You all know that." He looked around the room at each of them. "How can you think of letting it go?'' he demanded. "If she were here now she would slap your faces.''

"Mark, come on . . . '' Vita said.

"No. I won't agree. Ever.'' He got up and walked out.

After Mrs. Valerian's death, alone in the beach house, Mark had moved into her room and slept in her bed. This felt peculiar only on the first night. Margaret Valerian's room, with its large bay window on the ocean, was long and handsome, running the width of the house, with fine views up and down the coast. It was blue and white, with white taffeta curtains, Indian rugs, and white lacquer furniture. Through the line of windows the horizon stretched around like the true walls of the room, making it immense, bringing in the sea and sky with all its light. It was a room to wake up in. At sunrise the lemon, red, and orange colors of the sun revolved over the white curtains like flame, drifting down the wall as the sun rose, as in a stateroom on an enormous, slowly listing ship. Outside the sea slapped the beach resolutely, but he would be awakened by the clamorous light. Next to the blue room was a green room, and then a pink, no longer pink but referred to as such after so many years. The green room had been Mark's. Now he slept in the blue.

He felt that nothing was more important to him than this house, and since no one else stood in this relation to it they would not have understood the degree to which, day by day, the obsession grew. He saw himself as its custodian and protector, its Mrs. Danvers, the connection coming through the blue room, '' . . . *the loveliest room in the house, the loveliest room you've ever seen.*'' Like Mrs. Danvers he was proud to show it to anyone who called—though callers were not automatically interested—alluding in a fond crazy gaze over objects and views to a special, mysterious, nostalgic association with the past, never specified. Mrs. Warden, a neighbor passing by, had been brought into it on a bright sunny morning, when all the white and blue seemed edible, and had said excitedly that if this were her room she would never leave it. Exactly, Mark thought; a woman skilled in noisemaking. And in fact his mother had never left. Sometimes it seemed he might suddenly turn and catch a wispy glimpse.

But the others did not love the house in these terms; why should he so care? Its beauty, no doubt; its canopic aspects regarding his mother, and now, being ill, regarding him; the memory of thirty years there together. This, while enough, overwhelmingly enough for Mark, was insufficient to them, for whom it remained a pretty house by the sea with associations. They might say to him and to all this emotion: why and so what? Were it not for Mark, things would be different—simply the profit, really, instead of the expense and upkeep. He had no firm answer for himself or them, for whom beauty and recollection, like danger, glamour, greed, hunger—everything but disappointment and desire—were concepts belonging to other people. In fact, he thought, they might not see themselves for what they were, since what Mark saw and what they saw were not the same—when they should have been. House and mother had belonged to all. All had been children here; he and Tessa practically the same age, Vita just three years older, only George very grown at fifteen.

They had peered in at the misted, dusty windows. To one side Mark saw the dead startled Birds withdraw backwards through a doorway. His father signaled disapproval by keeping his hands in his pockets. Furniture lay in the middle of the vast room stacked like expensive fuel before the bulky fieldstone fireplace. Mark stood and turned toward the sea, which tilted over him at a slant like a picture, the line of the horizon that day blurring higher into the sky than might seem normal—it was all so important. "Only on the ocean," Mrs. Valerian had instructed the realtor. Downstairs the ancient furnace spread itself across the cellar like the roots of a banyan tree, funneling huge fat limbs along the ceiling and up through the house. Mr. Valerian shook his head, Margaret shuddered. She wanted to see the bedrooms.

He was ten, Tessa nine, the first summer, living like the Birds. Mr. Valerian was not yet so rich and they camped out at first. It was necessary to replace many of the windows right away. They were fake and did not open. Margaret Valerian repeated this unbelievingly. How could they be fake? The cost of thirty windows was thus added to the mortgage. The air then blew through it—as long ago Captain Bird, besides saving money, had feared the sea might some day enter at the portholes—and the long front room behind the porch became a deeper veranda in itself, open to the blue breeze. On the dune beside the house Mark built a network of sand channels down the incline, encouraging a pink rubber ball to travel from up there to down here as if under its own power, to fall with a snug plop into a pit at the end: the top, center, and bottom; the beginning, middle, and end; up coming down. As a metaphor it seemed to fit for a long time. Most things in life, including life itself, seemed to have articulated sections, discrete and separate and straightforward.

* * *

Some weeks after the meeting at Mr. Valerian's, Vita came to the beach house. On a late fall morning, the same as a summer day but for a faded difference in the light, they sat with coffee on the enormous porch. Up and down, the beach lay empty for miles. Boats in the offing, gulls and the changing light, the broad planes of sea and sky—these bright pictures were framed by the porch supports. Vita spoke first. Given the weight of his feelings she had changed her mind: she would not now agree to sell the house. For this was the most important thing, that when a person felt strongly about an issue in life, it mustn't be ignored by others; for if it was, everything subsequent to it would turn out badly, even though there should seem to be no direct connection.

"Then why did you say you would sell?" he asked.

"Because I was tired of Pop's games," she replied. "He thinks we're beyond his control here." Mr. Valerian, since being widowed, had not again set foot in the house. "I think," she said, "he believes that if it's sold we'll spend more time with him."

In the morning light, regarding the female version of his own face, Mark said, "Is it as simple as that?"

"In a way. But even without your objections they couldn't sell it now." *They* were the two Georges, father and brother. "Until other things are settled nothing will be done." Vita looked at him, took a sip of coffee. "Why is it so important to you?" she asked. "Have you thought?"

" . . . Because of everything."

"Right. You mean, all the years . . . "

"And Mom. And . . . "

Vita squinted into the sun.

"There's something about this place, you know," he went on after a moment. "It's not just me. I think of the pure chance of it being ours. Only chance. You could never arrange something like this again in a thousand years."

"Mark, it's just a house."

"But look at it!"

"Yes, I know," she replied, glancing around her as in a crowd. "But it's still just a house."

"You could say that's just an ass you're sitting on, but you would hate to lose it."

"You mean, it's part of you."

"It seems so basic," he said. "So obvious . . . The house is ours. It's been ours for so long. It's beautiful. To me it represents everything, the past, the future."

"—Yes," Vita interrupted him, "I see that. But I was wondering if you could see the less obvious reasons . . . "

"Such as."

" . . . Some sort of fear," she suggested.

He looked at her, startled. "Can't beauty be enough?"

"No," she replied. "Not usually."

Now when he entered a room or suddenly turned he encountered himself and his family, his siblings and nieces and parents, as if he had been mistaken in thinking them gone and himself alone. How could he be alone there again, except for a few moments at a time? It had become, besides, actually the sort of house that attracted people to it, in a daily ration of deliveries, the maid, plumber, carpenter, furnace man, the painter who never finished and seemed to work on his own; the alarm man, the gardeners. Mark would hear them on the gravel, or the too-loud bell would ring and he would see again the futility of thinking it was a house to be alone in. The others asked what he did with himself, knowing to themselves that he did, simply, everything and was endlessly busy. It was large, with every nook of it developed into something to be maintained. He would sit for a moment and realize the hatch at the top of the tower was ajar; when it was open the covers of magazines on the table by the fireplace, three floors below, lifted and settled on the coil of updraft swirling through the rooms. Or some quadrant of the lawn was being watered, or a storm the day before had misted the north-facing windows to a blur that must be squeegeed; or a drain at the back was loose, or moss had begun in the outdoor shower, as it did every year, a furry lime-green that called to mind the baroque grottoes of overachieved Italian villas. He was half inclined, scrubbing it away, to let it this year take hold.

With his mother gone, the house, far from ever being empty or complete or perfectly in order, was, beyond being a house, a place and monument. This is what the others did not see except in the passion with which he explained the undertaking of yet some new repair or project. For it was big enough never to be finished, and everything that was done to it—had been done to it—seemed to call up in him a progression of further things, as if it now itself kept a list for itself, a list far more ambitious than his own. When he tried to explain this to

Vita she characteristically voiced her opinion: that he liked to think this was true, yet of necessity he would have to say it did not come from the house. "These are your standards and ideals," she said. "Within the process, *you* decide." She was no doubt right. Her field. But the *impulse* she described in him was met by something in the house as palpable as its present shape: the shape it would have in the future. When Mark looked at it in a particular way, he saw it suddenly as it eventually would look. He said to Vita, "It's not imagination. I imagine different features and improvements all the time. They don't occur. But sometimes I see something already done, all its details at once, and after that it's not a matter of imagination but of recollection of the actual thing."

Vita shook her head, willing though temporarily unable to follow. "You mean of course the imposition of your will . . . " she suggested. But he had meant that with the warp of experience folding back on itself, as did time, it was all on a great tape—racial memory, the Collective Unconscious her colleagues had been talking about for so long: history itself, the future; the larger flavorsome bits. The house had a soul, it had a history.

"But not a destiny," she interrupted. "It could be sold tomorrow, and then who would interpret these—visions? Who would have them?"

This was precisely the point, he pointed out. No one would. That was his department. Vita did not doubt the potency of the scheme, as it inspired him, as it affected them all. Four or five weeks each summer she basked in this perfection like Princess Grace in the Monaco of her dreams. The rest of the year, with her children and their commitments, with her job and career, it was as with the others a question of the odd weekend. They might have held on to the place because the original investment was so eternally dwarfed by modern value—this was the Monaco of everyone's dreams—or now because of Mark; but without him keeping track none of it would have worked. Mrs. Valerian had managed it alone for thirty years. Now he did, in his own way. They all saw his reasons overlapped with their own in letting him.

Odd that four such people should turn up in the same family, or odd that he should be among them; for it was Mark who made the collection strange, who set the curve, with his inverted sexuality, sensitivities and thin skin, his standards and thoughts from some other, different place. While they seemed or were strange only in these comparisons

with him, which threw them to the opposite ends of all these spectra—
George Jr., practical and cunning; Vita, evolved and cool; Tessa the
winning, excitable wife and mother, still young, steeped in the details
of her children's lives—all so different from Mark and now abundantly
clear, after years when it had seemed otherwise. The gallant struggle
to convince themselves and the world that he was merely another sort
of Valerian—rather like Mrs. Valerian, whose instincts in all of this
had been unwavering—this struggle in the end had been incorporated
into the great Filial Wars, pitched battles between Mark and his father
that had dragged on for a decade, and in which the heaviest losses had
seemed as usual to be innocent civilians: the family itself. It seemed
to him his mother had given her life as part of this prolonged struggle,
the only evidence at first of how deadly such things became if not
settled early and wisely through ambassadors. They, he now supposed,
were the ambassadors. He felt that the exhausted truce lately reached
between his father and himself represented the world's last opportunity
to avoid catastrophe. It was, as Vita said, a question of not denying
something vitally important to someone else. If you did, it more than
harmed you; it destroyed you and your world to the extent it was itself
destroyed. Now his mother was dead, his father already old, and he
himself apparently dying, although you could never, he had learned,
be sure who would die before whom.

Vita did not in the least cavil, or hesitate. Like many of his conclu-
sions this came out in conversation with her. She thought the force of
Mark's will, being thwarted by this immovable object—his father—
had been turned back on himself with devastating results, and that
evidence of this effect would subsequently pull his father down.

"You must cure yourself," Vita said, going right to the payoff—
these were not office hours with a stranger, he thought. Meaning that
if he could turn the process off he might neutralize its effects in time,
and so at least slow the disease, or convert or divert it elsewhere. This
was the idea, to buy time.

The stupendous news of his illness had abruptly ended the Filial
Wars, like a smothered blaze. In the driveway of the beach house,
where Mr. Valerian would come to discuss it and see for himself, they
embraced and wept. It no longer meant a great deal that Mr. Valerian
could weep, although there had been an era—most of their lives—
when the idea itself represented a kind of doom not to be envisioned;
while Mark, in compensation, had been always a person to weep as
easily and effortlessly as an actor. Together they wept in each other's

arms in a way that might have obviated all unpleasantness, if only, if only; the unfortunate misapprehension of one person, meaning well but getting it wrong, by another; he and his father weeping beside the gleaming automobile that then, a moment later, slid across the white sweep of gravel and carried his father away.

In the huge unnaturalness of the world the most unnatural thing is the death of a child, which is to say death out of order. In Mr. Valerian's mind his son's illness sat at the top of a pile of problems that appeared to constitute this last segment of his own life. It took stepping back, but from his point of view it seemed, as he would presently say to Mark, that if they could only change places all this nonsense would be resolved, beginning with the medical thing which, of everything, was most beyond his control.

The other great problem in his life concerned the collapse at the last moment of the greatest deal of his long and profitable business career—the sale of Marval Products itself, Mr. Valerian's life work, to Court Industries. This collapse, coming only hours after he learned of his son's illness, had transpired with an equal force of devastation, like a second bomb dropped on rubble. In a long moment of realization Mr. Valerian had thought the two events to be in some way connected (as subsequently did Mark) beyond the usual compounded coincidences of life; as if, had you thought in astrological terms, which Mr. Valerian did not, you might find that on this day and at this hour several planetary masses had aligned themselves toward his specific ruination.

But that it should happen now, and so quickly, in this mad, last-minute upheaval of his life; that here at the top of the monument you found not a statue, not the figure of Victory poised for flight, but instead pigeon shit and disappointment—Mr. Valerian's disgust at this was less effective as a demonstration against life than it had been over the years against his mortified children. He was a man who had always intimidated people. He looked at them and dealt with them until he saw a light of defiance go out in their eyes. He kept on until he saw it, minutes or years. At last, in the driveway of the beach house, he saw it in Mark's eyes. Help me, they said: it was all Mr. Valerian had ever wanted to hear.

With something extra in her voice, due to the fact she was discussing her own father clinically, but also for what she considered the endless resourcefulness of the subject, Vita described Mr. Valerian as "very heavily defended.'' The fortress of their father's mind, Mark thought, thinking of something rocky and impregnable by Baldassare Peruzzi. ''If such a structure collapses, it comes down all at once,'' she said. ''At the end the mind is ruined. Much better if somehow it holds together.''

Mark's opinion of his father in these later years had thus been based, he felt, on this other resident expert—for what was Vita but court psychologist? the best money could buy, and right there in the family, rather like the best legal advice from their brother, George. Bolstered by the respect he felt for Vita's mind, Mark had applied these opinions to his own situation: the Filial Wars. It was from Vita he realized he would never convince his father of the legitimacy of his cause; quite simply because Mr. Valerian saw homosexuality in religious terms— as a sin—which then threatened the great buttress of his own defense system: religion. The top third of all widowers, Vita reported, meaning in health and adjustment, survived with the help of strong religious beliefs. Thus Mark's orientation ran in conflict with his father's concept of survival. Not a question of live and let live, Mark saw with dismay. It meant he must think of his father's generation as entrenched and lost—as of course they all thought of his.

For he *was* different from them—from his own father and sisters, especially different from his brother. He had something of his mother in him but this was because he realized that in the end only her love was unconditional, and in gratitude he had emulated her. Only that much of this appropriation did not sit so gracefully on him, the strapping male, as it had on her. And perhaps he had chosen some of her more problematic traits—the tendency to catastrophe, for instance, of immediately expecting the worst in an unpleasant situation, hardly important but negative, and which seldom turned out as badly as she expected. He heard a variant of this in himself and recognized it as surely as an old piece of clothing that fitted him but belonged to someone else: his mother's sense of catastrophe. This had stuck.

Ah, the victim. This, too, she had allowed, had encouraged in herself until too late. She had proved to him that the victim creates and perpetuates himself. This was the embarrassing part of being ill. The metaphor here was also too tellingly clear: the homosexual as victim. Unfair to pin it on his mother, who would be indignant to be thought of in these terms. But it was Vita's point that this was the cycle to be interrupted if he would break the pattern and save himself.

Yes, Vita, but how? And for a long time—most of his life, and often even now—he'd thought of this difference between himself and his family as evidence not of his failings, but theirs. Was not the absence of beauty the ugliest thing in life? (Vita would say no.) In the general scheme of things among the Valerians he often felt that wrong choices won out over right—wrong ideas, wrong directions, wrong fears. From an early age he had spoken up, feeling that in this small crowd was room—the dimensions—for more than one opinion; or even two. After all, a family might advance, as in certain quiz programs on TV in which a whole generation, sometimes two or three, put their heads together to define reality, and for their efforts won a car. It seemed the diversity he offered might be of use to them as a family, if they could only see it that way. In this his mother half the time had been his ally; half the time, with a gimlet eye, not. In matters of taste at least—of form, decoration, aesthetics: the usual homosexual métier—they had long since looked to him for quasi-professional guidance; so that George Jr. was legal, Vita psychological, Mark . . . artistic—though it might be argued that this end of things lay otherwise vacant of opinion for cultural, sexist reasons.

—Different, too, in that he was alone. This was it. Each of them had a unit of his own, while Mark clung to an order that had outgrown itself, whose vestigial remains could be found only in his father and himself, and in a ghost of the enmity between them, now laid to rest by . . . by It. The occasions on which the five of them might collude had been reduced to those of state—the meeting about selling the house, for instance—or perhaps when Tessa, whose instincts, though less developed, ran along similar lines, might suggest a public lunch on Father's Day—just them—which, however, George Jr. would be too busy and overworked to attend. It was not that they thought any less of the idea than Mark; if anything they thought more. Simply that family meant their own brood and not the abstract enshrinement, as if in retrospect, of the Valerians as they one day might have been but were no more—something in Mark's imagination. He might make every effort to impose this vision on them—the fight for the beach house had been one such effort—of a caring, interlocked group of siblings. But the demands of their own children made this difficult, except at intervals, or when a flare of need went up over the life of one of them. It was not that it didn't exist, this idea of family, but that it did not seem to exist always, and never as Mark saw it; or if it did, which he saw it did, it was really only among each of them and for their very own.

Meaning that he was not a member, in each case, of *their very own*. Here we had musical families, like musical chairs—life was nothing but quiz programs and time-passing competitions—and when the music stopped he alone stood in the circle of upturned, satisfied faces. None could feel this sense of estrangement, apartness, because all of life's institutions had seen to it that they didn't. Mates, children, parents, and other siblings all fitted into arrangements laid out for this specific accomplishment: to belong. So much easier, he thought, for them to go along—unnatural not to—because for them it was stupefyingly enjoyable, one small triumph of legitimacy after another.

But did he really expect family life to be arranged around the requirements of spinster aunts and bachelor uncles? Freud would say Grow up. The burden of neurosis added to the weight of history was too great. Darwin would call Mark's kind a mad biological experiment teetering on the edge of extinction and doomed to failure. Both privately would shake their heads; though Freud, being Jewish, would wonder. Vita, their avatar and spokesperson, would say that, considering the twenty-six million Americans extrapolated from Kinsey to be gay—one in ten—some people slipped through history without ever reaping its rewards.

It did not do to complain, but to understand. Her analogy was in this case the primeval tree of primitive man. Mark knew it as a two-story tree house he had built at an early age with Donny and Brock. It popped so immediately into mind that he knew she was right.

"But can we not provide some other service? Is it all just the timely impregnation of females?" he asked indignantly.

"What else did you have in mind?" Vita replied dryly. " . . . You may of course sound the alarm. But life is not that simple. Sometimes sounding the alarm arouses passions and causes trouble. In the commotion branches break, people fall and hurt themselves. The leopard grabs one of them . . . "

"But without them . . . " Mark said weakly. He would never be convinced.

In these conversations Mark was aware of this same weight of respect coming across the line from his sister. What was it in him that held her interest? Creativity, he thought; the position engendered by a combination of male egotism—the inculcation of centuries—and a feminine passivity, rarely mixed in those days, openly; or at least in her Philadelphia suburb. Only later did he see she had realized her professional luck in finding, in her own family, a fine pure example of something they were alluding to at school: Freud's obsessional neurotic. She of course made no effort to inform him of this conclusion, and he went on thinking she saw in him, at least potentially, the artist he wished to be. In any event, it would be one or the other; this was perhaps a matter of opinion, and too soon to say. Art, he thought too, was nothing but obsessional and neurotic. And what might have alarmed the sibling of another shrink seemed, to Mark, to be evidence of some sort of artistic progress not otherwise obvious.

He was less different from Vita, perhaps because they had in their own way each been made to follow their brother, George, with Mark's version matching hers in certain cross-gender ways; as if their parents, the Valerians, having thought just so far, had put everything into their first child and had made do, with the remnants of parentage, for the other three. George and Tessa were easier—not that *they* were similar—for being the first and the last. But Vita and Mark, appearing as if unbidden or at random, seemed to share the burden of catching their parents unawares, unprepared, or bereft, even though never in her marriage had Mrs. Valerian made love without the thought of conceiving a child. How for instance did a little girl differ from a little boy? Why then was this second son, who had come from the same people and in the same way, so shockingly different? The Valerians, smug, oblivious and proud, did the best they knew how, making an awful mess, Vita thought; Mark thought. But then in those days who hadn't?

Mr. Valerian stepped from the car and shaded his eyes from the sun. Perhaps he had been weeping on the drive down. Expecting him to the minute and hearing tires on the gravel, Mark came slowly out the door and through the garden, hands in his pockets, footprints blazing up behind him in tiny, sickle-shaped fires: his pockets spiritually picked, his life up in flames. Flowers in the border flashed dots of color at his feet, drifting by in focus within a long green blur. As he approached his father, they each wore the same ripening expression, of remorse and reproach, of colossal disappointment; this overlapping response paired their display—a sad caving-in of their feelings—and like two fine dynamos reaching tandem, they embraced. Mr. Valerian pounded once, twice, on Mark's shoulder in an excess not of tenderness but anguish. He said into Mark's ear, ''Believe me, if I could change places with you I'd do it in a second.'' It was what on the drive down he had decided to begin by saying. Holding his son by the shoulders, and at last seeing all defiance gone, he added, ''We're going to go through this together, and there's nothing we can't do if we want." This sent them back into the vortex. Mark felt infantile, helpless. He was ill: something between the two of them had shifted into something manifest on its own, a third, evil thing set loose, against which both now were helpless. An alliance of his own resolve coupled with his father's was meant to bear some force against this, which, coming from within, must be pursued from within; though it appeared now, even in the abstract, beyond spiritual, intellectual, even emotional measures. Perhaps only the medical remained. Strength of intention his father meant to give him, not realism or facts but something to use in the coming fight, something abstract to fight something real, against which as yet no real weapons existed.

They came through the house into the sitting room. Being alone, Mark had ordered it with the precision and flair of a photo-stylist. The vast blue plane of sea stretched around. Mark could almost feel the little hop his father's heart took, of pride, recognition and pain at the purity of sudden association with Margaret. Mr. Valerian looked out over the beach, nodded his head but sat in a chair with his back to the view—a gesture that meant here again were reasons why, with one thing and another, he was unable to enjoy this house further. They sat quietly. The waves squandered themselves. Two brown rabbits appeared on the lawn to feed, ears ruby sunlight. Mark watched them over his father's shoulder.

"Well," Mr. Valerian began. "Tell me about this . . . Tell me what the doctors said, what—y'know—what you know about it." Put me in the picture, Mark thought his father had with a certain delicacy refrained from saying. The terminology of a business meeting seemed appropriate to the situation, certainly automatic. He saw that sometime in the next few minutes he himself would say, "The bottom line is that there's no cure."

"Look," his father exclaimed when this remark had been delivered, "that's where you're wrong. It's not the bottom line. You mustn't think that way. They'll find a cure. They're all looking—"

"Utter bullshit," Mark interrupted. "It's not a cure they're looking for, it's a vaccine. Protect the healthy, let the sick die off."

"But, Mark . . . " Mr. Valerian protested, shaking his head.

"It's what they did with polio, and they were children."

"Well, you've got to think of yourself," his father went on. "You've got to be positive. You'll beat it one way or another. Either they'll find something or something will happen."

They regarded each other.

"And," his father said—these were the things he had driven here to explain—"I have a feeling this is a light case."

"A feeling?" Mark said.

"I just don't think it's as bad as you think."

"Dad, it's not what I think."

" . . . And there's experimental things. I read yesterday there's a guy in California immune to everything. They're studying his blood . . . "

"I don't think this is something we'll be able to buy."

"Why the hell not?" Mr. Valerian sat forward and went on in a fresh tone, "But you see, Mark, this is what I mean. You mustn't say, 'No, no, I can't, I can't, this is impossible, it won't work and I'm going to die . . . ' You've got to think something will happen. Some goddamn clever Swede or Frog will find the answer . . . And you'll see. It's not as bad as you think—in your case."

"You only say that because you can't face it."

"Then what the hell are you going to do!" his father snapped, "—Lay down and die? Is that it?"

"I'm not going to kid myself because you want to hear it."

"And that's where you're wrong, my friend," Mr. Valerian said derisively. "Why not a miracle? Open yourself up to the idea that anything can happen, and you're going to get through this in one piece."

" . . . Faith," Mark said quietly.

"Faith," Mr. Valerian repeated, adding a slight though unmistakable measure of reverence.

Mr. Valerian turned and they looked out the window together, each backing away from the idea just raised—Mark because he wished to avoid an argument about religion; Mr. Valerian because, while relieved to have hit on something tangible, he was not prepared to pursue it. He knew prayer and hard work were the answer—had already begun his own program along these lines—but not until you came to it yourself. And Mark thought it time to say something about his father's other great problem: the collapse of the deal to sell Marval.

"George told me," he began—out to sea two little sailboats took different tacks on the same wind, sails pinned to the opposite reach, the one crossing the other's wake; Mark thought of the currents as invisible streets—" . . . about the rest of your day. I'm sorry this happened all at once."

"I don't want you to think twice about that," Mr. Valerian replied.

"It's a disappointment, that's all. It means more hard work when I would've been retiring. But I can deal with that sort of thing. I've been doing it all my life."

"All in the same day . . . " Mark said wonderingly.

"Yes, well . . . " His father turned away from the window.

They put together a lunch of odds and ends and ate on the porch in front. Here Captain Bird had most seriously contrived to duplicate, on dry land and for the enjoyment of his dwindling days, the unique commanding experience of a ship's bridge. An end of the porch came around and finished in a circle topped with a pointed cone, like a gazebo jutting from a corner of the house. With the arrangement of a sand dune, a trellis, and the eastern orientation of the house, Captain Bird had created the illusion of being actually at sea, within a wheelhouse. If you sat or stood in a certain spot the horizon stretched three-quarters of the way around, the beach fell below the level of the porch railing, and all land disappeared, leaving only the sea. As they ate, a net of diamond shadows fell through the trellis, drifting over their shoulders and across the floor.

"What about George?" Mark said, to stay off It for a while. His father looked up. "What about him?"

"Well, he's disappointed, isn't he? He's worked hard on this, for a long time."

"Yes, he has." Mr. Valerian had thought to learn something about George. Sometimes his children told each other things that then he heard secondhand, as intended. "He's got his practice to repair. This thing took a lot of his time."

In conversation, as otherwise, Margaret Valerian had been their connection, the buffer between them—in a way demonstrated by the damage she herself had sustained; by the worry, never clearly stated, that the wrong person being right, the right person wrong, and she herself never sure, not enough had been said or felt for either. Instead she had worked hard to make them comfortable, knowing mere comfort was never enough. Mark and his father seemed only to disagree on principle, the principle of sex. This she held to be impossible, for love alone mattered, not principle. In fitting and tailoring their disparate responses to each other, she managed for years to fend off the implications and disasters of the Filial Wars, saying to one what the other could not. "Your father does not mean what he says. He loves you very much," and vice versa. So real was the need, any transparent effort worked. After her death the connection had devolved through

necessities surrounding her funeral and burial—the plot, the monument—for if the beach house meant the survival of her memory and
spirit in Mark's mind, even in her own, in Mr. Valerian's a cemetery
was where such things naturally came to rest. To him the beach house,
besides being a sad reminder of his dead wife, or the dying one, was
now his sole connection with Mark. And some months after Margaret's
death, at the change of seasons—when fifty steps to wintering an old
mansion on the water suddenly presented themselves—Mark had automatically taken up the job, interpreting this as an extension of his
mother's wishes—and now, being ill, it seemed he might belong there
as much as she—while Mr. Valerian saw the opportunity as both practical and wise. Several years into the arrangement it had become and
remained their subject. In every conversation, one or the other of them
brought it up.

"How's the house?" his father said, sociable over the food.

"That depends," Mark replied, "on where you look."

Mr. Valerian waved his hand in agreement. It was endlessly expensive, unfinished, yielding to salt air and sea. They were still compen-
sating, thirty years later, for Captain Bird's economies. "That Bird,"
Mr. Valerian would say, "had an anchor for brains." It had been some
years before they discovered all the drains simply stopped below grade.
All had to be dug up and connected. In his own mind Captain Bird
had been constructing a boat. Nothing except her moorings must hold
her. She must be free to sail at any moment, in the dead of night or
day, straight to sea on the course so carefully drawn through the hearth.
Now, Mark thought, the place was locked in—by water main, sewers,
gas lines, TV cables, telephone wires, even the thin lightning rod of
copper braid twisting from its height off the chimney and down the
sides of the house like a package tied with cord.

In Mark's mind, as opposed to Captain Bird's, in the moment before
setting sail, someone must sever these new connections one by one.
Where possible over the years he himself had felt inclined to keep the
boat idea in mind. An innovation of his own had been to shape the
ocean-side lawn into a bow, with a white, chevron bulkhead pointing
east into the waves. He thought that if this bow-shaped piece of earth
were included, giving her deck space all around, it would be easier to
fit the severed connections to a life-support system, all within a clear
crystal cube containing the earth's atmosphere—on a fresh morning,
the sun still on the water, or a starry night for sleeping, dreaming—a
crystal ship of lights that silently slips her lines and sails away.

From *Life Drawing*

Michael Grumley

Michael Grumley read parts of Life Drawing *at the Violet Quill, and Felice Picano published a section of the novel in* A True Likeness. *But for some reason Grumley found it harder and harder to make the novel work, and as his diary indicates, the last year of life was filled with both despair over ever getting the novel published and elation when it was accepted. However, he died before final revisions were completed, and Robert Ferro devoted the last months of his life to completing the manuscript. Ferro died, according to his sister, the day after she delivered to him the completed typescript.*

Millard Hughes used to come to school with his toenails painted. Red and chipped, shining like little shells at the bottom of his big-boned country frame. Nobody ever asked him why; big and tough, he did what he liked. It was Millard and his friend Joey Pinto who found poor Betsy Fiddler's body one morning on their way to school, close by Devil's Glen Trailer Park, stuffed in the bushes next to the bridge across the little river there. The killer was never apprehended, and Millard and Pinto shut up about it after the first two or three days. It was like a sudden explosion, a burst of random violence in a town where nothing seemed random. The white body found lying beside the black asphalt road, the photograph in the newspaper, then nothing. Someone passing through, someone from down by the railroad tracks, a friend?

Not too many mysteries in our small town. The mysteries would occur to us all later, when we had grown up and moved away. Our curiosity was about the future; the present was a closed book. Familiar people who acted strangely were still . . . familiar.

We liked the men who were tough and callous, men with tattoos winding up their arms. We were all going to be tough. One autumn, Franklin and I went with Gerald Page and his cousin Eddie out to the carnival at the county fairgrounds. The rides along the midway were spectacular; Gerald and Eddie smoked Camels as they strode along. We rode the Ferris wheel and the Tilt-a-Whirl and got sick, and recovered, and won kewpie dolls on silver canes at the shooting gallery.

The Page boys had an uncle who had been a juggler on the midway and who'd told them to say "I'm with it" to the barkers so they'd know not to hustle them. "I'm with it" meant you'd worked at carnivals and weren't just another rube. We tried it out, swaggering through the sawdust, hands deep in our pockets, looking tough. The man with all the stuffed animals abruptly stopped his spiel and flashed us a grin; the woman with yellowish skin at the bingo tent gave us a nod. We went into the sideshow tents, enthralled by the woman suspended in a vat of green water, the hairy "wolf child," the hermaphrodite wearing half a man's costume, half a woman's. Overconfident, we snuck through the back flap of the adults-only tent and crawled around behind the stage. A big nasty redhead moved around under a blue spotlight; beetles and river moths hit the light with a snapping sound, one after the other, in a kind of Morse code, and there was the sound of the rough men calling up to her and her yelling back. She moved to music from a record that had crowd noises on it, scratchy and overinflated, like something heard echoing from a distance. When we edged around to the front, we saw that she was stalking back and forth across the wooden stage, now and again crouching down at its edge. Every time she crouched, the men would cheer and whistle, and then we saw that she was picking up silver dollars the men placed on end there.

Her eyes were painted black and her hair was a taffy-apple red, and she wore black feathers in it; her breasts were white, scarlet at the nipples, and there was a kind of grass skirt tied at her waist. As she bobbed upright, her eyes scanned the dark enclosure, and she thrust out her tongue. Suddenly she caught sight of us, and pointed a long menacing finger. "Hey, you gents! What the hell are *you* doing in here?" she demanded. A few heads turned to look; she stood high above us and laughed, then again dropped down to the floor. We stood open-mouthed, then a big Hispanic man came after us, swearing and spitting, and we ran out through the exit flap and got away. We'd seen more than we bargained for. Eddie and Franklin said it was really cool, but I was deeply offended, came home and was sick again, didn't want to think about it.

My sexual education was patched together from such bright pieces. Sex, of course, was one of the main mysteries. I had learned from Franklin, earlier, that the way people made babies was for the man to pee in the woman when she wasn't looking. He had got this information from Danny Sujek down the block; Danny was already in high school at this point, and his opinion and store of knowledge counted for a lot. But the image was not what one had in mind. Incredulous, finally crestfallen, I had trouble looking Mom in the eye for a time.

Dad, getting wind of our misinformation, took Franklin and me out among the backyard four-o'clocks and disabused us of the toilet notion, illustrating with stamens and sepals what the process of fertilization was all about. The nonurinary function of our own equipment was explained to us, briskly and efficiently. Dad let us know that aggression was the key, that in sexual matters we were to take what we wanted without asking for a by-your-leave from our partners. Lust was acknowledged by all to be a relentless thing for the male—Sammy once asked me if it was true that the man, once he got started, couldn't stop. Telling her the truth, I felt myself traitorous, at odds with the prevailing winds of adolescence. Sexual arrogance was the habit we boys were to put on.

I never got it right, was something of a washout in the perseverance department. Tears (from Karla, or Candi, or Dora Mae) had on me an instant anti-aphrodisiac effect. I never arrived at that place where nothing mattered but getting it up and getting it in. "Never up, never in!" the golfers used to say to each other, with a wink, on the River Hills greens.

The girls in our high school were subdued about their own sexuality, and all one's gumption was needed to overcome their inertia. But one classmate of mine was rather less refined. In study hall and geography class, I used to receive notes from Roxanne Brewer that said simply, "Eat me." Square-shaped and sporting an auburn DA, Roxanne smiled her foxy smile at me across the pages of blue maps and yellowing desktops, slowly twisting the points of her upturned Judy Garland collar. I found her terrifying, never took a bite.

Sammy and I as a couple didn't make it through our senior year together. Just before school started up that August, she was spending

a lot of time around the club swimming pool. I found that the reason
was a member's son named Tom, a diver on vacation from Choate:
blond and heavy-limbed and intent on having his way with her. (I
ought to have known her question re male momentum wasn't strictly
academic.) He had it, finally, and to say I shrank from competition
thereafter would be cruelly correct. Who knows if we would have
stayed together, in our lustful if innocent state, if it hadn't been for
rude, unflagging Tom. At any rate, the world was getting larger for us
both that season.

In August, on the Mississippi, the mud of the riverbanks would cake
and split apart and peel up at the corners like the irregular sections of
an old jigsaw puzzle. The smell of the river, and the smaller streams
that led into it, was stale, and the flies and gnats and dragonflies hovering over the brown water's surface would give the impression of
movement where none occurred. It was as if the river stopped flowing
in August, and only sat there. Near the town of Muscatine were enormous sand dunes and mined-out quarries where couples would drive
to spend an afternoon or evening. It was a long drive from Lillienthal,
because it was hot, and the land was flat, with miles of cattails and
reeds on one side of the road and withered grassland on the other. By
the time you got to the dunes, you'd be so parched you'd splash down
into the water right away, tempted to drink from the still pools instead
of merely submerging yourself.

I came there when I was seventeen, three August Saturdays in a
row, with a student from the Palmer School of Chiropractic, who
worked part-time as a bellboy at the Blackhawk Hotel. He had a room
up above the pickles and beets and sliced roast beef of the smorgas-
bord; I stopped there for a cool drink after meeting him in the record
department of Whitfield's Department Store the first Saturday. He had
slick hair and soft eyes, and he showed me photographs of a summer
he'd been to Greece.

I knew we were going to do something, but I didn't know quite
what it was, and when he asked if I'd like to drive down to the quarries
with him, I remember I didn't hesitate for a second before saying yes.
My parents thought I was hot-rodding around with some of the other
guys from school, speeding along in somebody's raked and custom-
ized, turned-down and glass-packed pride-and-joy. But I was on my
own, with a 45 single of Jackie Wilson's ''Reet Petite'' clutched under

my arm and someone who'd been to Greece stepping on the gas beside me. We got to the dunes and out of our clothes—though we both kept on our Jockey shorts—and were down into the water in nothing flat.

He produced a half-empty bottle of sloe gin from his glove compartment, and I loved the sticky sweet taste of it. No one was anywhere near where we had parked the car—the beauty of the quarries was that with so many small coves and pools, it had the feel of a very private place. I've learned since that while we slowly approached each other above the surface, beneath us there was occurring even more rarefied sexual activity—the gestation of a species of mud turtle known nowhere else in the country or the world but in that sandy quarry. To think of it, then, I would have thought the Muscatine turtles to be as common as the mud on which Bayard and I lay. One's own singularity was all that mattered.

Before it got dark, and after we had taken off our cotton shorts and got ahold of each other, and spent ourselves in the water and on the sand and finally in the front seat of that old gin-smelling DeSoto, we drove back through the cattail marshes and fields of corn, to Lillienthal. I went on to where I was expected—a session of preseason weight training for the football team.

That first night after Bayard I felt something magical had occurred. I was a dynamo of prowess, filled with a rare strength, able to outshine the other guards and halfbacks. Exotic nights flashed before my eyes as I went through the exercises. Something like a moral invincibility cloaked me. The power of an undiscovered life—a truly adult way of being—came over me, and I outmuscled the rest of the team to set the evening's record in push-ups, sit-ups, and leg raises.

Afterward, at home in my bedroom, I didn't sleep. The adrenaline that had been unleashed in me kept barking through my veins. This body I had, this thing that had been lacking its own authority for so long, had suddenly come together, and hardened to a purpose I recognized as natural and just, no matter how outlandish it might seem to others. The secretness of it was part of it—I had never, as far as I could remember, been admonished *against* making love to a man. The subject hadn't come up.

The potency of unspoken sexuality filled the night around me that August. I stayed mum, and went on with my seventeenth year. But over my old life, a new life had formed.

* * *

In February of my last year of high school in Lillienthal, I came home from wrestling practice, went straight to my father's liquor cabinet, and finished off half a bottle of Old Crow. I was alone and got drunk and headed for New Orleans. Liquor was fuel for my impulse, and it kept me warm through the wet afternoon and evening.

I recall I started out down by the railway tracks, imagining I'd be able to find a boxcar headed south. Prowling among the ice-encrusted railway cars, I soon realized they were locked in for the night, if not the season. The local freight train I'd heard all my life didn't make a full stop in Lillienthal, as I'd always imagined—it slowed but continued its rattling journey at a nonnegotiable clip, and, running along beside it, I cursed its speed and heedless girth. I had to leave town, would leave town, though I couldn't then say why. The whiskey kept me chuckling to myself as I trudged along the tracks. It was warm in New Orleans, wasn't it?—and that was reason enough.

I was going to New Orleans, and the river would take me there. Down on the levee at night, men who worked on the paddle wheelers, or who were passing through, heading downriver to Memphis and the Gulf, would congregate. When we were younger, Mom and Dad had taken Franklin and me for walks along the levee, holding us up so we could look out over the loading of boats, the movements of winches and barges. Old Don Hammer sometimes worked on the levee, and when I was delivering newspapers he'd tell me about the accidents he'd seen—a man hit by a falling bale and paralyzed for life, a novice struck with a baling hook, a captain knocked overboard and nearly swept away. His accounts were gleeful, filled with the blood and thunder of a catch-as-catch-can life.

The levee in winter was bleak. Truck drivers collected around a drum fire: half a dozen men with dark faces, walking up and down, stretching their legs before they crossed the bridge and took the highway south through Illinois, down into Missouri, finally Arkansas, Louisiana. The river was open, and a barge was drawn up at the end of the loading pier—how long it had been moored there was hard to tell. Next to it lay the *River Queen*, and as I moved closer I could see light in its cabins and men moving along the passageways and decks. The *River Queen* churned up and down the Mississippi during the summer months. Once I'd gone for a ride on it with my girlfriend, Sammy. A band had been playing, and it was great fun slipping and sliding on the dance floor as the current changed and the band changed with it.

But I'd never thought about where it went or what it did during the winter when no pleasure-seekers queued up at the dock, no wedding parties waited to be carried away.

It must have been about nine o'clock at night now, and the damp winter rain was beginning to put a chill in my traveling plans. Steam rose up from the water, or a kind of fog. Laughter came from on board, and the smell of soup and cigarettes drifted out of the portholes.

I stood on the dock, watching the mysterious motions of the figures in the dark as they passed back and forth over the lighter surface of the paddle wheeler. Cigarettes lighted up like fireflies; lengths of white rope were tossed here and there.

The door of the cabin nearest the gangplank burst open then, and out of the swirl of swearing and yelling and the clank of pots stepped a figure I was sure I recognized. Not many black men were in my acquaintance—hardly any black families lived in Lillienthal—and so for a moment I pictured the faces I knew, or had seen. With the light behind him it was hard to see his features, but after another second I was sure who it was and called out his name: "Horace!"

He squinted down the gangplank. "Who's that calling my name?" he demanded, stepping closer to the edge. He looked at me curiously—hundreds of caddies must have worked at River Hills Country Club the same years I did, and Horace worked in the clubhouse, not on the greens.

"Are you Horace?" I asked, suddenly unsure of myself, and at the same time feeling dizzy. The smell of kerosene and of the muddy river came up from the space between us, and I put my hand on a timber that stood next to the gangplank, to steady myself. Whiskey flowed through me.

"Horace Olibanum Jefford, that's right. And if you know my name, you might as well come on inside and tell us what you're doing, wandering around this old levee looking like a half-drowned river rat. Come on, step lively now!"

He reached over and pulled me across, and I stumbled a little, and then was inside the cabin he'd stepped out of, amid tied-up bedrolls and wicker trunks and pans hung on a long trestle.

"This here is Sneezewood McKenna, and Ralph Scott. And this nasty-looking creature is my son James—don't you call him Jimmy—and somewhere or t'other is Curtis Stringfellow."

The men, who were seated around a table in the middle of the cabin, looked up from their cards and mumbled howdy, all except James, who stared at me close-mouthed. They were smoking, and the smoke was like a canopy over the table. Next to it was a stove as big as a sofa, and a sink, and vegetables and fruit in baskets, all in what seemed like one pile against the wall.

"Well?" Horace raised his eyebrows.

I came to myself enough to mumble my own name, and to tell Horace I'd seen him at the club. And I told him I was going to New Orleans.

At this the other men looked up again from the table, and James showed some teeth, and one of them, I think it was Sneezewood, said: "People all the while dying to come up north. What do you want to be heading the other direction for?" There was a pause. "Of course," he continued, going back to his cards, "some folks have more trouble traveling than others."

Horace said, "Now, now," and I suddenly felt foolish, and thought, What *am* I running off for, me so white and comfortable and all.

Then the boat gave a heave, as if the barge had bounced against it, and Horace said, "Current's turning. Better get at it." He looked at me quick and said, "You want some coffee," and took a cup from the trestle and a pot from the stove and put me off to the side to drink it. The boat moved again, and the men threw down their cards and together moved out the door.

"You, caddy . . . you stay here, and when we get back we'll talk about New Orleans!" He winked at James, who hadn't got up with the other men, but stayed at the table, his face rocking in the light, looking at me out of the brownest eyes I'd ever seen.

James was then eighteen, which meant he could drink and work on the river as a dealer. He was on his way south "to do a little business." When I knew him better and kidded him about the phrase, he'd laugh back at me, his laughter coming out from behind one of the cheroots he was always smoking. Cards were his business, and had been from an early age.

He got up from the table, and I could see he was taller than I was by an inch or so, rangy and wide-shouldered, with long arms—I thought of a spider.

"My papa doesn't know I'm in the life, so don't say nothing." He was rinsing out his glass at the sink as he said this, not looking at me, and his words fell from nowhere, landed nowhere, floated in the thick sweet air. He was shaking his head, and after a moment he did turn. He came back and took another look at me.

"You know what I mean?" he asked.

I didn't, exactly. I was excited in a way I hadn't been excited before, and waited to hear what else he might say.

"Forget it," he finally said, and sat down again.

Then Horace came back in and put on a yellow slicker over his jacket, and said the river was rising.

"So what about it, young bub? What's waiting for you in New Or- leans?" He stood at the door, expecting an answer.

"I'm going to school down there—college," I said, getting a hold of a lie by the tail and starting to twist it. "I go to Tulane University, and I had to come home for a while, and now I'm going back."

Father and son looked at each other, and then looked back at me.

"Well, that sounds right," said Horace.

James had pulled out a nail file and was moving it across his nails, frowning down at his hands. I imagined he was about twenty-five. I couldn't take my eyes off him.

Horace said, "James here is headed down that way himself. You sure you're not running away from something? No officers of the law after your little tail?"

Sneezewood came back in the cabin and, hearing Horace, made a loud guffaw. Then he put his lips together and shook his head. "What do you think we got here, a convicted felon?" He and James laughed.

"You never do know," Horace put in mildly, and seemed satisfied no trouble would come sniffing his way. He sat down at the table and picked up the cards.

"All right, then. When that barge gets done bumping up against us and knocking off my brand-new paint, it's going down the river. And James is going to be on it, and the captain—he's a real bulldog—can take along another boy if I say so." He pulled a card out of his hand and flipped it onto the table.

"And I guess I say so." He looked at James.

"That all right with you, James?"

James spread his hands apart, shrugged his shoulders, said, "Makes me no never mind," and then, giving it up, showed me a wide grin. The cabin rocked once more, Curtis Stringfellow made his appearance, blocking the doorway, as big and important as the night itself, and then James and I were down the gangplank, and across another one, and on our way.

* * *

The river was wide, and the river was long. By the time we got to the Missouri border the next day I felt as if I'd been on it all my life. We kept out of the way of Captain Eugene, who I gathered regarded us as no more or less interesting than the cargo that came on with us—soybeans from Clinton, wheat and alfalfa.

We slept next to the boiler that night, and nothing we said could be heard over its clanking, the repeated stanzas of iron grating against iron. I woke up and saw James watching me—we weren't very far apart, one bunk space between us—and he offered me a drink from a little silver flask he carried in his jacket, and I remember I took it from him just so I could touch his skin. I couldn't go back to sleep then, and we both were half sitting up, the early-morning light slipping in, as long as he was looking at me I was looking at him—as if we were both laughing, but neither of us was even smiling. The boiler chugged on, and no room for words; I sat up all the way and turned and leaned across to him, and handed back the flask—he took it, and kept hold of my hand with it, and the current ran through us both, and we bounced toward each other, and that was that.

One boy who thought he was pretty smart being outdone and out-classed, and turned, as Coach Mannucci used to say, every which way but loose. Other boy playing, then getting serious, playing again. I saw I knew nothing at all about giving someone pleasure, and I tried to do better, again and again. James was pleasure. Hot snake-smelling skin, knots of muscles hitting me like snowballs, breath like gin and jasmine—he was everything at once.

Whatever I'd been going to New Orleans for I'd found by St. Louis. When we finally got out on deck—which wasn't a deck at all but a big flat iron field moving through the water, lines looped all across it, and nowhere to walk but along the gangways—the captain grunted good morning, and the ugly little river towns spilled out their undersides like bunting. I was ready to take on the world, whatever the world happened to be.

But by then I was thinking about my family, wondering what they were thinking. James told me he lived off and on with his mother in Chicago, and didn't see his father but once or twice a year—he'd been staying on the *River Queen* with him for a week, before starting downriver to ply his trade on the gambling boats there—and he had older brothers whom he never saw. He was so out in the world, compared to where I was, that it seemed the world was written all over him, and he fairly glowed with it.

We stood behind the lines. The wind coming up from the south had a chance of spring in it, but the day was cold, no matter the clean white clouds snapping overhead, the bright blue tunnel of sky.

I took a breath and told him that I wasn't actually going back to school at Tulane, that I was just going to New Orleans plain and simple.

He let out a long low whistle.

"And your mama? She know that's where you're bound? Or did you just happen to run off without telling anybody?"

As pleased with me as he had seemed in the cabin, now he seemed as angry. He pulled away and walked along the gangway, and I followed after him.

When he turned around, it appeared the dark of his eyes had spilled over into the whites, they were so somber, so full of hurt.

"I thought you and me were going to be a team for a while," he said. "I thought you were your own man, but now I see you ain't even dry behind the ears."

I was confused, reached out for his arm, but he pulled it away, stood there looking at me with such reproach I felt I'd fallen overboard and was drowning.

Then he relented, said in a milder tone, "Nobody goes off and leaves their family, less they have a reason. Nobody lets them worry and carry on and wonder if they're dead or alive. Nobody I want to meet."

The softer voice eased the weight of his disapproval not at all; I was wretched. My brave freedom purchased at the price of my parents' worry hadn't been such a grand thing to achieve after all. Wouldn't they be calling the hospital by now?

I must have looked as bad as I felt, for he pulled me to him.

"Don't think I want to let you go, but seems like I'm going to have to." Then he turned me around and pushed me back toward the cabin.

"Time's got to be right," he said, and went to ask Captain Eugene how long before we tied up in East St. Louis. And that was how long we stayed in the cabin, pressed together, pulling the future out of each other, sweating and groaning and making sure each of us remembered.

An Oracle

Edmund White

"An Oracle" is one of three short stories Edmund White wrote for the collection The Darker Proof: Stories from a Crisis *(1988). Adam Mars-Jones wrote the other four stories in the book. White has not written a large number of short stories—much of the short fiction he's published over the years has been excerpts from novels—but "An Oracle" shows his mastery of the form, and he regards it as one of his finer pieces. One of White's rare ventures into the supernatural, "An Oracle" is a ghost story in a very Jamesian manner.*

for Herb Spiers

After George died, Ray went through a long period of uncertainty. George's disease had lasted fifteen months and during that time Ray had stopped seeing most of his old friends. He'd even quarreled with Betty, his best friend. Although she'd sent him little cards from time to time, including the ones made by a fifty-year-old California hippie whom she represented, he hadn't responded. He'd even felt all the more offended that she'd forgotten or ignored how sickening he'd told her he thought the pastel leaves and sappy sentiments were.

George had been a terrible baby throughout his illness, but then again Ray had always babied him the whole twelve years they'd been together, so the last months had only dramatized what had been inherent from the beginning. Nor had George's crankiness spoiled their good times together. Of course they'd lived through their daily horrors (their dentist, an old friend, had refused to pull George's rotten tooth; George's mother had decided to "blame herself" for George's cowardice in the face of pain), but they still had had fun. Ray leased a

329

little Mercedes and they drove to the country whenever George was up to it. A friend had given them a three-hundred-dollar Siamese kitten he'd found at a pet show and they'd named her Anna, partly because of Anna and the King of Siam and partly in deference to an ancient nickname for Ray. They both showered her with affection.

Which she reciprocated. Indeed, the more they chased away their friends, the more they relished her obvious liking for them. When they'd lie in bed watching television at night, they'd take turns stroking Anna. If she purred, they'd say, "At least *she* likes us." After George became very feeble and emaciated, he would ignore his mother and father and refuse to stay even a single night at the hospital and would play with Anna if he had the strength and berate Ray for something or other.

George would become very angry at Ray for not calling to find out the results of his own blood test. "You're just being irresponsible," George would say, "to yourself." But Ray knew that the test would tell him nothing—or tell him that yes, he'd been exposed to the virus, but nothing more. And besides, there was no preventive treatment. Anyway, he owed all his devotion to George; he didn't want to think for a second about his own potential illness.

Every moment of George's last four months had been absorbing. They quarreled a lot, specially about little dumb things, as though they needed the nagging and gibbering of everyday pettiness to drown out the roar of eternity. George, who'd never cared about anything except the day after tomorrow, suddenly became retrospective in a sour way.

They quarreled about whether Ray had ever needed George, which was absurd since until George had become ill Ray had been so deeply reliant on George's energy and contacts that Betty had repeatedly warned Ray against living forever in George's shadow. What she hadn't known was how much he, Ray, had always babied George at home—nursed him through hangovers, depressions, business worries, even attacks of self-hatred after he'd been rejected by a trick.

George, of course, was the famous one. Starting in the early 1970s he'd been called in by one major corporation after another to give each an image, and George had designed everything from the letterhead to the company jet. He'd think up a color scheme, a logo, a typeface, an overall look; he'd redo the layouts of the annual report. He'd work with an advertising creative director on the product presentation and the campaign slogans. He'd demand control over even the tiniest details, down to the lettering on the business cards of the sales force.

Since he was six-foot-three, rangy, and athletic, had a deep voice, and had fathered a son during an early marriage, the executives he dealt with never suspected him of being gay, nor was George a crusader of any sort. He liked winning and he didn't want to start any game with an unfair handicap. George also had a temper, a drive to push his ideas through, and he wasn't handsome—three more things that counted as straight among straights.

He'd also had the heterosexual audacity to charge enormous fees. His job as corporate image-maker was something he'd more or less invented. He'd realized that most American corporations were paralyzed by pettiness, rivalry, and fear, and only an outsider could make things happen. George was able to bring about more changes in a month than some cringing and vicious vice-president could effect in a year, if ever. George made sure he reported directly to the president or chairman, although as soon as he came "onstream" he solicited everyone else's "input."

On summer weekends George and Ray had flown in a seaplane to Fire Island, where they'd rented a big house on the ocean side complete with swimming pool. Around that pool they'd spent twelve summers with just a phone, a little acid, and thirty hunky men. They had, or Ray had, pounds of Polaroids to prove it. Here was the White Party and the house flying a thousand white balloons and Skipper in the foreground with his famous smile, the smile that earned him a hundred and fifty dollars an hour. Dead now of his own—not hand, but leap: he'd leapt from his penthouse on angel dust. And here was the Star Wars party with George as Darth Vader and his arm around little Tommy as R2-D2, the cute kid who wanted to be a DJ but never made it, though he did amazing disco tapes he sold to friends in editions of fifty.

And here was George as Darleen. Older guys hated George's dabbling in drag, since they associated it with the sissy 1950s. And the younger kids simply didn't get it; they'd heard of it, but it didn't seem funny to them. But for George's and Ray's generation, the Stonewall generation, drag was something they'd come to late, after they'd worked their way through every other disguise. For George, such a sexy big man with a low voice and brash ways, the character he'd invented, Darleen, had provided a release—not a complete contrast, but a slight transposition. For one thing, she was a slut, but an intimidating one who, when horny, yanked much smaller men to her hairy chest without a second's hesitation. For another, she had a vulgar but on-target way of talking over George's current corporation and reducing it to its simplest profile; it was Darleen in a drugged state who'd mumbled forth the slogans now selling seven of the biggest American products.

And Darleen had introduced a certain variety into Ray's and George's sex life, for she liked to be passive in bed, whereas George was tirelessly active. No one would have believed it, not even their closest friends, but Ray had fucked Darleen whereas he could never have fucked George. After sex they'd weep from laughter, the two of them, Ray sweaty and gold with his white tan line and George, foundered, skinny legs in black net stockings and the lashes coming unglued on his, yes, his left eye.

When George died, Ray thought of burying him in his drag, but the two people he happened to mention it to (although fairly far-out numbers themselves) drew back in horror. "You've got to be kidding," one of them had said as though Ray were now committable for sure. Ray had wanted to say, "Shouldn't we die as we lived? Why put George in a dark suit he never wore in life?"

But he didn't say anything, and George was buried as his parents wished. His father had been a cop, now retired, his mother a practical nurse, and in the last twenty years they'd made a lot of money in real estate. They liked fixing up old houses, as did George. Ray had a superstition that George had succumbed to the illness only because he'd worked so hard on his own loft. George was a perfectionist and he trusted no one else to do a job correctly. He'd spent hours crouched in the basement rewiring the whole building. Everything, and most especially the lacquering of the loft walls, was something he'd done by himself, again and again to get everything right.

Now he was dead and Ray had to go on with his own life, but he scarcely knew how or why to pick up the threads. The threads were bare, worn thin, so that he could see right through what should have been the thick stuff of everyday comings and goings, could see pale blue vistas. "You must look out for yourself," George had always said. But what self?

Ray still went to the gym three times a week as he'd done for almost twenty years. He never questioned anything here and resented even the smallest changes, such as the installation of a fruit juice bar or a computerized billing system always on the blink.

And then Ray had Anna to feed and play with. Since she'd been

George's only other real companion toward the end, she felt comfortable and familiar. They'd lie in bed together and purr, and that was nice but it wasn't a sign pointing forward to a new life, only a burned offering to his past, itself burned and still smoking.

He thought he was too young to have had to renounce so much. He'd always known that he'd have to end in renunciation, but he didn't like being rushed. He thought of George's long femur bones slowly emerging in the expensive coffin.

And of course he had his job. He did public relations for a major chemical company with headquarters on Sixth Avenue. It was a gig George had found him; George had done a total facelifting for Amalgamated Anodynes. Nearly everything about the company was reprehensible. It had a subsidiary in the Union of South Africa. Its biggest plant was in South Carolina, precisely because there the right-to-work laws, as they were called in the best Orwellian manner, had banned most of the unions. AA had produced a fabric for children's wear that had turned out to be flammable; Ray had even had to draft for the president's signature some very high-level waffling as a statement to the press. And Amalgamated Anodynes had a lousy record with women and minorities, although a creepy Uncle Tom headed the company's equal-hiring-practices commission.

Worst of all was Ray's boss, Helen, the token female vice-president. Helen was by turns solicitous and treacherous, servile to superiors and tyrannical to her staff, an old-fashioned schemer who knew more about office politics than her job.

Following a run-in with Helen a few days after the funeral (which, of course, he hadn't been able to mention), he'd locked himself in the toilet and cried and cried, surprised there was so much mucus in his head. Where was it stored normally, in which secret cavity? He was also surprised by how lonely he felt. Lonely, or maybe spaced. George had always been barking at him, scolding or praising him; now the silence was oddly vacant, as though someone were to push past a last gate and enter into the limitless acreage of space and night.

To cry he had had to say to himself, "I'm giving in to total self-pity," because otherwise he was so stoic these postmortem days that he'd never have let himself be ambushed by despair. Why did he keep this job? Was it to please George, who always wanted him to go legit, who'd never approved of his "beatnik jobs"? George had used "beatnik," "hippie," and "punk" interchangeably to dramatize the very carelessness of his contempt.

Ray had grown up on a farm in northern Ohio near Findlay and still had in his possession a second prize for his cow from the state fair; he'd sewn it and his Future Farmers of America badge to his letter jacket. What big-city sentimentalists never understood about the rural existence they so admired was that it was dull and lonely, unnaturally lonely, but it left lots of time for reading.

He'd read and read and won a first prize in the Belle Fontaine spelling bee and another as the captain of the Carrie debating team against Sandusky on the hot subject of Free Trade. His grades were so good he received a scholarship to Oberlin, where, in his second year, he'd switched his major from agronomy to philosophy.

From there he'd gone on to the University of Chicago, where he'd joined the Committee on Social Thought and eventually written a thesis on Durkheim's concept of *anomie*. His father, who wore bib overalls and had huge, fleshy ears and read nothing but the Bible, but that daily, would shake his head slowly and stare at the ground whenever the subject of his son's education came up. His mother, however, encouraged him. She was the school librarian, a thin woman with moist blue eyes and hands red from poor circulation, who drank coffee all day and read everything, everything. She'd been proud of him.

But she too had had her doubts when, after he received his doctorate, he'd drifted to Toronto and joined an urban gay commune, grown his blond hair to his shoulders, and done little else besides holding down part-time jobs and writing articles analyzing and lamenting the lesbian–gay male split. In the doctrinaire fashion of those days, he'd angrily denounced all gay men and assumed a female name for himself, Anna. The name wasn't intended as a drag name (although later George had insisted he use it as one), but only as a statement of his position against gender distinctions. Only his friends in the commune could call him Anna with a straight face.

Unlike most of the other early gay liberationists, Ray had actually had sex with other men. His affairs were shy, poetic, and decidedly unfancy in bed. Despite his political beliefs, he insisted on being on top, which he admitted was a "phallocratic" hang-up, although nothing felt to him more natural than lavishing love on a subdued man, similarly smooth-skinned, slender, and pigtailed.

Then one summer he'd met Jeff, a New Yorker and a contributor to the *Body Politic* who was every bit as ideological as Ray but much more muscular and amusing. When Jeff's Toronto vacation came to an end, Ray moved to New York to be with him. He justified the move to the other communards by pointing out that New York was a literary center. "So is Toronto!" they'd objected, for they were also Canadian patriots.

Ray had inchoate literary aspirations. For years he'd dutifully kept a journal. When he reread it after living in New York awhile, he found the voluminous self-analysis neither true nor false, the recorded ideas a good deal sharper than those he was currently entertaining, and the descriptions of nature accurate, and mildly, solidly of value.

When he looked for a job as a writer in New York, all he could find, given his lack of credentials (his Ph.D. in philosophy counted as a drawback), was a position on *Conquistador!*, a sleazy tits-and-ass magazine for which he invented the picture captions in the centerfold ("Lovely Linda is a stewardess and flies, natch, for Aer Lingus"). The indignities (plus low pay) of that job he tried to compensate for by reading manuscripts in the evening for Grove Press and evaluating them artistically and commercially. Since he'd read little except the classics in school, his standards were impossibly high, and since his aquaintanceship till now had included only Ohio farmers, Chicago intellectuals, and Toronto gay liberationists, his grasp of the potential market for any particular book was skewed.

He drifted from job to job, ghosted several chapters of a U.S. history college textbook for a tottering publishing house, worked as a bartender in a black-glass, red-velvet singles bar, taught one semester at a snooty Episcopalian boys' school in Brooklyn Heights, spent one winter as a stock boy at a chic Lucite boutique some friends owned, fled another winter to Key West, where he wore short shorts and served rum and coconut "conch-outs" around the pool of a gay guesthouse (he saw the shells as shrunken skulls). He was hired because he'd long since joined a gym, acquired a beefy but defined body, traded in his pigtail and severe manner for a ready laugh and a crewcut ("Wear a Jantzen and a smile," as the old swimsuit slogan had put it). Naturally he no longer insisted on being called Anna. He'd also moved bumpily from one affairlet to another and had been embarrassed that most of them had ended in squabbles over money or fidelity.

Into this confusion, so rife with opportunities he was unable to see how little hope it held out, George had entered. They were both guests at someone's house in New York, and when they helped out washing up, their hands met under the suds. When he later tried to pinpoint what had made this relationship take and stick he thought it could be seen as a barter—George's forcefulness for Ray's beauty, say. George was homely if sexy, yet he didn't sense his own appeal and he dwelled on all his imperfections. Ray on the other hand was "pretty" in the special sense that word acquired in the mid-1970s to mean massive shoulders, shaggy mustache, permanent tan, swelling chest. He was also pretty in the more usual sense, for his full lips seemed to be traced in light where a slightly raised welt outlined them, his deep-set blue eyes contained an implosion of gold particles falling into the black holes of his pupils, his jaw had comic-book strength, and his teeth were so long and white a dentist had to file them down once when he was twelve. And now that he was in his twenties one could discern brown-gold hair on his chest spreading wings over his lungs like that goddess who spreads her arms to protect the pharaoh from all harm.

Ray didn't take his own beauty too seriously, though he maintained it as one might conserve a small inheritance for the sake of security. His spell in the gay commune had made him suspicious of all "objectifications of the body" and "commodification of sex," but his years in New York had taught him the importance of precisely these two operations. He was a bit of a star on the deck during tea dance on Fire Island, for his years of training had in point of absolute fact turned him into a physical commodity—but one he was too ironic, too human to sell to the highest bidder. That George was not at all an obvious candidate, that he was too skinny, too pockmarked, a diligent but unsuccessful dresser, made him all the more appealing to Ray.

George had a ravenous appetite to win, even in the most trivial contests, and that made him both infuriating and appealing. Ray had always been accommodating—too accommodating, he now saw, in view of how little he'd accomplished. He deplored the way George cussed out every incompetent and sent back the wine and at every moment demanded satisfaction.

And yet George's life was royally satisfying. He drove his Chrysler station wagon full of friends to Vermont for ski weekends, he was doing the work he most enjoyed and making a minor fortune, and now, to put the final *u* on parvenu, he had . . . Ray. Until now, Ray had never thought of himself as primarily decorative, but George saw him obviously as a sort of superior home-entertainment center—stylish, electric. Ray didn't like to stare into this reflection, he who'd won the Belle Fontaine spelling bee and written one hundred and twenty closely reasoned pages on *anomie*. He saw that without noticing it he'd drifted into the joking, irresponsible, anguished half-world of the gay actor-singer-dancer-writer-waiter-model who always knows what Sondheim has up his sleeve, who might delay his first spring visit to the island until he's worked on those forearms two more weeks, who feels confident Europe is as extinct as a dead star and all the heat and life for the planet must radiate from New York, who has heard most of his favorite songs from his chronological adolescence resurface fifteen years later in their disco versions, at once a reassurance about human continuity and a dismaying gauge of time's flight.

Lovers are attracted by opposites and then struggle to turn them into twins. Ray worked to mollify George's drive to win and George wanted Ray to turn into a winner. Work hard and play hard was George's motto, whereas Ray, without admitting it, wanted lots less work than play and wished both to be not hard but easy. Nevertheless, George, true to form, won. He nudged Ray into a series of well-paying jobs that ended him up at Amalgamated Anodynes. "You must look out for yourself," George was always saying. He said it over and over: "Look out for yourself." Ray would sit on his lap and say, "Why should I deprive you of a job you do so well?" The one thing they'd agreed on from the first was not to be monogamous. Ray's ideological horror of marriage as a model and George's unreflecting appetite for pleasure neatly converged. What wasn't decided so easily were the terms under which they were to be faithful. George, who had a funny face, skinny body, and enormous penis, was always a hit at the baths; Ray, whose penis was of average dimensions ("a gay eight," meaning six inches), was more likely to attract another man for a lifetime than a night. Ray already had love, George's, but in order to get sex he had to seem to be offering love. When George would see some other beauty, as dark as Ray was fair, melting amorously around Ray, George would break glass, bellow, come crashing through doors, wounded bull in the china shop of Ray's delicate romantic lust. Of course Ray envied George his simpler, franker asset and wished he could score more efficiently, with fewer complications.

And now, a year after George's death, here he was learning all the ways in which he had accommodated George and was still doing so, even though George had broken camp. Ray saw how in their tiny group he'd been billed as the looker with the brain, exactly like the starlet whom the studio hypes wearing a mortarboard and specs above her adorable snub nose and bikini—yet he wasn't in Hollywood but New York City and he realized that he'd fallen way behind, hadn't read a book in ages or had a new, strenuous thought.

He still had the big showboat body that George had doted on and that Ray was vigorously maintaining two hours a day at the gym, even though personally (as in "If I may speak *personally* about my own life") he found the results caricatural and the waste of time ludicrous. And yet he was afraid to let go, stop pumping iron and deflate, sag, shrink, because if he was no longer the greatest brain he was at least a body; Some Body in the most concrete, painful sense. He looked around and realized he was still impersonating George's lover. He was even still using the same deodorant George had liked; George had had such an insinuating way of sticking his big, cratered nose into the most intimate aspects of Ray's habits. He'd made Ray switch from Jockey to boxer shorts, from cotton to cashmere socks, from Pepsi to Coke, from ballpoint to fountain pen; like all people who make their living from publicity, George had believed that products and brand names determine destiny. Ray was still walking around like a doll George had dressed and wound up before taking off.

In the corner bookstore he picked up a remaindered large-format paperback called *The Death Rituals of Rural Greece*, by Loring M. Danforth. He liked the way the widows resented their husbands' deaths and said, "He wasn't very kind to me when he left me." That was closer to the truth than this twilit grief one was supposed to assume. He liked the funeral laments, specially the one in which a mother asks her dead daughter how Death, called Haros, received her. The daughter replies, "I hold him on my knees. He rests against my chest. If he is hungry, he eats from my body, and if he is thirsty, he drinks from my two eyes."

When he had a Midtown lunch with Betty she told him he was having an identity crisis precipitated by George's death. "But your real problem," she said, warming unbecomingly to her subject, "is that you're still seeking an authority, the answer. If you don't watch out, you'll find yourself saddled with another dominating lover; it's your passive Aquarian nature."

Ray could scarcely believe how much his fur was being rubbed the wrong way, although he felt certain the prize had to go to Betty's insinuation that he was well rid of George. That night he found in an old linen jacket he took out of storage a joint of Acapulco gold George had rolled him—how long ago? two years—and he smoked it and

cried and ordered in Chinese food and sat in bed and watched TV and
played with Anna, who kept wandering over to the lit candle on the
floor to sniff the flame. When she felt the heat her eyes would slit shut
and she'd thrust her chin up, like a dowager who's smelled something
rude.

Even though George had been a baby, he'd fought death with a
winner's determination but he'd lost anyway. Ray thought that he himself wouldn't resist it for long. If and when the disease surfaced (for
it seemed to him like a kid who's holding his nose underwater for an
eerily long time but is bound to come gasping up for air), when the
disease surfaced he wouldn't much mind. In a way dying would be
easier than figuring out a new way of living.

Betty must have taken it on herself to contact Ralph Brooks and
suggest he ask Ray to Greece. Otherwise Ray couldn't imagine why
Ralph should have written him a belated condolence letter that ended
with a very warm and specific invitation.

Ray was flattered. After all, Brooks was the celebrated painter. Betty
would say that Ray accepted *because* Brooks was the celebrated
painter. Not that she ever accused Ray of social-climbing. No, she just
thought his "passivity" made him seek out authorities, no matter who
or of what. Oddly enough, Betty's nagging, grating Brooklyn accent
reassured him, because it was a voice that stylized suffering, domesticated it. Oy, Ray thought when he was with Betty. She wasn't even
Jewish, but she was from Brooklyn, and if he used her accent he could
actually say it to himself or to Anna: "Oy."

Ray welcomed the trip to Greece precisely because it didn't fit in.
George had never been to Greece; Ralph had never met George; Ray
himself scarcely knew Ralph. They'd become friendly at the gym and
worked out a dozen times together and Ralph had always asked him
his bright, general questions that didn't seem to anticipate anything so
concrete as an answer. Ralph, who'd worked out for years, had a big
bearish body that was going to flab—exactly what envious, lazy people
always say happens to weightlifters in middle age. His shoulders, chest,
and biceps were still powerful, but his belly was as big as a bus driver's. Ralph said he hated the ruin of his looks, but he seemed so relaxed
and sure of himself that this self-loathing struck Ray as an attitude he
might once have held but had since outgrown without renouncing.

Then again Ray would so gladly have traded in his own prettiness
for Ralph's success that perhaps he couldn't quite believe in Ralph's

complaints. As for the three weeks in Crete (he found the town, Xania, on the map), it would be all new—new place, new language, no ghosts. He even liked going to the country where people expressed their grief over dying so honestly, so passionately. In that book he liked the way a mother, when she exhumed her daughter's body after three years of burial, said, "Look what I put in and look what I took out! I put in a partridge, and I took out bones."

Betty agreed to take care of Anna. "You must look out for yourself," George had said, and now he was trying.

Ralph had rented a floor of a Venetian palace on a hill overlooking the harbor; at least Ralph called it a "palace" in that hyperbolic way of his. The town had been badly bombed during the war and empty lots and grass-growing ruins pocked even the most crowded blocks like shocking lapses in an otherwise good memory.

Nothing in town was taller than three stories except two minarets left over from the centuries of Turkish rule and allowed to stand more through indifference then ecumenism. At first Ray looked for the blazing whitewash and strong geometrical shapes he'd seen in trendy postcards from the Greek islands, but in Xania everything was crumbling brick, faded paint, mud or pebble alleyways, cement and rusting cement armatures sticking up out of unfinished upper stories, shabby exteriors and immaculate interiors, dusty carved-wood second stories overhanging the street in the Turkish fashion. Along the harbor a chrome-and-plastic disco, booming music and revolving lights as though it had just landed, made chic racket beside shadowy, abandoned arsenals where the Venetians had housed their warships. One of them had a stone balcony high above the harbor and two doors shaped like Gothic flames opening up on to a roofless void and a framed picture of the night sky—the half-waned moon.

Ralph and Ray ate fried squid and a feta cheese salad at a rickety table outside along the brackish-smelling harbor. The table could never quite find its footing. They were waited on by a Buddha-faced boy who smiled with mild amusement every time his few words in English were understood. The boy couldn't have been more than nine, but he already had a whole kit of skilled frowns, tongue-clicks, and body gestures, and his grandfather's way of wiping his forehead with a single swipe of a folded fresh handkerchief as though he were ironing something. Ray found it hard to imagine having accumulated so many mannerisms before the dawn of sex, of the sexual need to please, of the staginess sex encourages or the tightly capped wells of poisoned sexual desire the disappointed must stand guard over.

Ralph, who was shoe-leather brown and so calm he let big gaps of comfortable silence open up in the conversation, was much fatter—all the olive oil and rosé and sticky desserts, no doubt. A cool wind was blowing up off the Aegean, and Ray was glad he'd worn a long-sleeved shirt. Ralph had helped him unpack and had clucked over each article of clothing, all of which he found too stylish and outré for Xania. In fact Ralph seemed starved for company and gossip and far less vague than in New York. There he seemed always to be escaping sensory overload through benign nullity, the Andy Warhol strategy of saying "Oh, great" to everything. Here he took a minute, gossipy interest in the details of everyday life. Ray thought, We each need just the right weight of pettiness to serve as ballast. George's death had tossed all the sandbags overboard and Ray had been floating higher and higher toward extinction.

Ralph was specially interested in the "locals," as he called the young men. "Now this is the Black Adonis," he said of one tall, fair-skinned twenty-year-old strolling past with two younger boys. "He's in a different shirt every night. And would you look at that razor cut! Pure Frankie Avalon . . . Oh, my dear, what fun to have another old-timer from the States with me, no need to explain my references for once."

Ralph had a nickname for every second young man who walked past in the slow, defiant, sharp-eyed parade beside the harbor. "This is the tail end of the *volta,* as we call the evening *passeggiata,*" Ralph said, typically substituting one incomprehensible word for another. "There's absolutely nothing to do in this town except cruise. In the hot weather they all stop working at two in the afternoon. Now here comes the Little Tiger—notice the feline tattoo?—a very bad character. He stole my Walkman when I invited him in for a nightcap; Little Tiger, go to the rear of the class. He's bad because he's from the next town and he thinks he can get away with it. Stick with the locals; nothing like the high moral power of spying and gossip."

Ray had always heard of dirty old American men who'd gone to Greece for the summer "phallic cure," but he'd assumed gay liberation had somehow ended the practice, unshackled both predator and prey. Nevertheless, before they'd left the restaurant two more Americans, both in their sixties, had stopped by their table to recount their most recent adventures. Ray, used to fending off older men, was a bit put out that no one, not even Ralph, was flirting with him. In fact, the assumption, which he resented, was that he too was an old-timer who'd come here "for the boys" and would be willing to pay for it.

"Aren't there any Greeks who do it for free?" Ray asked, not getting the smiles he'd anticipated.

"A few frightful poofs do, I suppose," Ralph drawled, looking offended by the notion. "But why settle for free frights when for ten bucks you can have anyone in town, absolutely anyone including the mayor and his wife, not to mention the odd god on the hoof?"

For a few days Ray held out. Betty, morbidly enough, had made a tape of all the crazy messages George had left on her answering machine during his last year. She'd given Ray the tape just before he'd left, and now he sat in his bedroom, wearing gaudy drawstring shorts, and looked at the harbor lights and listened to George's voice.

Ray remembered a remark someone had once made: "Many people believe in God without loving him, but I love him without believing in him." Ray didn't know why the remark popped into his head just now. Did he love George without believing he existed? Ray described himself as a "mystical atheist." Maybe that was a complicated way of saying he believed George still loved him, or would if God would let him speak.

In his New York gay world, which was as carefully screened from men under twenty-five as from those over sixty, Ray counted as young. That is, some old flame whom Ray had known fifteen years ago—a guy with a mustache gone gray and fanning squint lines but a still massive chest and thunder thighs under all that good tailoring—would spot Ray at a black-tie gay-rights dinner or health-crisis benefit and come up to him murmuring, "Lookin' good, kid," and would pinch his bottom. It was all continuing, and Ray knew that despite the way his body had acquired a certain thickness, as though the original Greek statue had been copied by a Roman, he still looked youthful to his contemporaries.

In the first two weeks after George's death Ray had picked up three different men on the street and dragged them home. Ray had clung to their warm bodies, their air-breathing chests and blood-beating hearts, clung like a vampire to warm himself through transfusions of desire. He and Anna would sniff at these bewildered young men as though nothing could be less likely than a scabbed knee, furred buttocks, an uncollared collarbone, or the glamorous confusion of a cast-aside white shirt and silk rep tie. What they, the pick-ups, wanted, heart-to-heart post-coital chat, appealed to him not at all; all he wanted was to lie facedown beside tonight's faceup partner and slide on top of him just enough to be literally heart-to-heart. Their carnality had seemed very fragile.

After this brief, irresponsible flaring up of lust, which had followed the sexless year of George's dying, Ray had gone back to celibacy. He thought it very likely that he was carrying death inside him, that it was ticking inside him like a time bomb but one he couldn't find because it had been secreted by an unknown terrorist. Even if it was located it couldn't be defused. Nor did he know when it might explode. He didn't want to expose anyone to contagion.

He wrote his will as he knew everyone should. That was the adult thing to do. But the paltry list of his possessions reminded him of how little he'd accumulated or accomplished; it was like the shame of moving day, of seeing one's cigarette-burned upholstery and scarred bureau on the curb under a hot, contemptuous sun. His relatively youthful looks had led him to go on believing in his youthful expectations; his life, he would have said as a philosophy student, was all becoming and no being. All in the future until this death sentence (never pronounced, daily remanded) had been handed down.

Occasionally he jerked off with poppers and dirty magazines. Although he found slaves and masters ludicrous and pathetic, his fantasies had not kept pace with the fashions and were mired somewhere in 1972, best simulated by the stories and photos in *Drummer*. He would read a hot tale about a violent encounter between two real pigs, sniff his amyl, even mutter a few words ("Give your boy that daddy-dick"), and then find himself, head aching, stomach sticky, heart sinking, erection melting, alone, posthumous. Anna wrinkled her nose and squinted at the fumes. He hoped his executor, who was his lawyer, would be able to bury him next to George as instructed, since he only slept really well when George was beside him. Once in a Philadelphia museum he'd seen the skeletons of a prehistoric man and woman, buried together (he couldn't remember how they'd come to die at the same time). He was lying on his back, she on her side, her hand placed delicately on his chest.

The days in Crete were big, cloudless hot days, heroic days, noisy with the saw rasp of insects. They were heroic days as though the sun were a lionhearted hero ... Oh, but hadn't he just read in his beach book, the *Odyssey,* the words of the dead, lionhearted Achilles: "Do not speak to me soothingly about death, glorious Odysseus; I should prefer, as a slave, to serve another man, even if he had no property and little to live on, than to rule over all these dead who have done with life.'' He'd cried on the white sand beach beside the lapis-lazuli water and looked through his tears, amazed, at a herd of sheep trotting toward him. He stood and waded and waved, smiling, at the old shepherd in black pants and a carved stick in his hand, which itself looked carved; Ray, expensively muscular in his Valentino swim trunks, thought he was probably not much younger than this ancient peasant and suddenly his grief struck him as a costly gewgaw, beyond the means of the grievously hungry and hardworking world. Or maybe it was precisely his grief that joined him to this peasant. Every night he was dreaming about George, and in that book about the Greek death rituals he'd read the words of an old woman: ''At death the soul emerges in its entirety, like a man. It has the shape of a man, only it's invisible. It has a mouth and hands and eats real food just like we do. When you see someone in your dreams, it's the soul you see. People in your dreams eat, don't they? The souls of the dead eat too.'' Ray couldn't remember if George ate in his dreams.

Ralph and Ray rented motor scooters and drove up a narrow road through chasms, past abandoned medieval churches and new cement-block houses, high into the mountains. They chugged slowly up to and away from a goat stretching to reach the lower branches of a tree. They saw a young Orthodox priest in a black soutane out strolling, preceded by a full black beard he seemed to be carrying in front of him as one might carry a salver. He remembered that Orthodox priests can marry and he vaguely thought of that as the reason this one seemed so virile; he looked as though he'd just stepped out from behind the plow into this dress.

The summer drought had dwindled the stream to a brook within its still green bed. At a certain turn in the road the air turned cool, as though the frozen core of the mountain had got tired of holding its breath. In the shepherds' village where they stopped for lunch a smiling boy was found to speak English with them. He said he'd lived in New Zealand for a year with his aunt and uncle; that was why he knew English. Laughing, he offered them steaks and salads, but it turned out the only food available in the village was a runny sour cheese and bread and olives.

Every day, despite the climate's invitation to languor, Ray did his complete workout, causing the heavy old wardrobe in his room to creak and throw open its door when he did push-ups. Some days, specially around three, a wind would suddenly blow up and he and Ralph would run around battening down the twenty-three windows. At dusk on Sundays a naval band marched all the way around the harbor to the fortress opposite the lighthouse and played the national anthem ("which was written by a German," Ralph couldn't resist throwing in) while the blue and white flag was lowered.

Although the days were cheerful—scooter rides to a deserted beach, vegetable and fish marketing, desultory house-hunting out beyond the town walls on which the Venetian lion had been emblazoned—the nights were menacing. He and Ralph would dress carefully for the *volta,* Ralph in a dark blue shirt and ironed slacks, Ray in a floating gown of a Japanese designer shirt and enormous one-size-drowns-all lime-green shorts, neon-orange cotton socks, black Adidas, and white sunglasses slatted like Venetian blinds angled down ("perfect for the Saudi matron on the go," he said).

At least that's how he got himself up the first few nights until he sensed Ralph's embarrassment, the crowd's smiling contempt, and his own . . . what?

Desire?

Every night it was the same. The sun set, neon lights outlined the eaves and arches of the cafés, and an army of strollers, mostly young and male, sauntered slowly along the horseshoe-shaped stone walk beside the harbor. Sometimes it stank of pizza or what was called Kantaki Fried Chicken or of the sea urchins old fishermen had cleaned on the wharf earlier in the day. The walk could be stretched out to twenty minutes if one lingered in conversation with friends, stopped to buy nuts from one vendor and to look at the jewelry sold by Dutch hippies. A drink at an outdoor café—ouzo and hors d'oeuvres (*mezes*)—could while away another forty minutes.

The full hour was always devoted to boy-watching. Ray looked, too, at the wonderful black hair, muscular bodies, red cheeks under deep tans, flamboyant mustaches, big noses, transparent arrogance, equally transparent self-doubt, black eyebrows yearning to meet above the nose and often succeeding. "Of course they need reassurance," Ralph said. "What actor doesn't?" These guys had loud voices, carnivorous teeth, strutting walks, big asses, broad shoulders. Ray thought they were more like American teenage boys than other European youths; they were equally big and loud and physical and sloppy and unveiled in their curiosity and hostility.

One of the sixty-year-old Americans, a classics professor in the States, was an amateur photographer of considerable refinement. He'd persuaded, it seemed, dozens of locals to pose nude for him. He paid them something. He was discreet. He flattered them as best he could in the modern language he'd pieced together out of his complete knowledge of ancient Greek. "Sometimes," he said, "they say a whole long improbable sentence in English—picked up from an American song or movie, no doubt."

Among the locals his ministrations to vanity made him popular, his scholarship made him impressive, and his hobby risible, but since he always seemed to be laughing at himself in his ancient, elegant prep-school way, his laughter softened theirs. His photographic sessions he dismissed airily but pursued gravely.

Homer (for that was his name, absurdly; "Stranger than epic," as he said) took a polite but real interest in Ray—but strictly in Ray's mind. Ray, who expected, invited, and resented other men's sexual attraction to him, found Homer's sex-free attentiveness unsettling. And appealing. Maybe because Homer was a professor and had a professor's way of listening—which meant he winced slightly when he disagreed and cleaned his glasses when he deeply disagreed—Ray felt returned, if only for an instant, to his school days. To the days before he'd ever known George. To the days when he'd been not a New York know-it-all, but a Midwestern intellectual, someone who took nothing on authority and didn't even suspect there were such things as fashions in ideas.

This repatriation cheered him. Ralph had made a spaghetti dinner at home ("Enough with the swordfish and feta, already") and invited Homer. Ray's and Homer's conversation about the categorical imperative, the wager, the cave, the excluded middle, astonished Ralph. "You girls are real bluestockings," he told them, "which is OK for a hen party, but remember men don't make passes at girls who wear glasses." Ralph even seemed disconcerted by their intelligence, if that's what all this highbrow name-dropping had revealed.

After the wine and the laughter Ray thought it only natural to go on to the bar with his friends, the gay bar where they met with "true love" every night, as Ralph said. On the way along the harbor, Ray told Homer all about his sexual qualms. "I just don't think I should expose anyone else to this disease in case I've got it or in case I'm contagious. And I'm not disciplined enough to stick to safe sex."

Homer nodded and made the same noncommittal but polite murmur as when earlier they'd discussed the *Nicomachean Ethics*. Then, as though shaking himself awake, he asked, "What *is* safe sex, exactly?"

"Strictly safe is masturbation, no exchange of body fluids. Or if you fuck you can use a rubber. But I'm not worried about myself. The only one in danger where fucking and sucking is involved is the guy who gets the come."

Silence full of blinking in the dark, blinking with lashes growing longer, darker with mascara by the second. "But, darling," Homer finally confided, hilariously woman-to-woman, "then the Greeks are *always* safe. They're the men; we're the girls."

"Call me square," Ray said, "but that's old-fashioned role-playing—and I've never, never paid—"

Homer interrupted him with a soft old hand on his arm. "Give it a try. After all, it's your only option."

The alley leading to the bar was too narrow for cars but wide enough to accommodate four noisy adolescents walking shoulder-to-shoulder; one of them stepped drunkenly down into the grass-sprouting ruins and pissed against a jagged wall. The kid had a foolish grin and he seemed to have forgotten how to aim, shake, button up. The others started barking and mewing. Ray found the situation and the hoarse voices exciting. Had these guys come from the bar? Were they gay?

The bar was a low room, a basement grotto, one would have said, except it was on the ground floor. There were several dimly lit alcoves just off the room in which shadowy couples were smoking and drinking. The waiters, or "hostesses," were two transvestites: Dmitri, who was chubby and brunet and kept a slightly deformed hand always just out of sight, flickering it behind his back or under a tray or into a pocket, and Adriana, who was slender, with straight, shoulder-length blond hair and who responded to open jeers with a zonked-out grin that never varied, as though she were drugged on her own powerful fantasy of herself, which made her immune. Both were in jeans and T-shirts; Adriana had two small, hormone-induced breasts, but his arms were still muscular and his hips boyishly narrow. Dmitri, the brunette, had less beauty and more vitality, a clown's vitality; he was the stand-up or run-past comic. He did pratfalls with his tray, twinkled past on point, sat on laps, or wriggled deliciously against sailors, always keeping his hand in motion, out of focus. The bar was called Fire Island.

At first this gay bar seemed to Ray an unexpected trove of sexy young guys until Homer explained that, technically, they (Ralph, Ray, and Homer) were the only gays, along with the two hostesses, of course. Everyone else was, well, a gigolo, although that was too coarse a word for it. "Greek men really do prefer male company. All their bars are like this one," Homer said with that ornithological pride all old-timer expatriates exhibit to the newcomer. "The women don't go out much. And the men all think it's normal to get money for sex— just remember the dowries they receive. And then they're terribly poor, the sailors, five bucks a week, that's all they get. So, you take all these horny nineteen-year-olds away from their villages for the first time in their lives. Here they are, bored, lonely, with too much time on their hands, no unmarried Greek girls in sight . . . "

"Where are the girls?" Ray asked, embarrassed he hadn't noticed their absence till now.

"Their mothers quite sensibly keep them under lock and key. I myself feel an infinite reverence for the intact maidenhead. Of course you know these scandalous mothers teach their daughters to take it up the ass if they must put out; anything to stay intact. Although why am I complaining? That's my philosophy exactly."

"So the sailors are alone and horny . . . "

"And naturally they want to party. That's how they think of it. You buy them drinks and you're a real sport. You ask them home. It's a party. The only problem is how to wean them away from their *parea*."

"Come again?"

"*Parea*. That's their group, their friends, oh, a very useful word. If you want to pick someone up, point to him, then yourself. Say, 'You, me, *parea*?' "

"And what do they call us, the faggots?"

Homer smiled and lowered his voice: *"Poosti."*

"So we're *poosti* on *parea* . . . Don't rain on my *parea*."

"Yes," Homer said somewhat primly, "but not so loud. You'll scandalize the seafood," nodding toward a *parea* of five sailors, smiling at them with lofty politeness.

After two hours of drinking gin and tonic, Ray realized most of the boys weren't drinking at all and were just sitting over empty bottles of beer, bumming cigarettes from one another and hungrily staring at the door as each newcomer entered. Only a few were talking to each other. Sometimes they seemed to be inventing a conversation (involving lots of numbers, as even Ray could decode) and an emotion (usually indignation), but purely as a set piece to show them off to advantage to potential clients. The same tape of "Susanna" kept playing over and over, last year's disco tune, which didn't mean much to him since it had been popular when George was already sick and they had stopped going out dancing.

He excused himself, pecked Homer on the cheek, and squeezed past a suddenly amorous Dmitri, the hefty hostess, who smelled of sweat and Chanel.

Outside the night was airless, fragrant, the sky an enormous black colander held up to the light. Since it hadn't rained in months, dust filled the streets, dulled the store windows examined by veering headlights, rose in lazy devils behind passing shoes. In a bridal store the mannequin of the bride herself was snub-nosed and blond, her hair bristling up under her veil at crazy shocked angles as though she'd stuck her finger in an electric socket. She was flanked by curious white cloth bouquets trailing white silk ribbons. Were they held by her bridesmaids? Ray had seen a woman bringing such a bouquet here on the plane from Athens. In that book he'd read, the exhumation of a dead person's bones three years after death was compared to a wedding. The same songs were sung; the words varied only slightly. Both songs had begun with the words: "Now I have set out. Now I am about to depart . . . " Something like that.

On the corner a man was selling round green melons out of a cart. Everywhere people seemed awake and watching—from a trellised balcony, from a waiting cab, from a rooftop café. In such a hot country, people stayed up to enjoy the cool of the night. Kids, calling out to one another, sped by on bicycles. In the square in front of the cathedral a whole line of taxis waited, five drivers standing in a circle and disputing—what? Soccer? Politics?

Ray turned onto a deserted street lined with notions shops displaying lace trimmings and bolts of fabric and spools of thread. At the corner an old man with yellowing hair, worn-down shoes, and no socks had fallen asleep with his feet up on his desk in an open-air stand that sold ex-votos in tin—a bent arm, an ear, an open eye, a soldier in World War I uniform and helmet—and also tin icons, the metal snipped away to frame crude tinted reproductions of the Virgin's face. He also had long and short candles and something (incense?) wrapped in red paper cylinders, stacked high like rolled coins from the bank.

Cars with bad mufflers blatted and farted through town or throbbed beside a lit cigarette kiosk in front of the dim covered market. The cars were always full of teenage boys, but when they'd get out to buy cigarettes or to go into a bar and buy a paper, he'd see they were fat or thin, usually big handsome guys with black mustaches or the first faint charcoal sketches of mustaches.

It struck Ray that it had been years since he'd seen guys this young. Expensive, childless Manhattan had banned them. Ray imagined that he was back in Findlay, Ohio, on a Saturday night, the dark silent streets suddenly glaring and noisy with a gang in two hot rods. He forgot for a moment that he was forty; he felt he was sixteen, afraid of the hoods who'd driven in from Sandusky or even from as far away as Toledo. He was afraid and curious and contemptuous and excited as he darted along under the old trees, hoping he was invisible.

He crossed the street to avoid two strolling straight couples, and now he did feel forty. And queer. And foreign. He wouldn't even know if they were gossiping about him. Worse, he knew he didn't exist for them, he was invisible.

As he headed up the gently winding street toward the town zoo, he passed a lone young guy coming down toward him, who stared at him hard, harder and longer even than the other Cretan men normally stared. The boy spat through his teeth as they passed. He struck his heels with spark-making violence against the pavement. And then he stopped. Ray heard him stop behind him. If I turn around will he punch me?

When Ray finally turned around the young man was standing there staring at him. *"Ya,"* he said, that short form of *yassou,* the all-purpose greeting. Ray could see he was handsome with regular features, an upper lip pulled back to show white teeth made whiter by his mustache and a black beard that he was letting grow in. He had on jeans and a denim jacket, and the jacket sleeves were tight enough to reveal well-muscled upper arms, not the netted cantaloupes Ray had for biceps, but longer, grooved haunches, the tightly muscled arms that the ancient Cretan youths had in those wall-paintings at absurdly overrestored Knossos: murderously slim-waisted matadors.

He was either very tanned or very swarthy. His hair was long and pushed back behind his ears. His slightly unshaved face (the look of the New York model who wears a two days' growth of beard as an accessory to his smoking jacket or white silk pajamas), his obviously American jeans jacket, and his long hair were the three things that made him look fractionally different from all the other young men in this city of young men.

He kept staring, but then when Ray looked away for an instant, he slipped into a side street. Ray wondered if he'd be jumped when he followed him. As he turned the corner, the boy was standing there and asked aggressively, "What you want?" and his faint smile suggested he already knew and that Ray's desire was disgusting and entirely practicable.

Ray said, "You," with the sort of airiness that ruined Oscar Wilde, but that word apparently was not one of the boy's dozen English words. He frowned angrily.

"Sex," Ray said, and this time the boy nodded.

"But money!" he threatened, rubbing his thumb and forefinger together. Ray nodded with a face-saving smirk he regretted but couldn't wipe away. "I fuck you!" the boy added. This time as Ray nodded his smile vanished, a little bit in awe at the mention of this intimacy, once so common, now so rare, so gravely admonished, so fearfully practiced in his plagued city.

"*Profilatikos*. You buy. Here." He pointed to the lit cigarette kiosk on the corner.

"No! *You* buy," Ray said, the facetious smile back in place but genuine alarm in his heart.

"You," the boy insisted, stepping into the shadows of a building.

Now all of his teenage qualms did come rushing back. He felt his fear of and fascination with the prophylactics dispenser in a Kentucky filling-station toilet he'd glimpsed once during a family trip through the Smokies. Or he remembered the time when he'd helped his mother turn back the covers for a married couple who were visiting them, and he'd seen under the pillow the raised circle of the rolled rubber in its foil wrapper. The very width of that circumference had excited him.

He said the word to the impassive middle-aged woman in the kiosk. She lowered her head on an angle, dropped her eyes, said, *"Ne,"* which means "yes" but sounds to English-speakers like "no." A second later she'd fished up a box that read, in English, "Love Party," above a photo of a woman in provocative panties, one nyloned knee resting on the edge of a double bed.

Why rubbers? Ray wondered. Has he heard of our deadly new disease way out here at the end of the world, in a country where there are only two recorded cases, both of whom were visitors to New York? No, he must have in mind the old, curable maladies. Or maybe he just wants to dramatize our roles. I don't mind. Rubbers are terribly 1958 Saturday night at the drive-in. Maybe he needs a membrane intact to suggest his own virtual virginity.

A moment later, Ray was pursuing the boy through deserted night streets under big trees, big laurels so dry their gray-green leaves had started curling laterally. Distant motorbikes were test-drilling the night. The turn-of-the-century mansions lining these blocks were dilapidated, shuttered, and unlit behind rusting wrought-iron balconies, although trimmed hedges proved at least some of them were inhabited. The smells of garbage on a hot night alternated with the smell of jasmine, at first sniff slightly sweet, then ruttishly sweet. The boy wouldn't walk beside Ray, although Ray thought it must look much odder, this strange parade. They turned right off the boulevard and walked up, up a hill through residential streets. The boy's Keds shone almost phosphorescently white in the dark. Ray was calculating how much money he had in his wallet, while in his heart, his suddenly adolescent heart, he was exulting: "George, I've escaped you, I've gotten away from you."

In one sense he knew he was a slightly sissified middle-aged New York muscle queen somewhat out of her depth. In another sense he felt he was the teenage debating-team captain in love again with Juan, son of a migrant Mexican worker who'd been brought to northern Ohio to pick fruit. The first confused conversation with Juan, the visit to the workers' compound, the smell of cooking chili, the sight of candles burning even by day before the tin shrine of the Virgin . . . The one thing certain was that whatever was going on in Crete came before or after George and precluded George.

As they walked along, the boy clicked a key chain, vestigial worry beads. Cats were everywhere, gliding in and out of shadows, daintily pawing black plastic garbage bags, slithering through gaps in fences, sitting on top of parked cars. Twice the boy stopped and scented the path—and now he looked like an Indian brave. Or so Ray thought, smiling at his own way of leafing through his boyhood anthology of erotic fantasies.

They reached what looked like a school-yard, dark and empty because it was summer and night, but otherwise like any school-yard in Ohio—broken concrete playing area, an orange metal basketball hoop dripping rust stains on to the wood backboard, peeling benches, a toilet with separate entrances for boys and girls, a high fence surrounding the whole. The boy scrambled over the fence in two quick steps up and a graceful pivot at the top. Ray followed fearfully, awkwardly ("Here, teach, lemme give you a hand"). The boy gave Ray his hand and produced his first real smile, as dazzling as a camel boy's (a new page in the erotic anthology flipped open). His skin was surprisingly warm and plush and there were no calluses on his palm. Homer had told Ray that if parents could afford the luxury, they preferred to shield their kids as long as possible from work. The boys, their adolescence extended well into their twenties, sat idly around the harbor at night, trying to pick up foreign girls (the sport was called *kemaki*, ''harpooning'').

When they ducked into the toilet, in the second that Ray's eyes took to adjust to the deeper dark, he walked by mistake right into the boy. They both gasped, the boy laughed, maybe a bit insultingly, his teeth lit up the room. Ray started to draw away but his hand had brushed against what could only be a big erection, ''big'' because of normal size; the boy's youth, the night, the danger, the fact he would be getting some money later on, all these things made it ''big.'' Ray noticed the boy had already unzipped his fly. Out of eagerness?

Ray wanted him to be eager.

And then Ray, a famous beauty in his own right, a perennial hot number, hard to please, easily spooked by a maladroit cruiser, pursued throughout his twenty years of gay celebrity by hundreds of equally beautiful men, that elite corps of flight attendants, junior executives, and models—this Ray (he was trembling as he knelt) knelt before what could only be white Jockey shorts, yep, that's what they were, luminous under undone fly buttons, tugged the jeans down a notch, pulled down the elastic waist of the underpants, and tasted with gratitude the hot, slightly sour penis. He whose conscience years of political struggle had raised now sank into the delicious guilt of Anglo fag servicing Mexican worker, of cowboy face-fucked by Indian brave, of lost tourist waylaid by wily camel boy. He inhaled the smell of sweat and urine with heady, calm pleasure. He felt like ET being recharged by spaceship transfusion.

His mouth had been dry with fear. Now the penis striking his palate drew forth a flow of water in the desert. His knees already ached where he knelt on the wet cement floor. He took the boy's limp, hanging hand and laced his fingers into his. He looked up to catch the glance, but his eyes were shut and his face blank, which made him look much younger and almost absurdly unintimidating. At a certain point Ray pressed the unopened rubber into the boy's hand. Like a child peeping through a keyhole, Ray continued to kneel to watch the boy breaking open the packet and methodically unrolling the rubber down the length of his penis. He got it going the wrong way, lubricated side in, and had to start over. Then the boy gripped him from behind and Ray felt the invasion, so complex psychologically, so familiar but still painful or pleasurable to accommodate, he couldn't tell which, he'd never known which. The boy breathed on his shoulder; he smelled of Kantaki Fried Chicken.

When Ray paid the boy, who aristocratically palmed the money without bothering to see how much it was, Ray used one of the few Greek words he'd picked up (this one at the laundry), *"avrio,"* the word for "tomorrow." The boy nodded, or rather did what Greeks do instead of nodding, he clicked a *tsk* between his teeth and jerked his head down, lowering his eyelids. He pointed to this spot, to the ground in front of them. Then he flashed ten and two fingers. "You like?" he asked, pointing to his own chest.

"Yes, of course," Ray whispered, thinking: These men . . .

He told the whole story at breakfast the next morning to Ralph, who was courteous enough to appear envious. After their yogurt and honey and the French-roast coffee Ralph was at such pains to secure, they moved into Ralph's studio with its one small window looking down to the sea and the lighthouse. The studio had little in it besides a rocking chair, an old battered desk, a small kitchen table freighted with tubes of acrylics, a big, heavy wood easel, and a rack for finished paintings. On the wall was a watercolor, poppies brilliant in a silky field of green and tan grasses. "Well, it's the only solution. For you," Ralph said.

Oh, he's turned his envy into pity, Ray thought, pity for me, the ticking time bomb, the young widow, but my only solution doesn't seem all that much of a hardship.

As Ray napped in the hot, airless, late afternoon he could feel a small painful spot inside him where the boy had battered into him and he smiled to feel that pain again. "Oy," he said to himself in Betty's accent.

That night the boy was there exactly on time. His hair was cleaner and shinier, and he'd shaved (not the mustache, of course). But he was wearing the same jeans jacket, although the T-shirt looked clean. They went through exactly the same routine, for Ray didn't want to scare him off. He wanted to build up a fixed routine, the same place, the same acts, the same price. Tonight the only innovation was that Ray pulled the kid's jeans and underpants all the way down below his knees and discovered that his testicles hadn't descended and that his ass was hairy with nice friendly fuzz. Nor did he have a tan line; his skin was naturally just this dark.

After sex the kid hopped over the fence and disappeared into the night and Ray walked home, downhill all the way through the silent, cat-quick, jasmine-scented streets. He felt sad and lyric and philosophical and happy as he'd felt as a teenager; since these encounters with the boy—strictly sexual—seemed a strangely insufficient pretext for so much emotion, he also felt something of a charlatan. Objective correlative. That was the term. T. S. Eliot would have said that his emotion lacked an objective correlative.

The next night he asked him his name, which he discovered was Marco. "You must remember," Homer said during the *volta* the following evening, "the Italians ruled Crete for hundreds of years. Maybe he has some Italian blood." And again Ray had to describe his "find," for that's how the connoisseurs judged Marco. "Not the usual harbor trash," Homer said, and he announced that he was going to start harpooning in the zoological gardens again, which he'd assumed had long since been fished out. Ray refused to divulge where he met Marco every night. He wanted one secret at least, his dowry, the smallest secret he could keep and give to Marco, and again he thought of that book and the way they'd compared marriage to death, or rather marriage to the exhumation of bones.

Once he asked Marco where he lived, but Marco only waved vaguely in the direction of the shantytown inland and to the west of the harbor. *"Spiti mou, to limani,"* Ray announced, which he thought meant "My house is on the harbor," but Marco only lifted an indifferent eyebrow, the counterpart to the Frenchman's weary *"Eh alors?"* when smothered by Americans' doggy effusiveness. That night, Ray broadened his area of conquest and explored Marco's taut brown stomach up to his chest. By now there were several white rubbers on the wet cement floor like jellyfish washed up on the bleak shingle.

By day, Ray would go swimming or motorbiking to old churches or ruined monasteries or hidden beaches, but all day long and during the endless evenings, he'd daydream about Marco. He bought a phrase book and pieced together Greek words for that night's rendezvous.

Once Marco asked Ray if he should bring along a friend, and Ray agreed because he thought Marco wanted him to. But the friend was a portly sailor ("Greeks go off early," Ralph had said, as though they were a temperamental triple-cream cheese, a Brillat-Savarin, say). Ray sucked them both at the same time, doing one then the other, back and forth, but his only pleasure was in imagining reporting it to the other Americans tomorrow. The boys seemed embarrassed and talked loudly to each other and joked a lot and Marco kept losing his erection and he sounded nasty and used the word *"putana,"* which surely meant "whore" in Greek as well as Italian.

Ray paid them both and was tempted to mutter *"putana"* while doing so, but that might queer the deal, so he swallowed his resentment (yes, swallowed that, too) and drew Marco aside and said *"Metavrio,"* which meant "the day after tomorrow" (*meta* as in "metaphysics," "beyond physics"). The delay was meant as some sort of punishment. He also indicated he wanted to see Marco alone from now on. Marco registered the compliment but not the punishment and smiled and asked, "You like?" pointing to himself, asked it loud and clear so the other guy could hear.

"Yes," Ray said, "I like."

As he walked home, Ray took a stroll through the zoological gardens, where there was also an outdoor movie theater. Inside, people sat on folding chairs and watched the huge screen on which a street-lamp had disobligingly cast the shadow of a leafy branch. Tonight he sat outside but he could hear the end of *Querelle,* of all things, dubbed into Greek and offered to the extended Cretan family, who chuckled over the perversities of northern Europe. In the closing sequence, Jeanne Moreau laughed and laughed a shattering laugh and the caged egrets dozing beside Ray awakened and started to chatter and call. Then the houselights came up, the families streamed out, for a moment the park was bright and vivid with crunched gravel and laughs and shouts, then car doors slammed and motorbikes snarled, the lights were dimmed and finally, conclusively, everything was quiet. Ray sat in the dark, listening to the awakened birds paddling the water, a leaf spray of shadows across his face like an old-fashioned figured veil. The jasmine gave off a shocking body odor, as though one were to discover a pure girl was really a slut.

Ray regretted his spiteful decision to skip a day with Marco. The depth to which he felt Marco's absence, and his anxiety lest Marco not show up at their next appointment, made Ray aware of how much he liked Marco and needed him. Liked him?

There was nothing to like, nothing but a mindless, greedy Cretan teen who was, moreover, heterosexual. Or worse, a complete mystery, a stranger, a minor tradesman with whom he was only on fucking terms.

Then Ray told himself he liked his own sense of gratitude to Marco, the silence imposed on them by the lack of a common language, liked the metered doses of sex fixed by fee and divergent appetites. He liked the high seriousness of the work they did together every night. He also liked stealing bits of affection from his co-worker, whose mustache was coming in as black and shiny as his eyebrows and whose chest (as Ray's hand had just discovered) was sprouting its first hair, this young man who would never love anyone, not even his wife, as much as Ray loved him.

One weekend Ralph went off on a yacht with a Greek collector of his paintings; they were sailing over to Thera and wouldn't be back till Monday. "Feel free to bring your child husband to the palace while I'm away," Ralph said as he pecked Ray on both cheeks in the French manner. And indeed that night Ray did say to Marco, *"Spiti mou,"* showed him the house keys, and led him through town, walking a few paces ahead just as on that first night Marco had preceded Ray. On the street of notions shops someone hailed Marco (*"Yassou"*) and talked to him, and Ray, smiling at his own quick grasp of things, didn't look back but turned the corner and waited there, in the dark. After all, it was a little town. And only last week a shepherd had discovered his son was getting fucked and had killed him, which Homer said most of the locals had considered fair enough.

Marco in his white Keds and Levi's jacket came treading stealthily around the corner, noble and balanced as a lion; he winked his approval and Ray felt his own pleasure spread over his whole body like the heat of the sun.

Marco was obviously impressed by the palace—impressed by its grandeur and, Ray imagined, proud that foreigners had furnished it with old Cretan furniture and folk embroideries.

Impressed? Nonsense, Ray thought, catching himself. Purest sentimental rubbish on my part. No doubt he'd prefer lavender Formica with embedded gold glitter.

Ray, who liked Marco and wanted to show that he did, felt a new intimacy between them as he led him into his bedroom. He gently pushed him back on the bed and knelt to untie the Keds and take them off, then the smelly socks. Then he made Marco wriggle out of his jeans; he started to pull the T-shirt over his head but Marco stopped him, though he, too, was gentle. Every one of Marco's concessions meant so much more to Ray than all the sexual extravagances of New York in the old pre-plague days—the slings and drugs and filthy raps.

Ray undressed himself. He wondered what Marco thought of him, of this naked adult male body which he'd never seen before. How old does he think I am? Does he admire my muscles? Or does my role as *poosti* on *parea* keep him from seeing me?

Ray worried that the whole routine—nakedness, a bed, privacy—might be getting a little too queer for Marco, so he was quick to kneel and start sucking him, back to the tried and true. But Ray, carried away in spite of himself, couldn't resist adding a refinement. He licked the inside of Marco's thighs and Marco jumped, as he did a moment later when Ray's tongue explored his navel. Strange that his cock seems to be the least sensitive part of his body, Ray thought.

When the time for the rubber arrived, Ray thought that surely tonight might make some difference, and indeed for the first time Marco gasped at the moment of his climax. Ray said, "You like?" and Marco nodded vigorously and smiled, and a young male intimacy really had come alive between them, glued as they were together, their naked bodies sweaty.

Almost instantly Marco stood and dashed into the bathroom, pulled off the rubber, and washed while standing at the sink. Ray leaned against the door and watched him.

In this bright light the boy looked startlingly young and Ray realized, yes, he was young enough to be his son. But his other feeling was less easy to account for. It was of the oddness that a body so simple, with so few features, should have provoked so much emotion in him, Ray. Clothes with their colors and cuts seemed more adequate to what he was feeling.

Once again Ray noticed that he was feeling more, far more, than the occasion warranted. No objective correlative. Ray took Marco up to the roof to see the panorama of the sea, the harbor, the far-flung villages, a car burrowing up the mountain with its headlights like a luminous insect. But now that the transaction was over, the tension between them had been cut.

The next night Marco came directly to the palace and Ray persuaded him to take off his T-shirt, too, so that now there was no membrane except the rubber between them. Before they got to the fucking part, Ray paused in his exertions and crept up beside Marco and rested his head on Marco's thumping chest. Marco's hand awkwardly grazed Ray's hair. Ray could smell the rank, ingenuous odor of Marco's underarm sweat—not old sweat or nervous sweat but the frank smell of a young summer body that had just walked halfway across town.

On the third and last night they'd have alone in the palace, Marco came up the steps hanging his head, not giving his hearty greeting: *"Ti kanes? Kala?"* He simply walked right into the bedroom, threw his clothes off, fell back on the bed, and with a sneering smile parodied the moans and squirmings of sex.

"What's wrong?" Ray asked. Marco turned moodily on his side and Ray was grateful for this glimpse into the boy's discontent. When he sat down beside Marco he could smell beer on his breath and cigarette smoke in his hair, though Marco didn't smoke. At last, after a few words and much miming, Marco was able to indicate that he had a friend who was leaving the next morning for Athens to begin his compulsory military service and the guy was waiting for him in a bar down below alongside the harbor.

Ray pulled Marco to his feet, gave him double the usual thousand drachmas, helped him dress, set tomorrow's date back in the school-yard, and urged him to hurry off to his friend. He had a half-thought that Marco understood more English than he was letting on. For the first time Marco seemed to be looking at Ray not as a member of another race, sex, class, age, but as a friend.

Friend? Ray laughed at his own naïveté. The boy's a hooker, he told himself. Don't get all moony over your beautiful budding friendship with the hooker.

After Marco had run down the steps, the thuds rattling the whole house, Ray was alone. Definitely alone. He walked to the balcony and looked down at the harbor, most of its lights extinguished, the last waiters hosing down the boardwalk. He put on his headphones and listened to George's telephone messages to Betty. "Hi, doll, this is Darleen, now a stylishly anorectic 135 pounds. The Duchess of Windsor was wrong. You can be too thin." Oh yes, four months before the end. "Hi, doll, I know you're there with the machine on watching "The Guiding Light." Can you believe that bitch Vanessa? Hi!" and a sudden happy duet of overlapping voices, since just then Betty picked up and confessed she had indeed been pigging out on the soaps and a pound of chocolates.

Ray snapped it off. "You must look out for yourself," George had said, and just now the best way seemed to be to forget George, at least for a while, to forget the atmosphere of dread, the midnight visits to the hospital, the horrifying outbreak of disease after disease—fungus in the throat, a bug in the brain, bleeding in the gut, herpes ringing the ass, every inch of the dwindling body explored by fiber optics, brain scanner, X rays, the final agonies buried under blankets of morphine.

Ray received a call from Helen, his boss, and her tinny, crackling tirade sounded as remote as the final, angry emission from a dead star. He had no desire to leave Xania. With Homer as his translator he looked at a house for sale in the Turkish quarter and had a nearly plausible daydream of converting it into a guesthouse that he and Marco would run.

He started writing a story about Marco—his first story in fifteen years. He wondered if he could support himself by his pen. He talked to an Irish guy who made a meager living by teaching English at the prison nearby in their rehabilitation program. If he sold George's loft he could afford to live in Greece several years without working. He could even finance that guesthouse.

When he'd first arrived in Crete he'd had the vague feeling that this holiday was merely a detour and that when he rejoined his path George would be waiting for him. George or thoughts of George or the life George had custom-built for him, he wasn't quite sure which he meant. And yet now there was a real possibility that he might escape, start something new or transpose his old boyhood goals and values into a new key, the Dorian mode, say. Everything here seemed to be conspiring to reorient him, repatriate him, even the way he'd become in Greece the pursuer rather than the pursued.

One hot, sticky afternoon as he sat in a café with a milky ouzo and a dozing cat for company, a blond foreigner—a man, about twenty-five, in shorts and shirtless, barefoot—came walking along beside the harbor playing a soprano recorder. A chubby girl in a muumuu and with almost microscopic freckles dusted over her well-padded cheeks was following this ringleted Pan and staring at him devotedly.

Ray hated the guy's evident self-love and the way his head drooped to one side, and he hated the complicity of the woman, hated even more that a grown-up man should still be pushing such an overripe version of the eternal boy. He really did look overripe. Even his lips, puckered for the recorder, looked too pulpy. Ray realized that he himself had played the boy for years and years. To be sure, not when he'd chronologically *been* a boy, for then he'd been too studious for such posturing. But later, in his twenties and thirties. He saw that all those years of self-absorption had confused him. He had always been looking around to discover if older men were noticing him and he'd been distressed if they were or weren't. He hadn't read or written anything because he hadn't had the calm to submit to other people's thoughts or to summon his own. George had urged him to buy more and more clothes, always in the latest youthful style, and he'd fussed over Ray's workout, dentistry, haircut, even the state of his fingernails. When they'd doze in the sun on Fire Island, hour after hour George would stroke Ray's oiled back or legs. Ray had been the sultan's favorite. Now he'd changed. Now he was like a straight man. He was the one who admired someone else. He wooed, he paid. At the same time he was the kneeling handmaiden to the Cretan youth, who was the slim-waisted matador. This funny complication suited him.

A journalist came down from Athens to Xania to interview Ralph for an Athens art magazine or maybe it was a paper. Since he was gay, spoke English, and was congenial, Ralph invited him to stay on for the weekend. The day before Ray was due to fly back to New York, he asked the journalist to translate a letter for him into Greek, something he could give Marco along with the gold necklace he'd bought him, the sort of sleazy bauble all the kids here were wearing. Delighted to be part of the adventure and impressed by the ardor of the letter, the journalist readily accepted the commission. Ralph arranged to be away for a couple of hours on Ray's last night and insisted he bring Marco up to the palace for a farewell between sheets. Covering his friendliness with queenliness, Ralph said, "How else can you hold on to your nickname, La Grande Horizontale?"

In the palace bedroom that night, just as Marco was about to untie his laces and get down to work, Ray handed him the package and the letter. Before opening the package, Marco read the letter. It said: "I've asked a visitor from Athens to translate this for me because I have to tell you several things. Tomorrow I'm going back to New York, but I hope to sell my belongings there quickly. I'll be back in Xania within a month. I've already found a house I'd like to buy on Theotocopoulos Street. Perhaps you and I could live there someday or fix it up and run it as a guesthouse.

"I don't know what you feel for me if anything. For my part, I feel something very deep for you. Nor is it just sexual; the only reason we have so much sex is because we can't speak to each other. But don't worry. When I come back I'll study Greek and, if you like, I'll teach you English.

"Here's a present. If you don't like it you can exchange it."

After Marco finished reading the letter (he was sitting on the edge of the bed and Ray had snapped on the overhead light), he hung his head for a full minute. Ray had no idea what he'd say, but the very silence, the full stop, awed him. Then Marco looked at Ray and said in English, in a very quiet voice, "I know you love me and I love you. But Xania is no good for you. Too small. Do not rest here. You must go."

Although Ray felt so dizzy he sank into a chair, he summoned up the wit to ask, "And you? Will you leave Xania one day?" for he was already imagining their life together in New York.

"Yes, one day." Marco handed the unopened package back to Ray. "I won't see you again. You must look out for yourself."

And then he stood, left the room, thudded down the front steps, causing the whole house to rattle, and let himself out the front door.

Ray felt blown back in a wind-tunnel of grief and joy. He felt his hair streaming, his face pressed back, the fabric of his pants fluttering. In pop-song phrases he thought this guy had walked out on him, done him wrong, broken his heart—a heart he was happy to feel thumping again with sharp, wounded life. He was blown back onto the bed and he smiled and cried as he'd never yet allowed himself to cry over George, who'd just spoken to him once again through the least likely oracle.

Bearing Witness

George Whitmore

"Bearing Witness" was the second of two articles that George Whitmore wrote for The New York Times Magazine. *The articles became part of* Someone Was Here, *his last book and one of the first, and still one of the best, accounts of the human aspects of the AIDS epidemic. Whitmore was particularly suited for this article not only as a person with AIDS and a writer with long experience as a journalist, but also as a social worker with Planned Parenthood and the Citizens Housing and Planning Council. Whitmore died of complications resulting from AIDS in April 1989.*

> And we go,
> And we drop like the fruits of the tree,
> Even we,
> Even so.
>
> —GEORGE MEREDITH
> "Dirge in Woods"

Three years ago, when I suggested an article to the editors of this magazine on "the human cost of AIDS," most reporting on the epidemic was scientific in nature and people with AIDS were often portrayed as faceless victims. By profiling a man with AIDS and his volunteer counselor from Gay Men's Health Crisis, I proposed to show the devastating impact AIDS was having on a few individual lives. It had certainly had an impact on mine. I suspected that I was carrying the virus and I was terrified.

Plainly, some of my reasons for wanting to write about AIDS were altruistic, others selfish. AIDS was decimating the community around me; there was a need to bear witness. AIDS had turned me and others like me into walking time bombs; there was a need to strike back, not just wait to die. What I didn't fully appreciate then, however, was the extent to which I was trying to bargain with AIDS: If I wrote about it, maybe I wouldn't get it.

My article ran in May 1985. But AIDS didn't keep its part of the bargain. Less than a year later, after discovering a small strawberry-colored spot on my calf, I was diagnosed with Kaposi's sarcoma, a rare skin cancer that is one of the primary indicators of acquired immune deficiency syndrome.

Ironically, I'd just agreed to write a book on AIDS. The prospect suddenly seemed absurd, but "Write it," my doctor urged without hesitation. And on reflection, I had to agree. I don't believe in anything like fate. And yet clearly, along with what looked like a losing hand, I'd just been dealt the assignment of a lifetime.

That I was able to take it on isn't as remarkable as some might think. Kaposi's sarcoma alone, in the absence of the severe opportunistic infections that usually accompany AIDS, can constitute a fortunate diagnosis. Many Kaposi's sarcoma patients have lived five years and beyond. Although my own disease has steadily accelerated, I'm one of the very lucky ones. Although increasingly disabled, I haven't even been hospitalized yet.

I'm also hopeful—though it gives me pause to write that, since I value realism and pragmatism over the ill-defined "positive attitude" I'm often counseled to cultivate. Last summer, I began taking the antiviral drug AZT in an experiment to test how it works in people with Kaposi's sarcoma. Partly because testing has been completed on so few other drugs in this country, AZT or something like it is our best hope for an AIDS treatment and, in spite of possible severe side effects, it has already been shown to benefit other categories of people with AIDS. I have no doubt that, administered in combination with drugs that boost the immune system, antiviral drugs like AZT will eventually prolong the lives of countless people like me.

But I don't want to give the impression that I'm patiently waiting, hands folded, for that day to come.

When I began taking AZT, I bought a pill box with a beeper that reminds me to take the medication every four hours. The beeper has a loud and insistent tone, like the shrill pips you hear when a truck is backing up on the street. Ask anybody who carries one—these devices insidiously change your life. You're always on the alert, anticipating that chirp, scheming to turn off the timer before it can detonate. It's relentless. It's like having AIDS. At regular intervals your body fails to perform in some perhaps subtle, perhaps not new, but always alarming way. The clock is always ticking. Every walk in the park might be your last. Every rent check is a lease on another month's life. The beeper is a reminder that with chronic illness, there is no real peace and quiet and no satisfaction, not without the sure prospect of complete health. Paradoxically, this same sense of urgency and unrest enabled me to write my book.

Needless to say, reporting on the AIDS epidemic from my particular point of view has had its advantages and handicaps. My book includes my original article on Jim Sharp, then thirty-five, a New Yorker with AIDS, and Edward Dunn forty-three, his counselor from Gay Men's Health Crisis, both white gay men, like myself. But it also profiles men, women and children, black and brown, in all walks of life, who have been touched profoundly by AIDS, too. We are more alike than not. If I felt a special affinity for Manuella Rocha, a Chicano woman in rural Colorado who defied her family and community to nurse her son at home until his death in 1986, it was in no small part because I recognized in her eyes the same thing I saw in my own mother's eyes the day I gave her the news about myself. If I was scared sitting for hours in an airless room in the South Bronx with a bunch of junkies with AIDS, it wasn't because I was scared of *them*. It was because their confusion and rage were precisely what I was feeling myself. The journalist's vaunted shield of objectivity was of little use at times like those. On the contrary, what often counted most wasn't my ability to function as a disinterested observer, but my ability to identify with my subjects.

Although some reporters might, I didn't need to be told what it feels like to wait a week for biopsy results or to be briefed on the unresponsiveness of governments and institutions. Nor did I need to go out of my way to research issues of AIDS discrimination—not after I was informed at my neighborhood dental clinic, where I'd been treated for years, that they would no longer clean my teeth.

So, there's much to be said for subjective truth. Nevertheless, I worried for a long time about the morality, even the feasibility, of producing a documentary-style piece of reportage like the one I'd contracted for—that is, without literally putting myself into it, in the first person. It wasn't until I found myself alone in a cabin in the woods, poised to write, that I began to confront just who that "first person" had become.

* * *

The MacDowell colony in Peterborough, New Hampshire, is a collection of quaint artists' studios, each isolated from the others on 450 acres of dense woodland. Since 1907, the colony has served as a retreat and a safe haven for generations of writers, composers and other artists, and it surely did for me. But it would be a lie to say that people who go there can escape; up there, in the woods, the world is very much with you. Up there, away from my constant lover and loving friends, at a certain remove from the Catherine wheel of death and mourning that my life in New York had become, off the treadmill of interviews and deadlines, I came face to face with everything I'd successfully evaded about AIDS.

Having it, for instance. Before I went to New Hampshire, it was still possible, even necessary, to pretend that in some essential way I didn't have AIDS in order to keep working. As far as I know, no one I interviewed during the course of researching my book knew that I had AIDS. And the telltale marks hadn't spread to my face.

My body. I hadn't looked at it much.

Before I left for New Hampshire, at the Passover seder with my lover Michael's family, we took turns reading the Haggadah in booklets illustrated with line drawings. When we reached the page with the plagues God brought down on the Egyptians, there was a locust, there was a dead fish with X's for eyes, there was the outline of a man with dots all over him, signifying boils. I stared at the cartoon of the man with the boils. I knew Michael, sitting next to me, was thinking the same thing. My body was like that now. I'd had three lesions twelve months before. Now there were three dozen.

One day in New Hampshire, in the shower, I looked at my body. It was as if I'd never seen it before.

A transformation had taken place and it was written on my skin. When I met Jim Sharp three years ago, I have to confess, I could only see a dying man. A chasm had separated me from him and the other men with AIDS I interviewed for the *Times*. Even though they were gay, even though most of them were my own age, each one of them remained safely at arm's length. But now that chasm was breached and there was no safety.

Grief, despair, terror—these feelings easily come to mind when AIDS does. They threatened to engulf me when I began writing my book. But what about anger?

When you have AIDS, the fear and loathing, the black paranoia, the everlasting, excruciating uncertainty of AIDS colors everything. When you walk down the street with AIDS, everything in your path is an aggravation, an impediment, a threat—for what in your life isn't now? A cab over shoots the crosswalk. Someone at the head of the line is arguing with the bank teller. All the petty frustrations of urban life get magnified to the limit of tolerance. Not even the infirm old man counting out his pennies at the newsstand is exempt from your fury—or perhaps especially not him, for in the prime of life aren't you becoming just that: elderly and infirm?

It wasn't until I returned to the transcripts of my original interviews with Jim that I realized that he—a voluble ad man with a wicked sense of humor, a short fuse and an iron will to live—had a special gift for anger, and Jim was now speaking for me, too.

Anger, life-affirming anger was the lesson Jim, Manuella Rocha and that room full of addicts taught me. Without it, I couldn't have written about the ocean of pain and loss that surrounds us without drowning in it.

My article about Jim Sharp and Edward Dunn was a portrait of two strangers united in adversity. In 1984, after his lover died of AIDS, Edward felt compelled to volunteer at Gay Men's Health Crisis. He couldn't, he said, sit passively on the sidelines while the epidemic raged on. Jim's case was the first one assigned to Edward when he finished his training as a crisis counselor. It was Edward's job to help Jim negotiate the labyrinth of problems—medical, financial, legal—that an AIDS diagnosis entails. In time, they became remarkably good friends as well.

An intensely private person, Edward was willing to expose himself in a series of grueling interviews because he was, I think, desperate to make a difference. The sole stipulation he attached to our work together was that his lover be given a pseudonym. Edward wanted to spare "Robert" 's family—who had never been able to acknowledge their son's homosexuality, even unto death—any possible hurt.

Soon after the article came out, Edward brought me a gift. It was a little teddy bear—a nice ginger-colored bear with a gingham ribbon tied around its neck—and I didn't know quite what to make of it. But Edward explained to me that he often gave teddy bears to friends, as they represented warmth and gentleness to him. Later, he asked me what I was going to name mine.

"I hadn't thought of naming it . . . "

"Oh, you have to name him," Edward said.

"I don't know, what do you think?"

"I thought you might call him Robert."

That summer, Jim, a transplanted Texan, moved back to Houston from New York. Then, Edward moved to Los Angeles, saying it was time to begin a new life. Perhaps grandiosely, I wondered if our interviews hadn't played a part in Edward's decision to leave the city— that perhaps they'd served as something of a catharsis or a watershed.

Over the next year and a half, Robert the bear sat on the bookshelf in the hall and only came down when the cat knocked him down. Every once in a while, I'd find Robert on the floor, dust him off and put him back on the shelf. I felt vaguely guilty about Robert. I was no longer in touch with Edward.

It has been called "the second wave" of the AIDS epidemic. Its casualties include, in ever-increasing numbers, drug abusers, their wives and lovers, and their babies. I knew one of those babies.

I first saw Frederico—this is not his real name—one gloomy day last March, in the pediatrics ward at Lincoln Hospital in the South Bronx. Room 219, where Frederico was kept out of the way, is down the hall from the nurses' station. Not many people pass by its safety-glass windows. I doubt that I would have known Frederico even existed had I not been told about him by Sister Fran Whelan, a Catholic chaplain at the hospital.

Sister Fran, a petite woman with a neat cap of salt-and-pepper hair, was instrumental in getting me permission to visit Lincoln to observe its "AIDS team." For a few months, I sat in on meetings, went on rounds with its members, interviewed patients and health-care workers, and attended the weekly support group for people with AIDS.

In the early years of the epidemic, when Sister Fran, a member of the Dominican Sisters of the Sick Poor, began working at Lincoln, there were no more than one or two people with AIDS in the hospital at any given time. By last winter, there were always more than two dozen, with dozens more on the outpatient rolls. Virtually all of the AIDS patients at Lincoln, a huge municipal hospital, were heterosexual, virtually all were black or Hispanic. Although blacks and Hispanics account for some 20 percent of the United States population, they now represent, nationwide, 39 percent of those with AIDS. In the Bronx, rates of AIDS infection are believed to be among the highest in the nation. Currently, one out of forty-three newborn babies there carries antibodies to the HIV virus, indicating that their mothers were infected.

When I first saw him, Frederico was two and a half years old and had been living at Lincoln for nine months. His mother, an alcoholic and former drug addict, had apparently transmitted the AIDS virus to him in the womb. The summer before, a few weeks before Frederico's father died from AIDS, his mother had left him in the hospital. Then she died of AIDS, too. From then on, Frederico was a "boarder baby," one of about three hundred children living in New York City hospitals last March because accredited foster homes couldn't be found for them. Frederico happened to be disabled—he was born with cerebral palsy in addition to his HIV, or human immunodeficiency virus, infection— but lots of other children who were no longer ill and had no handicaps remained in hospital wards indefinitely.

Frederico's only visitor from the outside was a distant relation, a Parks Department worker named Alfred Schult who came to the hospital religiously, on Tuesdays and Sundays. Frederico's mother had been, Mr. Schult later told me, "the daughter I never had." When she died, Mr. Schult sent a telegram to her widowed father in Florida. The telegram wasn't returned but it wasn't answered, either. Frederico's father's mother, who lived in the Bronx, visited him in the hospital once, I was told. She had custody of Frederico's five-year-old brother, whom she'd sent to Puerto Rico to live with relatives. But no one in Frederico's father's family was willing to take Frederico. Nor was Mr. Schult, ailing himself, able to.

At two and a half, Frederico couldn't talk. He couldn't sit up or stand. He couldn't hold a bottle. Since he'd never had any of the cancers or opportunistic infections that spell AIDS, his official diagnosis was AIDS-related complex, or ARC. He had not, however, escaped the stigma of AIDS. Sister Marie Barletta, his patient advocate at the hospital, had to argue long and vigorously with authorities and submit reams of paperwork to get Frederico into a rehabilitation daycare program elsewhere. Unfortunately, just when he was about to go to day care, Frederico got a temperature, so day care was postponed.

The hospital personnel and the volunteers who held and fed Frederico did the best they could.

The day Sister Fran took me to see Frederico, he was sleeping. We stood side by side, peering into his crib.

That day, he was wearing mitts made of stretch-knit bandage material knotted at one end and fastened around his wrists with adhesive tape. These were to keep him from scratching himself or pulling out tubes; sometimes Frederico had to be fed formula through a nasal-gastric tube taped to his cheek and nose, and sometimes he had to be given antibiotics intravenously.

The nurses on Frederico's floor noticed that he picked up everything, every little fungus, every little infection.

Stuffed animals were lined up at the head of Frederico's crib. A musical mobile of circus animals in primary colors was fastened to the headboard. A heart-shaped balloon with the words ''I Love You'' was tethered to the rail. Frederico was propped up in an infant carrier in the crib, facing a blank wall with a bed-lamp on it and a red sign that said NO SMOKING/NO FUMAR.

I stood next to Sister Fran, looking at Frederico. I heard a ringing in my ears. I almost bolted out of the room. Somehow, I kept my feet planted where they were on the floor.

I'd seen eyes unblinking from lesions. I'd spoken into deaf ears. I'd held the hand of a dying man. But nothing prepared me for this.

Frederico was beautiful. In his sleep, he expelled little sighs. His eyelids twitched. He was very fair, with light brown curly hair. His skin was translucent. You could see violet veins through the skin of his eyelids.

I wanted to snatch him out of his crib, snatch him up and run away with him. It was all at once horribly, cruelly clear that I wanted for Frederico what I wanted for myself, and I was powerless.

Later, walking down the hall beside Sister Fran, I struggled to retain my composure.

''It's good the nurses saw you with me,'' Sister Fran was saying. ''Now you can come visit him lots, whenever you like, and there'll be no questions.'' Sister Fran has her ways. She knew I'd come back.

And I did, more than once. I held Frederico in my arms. He smelled like urine and baby powder, and he was quite a handful. He squirmed in my arms. I was a stranger. He didn't know me. He wanted to be put down.

The day I first saw Frederico, when Sister Fran was distracted for a moment, I took Robert the bear out of the plastic bag I was carrying and set him down among the other stuffed animals in the crib. I had felt I shouldn't come empty-handed. I knew Edward would approve. What I didn't know was that Edward had AIDS and would die before the year was out.

* * *

Irony of ironies, Jim outlived Edward, the counselor sent to aid him in his affliction.

Today, Jim lives in a modest bungalow house on a tree-lined street in Houston, where I visited him last June. He's something of a celebrity and has served on the board of the local AIDS foundation. He spends lots of time every day on the phone, dispensing comfort and advice to other people with AIDS. Among his other distinctions, Jim is probably the only man with AIDS in Texas who has lived through the mandatory two-year waiting period there to collect Medicare.

As we sat talking in Jim's living room, I noticed, on the mantelpiece, the stuffed piranha Edward once brought back from Brazil and gave to him, joking, "This is what you look like when you don't get your way."

I remember vividly my reaction to the piranha, when I first interviewed Jim in New York three years ago—with its slimy hide and repulsive grin, it was the perfect image of AIDS to me. Now it seemed strange to see it in a living room in Texas, alongside all the ordinary things people accumulate. Still fearsome, still bristling with malevolence, the piranha had nevertheless somehow grown familiar, almost domesticated, like the gnawing terror Jim and I and thousands like us have had to learn to accommodate. Every time he has to go to the hospital, Jim told me, he takes along the piranha. It's a kind of talisman.

A week after I got back from Texas, Mr. Schult called to tell me Frederico was dead.

Things had been looking up for Frederico. Sister Barletta had finally gotten him into day care. The agency had placed him in a foster home. But on his second night outside the hospital, inexplicably, Frederico turned blue. By the time the ambulance arrived, he was dead. And for some reason, I was told, the emergency medical service didn't even try to revive him.

I went to the funeral parlor. The long, low, dim basement room in East Harlem seemed full to overflowing with grieving women—Sister Barletta, the women from Frederico's day-care center, nurses and volunteers who'd taken care of Frederico in the hospital—all of them asking why.

Frederico's body lay up front in a little coffin lined with swagged white satin. He was dressed in a blue playsuit with speedboats on it.

"You dressed him in a playsuit," I said to Mr. Schult, at my side.

"And now he's at play," Mr. Schult sobbed. "He's romping in heaven now with Jesus like he never was able to down here."

I held Mr. Schult's arm tightly until the sobbing passed. I couldn't help but notice, the coffin was too small for the top of the catafalque. You could see gouges and scrapes and scars in the wood in the parts the coffin didn't cover. I looked down into the coffin, at the body beyond help. I agreed aloud with Mr. Schult that Frederico was in heaven now, because it seemed to make him feel a little better.

I don't know why, but I always thought Frederico would live.

The Symmetry!

Felice Picano

Felice Picano continues to explore and hone his craft. His newest novel, Like People in History, *is a large work that stretches over a long period of time. "The Symmetry!" is part of the first chapter, exploring the tension not only between pre- and post-AIDS generations of gay men, but also between different styles of post-Stonewall sexuality.*

"Are you sure?"

The last thing I was was sure.

"Are you sure about this?" Wally repeated.

I must have looked dumbstruck, because he went on: "Going up there? Now? Tonight?"

That at least was a question I could answer.

"We've *got* to go up there," I said. "It's Alistair's birthday!"

We were standing in the lobby of Alistair's building, the last shafts of a cerise sunset reflecting off the Hudson and somehow managing to obliquely strike this one marble wall. It's not the grandest building Alistair has ever lived in, nor was the man in uniform behind the desk the most pretentious I'd ever dealt with for Alistair's sake, but he was tall, with skin the color of whole nutmeg, and quite stately in that Russian-green uniform and he was quite ready to, at any minute, either sneer at us or call some janitorial person to sweep us out.

"We're going up!" I said, with tons of pseudo-decision.

"Name?" the man in uniform asked, although he'd had me tell it a dozen times earlier that month.

"Sansarc," I replied. "Roger."

He picked up the desk phone—a faux-marble affair with scores of buttons matching his epaulets—and without looking at it impressively struck the correct number.

I moved Wally away from the desk far enough to say, "If we didn't appear at his forty-fifth birthday, Alistair would hunt us down through the streets of the city, through the alleyways and sewers and . . . ''

Behind me I heard the uniform mispronounce my name. Which whoever answered—doubtless The White Woman—evidently was used to, as the man in uniform hung up and said, as if I didn't already very well know, "16J."

"If *you* don't show up," Wally corrected me.

We walked through about a quarter mile of postmodernist interior décor to the elevators, pretty well disguised as fake ecru adobe. At the far end was a wall-sized mirror, enough for me to glance at what the building staff had seen and snorted at—two homosexuals in black denim with black leather Patrick sneakers and worn leather bomber jackets of slightly differing cut and shades of brown. Wally of course had his Miss Porter's School posture and his shock of auburn hair to set him apart. And his youth. And his beauty. Whereas I . . .

The elevator door opened and a mixed-gender couple in matching black skintight Lycra bicycle outfits—hers striped hot pink, his aqua— shoved their eighty-speed mobelium sprocketed-to-death machines at us until we were pinned against the far wall. They pointedly ignored us in their perfectly coordinated twenty-four-year-old blindness.

"Fucking breeders!" Wally shouted after them.

" 'Scuse me?" The male member of the duo turned around. Completely oblivious.

I pushed Wally into the elevator and, mercifully, the door shut.

Wally checked his widow's peak in the fish-eye corner mirror, then slid me against one wall and began to tongue-kiss me as though he were trying to ingest both my tonsils simultaneously. This of course was intended to shut me up and to incite any purple-haired woman with a Lhasa apso unfortunate enough to have rung for the elevator.

None rang, however, so I enjoyed having my epiglottis ravaged before he pulled away to the far wall and began to sulk.

"Getting excited about the action at Gracie Mansion?" I asked.

"Are you going to give it to him?" Wally asked back.

Neither of us was prepared to answer the other's question. So instead we smiled stonily at each other.

"You did bring it, didn't you?" Wally nudged.

"Them! Not it. Them. Sixty of them! Yes, I brought them."

"Wrapped in what? Some cutesy little malachite box in the shape of Minnie Mouse's vulva?"

The door opened at floor 16.

"It's none of your business."

Wally stood in front of the door, trapping me, keeping it from closing.

"You've made it my business over the past two weeks of breast-beating, moaning, sighing, outbursts, tears, and pacing the damned floor!"

"You're right, Wals. I've been a complete turd about it."

That admission so surprised him he let me slip out. I skipped down the hallway to the noise at 16J and rung the bell.

"I'm not staying," Wally whispered Hecate-like into my ear as the door was opened by Alistair's latest in a series of what he affectionately called his "amahs," one James Orkney Downes, a pale fattish man somewhere between thirty and Alzheimer's whom Wally called "Dorky" to his face and whom at home we referred to by Alistair's initial description of him as "The Last Truly White Woman in America."

"Oh, it's you," The White Woman intoned and moved aside to let us in. Somewhere from within we heard what sounded like Ustad Akbar Khan playing the Final Sunrise Raga. "He's over there, with the crowd." The White Woman politely lifted a snub nose to point.

Then, blessed by that muse of wit that sometimes descends even to the gutter, The White Woman looked at Wally's T-shirt—white block letters on a pure black background reading DIE YUPPIE SCUM!—and uttered, "That's cute."

I dragged Wally away before mayhem erupted, toward the group I assumed to be surrounding our host.

One hand searched like a living creature through a phalanx of backs ranged before us until fingertips touched my chin. The various backs between us were divided, and Alistair's face popped out, mostly eyes and cheekbones.

"Welcome to Mother Gin Sling's!" he shouted. Then, glancing seductively as he could at Wally, "Mother Gin Sling's never closes!"

The others were swept away and the two of us engulfed in Alistair's arm-and-leggy ambience. He gestured at a large fake Louis Quinze fauteuil, onto which he dropped.

"Dearest Cuz." Alistair smiled benevolently upon me, at the same time gesturing in the direction of two stools he wanted us to pull up and sit upon so as to be closer to him. "And you, Wallace, you shockingly handsome child stolen by my cousin germane out of your happy bassinet," gesturing for Wally to sit also. "How sweet of you to come celebrate with me. How beyond sweet!"

I am always surprised how Wally—who dishes Alistair to filth behind his back—simply basks almost openmouthed in his presence. Hypnosis, Wally always insists, and it is true that he usually snaps out of it, if not completely, then usually within five or ten minutes.

"How especially sweet of you," Alistair went on, "since I know you have Serious Business to attend to tonight. The demonstration. I know that you, especially, Wallace dear, must be itching to get out of this lumber room of deadwood and get over there with all your angry little friends."

I was checking Alistair over. He looked no worse tonight than recently. Indeed, somewhat better than lately. I decided he was wearing cosmetics.

"We can't stay long," I said for the two of us.

"Naturally," Alistair allowed. Then he took Wally's hand in his and put on what I've come to know as Sincere Personality #3. "Joshing aside. I think it's terribly important what you ACT OUT people are doing."

"ACT UP," I corrected. Wally was too transfixed by Sincere Personality #3 to notice the libel. Or to notice that those streaks of gray in Alistair's hair were gone, erased no doubt by The White Woman's liberal application of Loving Care mousse, Ash Blonde. . . . Not that I don't myself sometimes "touch up."

"We do appreciate it. Really we do," Alistair said. "We depend upon it at times to get through the day."

I thought, Now really, you've gone too far.

Wally, evidently still stupefied by whatever mesmeric pheromones Alistair was emitting, said, "We're doing it for ourselves, too."

"I'm doing it for the B.V.M.," I said. "I'm dedicating this entire action to her, you know. I'm wearing a blue shift under this, and at the crucial moment I'll strip and reveal it."

This is called "cutting through the shit with garden shears."

"Isn't Cuz a pill?" Alistair said, and laid a hand upon my knee. I couldn't help but feel it flutter there. And suddenly I realized what was different about him. The tic was gone. The bunched-up Guillain-Barré tic that had disfigured the left half of Alistair's face for weeks.

Replaced by this unceasing subtle shaking. A form of Parkinson's, I guessed.

I was about to ask Alistair about it, and to find out the clever little name he and The White Woman had given it, when we were all saved by the bell. Someone from Showbiz had just been admitted, and Alistair's sixth sense about The Rich and Glamorous went on full Red Alert. He removed his hand from my knee to pat his over-perfectly coiffed hair in preparation for Meeting.

I got up and grabbed Wally.

"Let's get a drink."

"Can't have any liquor on our breath," Wally insisted. "The marshals insist on that."

"Cream soda," I protested, "Cel-Ray!" None of which, I was certain, he'd ever heard of, growing up as he had somewhere in Montana.

"Tonic water and lime," Wally said to the bartender standing behind the cloth-draped table set up between the kitchen and living room. "Who the hell is Mother Gin Sling?"

"You had to be there," I said.

"Another one of your Alistair stories?" Wally asked with a hint of scorn. I wondered if he knew he had a blackhead. Probably not. He'd scream if he did, drag me into the john and insist I help get it out.

"A minute ago Alistair could have fed you a live baby and you would have gobbled it down without salt," I said haughtily. Then, "It's not another Alistair story. It's from a Josef von Sternberg movie. *The Shanghai Gesture.*"

"Dietrich?" Wally asked, and in that second I knew why I loved him—he tried, he actually tried to know about something that interested me, even though to someone his age it must seem chronologically about equal to the Parting of the Red Sea.

"Actually, it was someone named Ona Munson no one ever heard of before or since," I explained. "She was probably sucking Sternberg's boot tips at the time. But she made a terrific Mother Gin Sling. Victor Mature was Dr. Omar. Very handsome with oiled hair and a fez. Very decadent. He seduces Gene Tierney into gambling."

"Tierney ended up in a nut house, didn't she?"

I beamed with pleasure. I could take Wally anywhere. Sequoia on the shoulder or not.

"Not until after *Laura.* In this film she was unbelievably beautiful," I said, remembering the clean new print on videotape I'd recently seen.

Wally had meanwhile become aware that he was being eyed by the bartender, a model-actor-waitress of no discernible attractions. To be nice to me and nasty to the flirter, Wally grabbed and kissed me, perfectly in profile to the bar.

"So when are you going to give him your gift?" Wally asked.

"I thought . . . as we leave?"

"You're still not sure whether you should give it to him?"

"Of course, I'm not sure. They're not Sen-Sen!"

"You got them. You spent two weeks among some of the scrungiest faggots I ever laid eyes on, in dives even *I* wouldn't go near, for two weeks, collecting enough of them. And you're *not* giving them to him?"

"Look, Wally, I know you don't approve."

"I told you before—"

"Some smidgen of religion or something your grandmother once said or some item in *Senior Scholastic* or—"

"Whatever you do, just fucking do it. Okay!"

"So I can't blame you for not approving," I continued, unfazed. "But he came to me. He asked me. I couldn't refuse him. Could I?"

"You've never refused him before."

"That's not true."

"When?" Wally demanded.

"I have."

"When?"

"Sometime I'll tell you."

Of course he was 99 percent right.

"Well, I'm tired of the suspense," Wally said. "I'm not hanging around here for you. I'm leaving now. I'll be downstairs at Hunan Hell eating Hummingbird Scrota in Oyster Sauce."

I could have stopped him, but the truth was I was conflicted enough without having Wally's presence and disapproval to add to it.

And there was Alistair, still enthroned, surrounded by admirers new and old, common and semi-regal, and I didn't know when I could, or if I could, or even if I should give him the sixty electric-blue-and-red Tuinals with which he fully intended to end his life tonight.

"So how do you think he looks?"

I smelled The White Woman before I heard his words. An odor close to that of brand-new Naugahyde in a late-sixties model Chevy. Actually, I felt him before I smelled him. He's like one of those black holes in space: He absorbs everything around him for about a yard circular. On his approach, molecules shed their magnetic and electrical charges: It's depressing and draining, like the few minutes immediately preceding a spectacular thunderstorm. Except, in his case, the storm never arrives.

"He looks tarted up," I said.

"That's what he wanted."

"At least the tic's gone."

"Did you notice his hands? He can hardly use them. I have to cut up his food. Sometimes even feed him. He's got medicine for it, but he says it makes him so sleepy he calls himself Parko the Narko."

Voilà! The cutesy name I'd been waiting for.

"You're a saint, Dorky. You'll go to heaven with your shoes on. Bally oxblood wing tips," I specified.

"I don't mind. I'm—"

"—nothing. Alistair's everything," I finished the sentence.

"You're in a bad mood," The White Woman concluded without rancor, and swept his electron-removal off to de-Gauss someone else.

Well, we'd talked, and I'd been rude to him. As usual.

"Someone told me that absolute hunk is your lover."

The speaker was the bartender, mercifully silent until then.

"I don't get it," he went on, fatuous as predicted. "You're nothing special."

"I have a huge dick. Size of a small child's arm."

"You're kidding," he said, checking my crotch.

"Left it at home tonight. Actually," I intimated, crooking a finger for him to lean over the bottles and glasses and lemon wedges, "I do have a secret weapon."

"You do?"

"Seems that Socrates was right: Virtue does attract Beauty."

"Hu-uh?"

I breezed away into a corner where I could sip my vodka-less tonic and mope. As usual, someone located the record collection and put on Gloria Gaynor's first LP. In fact, everything so far tonight had been so mundane I felt in my pocket to make sure the Tueys—that alone made this night Significant and Different—were still there.

As usual. All of it as usual.

I found myself placed in a sort of cul-de-sac behind the enormous fake columns Alistair had installed a year ago and then had painted faux marble by a former trick, once a promising artist, now the beneficiary of some rehab program fund to "aid the arts" that Kuwaiti or

Afghani billionaires finance and, by the way, help some of their best former customers recover from decades of hard drugs. From here, the columns framing it all, I could see the party almost as though it were on stage.

Who knows how memory works? Neurologists have studied the physical and electrochemical aspects of the human brain for decades and think they've got some clues. But ask them why it is you can't find your car keys and yet can recall with absolute precision a letter you received when you were six and they'll shrug.

Due to whatever conjunction of synapse and neurons, as I stood there I remembered something Madame de Maintenon had reportedly said, quoted in some book or other I must have read in college. Maintenon, the powerful, manipulative, overly pious old mistress and secret wife of Louis XIV, spent most of her adult life within the palace at Versailles. A beautiful building still, but made even more special then by its newness and by the newness of its theme: The architect had designed it so that every single aspect was perfectly symmetrical. Which, artistic as it might be, did have drawbacks. One was drafts: Winter winds would slide between cracks and openings and under doors, and propelled by hard surfaces and little interference from the sparse furnishings in the yawning spaces would travel unimpeded the length of frigid corridors, chilled salons, and shivering chambers. It was in one such chamber, barely warmed by a gigantic fire in a vast ingle, that a visiting potentate tracked down La Maintenon and enthused, "The symmetry, madame! And imagine abiding *within* such symmetry!" To which the king's favorite had allegedly replied, I take it a bit icily, "You're right, sir! The symmetry! At times, one all but perishes from the symmetry!"

"Missing him already?"

I snapped to attention: Alistair, leaning close.

"Him who?" I asked.

"Whom else? Wallace the Red. I saw him vanish into the crowd and out the door like a sword through hot butter."

"He was hungry for Szechuan food."

"Bless his metabolism," Alistair said, with less irony than usual. "Indeed. Bless anyone for still *having* a metabolism! I was thinking of installing paramecia or something prevertebrate like that into my intestine so I might once again recognize what used to be called an appetite."

"You don't look that bad," I lied.

"You mean I don't have that I've-been-in-Auschwitz-and-I-managed-to-get-out look yet?" Alistair asked. "Babe Paley was wrong. You *can* be too thin. Give me a hand," he added, literally dropping a nearly fleshless and thus lightweight and fragile arm onto my shoulder.

"Where are we going?"

"The loo."

"What happened to whatshisname?" I asked as I steered Alistair into the hallway. "The star?"

"He left."

"How was he?"

"Flawless. He didn't once mention *It*," Alistair said.

"Is that good or bad?" I asked; these days one could never be certain whether one should or shouldn't. The epidemic seems to have developed an ever-metamorphosing construct of etiquette. I sometimes think there should be an Illness-Manners Crisis hot line you can phone to get the latest subtle twist.

"Good for him," Alistair explained. "He'd only say the wrong thing."

We'd gotten to the john, and I knocked hard enough to awaken anyone catnapping within.

"It's all yours," I declared, opening the door.

"Come in with me."

"It hasn't come to that, has it?"

"No, silly. I want you to fix my face."

Alistair's bathroom had always been large, but when he'd redone the apartment during a burst of unexpected energy, he'd enlarged it further by absorbing two closets; then he'd followed through the post-modern architectural theme of the building to what I considered illegal lengths. If the large living-dining era was post-Pompeii, the bathroom was late Dark Ages. The stall shower—big enough to hold a medium-sized dyers' guild—was in the color of and with that pudding-like texture of alabaster you see only up at the Cloisters. The floorboards had come from a twelfth-century Norman mill. The sliding doors were artfully mosaicked chunks of stained glass of the same period but from a Silesian monastery. The rest of the large room followed the motif: The fixtures looked like baptismal fonts, the walls were scattered with sour-faced Madonnas holding goggle-eyed infants against fields of ancient gold leaf, each set within their own little house—frames resembling nothing more than cowsheds behind which lurked cabinets for toiletries. Next to these floated antique mirrors of varying sizes, the bluish glass much impinged upon by thick frames filled with hordes of pouting, rather bony cherubim. It was into one of these that Alistair thrust his face.

"Hit those pin spots," he commanded. "The controls are inside that little baldachin right by your hand."

After some hit and miss, I found the correct button and Alistair's head was thrown into strong, white illumination.

He'd opened a cabinet and withdrawn two vials of ecru liquid.

"Where would we be without Cover-Up?" Alistair sighed, handing the two little bottles to me. "You'll have to do it for me. The way my hands shake I'll end up looking like Clarabell."

"You don't need it," I said. But of course in this light I could very clearly see he did. The White Woman had been far too stinting earlier and I could see three KS lesions already showing through his ministrations.

"Use the darker color in front, the lighter on my neck," Alistair said, as I chose and began applicating. "Old trade secret of the stars, that!" Alistair went on. "Keeps the wrinkles from showing under strong key lights."

His skin looked papery as a wasp's nest wherever a bone was prominent—on the bridge of his nose, at either eyebrow ridge, under his imperfectly shaven chin.

"Garbo teach you this?" I asked.

"Actually it was Bette Midler. Before she got it fixed, her nose bone bent like that road sign in Monterey spelling out 'Curves Next 120 Miles'! I watched her paint a line straight down it, and shade in both sides. Not that it was ever a petite button, but she made herself look like Esther the Queen redivivus."

"When was that?"

"Continental Baths. Seventy-two? Seventy-four?" Alistair slowly shifted the planes of his face in the mirror. "You're in love with that little schmuck, aren't you?"

"Hold still."

"I can tell. All the signs are there," Alistair said.

"Nefertiti, gone four thousand years, could tell," I said. "I mean, Wally's only been living with me over a year."

"Have you awakened in the middle of the night yet and wanted to strangle him in his sleep? That's the only way I've ever been certain I loved someone."

"There are less homicidal ways."

"None as certain," Alistair argued. "You're not bad at this. I guess it was all your zits that made you master of the makeup jar."

"I never had zits," I said. "You taught me how to do this."

"I did?" Alistair seemed amazed. "When?"

"When we were adolescents. We practiced on that pretty girl with all those beauty marks she hated. Judy something. In California."

"She married a maharaja," Alistair mused. "Or became a maharishi. I don't remember which. So are you and the little beast going to exchange rings in the Sheep Meadow and all that homo-tripe?"

"Wally would rather blow up Sheep Meadow," I said.

"He sort of reminds me of myself at that age."

"Come off it. At Wally's age all you wanted was your name etched on double glass doors on Fifty-seventh and Fifth."

"That's enough," Alistair said. "I don't want to look like Dietrich."

I pulled back a second, then placed my own face in the mirror next to Alistair's. Difficult to believe we'd once looked so alike. Oh, the structure was there, all right: the identical wide brows, the little dents at each temple, the long, somewhat aristocratic nose. But the lower part of my face was round—though not yet jowly—whereas his was pointed. And my lips were thinner. Features even the gauntness of his illness hadn't affected.

"You do!" I said, louder than necessary. "You look like Dietrich in the sixties in Paris. When she was wearing those silver sequined gowns they had to break several ribs to stuff her into and singing 'Lili Marlene' for the eleven-thousandth time during yet another of her innumerable farewell performances at the Paris Opera House."

"Shameless flattery," Alistair sniffed, but he preened, too.

He was busy making big lips at himself in the mirror and saying "Daw-a-ling" when he suddenly asked, "You did bring my gift?"

I turned away and began deliberately shoving the little brushes inside each vial of Cover-Up and carefully screwing closed each cap.

"Remember when my mother called us the Gold Dust Twins?"

"Your mother was a doll, but she saw things no one else did," Alistair said.

"Must run in the family. Remember Great-aunt Lillian? How she used you in her séances?"

"Did you bring my gift?" he repeated quietly but firmly.

"I brought it, but I still don't think—"

"What you think is inconsequential at this late date, Cuz."

"It's not that late."

"Be real for once. Nothing is working anymore."

"Nothing?"

"Doctor Jekyll says he recently discovered a T cell, and my Billy Rubin is about the same as that of an arctic sardine." He turned to me. "But do let's face facts. I spike a fever to 104 every other day. And it's already passed the brain-blood barrier and damaged my cerebral cortex. I can't remember anything anymore. Orkney's taken to attaching little yellow glue-on notes to things like salad forks and needle cases so we won't be *too* embarrassed."

"It's age. My own memory is—"

"Shut up and listen, Rog. My boats are burned," he said, carefully enunciating. "And I'm a big enough girl to realize it's time for a final Viking do. Shields inverted! Flames to the top of the mast! Floating out in Long Island Sound!"

I half collapsed on the toilet.

"Come on! Don't be like that!" Alistair said brightly. "We've planned this for weeks. Don't spoil it."

"I can't believe it's . . . over."

"Look on the bright side, Cuz. You'll soon be the last queen left in New York who necked at Le Jardin with the son of a President in Office."

"I never did that."

"You did too! Stephen Ford. Or was it Jack Ford? One of those Ford boys."

"Not me," I declared.

"Big beefy blond. Remember? Fran Lebowitz was at the next table, and as we entered you said, 'Don't let her see me,' even though she wouldn't have known you from Mighty Joe Young. Ultra Violet came over to her table with Jack or Steve or whomever Ford in tow, and he sat down next to you while she joined Fran and next thing I knew you two were gone. I later found you in the men's-room lounge pressed into the wallpaper doing the heaviest fully clothed petting act I've seen outside of Tijuana."

I remembered the incident, and the boy, but I still disbelieved him about it being one of President Ford's sons.

"If it is true," and I stopped him from interjecting, "who'll be around to remind me?"

"You'll remind yourself. You'll sit yourself down with magnums of Dom Pérignon and write your memoirs."

"I never did anything, and what I did I'll need you to remember."

"It would be fun if I remained as a tiny voice. Who was that pretty boy in Ovid? Tithonus? He became Aurora's lover and she managed to get him eternal life, but she forgot to ask for eternal youth too, and he shriveled away to the size of a cricket."

"Tennyson," I said. " 'The woods decay, the woods decay and fall.' Don't take them, Alistair!"

"Of course I'm going to take them. And you know what? I found these clever little things." He pulled out a little plastic packet of flesh-colored patches, each the size of a nickel. "Anti–Lupe Velez Syndrome patches," he said. "I place one on each pulse point on the back of my neck and these'll keep me from getting nauseated and looking like shit when they find the body."

"Does The White . . . Does Orkney know about this?"

"He'll go to sleep in his usual sublime ignorance and awaken to what I trust is only a tiny iota less ignorance tomorrow morning."

"What if something goes wrong? Shouldn't he know?"

"Be real, Cuz. He's one of those Vermont WASPs who'd cut open their bellies to keep their babies warm in winter. He'd never approve me escaping from one second of earthly suffering."

"Wally, too. We've argued over this all week."

"I'd think he'd want to see me out of the way!"

"He's conflicted," I temporized.

"Neither of them have suffered as you and I have, Cuz. Physically. Or ethically."

"And neither of them ever had as much fun."

"Or fought as bitterly."

"Or loved as hopelessly."

"Or—"

I hung on Alistair's breath.

"—Saw as many bad movies!" he exploded.

We both laughed till I said, "Or screwed as many pretty boys."

"Or been as badly screwed by as many pretty boys," Alistair completed the list. "One of whom was inconsiderate enough to have led us to this very moment."

My high spirits sank.

"Which is about to end as planned. You will give me my forty-fifth birthday present. Then kiss my well-cosmeticized cheek, and leave me. Forever."

He was serious now. Exhausted, too.

I stood up, dug into my deep pocket, and handed over the little package. It was wrapped in black paper with a narrow black ribbon.

"Happy forty-five," I said. And as he collapsed onto the toilet seat I'd just vacated, I kissed one of the cheeks I'd just made up.

"Thank you, Cuz. These wrappings! Couldn't you find anything with a skull-and-crossbone motif?" He ripped off the paper and held the metal palm-sized ebony-colored Sobranie cigarette box in one skeletal hand, then lifted its lid and said in a voice I'd never before heard out of him, "Ah, my hot-pink-and-electric-blue darlings!"

Alistair looked up at me as though surprised I was still there. "What are you waiting for? Go."

"I'm waiting for you to say something final to me."

"Make sure they play Ravel's *Mother Goose Suite* at my memorial service. The four-hand piano version."

"Oh, Alistair! That's not what I mean!"

He smiled an odd, crooked smile, doubtless twisted by the same Parkinson's that had affected his hands. "What's left to say? No, really, Cuz. What haven't we said? What haven't we *done* to each other?"

I left the bathroom. Left the apartment. Got into the elevator and descended.

When it arrived at the third floor and opened its doors for the blue-haired old woman with the beribboned dachshund to get in, she was treated to the possibly not-too-daily sight of a grown man soundly and methodically banging his head against the cleverly pre-aged wood paneling.

Gay Literature Today

Robert Ferro

Jordan Balter, a student at Oberlin College, conceived the idea of inviting the leading gay novelists of the time to speak on gay fiction. Three novelists, Robert Glück, Andrew Holleran, and Robert Ferro, gave talks over the years. Robert Ferro took this assignment seriously, as Michael Grumley's last diary shows, and he labored over this talk, whose text is presented here for the first time. Writing in the last year of his life, Ferro takes pains to place himself and his work in a tradition of gay writing.

A writer's perspective on gay literature, today as in the past, is different from that of those who publish, those in the market, those who read, or those in academia who, from a great height and after some long or short period of time, judge and consign the work either to the library or into the dustbin. In fact, gay literature—no longer new—has in recent decades been in such a state of becoming as to render any single view of it incomplete and undependable, save that of the purely personal. As a novelist I am best advised to ignore most conceptions of what gay literature may be, just as any writer had better ignore most of literature if he or she expects to get anything done. It is useful to understand the market, the reader, and even somehow academia, but in the end, literature—gay or otherwise—is never a question of perspectives or trends but of free creativity, individual art. Artistic genius may be defined in some way as the ability of an individual to find a way through dilemmas, the paradoxes of history, culture, human nature, life, sometimes with ideas that would have seemed to others unlikely or impossible or, in the case of gay literature, not in the best of taste.

From the gay writer's point of view, it is helpful, although not es-

sential, to place oneself within a context, even after inventing a world
of one's own, remembering of course that the writer's appraisal of his
situation is often wrong—wrong for his own reasons. In my view, what
is happening today—the context in which we work—has so changed
and will so continue to change as to foment a renaissance of activity
we consider a true movement, one of the important movements of the
century. Perhaps this renaissance appears clearer because it comes at
the end of a period of intense literary activity, a period that has seen
what some have called "the Death of the Novel" itself.

But "Death" in this slogan means change, not the end, and not, I
believe, the death of the novel but of the narrator. And it may be that
in the return of the narrator from his grave in the 1950s—a return
effected to retell properly and subjectively the inside story of homosexuality—that the novel form becomes at last either the coda to an
enclosed art form, or the greater prelude to what is to come: a renaissance of gay writing and the literature of the new age.

Gay literature today is the collective result of small and large forces,
old and new, and the choices of many individual writers. It is something new in dimension that is part of something very old, and is, in
this sense, today in a renaissance. For those now at work tie into earlier
accomplishments, consciously or not; most immediately as a consequence or reaction to those who came immediately before us; or on
the shoulders of those who connect us to an earlier but similar reality,
an earlier literature. Once this connection with the past is made, it
stretches back through history, most directly and immediately to the
Edwardians, but before that to the end of the Roman Empire on the
verge of Christian conversion in the third century, when a large gay
canon was published and circulated, and would, it was hoped, be included in the official Gospels of the Church. Of course, other choices
were made, and the precepts and spiritual ideas of a group called the
Gnostics—the Gnostic Gospels—were lost. For homosexuals and lesbians this was the exact point of expulsion from the Church. However,
a long and healthy tradition of homoeroticism existed all through the
Italian Renaissance, as art historian James Saslow has recently and
helpfully demonstrated, beginning with the seminal application of the
Zeus/Ganymede myth in the poetry and drawings of Michelangelo.
And most recently, the Edwardians provide us with a bridge to the
past—a connection to all that had come before—in the life and times
and fall of Oscar Wilde.

The history of gay literature reaches back to a different world, to a world in fact before literature. Gay history, to be properly understood, must be pursued back to a period before books, back to an ancient time before the Church, before the Bible, before monotheism, before Moses, practically before God. It is not my intention to trace seriously any of this today, except to say that gay literature is the result of many convergent cycles in history and the work of many people. It is a thread running through history, often broken, or lost between the lines, but always taken up again by individuals working on their own, either with a self-conscious knowledge of older traditions, or with an instinct for the truth of the matter which apparently is never completely lost; or because, from the beginning of human existence, homosexuality itself has never been far from the center of culture.

The low social status of homosexuals from the third century A.D. until the near past largely prohibited and discouraged the composition and publication of literature in which the homosexual was not depicted, in some specific way, as a victim. The literature of homosexuality has long centered on the myth of the victim who must die to assuage an intolerable moral guilt.

In 1969, a group of patrons at a New York gay bar called the Stone-wall replied with thrown bottles and resistance when police, as was routine, tried for the second or third time that night to shut the place down. It was the first time that anyone questioned their authority to harass homosexuals. Known now as the Stonewall Rebellion, this event marked the beginning of gay liberation, ushering in a period of unprecedented political and literary activity in the gay world. Most important, it marks a major shift in self-perception from the myth of the victim to activist. The ensuing twenty years have seen a general restructuring of the gay ethos by a growing army of writers whose work has helped to redefine the psychological, social, sexual, spiritual makeup of American gay people.

These writers—and I flatter myself to think I have been one of them—have done this primarily through the art of autobiographical fiction, on the theory that when a particular story must be told, invention may be superfluous, and even at times counter-indicated.

Autobiography has long been misrepresented in American fiction. It has often been considered the recourse of a limited imagination and, as such, writers have long suppressed or disguised that their writing was based not on imagination but on the facts of their own lives. This does not mean that autobiography is new to fiction; simply that within gay writing it has found new acceptance and utility. The relationship between the frankness of autobiographical fiction and fiction itself has changed. What is different now is the perception that one's own version of one's own life is any less valid or successful than the purely fictional product of the imagination. In other words, one writer's attempt to construct a reality from autobiography may then be no less fictional or inspired than an invented novel, but will, in certain respects, reflect the range and depth of a new personality in ways never attempted or achieved in fiction. It is through autobiography that we best investigate a taboo. It can be said that autobiography has been used by gay writers to fill in the gaps left by the removal from fiction of various negative and stereotypical myths. This is not to say that invention, within the autobiographical framework, cannot be manipulated into a vital role. For it has been the secondary directive of these writers, after telling their own stories, to invent new myths, new themes, for gay fiction, and this continues to be largely a question of inspiration and imagination.

As mentioned earlier, the death or decline of the narrator took place in the fifties, principally in the English novel, culminating in the work of writers like B. S. Johnson, whose disillusionment with fiction also crossed over into his private feelings, causing him eventually to take his own life. Johnson, whose publisher was apparently most cooperative, once published a novel with a hole cut through the center; another with interchangeable unnumbered pages. Johnson's work is the history of the narrator on trial. At the end of the trial the narrator is found guilty of incompetence and irrelevance, and is executed before our eyes. Meanwhile, in Paris, the vestigial remains of the French novel were being slowly beaten to death by Samuel Beckett. Again the idea is the same: futility and chaos, truth overwhelmed. It can be said of Western literature in this period that writers lost faith with a central idea that had been prevalent since the rise of the realist tradition in nineteenth-century France, of the possible encapsulization of truth, large or small, in fiction. This loss of faith was brought about by a failure of confidence, on the part of the writers themselves, to find a point of view from which the increasingly complex and bewildering implications and revelations of modern life could be truthfully, adequately, or even competently represented. In this new postwar chaotic world, a world of huge population growth and strange juxtapositions of cultures and ambitions, the concept of "Art as a Lie" was increasingly, obviously, inadequate. To the writers of the period it did not seem to be art but life that was the lie.

The resulting fiction and theatre of the period, epitomized in Beckett and Johnson, is a narrative constantly interrupting itself to the point of distrust and confusion—books without plot, without stories, without characters, devoid of point of view.

I will not make the case myself here but think a connection can be made between the death of the narrator and subsequent schools of American fiction: dirty realism, for instance, and what is now called *New Yorker* fiction—in which the quotidian is approached carefully and meticulously, and without particular emphasis.

American fiction today, with exceptions, seems the result of a philosophy of the limited in the face of the too great. It is the writer himself made small in reaction to the sudden revelation of the complexities of life, of nature and the cosmos—the overwhelming revelations of the moderns.

However, it has not been difficult for gay writers today to step lightly over all of his, and to seek out earlier models—in particular, in my view, the great nineteenth-century realists of England and France. For unlike those of other writers—intimidated and beleaguered by modern chaos and its plethora of possibilities—the problems of the gay writer have been all too clearly laid out and defined. In fact, these problems themselves constitute the first fresh ideas in literature in a generation, and, perhaps, in a hundred years. For it can be said that the moral barriers erected around the subject of homosexuality have remained standing even after those of sexuality itself were dismantled. And the effect has been to keep the whole theme of flesh untouched as an idea. In claiming this territory for our own, gay writers lay claim to something new. And in ignoring the subject, or avoiding it, we waste a unique and valuable resource—ourselves.

The resuscitation and return of the narrator in gay fiction is in fact a return to the early models of the great realistic novel of the late nineteenth and early twentieth centuries. It cannot be said that we have had a monopoly on this return, for others have managed to get their feet under them with regard to a new vision of the world that allows them a specific narrative point of view. Blacks, certain women writers, Jews—in fact, the return of the narrator has been effected by those with a story to tell, and for whom the particularized devices of realism are again useful. Flaubert said, *"Madame Bovary, c'est moi."* It is a motto easily applied to the workers of modern gay fiction, in which the teller of the tale is him- or herself.

My point is that no one else is qualified to do the thing justice, and as such the gay writer faces a responsibility relatively rare in modern fiction: commitment to an idea, to a truth that flies in the face of convention and persecution. It may seem to you, as young students of the novel, that the large spate of coming-out books in the seventies broke enough ground and ice for the next generation to slip through without incident. This perhaps might have been true before AIDS, perhaps not. But it is quite clear that the pendulum theory, of accomplishment and setback, of advance and retreat, is as applicable to literature as it is to law and social justice. In certain ways, the battle for the liberation has been fought and won; in others, it has amounted so far to little more than a few bloody, and rather private, skirmishes.

It is not surprising or profound that the age-old enemy both to gay literature and homosexuality has been the same: homophobia. For if there is a single irreducible message to the literature of homosexuals it is that homophobia is the aberration, not homosexuality. Or, put another way, it will perhaps have been the lesson of our age, both in literature and religion, that there are so many different kinds of people in the world and that no one of them is any better than anyone else. Disparate types from the far corners of the world thrown into a single room, or into a single bed, seem to have been the mise-en-scène of the postmodern world. And discrimination, racism, anti-Semitism, misogyny, misandry, homophobia—these are failures of the human spirit, of the human soul and psyche. Religion has so far failed to rid us of these things; to some it appears that religion has only made them worse. Another topic for another day. But it may be in literature, as in the past, that the lessons of the future are to be learned.

Any course in the gay novel—and there should be such an offering in every college curriculum in the country—would name as our literary forebears the same eight or ten great homosexual writers, some living, some dead: Baldwin, Burroughs, Williams, Genet, Isherwood, Forster, and a few others. It is a rich list steeped in literary and moral bravery: *Another Country, Giovanni's Room, Naked Lunch, Our Lady of the Flowers, A Single Man, Maurice.* Homosexual literature is measured by these artifacts, assembled in the last fifty or sixty years in a still growing body of work comparable in quality and cohesion to any movement of the century.

As indicated, the central myth governing and informing homosexual literature of the twentieth century, and certainly dominating the novels I have listed, has been the myth of the victim, the martyred homosexual. In fact, it is this myth—which by its presence or absence in twentieth-century literature, before or after Stonewall—which defines it as homosexual or gay. At the center of the myth is the idea that the homosexual is doomed, and in this century few homosexual heroes of novels have survived. He is doomed by the weight and force of his own moral guilt in the eyes of society. This imagined moral guilt, based on a two-thousand-year-old conflict with the male-dominated Judeo-Christian ethic, is the basis for one of the last lingering aberrations, homophobia, and it is within the context of homophobia that this myth has been generated and perpetuated.

If there is one historical figure who epitomizes the victim myth it is the great poet, aesthete, playwright, aphorist, and novelist Oscar Wilde, leader and inspiration of the English Aesthetic movement, an early gay movement. Oscar Wilde is the pivotal figure in homosexual literature, not only for his work but also for his life, which qualified him—some would say doomed him—to this position and fate. Wilde was arguably the most important and certainly the most visible artist of his time, with perhaps only Yeats challenging this position. The Victorians had been the first and only people in Western society to discuss sex openly and publicly. The celebrated and scandalous sex trial, *Oscar Wilde v. the Marquess of Queensbury*, was the occasion on which they brought the subject up. It both ruined Wilde and established him at the center of the myth of the victim.

Here is a passage from a recent *New York Times Book Review* by the novelist Peter Ackroyd:

> *But it was not just the bravura of Wilde's self-expression that gave him such a hold on his contemporaries. It was something much more profound and perhaps more dangerous, for, if he was a man of genius, he was one because he came to embody the obsessions of his own period. He said of himself, "I was a man who stood in symbolic relation to the art and culture of my age," but it was both his blessing and his eventual tragedy that the age itself might most aptly be termed fin de siècle. Since we are now entering an equivalent period, perhaps we are in the best position to understand that joy in artifice and parody, the celebration of style and pastiche, that mockery of previous values, which such a time seems to encourage. In Wilde's lifetime the end of "Victorianism" (and all that it had come to represent) was in sight, but nothing had come to take its*

394 / Robert Ferro

> *place: it was a time of spiritual, moral, social and artistic chaos, when even the most formidable conventions and the firmest convictions began to crumble, to slide and eventually to dissolve. In many ways it was a worn-out society, theatrical in its arts, theatrical in its life, theatrical even in its devotions. It happened to be Wilde who defined both the conscience and the consciousness of the artist at a time when all the other values were thrown into doubt. Indeed, it was from the wreck of those values that he tried to save the concepts of beauty and pleasure.*

Moreover, Wilde's only novel, *The Picture of Dorian Gray*, called the only French novel written in English, is the connection between the English novel and the realist tradition of nineteenth-century France which dominates Western literature throughout the twentieth century, and which with the return of the narrator in modern gay fiction is the early model for much work being done today. In his audacity, in his inability either to hide or abnegate his responsibilities—to himself or his art—and as the most visible proponent of what Edward Carpenter and others called Uranian philosophy, Oscar Wilde was a logical choice for the martyrdom required by Victorian morality, once its austere attention had been drawn by Wilde himself to the subject of homosexuality. Judeo-Christian morality, the assumption of Wilde's guilt in the eyes of God, was the basis of the trial, as it has been the basis of homophobia throughout the history of Christianity. For the ensuing hundred years, until the literature of the post-Stonewall era in the 1970s, the myth of the homosexual as victim has held dominion. It still lies at the heart of many novels dealing with the subject, from the First World War all the way to the age of AIDS.

It would appear that the primary argument today in gay-studies circles is the discussion of the legacy of the Essential poets—Blake, Whitman, Wilde—and the development of the Uranian philosophy of Edward Carpenter and others, which posited a magical quality developed in those who are freed from the constraints of conventional human response, and who find in themselves a sympathy with what we would call the mystical. This is a pre-Judeo-Christian notion, referring to what is called the Old Religion, or paganism, which it was the early and continuing goal of Christianity to eradicate. Essentialism is in many respects the vestiges of that Old Religion, based not on a militaristic patriarchy but on the permanent sensibilities of matriarchy, including shamanism and the worship of the White Goddess, the center of the first cults and the first religion. By this view, the history of religion is the history of the transfer of the control of society from woman to man, from matriarchal to patriarchal system. Under the former, those instincts which Essentialists marked for value were treasured and developed. Under the later patriarchal system they have been considered as threats and systematically eradicated.

The alternative view to Essentialism is Constructionism, which holds that we are what society makes of us in any given age, rather than what we have, under Essentialism, has always been within ourselves and can be again.

E. M. Forster is the time bomb gay literature set in 1913 and exploded in our day with a great novel called *Maurice*, which is very much the image of homosexuality that modern society is prepared to accept and the point to which gay people have developed.

There has always been a lag between the pronouncements and discoveries and advancements of a minority group, and the opinion in which that group is held by everyone else. In our case I would have thought that lag amounted to something like twenty or thirty years, but Forster and others, including Wilde and Carpenter and most especially the Essential poet Walt Whitman, have shown us that this lag may be far longer—as much as eighty or one hundred years. It is Forster who takes from Wilde and the English Aesthetes the visionary, romantic ideals of the Essentialists and transforms them into concepts that a nation might sit down and discuss over coffee. *Maurice* demonstrates as clearly as any novel of the century how little these issues have changed in sixty years.

Forster is an Essentialist in his belief in the survival of the homosexual, and in *Maurice* he was generations ahead of his time. Forster's belief is based largely on old instincts of anti-militarism, of sensibility and honor, which to him is a belief in self. The ending to *Maurice*, which Forster himself characterized as a fairy-tale ending, in which the upper-class Maurice runs away from his life, class, family, his very future, with an assistant gamekeeper named Scudder, is Forster's triumph in that in our day this ending has descended to the realm of possibility and even cliché.

Since the small but symbolically important act of rebellion in a gay bar in 1969, which was a long-needed symbolic shift from victim to activist, an army of scribes have attempted to replace this central destructive myth with others. It has been a collective effort to change the perception of homosexuality in society, to write ourselves out of one role and into something more workable and self-assigned. And as such this is a movement, like those of women and blacks before us, like also Jews, whom, with supreme irony, we most resemble. We, too, have been murdered and burned, gassed and clubbed, persecuted for centuries, reviled and treated with contempt.

The myth of the victim, it could be argued, is the setup for AIDS itself, as a central part of the idea that AIDS is our fault; for in the old metaphor, illness is punishment brought by the wrath of God, in this case for the contamination of society by gay people. The inclusion of the wrath of God is mythic indication of a millennium of conflict between the Catholic Church and gay people. To a lesser degree, but importantly, Jewish orthodoxy has abetted the Church in support of the major development of Western thought: the Judeo-Christian ethic, which, because of the teachings and amendments of Saint Paul, Saint Augustine, and other subsequent interpreters of the *intentions* of Christ, has pitted the Church against sexuality, particularly the so-called unnatural sex acts: anal intercourse and fellatio. Simply stated, the Church's opinion of sodomites is based on the belief that only the Devil would contemplate sex between men; and thus, coming from the Devil, such acts were considered heretical and punishable throughout the Inquisition by death. There is irrefutable evidence—unearthed and published by an ever-growing discipline of gay studies—of the unbroken persecution of gays and lesbians by the Catholic Church from the fourth century A.D. to, in subtler forms, the present. The Judeo-Christian ethic established a patriarchal dictatorship-religion, a religious world of masters and slaves, a cause for which, over the centuries, more blood has been shed than in all the wars of history. Its conflict with homosexuality predates religion itself, and is resolved only in anthropology, in the Darwinian horde where, as Freud has shown, nondominant males lived together after expulsion from the tribe, and where homosexuality was born. Church dogma is at the true heart of the victim myth. The modern effort of gay literature seems to be to change those myths and thus alter dogma.

It usually takes literature four or five years to get its feet under itself on a major issue, like Vietnam, or AIDS, whereas music and drama are on the case immediately. A longish period is necessary for literature to see what is happening and to figure out what it all may mean, how it began, and how it may stopped. And then there is the interval of composition, which may take years, and the publishing process, which takes more time. And in the actual event, AIDS has killed many before they were able to control creation, or finish it, overwhelming them beyond the demands of fiction.

It seems to me that if our movement is to produce something truly worthwhile, it will do so in the literature which is a response to AIDS. Several new books we know to expect, and have long been waiting for. And there will be others, as from this dreadful calamity, which touches all our lives, new directions are chosen and new myths are made.

The new direction, to me, appears to be at once spiritual and pragmatic: combining the Essentialist *and* Constructionist. It is spiritual in the sense of going beyond principles of pleasure and gratification learned in the Sexual Revolution—not the spirituality of religious faith but the magic of belief and the confidence in self, not in the rewards of an afterlife, but in the development of the continuing moment of life. It will also be pragmatic in the sense that it rests with ourselves to change the world if the world does not suit us, to dispel the ignorance and fear that is homophobia with knowledge, openness, and achievement.

As the poet James Broughton has recently pointed out, we are in a meridian/central position of human existence, not its lunatic fringe. The lessons we must learn are the lessons of the age, and much depends on our learning them.

A Place of Their Own

Andrew Holleran

Of the friendships that bound the Violet Quill together, the oldest was between Robert Ferro and Andrew Holleran. Indeed, their friendship may have predated the one between Ferro and his lover Michael Grumley. This remembrance of the two was published in Christopher Street *after Ferro's death. In a letter to Ferro at the time of the demise of the Violet Quill, Holleran wrote, "It doesn't even seem necessary to me to declare the Club finished—since it is something that by nature goes dormant, then is called up again, then fades—because that is how it's useful to us. The VQ Club has no QUORUM." Holleran's memorial to Robert Ferro and Michael Grumley celebrates the moveable feast of friendship called up for the last time.*

I met Robert Ferro at the Writers' Workshop at the University of Iowa, in Iowa City, Iowa, the fall of 1965. So did Michael Grumley. Years later, when they were living in New York, the magazine *W* sent a subscription enticement addressed to "the Ferro-Grumleys." They saved the address label, the name stuck, and we ever afterwards referred to them as the F-Gs. They were a couple as married as any could be; when shortly before their deaths, Robert remarked to me that he and Michael had not spent more than six days apart from each other in the past twenty years, it startled me for a moment and then I realized it was probably true. As Robert also said to me early in their relationship: "It's easier facing the world as two people than as one."

I don't remember Michael Grumley at Iowa—he studied with another writer—but I do remember Robert. Not only did we both end up in the classroom of the same instructor, a Chilean novelist of considerable charisma, but Robert had charisma of his own. He was good-looking. He had an excellent physique—if I'm correct, he had been on the diving team at Rutgers—both muscular and proportioned. ("In life," our favorite teacher said, "as in art, proportion is everything!") He also had long, long auburn hair, a beard, a nose, that same professor joked, "like a baroque instrument," and brown eyes that regarded you with a look that was an odd combination of Bambi and the Lord High Executioner. He wore jeans, black T-shirts, a silver bracelet of austere design, and boots. He reminded me of a horse, a beautiful Arabian horse, stamping its hoof and tossing its mane from time to time. Sometimes he did toss his mane, that long hair he never abandoned. ("Yesterday someone asked me what I was," he joked years later in a letter from New York, "and I replied that I am an idea in the mind of my hairdresser.") He belonged to a small set of Easterners who also wore black, had long hair, and Indian jewelry (not to mention an Indian name, in the case of the daughter of a New York psychiatrist who christened herself Morning Mist after taking a part-Cherokee lover), and when Robert told me his literary idols were Isak Dinesen and Virginia Woolf, it only confirmed my impression of him as something rarefied, European, outré. He was working on a novel about a pensione in Florence he had lived in before coming to Iowa, about an affair with the older Italian woman who ran it, and all of this contributed to my certainty that he had what I did not: an adult sexual past, an adult sexual present. He lived downtown in a dark, wood-paneled apartment with a loft, and I could only imagine what went on in there. He was just a few years older than I, but from the very start seemed further along in life; initiated into the secrets of sex, and the real world, in a way I was not. When we left Iowa two years later, with only a few friends, our teacher, and our determination to be writers in common, I allowed him to play Auntie Mame to my Agnes Gooch; that is, I went to law school, and he went to Rome.

From Rome he wrote letters—letters that seemed in 1968 very funny, confident, and glamorous, and still do. They came from places like Largo Febo (Square of the Sun God, Phoebus), were typed on thin crinkled sheets of notepaper, and mailed in envelopes whose faded brown contrasted with the red and green of the Italian stamps. Like everything about Robert, they were evidence of taste, a taste he loved to exercise, I think, on all aspects of his life, and writing: aesthetics and ethics were not far apart in his view of life. Sometimes the letters were typed—on a portable I imagined on his lap on a sunny terrace lined with geraniums. The letters were large, airy, with a lot of space between the lines. (Hadn't our professor once said his reaction to a student's novel was completely different when he read it in double-space?) Sometimes he wrote them out—in a script whose *f*'s and *s*'s resembled the prow of a gondola. In either form they came from some-one who conceived of himself as an artist—a vocation he viewed in almost Renaissance terms; he the poet, deserving a patron. (''If you had spent half the time educating your parents as you have educating yourself, you'd be propped up here in Rome in a small, rather inex-pensive but nice flat down the street from me.'') Lectures on leaving law school accompanied this: ''Drop out before it's too late. It's so much easier to suffer in a four-hundred-year-old palazzo than in the University of Pennsylvania Dining Hall. Studying all that stuff will addle your brain. Your characters will start saying things like 'I've just fallen in love with the party of the first part,' and 'behoove,' and 'right of way.' And so on.'' As for himself: ''I've just put on my white tie and white tails and white hat and there's all those white steps to go down, out into the city, dancing. Oh Budapest!''

The next year, a letter came from Rome with news of some success; he and Michael Grumley had gone scuba-diving in the Bahamas, dis-covered the lost city of Atlantis (''One only had to don one's pink aqua-lung and mask, drop over the side, and hover a bit. . . . ''), and written a book about it: *Atlantis: The Autobiography of a Search.* He was a writer, after all. ''Meanwhile,'' the letter goes on, ''we are propped up in a very showy, though empty, five-terraced apartment, high above Rome, close by the Piazza Navona. . . . I have gotten my-self to the point where I loathe crowds of more than three people, except sexually, and this of course lets out the entire United States. Here, in Rome, one floats above the language (a line from the book) and, up in this blimp of an apartment, one floats above everything.''

Atlantis floated them right out of the apartment onto a book tour, the sort we all secretly dreamed of in Iowa—a talk show in Los An-geles, hotel, limousine—but then they hit what turned out to be a very large air pocket, and, their fifteen minutes (not so much of fame as of attention) over, they fell down into the vast vacuum of the poor and ambitious. Once Robert remarked that when he got on the Fifth Av-enue bus, he felt he was in reality the king of Crete; but that, as they say, and a subway token will get you nowhere. We moved to New York, they from Rome and I from Philadelphia, but the city swallowed us up separately. I'm not sure why; perhaps the warm confidence engendered by Iowa had spent itself. Perhaps the relationship—the correspondence, certainly—had been based all along on glamour, a word whose root is "distance," and, there being no distance anymore between us, there could be no letters, much less air-mailed envelopes from Roman palaces, with advice to the bookworm law student.

Robert and Michael lived uptown on Ninety-fifth Street, and I in the East Village on St. Marks Place. He had a social life I knew nothing of; I spent those years going to Fire Island as often as I could, visiting the Eagle's Nest, the Everard, and whatever dance club happened to be the one that winter. Once I came upon Robert and Michael by accident, reading the morning paper in the stern of a cabin cruiser tied to a dock in the Pines; we spoke briefly, but I never saw them again that weekend. Whereas the Pines was Mecca to me, to them it was a place to drop anchor once, I assumed. We had different objects of glamour: I was a clone; Robert was not. Both he and Michael had, I felt sure, a sexual and social life that did not require the throngs of moustached men who filled the gyms, baths, and bars I went to; they had, I suspected, their own contacts. (In 1980, when I was in Florida and we were again corresponding, he wrote: "I am developing a rudimentary list of private acquaintances into something between a social life and a hobby. It has a house-of-cards quality to it. . . . Someone is always in the hospital, has the clap, has to work the next day, is depressed. As in Marrakech, it takes ten men to make a decent date lately.")

Years later, around the time *The Family of Max Desir* was published, I learned Robert did have a life downtown, tangential to the circuit, but it was a particular subculture that consisted of private parties, and men of color. He became a sort of cult figure among these people—a drawing of him was engraved on the invitations sent to this special guest-list—and he must have felt slightly like the idol cited in the beautiful closing pages of his novel about that world, a world in which he used the name "Max," as if that person—the man who went downtown for pleasure—was not the same as the one who wrote *The Others*.

The Others was the novel Robert published several years after *Atlantis*, before *Max Desir*—it was, in its way, his homage to that writer he most admired at Iowa: Isak Dinesen. It is pure fable, allegory, a gothic tale, if you will, containing the things he loved that would appear in all his novels thereafter: ships, secrets, mystery, Italy. It was a slim novel whose handsome dust jacket was designed by Michael. It left them no less poor after its publication than before.

Michael was working at this point in the Endicott bookstore on the Upper West Side. I had just published a novel about gay life; and either this, or the sudden awareness on Robert's part that this sort of material—homosexual society—might be something he could use, impelled him to suggest we revive those customs we'd shared years ago in Iowa City—that is, form a little workshop on our own, writers who would meet periodically, read their work aloud, and accept criticism from the others. This we did. I'm not sure really whose idea it was, or how it began, but I would not be surprised if it was Robert's, or if the name, the Violet Quill, came from him, too; for no one took our literary group more seriously, joyously, than he. No one conceived of what he used to call "gaylitter" more idealistically—it really was a brotherhood, imbued in his mind with some of the drama, no doubt, he brought to Freemasonry in *The Blue Star*. "I was sitting there last night," he wrote in 1981, "wondering about all of us . . . and I realized why the thing works. . . . Simply this: an attitude in common toward the cold realities of publishing a book, juxtaposed against our everyday lives. We all have this incredible thing in common. . . . That is why gay society has a chance. It is the other side of the balance. Pressures from the real world make us deal with each other." On the other hand, discussing a plan to have a photograph of the VQ club taken: "The finished portrait is to hang *either* on the rear wall over the jukebox in Boots and Saddles or in the third tollbooth from the left as you are approaching the Lincoln Tunnel from the New Jersey side."

That was more the reality, actually—though the academic world may thrive on such suggestions of a "movement" that dessert-and-short-story clubs like the VQ provide, in fact we met only seven or eight times before an internecine feud rent us apart; and short of the realization that several of us were writing autobiographical works dealing with the same material, the VQ Club's dissolution left us pretty much in the same places we were before. Robert and Michael were still poor, for one thing. Robert got work as a waiter. The friend who had written me initially from the terrace of a four-hundred-year-old palazzo, who had floated above everything in "this blimp of an apartment," was now shuttling dinner plates from kitchen to "a dinner for four hundred in a rain-soaked tent that leaked like a sieve—yards and yards of limp tulle and muddy spikes—a really ornery crowd of decorators who had assembled, apparently, to congratulate themselves for having Bloomingdaled forty rooms of the Gould-Guggenheim mansion in Sands Point into forthright ugliness. God and the metereologists proved to be severe critics." And: "Sunny afternoons find us mooning up at the St. Urban from our bench in the Park at 89th Street (where eventually we will be found, dribbling and farting, with a nurse sitting between us). . . . [Richard] is doing a book for Random House on his favorite places [in Europe]. I'm doing one on my favorite potholes. I drove into one on Tenth Avenue yesterday and have not been heard from since."

It was a car—a black, battered Pontiac Trans Am—that Robert drove, as he did everything else, confidently. He used to take himself and Michael (and on weekends, friends) down to a house his family owned on the Jersey shore, in an immaculate town whose church was a simulacrum of St. Peter's in Rome. There the writer, the waiter-on-tables-of-decorators-in-soaked-tents, could express his own dream of creating a beautiful place. ("You ask about what is glamorous now, or to me," he wrote once. " . . . To me, still, place is glamorous, is real, is life. Place. The house in my novel is a glamorous character to me. . . . ") Once, when he was poor, Robert mused on the fact that, had he just been a decorator, he might not have had to be poor. Well, the house on the Jersey shore—the house in both *Max Desir* and *Second Son*—was his, and Michael's, character; their escape from everything: poverty, New York, limitations—where he and Michael made muffins, tea, dinners, assigned rooms to guests, planted flowers, created, somehow, that place for which part of their imaginations longed, I think: a dream of people and place together. He called the house "Gaywyck" after the novel by Vincent Virga. And it was to Gaywyck they would fly as in a gothic novel—in that black Trans Am.

Robert once said that before writing a story, it should already be there, in life; one had only to present it. If the key to autobiography, as he said in an interview, was knowing what to leave out, it was also knowing, finding, finally, what to put in. What to put in was now the life he was leading. "*Max Desir* lives," he wrote April 6, 1980. " . . . I have been writing fragments, notes, bits here and there, and now in going over them I can see, as if at night in a fog wearing sunglasses, a very faint outline of a shape. As Michael says, a book accrues. . . . " It not only accrued, it was published; and the very fragmentation his life seemed to consist of (family sorrows, New York sex) was brilliantly juxtaposed on that most unifying of places, the page. He was now his subject. (Even the novel he had been working on at Iowa would not see the light till the homosexual facts of his year in Florence were no longer disguised in heterosexual trappings; they then became the first seventy or so pages of *The Blue Star*.) Fifteen years after going to Iowa, he had found his subject, his audience, his place—his literary place, at least. He was very happy. No one loved the minutiae of publishing more than Robert. He chose the book jacket with the same care he gave to muffins, *faux marbre*, and guests for tea. The F-Gs were what they had wanted to be when young; Michael was working on a novel himself; and with this new confidence, Robert could return to the book he'd been working on at Iowa, under the spell of Dinesen, and do it again in his own voice as *The Blue Star*.

Life, in short, was fun—till one day Robert discovered a Kaposi's sarcoma lesion. He told me he found it just when he thought he'd escaped. He wanted us to tell no one else. Robert had a distinct sense of how things should be done—when you violated it, you were told so in no uncertain terms—and we kept quiet. And life went on pretty much as it always had. He had what the doctor called "indolent" lesions and, save for an afternoon nap, his life altered little externally.

He even went back to Europe. "It's that terrifying moment of first sitting down to one's new Roman desk," he wrote on August 4, 1985, "on the first real morning of settling in. . . . It had not been properly cleaned before we arrived. . . . When the American woman who is renting it to us arrived, we dined on her head and limbs. But I have now rearranged the furniture and taken down the bad pictures. . . . " (He would even, his sister said, rearrange the furniture in the lobby of a hospital where he stood waiting for an elevator to take him up for more tests.) As for the new reality: "I simply don't think about it here as much, and feel less self-conscious, and therefore more normal. People look at one here, in a way they don't in New York, or at least haven't in years. And such beautiful men everywhere. My new stance in the face of scrutiny or interest is of course demurral. . . . You look at your feet, to disengage. It's all I want." Except a cure: he watched the newspapers, as everyone did, for news from Stockholm or Israel or France or Washington or someplace, for the medicine that would restore his health. He felt, he said, as if he might meet a woman on a bridge, someone who would tell him where a door was he only had to knock on—as in one of his novels. In fact, he consulted a witch, I believe; he and Michael were the only people I knew who could use that word in its literal sense, calmly, over tea; they had, all the years I'd known them, consulted people in the world they referred to as "spooks and kooks"—that raffish demimonde filled with decorators, witches, movie extras, fake principessas, clairvoyants, and gigolos, to which they had once belonged. So when the characters in *Second Son* listen to plans for a spaceship to a planet free of AIDS, it was neither out of keeping with Robert's fictional method—he was what Richard Howard called a "fabulist"—nor his own imagination, though he saw it as, and it should have been treated by the critics as, simply the poignant wish of the imagination it was: a wish to be free, to escape from this nightmare.

On their last trip to Rome, the following year, Michael—the one on whom Robert had been relying for help—suddenly developed a high fever that turned the penthouse overlooking the Old City into a sick-room. They returned to New York, and, since I'd not been in New York since 1981 for any length of time, I followed their progress with letters and phone calls. "I am hoping that in the next month or two," Robert wrote in 1986, "they will get into trying combination tests of several drugs—the soup, Alphabet soup. A hot cup of AZT and In-terleukin-II, please. The genetic vaccine and Dr. Lo's new virus. Hold the mayo," he wrote in August of 1986, from the lake in the Berkshires on which they'd rented a cottage, the lake that was to be so lovingly described in *Second Son*. Gaywyck itself was a problem now; someone had sold the empty lot next door, and a huge new house had gone up in record time. ("New house owner is about thirty, a super stockbro-ker . . . and is yes handsome. Last week he told me he was not the sort of person who could be pushed. How 'bout poisoned?") The new house was so big and so close, Robert had done what only Robert would do: create a berm between Gaywyck and the new building. ("I am considered the cleverest woman in Sea Girt for causing such a thing to be built—the great wall of China, visible from the moon.")

And yet some discouragement must have come over him at this point; they went to Massachusetts to escape this time, instead, and the difficulty of shutting out the insults of real life—the house next door and its floodlights, with a berm; AIDS itself, with the drugs he'd been postponing till now—must have struck him. He was going to have to look elsewhere. "I've made the discovery that it is not just [Gaywyck] that I can love," he wrote from the Berkshires in the last letter of his

I have. "This perhaps sounds odd . . . but I realize after living in all the places we have, that all I want is a place of my own, a private place. It doesn't have to be the family manse. It doesn't have to reverberate with generations of family talk and tradition." As for his novel: "Now I am simply looking for the back door. So hard to get to the end because one hasn't come to the end, or seen it clearly. I don't want to insist. It's a mistake to force yourself on the book at the end. But to what extent is a wish to survive an analogue of the novel?" And the world itself: "But, darling, the ignorance of the people in charge. . . . We were, we are, the guardians, the givers of the alarm; and of course nobody listened. Listen to the fagoons?"

That was how things stood when he did finish *Second Son* and went on a tour to give readings and sign copies. Michael, who was scheduled to go too, came down with TB just as they were to leave. He insisted Robert go alone. Robert did, carrying on with dignity and aplomb a struggle which no one who saw him realized was going on at all. The word for this is gallant. Gallantry which rose to another level when I next saw Robert, in the hospital room in New York where Michael had been assigned. "I can't tell you how bad it's been," he said, only once, in a soft voice in the other room. The next time we spoke, on the phone a few weeks later, he lambasted me for saying I was not going to be able to fly up for the memorial he had arranged for Michael; a phone call that was like opening the door of a furnace, a furnace in hell in which someone I had known for twenty years was burning up. The next week he greeted me in a big, palm-filled room he had rented on Central Park for the memorial. Both families were there; friends, writers, a pianist who played not only Schubert but a song Robert and Michael had written for a musical they had been planning. Robert was still handsome—slender, burnished by the sun. Only his eyes, those intense, glowing eyes, betrayed the fact that he was running on merely his devotion to Michael; whose gravesite, beside his own, he had just selected on a bluff overlooking the Hudson River—"the most beautiful place," he said. Throughout the service I kept thinking of the opening line from *The Good Soldier* by Ford Madox Ford: *"This is the saddest story ever told."* Yet the day was splendid; including the reception at a friend's apartment afterwards ("This is *just* enough chintz," was Robert's joke), where the family he had written about all these years, the nieces and nephews, were all assembled like some graduation party on a sunny June day. He told me he'd felt Michael leave at the memorial—his soul, that is—but that he, Robert, was not even sure anymore if there was anything to all that: souls, spirits, their meeting on the other side. On this side, we were happy to learn he planned to visit a friend in France in a couple of weeks. But when the day came to go he was too sick. He did not want to enter the hospital; he'd had enough of that; he went back to his father's house in New Jersey and shocked everyone by dying just a few days later.

Years ago, in 1968, in an early letter I got from Robert Ferro, there is this: "Have been reading Wilde myself—*De Profundis*. It's a shock to find him without, for once, his sense of humor. I think it was his real disgrace—not the trial and prison, etc.—but that treatise on gloom and sadness. He should never have admitted to us that he was wrong. Because, of course, he wasn't. What will life do to us, if it did that to *him*?"

Bibliography

WORK BY CHRISTOPHER COX
A Key West Companion. New York: St. Martin's Press, 1983.

WORKS BY ROBERT FERRO
Atlantis: The Autobiography of a Search. With Michael Grumley. Garden City, N.Y.: Doubleday & Co., 1970.
The Others. New York: Scribner's, 1977.
The Family of Max Desir. New York: E. P. Dutton, 1983.
The Blue Star. New York: E. P. Dutton, 1985.
Second Son. New York: Crown Publishers, 1988.

WORKS BY MICHAEL GRUMLEY
Atlantis: The Autobiography of a Search. With Robert Ferro. Garden City, N.Y.: Doubleday & Co., 1970.
There Are Giants in the Earth. Garden City, N.Y.: Doubleday & Co., 1974.
After Midnight. New York: Scribner's, 1978.
Hard Corps: Studies in Leather and Sadomasochism. New York: E. P. Dutton, 1977.
Life Drawings. New York: Grove Weidenfeld, 1991.

WORKS BY ANDREW HOLLERAN
Dancer from the Dance. New York: William Morrow and Co., 1978; New York: New American Library, 1986.
Nights in Aruba. New York: William Morrow and Co., 1983; New York: New American Library, 1984.
Ground Zero. New York: William Morrow and Co., 1988; New York: New American Library, 1989.

408

WORKS BY FELICE PICANO

Fiction

Smart as the Devil. New York: Arbor House, 1975.

Eyes. New York: Arbor House, 1976.

The Mesmerist. New York: Delacorte Press, 1977.

The Lure. New York: Delacorte Press, 1979.

(Editor) *A True Likeness: An Anthology of Lesbian and Gay Writing Today.* New York: Sea Horse Press, 1980.

An Asian Minor: The True Story of Ganymede (novella). New York: Sea Horse Press, 1981.

Late in the Season. New York: Delacorte Press, 1981.

Slashed to Ribbons in Defense of Love and Other Stories. New York: Gay Presses of New York, 1983.

House of Cards. New York: Delacorte Press, 1984.

Ambidextrous: The Secret Lives of Children (memoir), vol. 1. New York: Gay Presses of New York, 1985.

Men Who Loved Me: A Memoir in the Form of a Novel. New York: New American Library, 1989.

To the Seventh Power. New York: Morrow, 1989.

Poetry

The Deformity Lover and Other Poems. New York: Sea Horse Press, 1978.

Window Elegies. Tuscaloosa, Ala.: Close Grip Press, 1986.

WORKS BY EDMUND WHITE

Forgetting Elena. New York: Random House, 1973.

The Joy of Gay Sex: An Intimate Guide for Gay Men to the Pleasures of a Gay Life Style. With Charles Silverstein. New York: Crown Publishers, 1977.

Nocturnes for the King of Naples. New York: St. Martin's Press, 1978.

States of Desire: Travels in Gay America. New York: E. P. Dutton, 1980.

A Boy's Own Story. New York: E. P. Dutton, 1982.

Caracole. New York: E. P. Dutton, 1985.

The Beautiful Room Is Empty. New York: Alfred A. Knopf, 1988.

The Darker Proof: Stories from a Crisis. With Adam Mars-Jones. New York: New American Library, 1988.

Genet: A Biography. New York: Alfred A. Knopf, 1993.

The Burning Library: Writings on Art, Politics and Sexuality, 1969–1993. David Bergman, ed. New York: Alfred A. Knopf, forthcoming.

WORKS BY GEORGE WHITMORE

Getting Gay in New York. New York: Free Milk Fund Press, 1976.

The Confessions of Danny Slocum, or Gay Life in the Big City. New York: St. Martin's Press, 1980. Rev. ed. San Francisco: Grey Fox Press, 1985.

"Deep Dish" (serial in 29 episodes). *New York Native* 1–30 (December 29, 1980–February 1, 1982).

Nebraska. New York: Grove Press, 1987. Rev. ed. New York: Washington Square Press, 1989.

Someone Was Here: Profiles in the AIDS Epidemic. New York: Penguin Books, 1988.